Healthy Eating in Relation to National Dietary Guidelines

Healthy Eating in Relation to National Dietary Guidelines

Editors

Clare Collins
George Moschonis

MDPI

Basel • Beijing • Wuhan • Barcelona • Belgrade • Novi Sad • Cluj • Manchester

Editors

Clare Collins
University of Newcastle
Callaghan, Australia

George Moschonis
La Trobe University
Melbourne, Australia

Editorial Office
MDPI
St. Alban-Anlage 66
4052 Basel, Switzerland

This is a reprint of articles from the Special Issue published online in the open access journal *Nutrients* (ISSN 2072-6643) (available at: https://www.mdpi.com/journal/nutrients/special_issues/dietary_guidelines).

For citation purposes, cite each article independently as indicated on the article page online and as indicated below:

Lastname, A.A.; Lastname, B.B. Article Title. *Journal Name* **Year**, *Volume Number*, Page Range.

ISBN 978-3-0365-9692-1 (Hbk)
ISBN 978-3-0365-9693-8 (PDF)
doi.org/10.3390/books978-3-0365-9693-8

Contents

About the Editors

Clare Collins

Dr Clare Collins is a Laureate Professor in Nutrition and Dietetics at the University of Newcastle, and Director of the Food and Nutrition Program, Hunter Medical Research Institute, Australia. L/Professor Collins' research expertise spans evidence synthesis using systematic review methodology, nutrition epidemiology, dietary assessment methods, nutritional biomarkers and dietary metabolomics, and personalized nutrition interventions based on life stage and chronic disease risk, delivered using eHealth technologies.

George Moschonis

Dr. George Moschonis is a Professor in the Discipline of Food, Nutrition and Dietetics at La Trobe University in Melbourne, Australia. Professor Moschonis' main research area of expertise is the identification of determinants or predictors (starting from very early life stages) of obesity and obesity-related cardio-metabolic complications, and the design and evaluation of the clinical effectiveness of nutrition counselling programs, which aim to tackle the societal challenge of chronic disease including obesity, type 2 diabetes, cardiovascular disease, etc. In addition, his research expertise also extends to the design of new functional food products, as well as to the design and implementation of human clinical trials that set the basis for the assessment of the clinical effectiveness of functional foods and supplements in tackling nutrition-related health conditions.

Preface

This Special Issue of Nutrients includes a variety of original research studies, as well as systematic reviews and meta-analyses coming from a wide range of related disciplines (i.e., human nutrition and dietetics, public health, epidemiology, and non-communicable chronic diseases). The Special Issue "Healthy Eating in Relation to National Dietary Guidelines" represents a unique selection of original research and review articles that highlight the importance of adhering to National Dietary Guidelines in maintaining health and preventing disease.

Clare Collins and George Moschonis
Editors

nutrients MDPI

Article

Caffeine, D-glucuronolactone and Taurine Content in Energy Drinks: Exposure and Risk Assessment

Carmen Rubio [1,*], Montaña Cámara [2], Rosa María Giner [3], María José González-Muñoz [4], Esther López-García [5], Francisco J. Morales [6], M. Victoria Moreno-Arribas [7], María P. Portillo [8,9,10] and Elena Bethencourt [11]

1 Toxicology Department, Pharmacy and Health Sciences Faculties, Universidad de La Laguna (ULL), 38071 San Cristóbal de La Laguna, Spain
2 Nutrition and Food Science Department, Pharmacy Faculty, Complutense University of Madrid (UCM), Plaza Ramón y Cajal, s/n, 28040 Madrid, Spain
3 Department of Pharmacology, Faculty of Pharmacy, University of Valencia, 46100 Burjassot, Spain
4 Department of Biomedical Sciences, Toxicology Unit, Faculty of Pharmacy, University of Alcalá, Alcalá de Henares, 28871 Madrid, Spain
5 Department of Preventive Medicine and Public Health, School of Medicine, Universidad Autónoma de Madrid, Spain/IdiPAZ, CIBER of Epidemiology and Public Health (CIBERESP), 28029 Madrid, Spain
6 Institute of Food Science, Technology and Nutrition (ICTAN-CSIC), 28040 Madrid, Spain
7 Institute of Food Science Research (CIAL), CSIC-UAM, 28049 Madrid, Spain
8 Nutrition and Obesity Group, Department of Pharmacy and Food Sciences, University of the Basque Country (UPV/EHU), 01006 Vitoria-Gasteiz, Spain
9 CIBERobn Physiopathology of Obesity and Nutrition, Institute of Health Carlos III, 28029 Madrid, Spain
10 BIOARABA Institute of Health, 01009 Vitoria-Gasteiz, Spain
11 Elena Bethencourt Barbuzano, Toxicology Department, Pharmacy and Health Sciences Faculties, Universidad de La Laguna (ULL), 38071 San Cristóbal de La Laguna, Spain
* Correspondence: crubio@ull.edu.es

Citation: Rubio, C.; Cámara, M.; Giner, R.M.; González-Muñoz, M.J.; López-García, E.; Morales, F.J.; Moreno-Arribas, M.V.; Portillo, M.P.; Bethencourt, E. Caffeine, D-glucuronolactone and Taurine Content in Energy Drinks: Exposure and Risk Assessment. *Nutrients* **2022**, *14*, 5103. https://doi.org/10.3390/nu14235103

Academic Editor: Marilyn Cornelis

Received: 24 October 2022
Accepted: 25 November 2022
Published: 1 December 2022

Abstract: The consumption of energy drinks (EDs) is increasing globally while the evidence and concern about the potential health risks are also growing. Caffeine (generally 32 mg/100 mL) together with a wide variety of other active components such as taurine (usually 4000 mg/L) and D-glucuronolactone (generally 2400 mg/L) are the main ingredients of EDs. This study aims to assess the exposures to caffeine, taurine and D-glucuronolactone from EDs in various consumption scenarios and consumer profiles and to characterize the risks by evaluating caffeine and taurine intakes with their reference values and by calculating the margin of safety (MOS) for D-glucuronolactone. While the exposure assessment results showed that caffeine intakes from EDs ranged from 80 to 160 mg (1.14–4 mg/kg b.w.) for the considered scenarios, the risk characterization estimated some risks that could be managed with consumption recommendations such as limiting EDs in 40, 60 and 80 kg b.w. consumers to 175, 262.5 and 350 mL, respectively, to prevent sleep disturbances and to 375, 562.5 and 750 mL to prevent general caffeine adverse health risks, respectively. Dietary exposure to D-glucuronolactone from EDs ranged from 600 to 1200 mg (7.5–30 mg/kg b.w.). As D-glucuronolactone MOS $\geq$ 100 is only observed when EDs consumption is limited to 250 mL, for individuals weighing above 60 kg, some risks were observed in some of the studied scenarios. A taurine exposure from EDs varied from 1000 to 2000 mg (12.5–50 mg/kg b.w.) and consumptions over 500 mL were estimated to generate intakes above the reference value. In conclusion, the management of these risks requires a European legal framework for EDs with maximum limits for the active components, volume size limitations and labeling improvements along with the development of education and awareness programs and risk communication actions in collaboration with the industry and society.

Keywords: energy drinks; caffeine; taurine; D-glucuronolactone; exposure assessment; risk characterization; risk management

1. Introduction

The energy drinks (EDs) market is estimated to be 1% of the non-alcoholic drinks market and this may be attributed to the well-thought-out design process in the food industry. The consumption of EDs has considerably increased worldwide [1–11], especially among male adolescents and young adults. The European FoodEx2 classification classifies EDs in the non-alcoholic functional drinks category [12].

EDs consumption was estimated to be at 30% in European adults (18–65 years; 16% corresponding to chronic consumers) and at 68% in European adolescents (10–18 years; 10% classified as chronic consumers). Almost 12% of all adult Europeans (13.3% of "young adults") described themselves as regular consumers, drinking EDs 4–5 times a week or more and consuming a mean average volume of 4–5 L/month [13]. The Spanish Survey on Drug Use in Secondary Schools (ESTUDES) estimates the prevalence of EDs use among students at 50.7% and 39% for young males and females, respectively [14].

Recent studies report that, during the COVID-19 pandemic, not only has the frequency of the consumption of EDs increased but also the amount ingested, which was probably due in part to the need to cope with stress, boredom and the desire to improve attention when using screens and playing video games [15,16].

There is a global growing concern about the potential risks and the existing low-risk perception associated with these drinks [2,9,10,17–19]. In general, the evidence correlates EDs with a significant increase in the odds of insomnia (and jitteriness/activeness) [11], anxiety, depression, impulsivity and poor academic performance, among others. While frequent Eds consumption generates stimulation (nervous and cardiovascular), hypertension, bone density loss, osteoporosis, low psychological, physical, educational and overall well-being, among other consequences [2,11,20,21], acute Eds consumption not only generates a caffeine overdose but has also been identified as an indicator of the use/abuse of other psychoactive substances (tobacco, sedatives, cannabis, cocaine and ecstasy) and risky behaviors [1,14,17,22–24]. The combined consumption of EDs with alcoholic drinks is known to generate, among other effects, a decreased sense of drunkenness [17], and this has been a growing cause of concern since more than half of young European consumers said they occasionally consumed EDs mixed with alcohol [13].

Despite the variety of ingredients, most EDs share the same composition of caffeine, taurine and D-glucuronolactone in varying proportions, along with other minor components such as B vitamins and L-carnitine that increase their attractiveness, especially among young consumers [25,26]. While the European Food Safety Authority (EFSA) found that forty-nine of the fifty-three EDs distributed in Europe contained taurine in their formula [13], the French Agence Nationale de Sécurité Sanitaire de l'alimentation, de l'environnement et du travail (ANSES) reported that only 103 out of 126 of the EDs marketed in France showed a complete list of ingredients on the packaging and, of these, only 52% contained taurine [27]. Additionally, 33% of the EDs on the French market contained D-glucuronolactone and 59% of the EDs did not state the amount on the labeling [27].

The caffeine content in EDs usually ranges between 15 and 55 mg/100 mL [28], although the most common concentration is 32 mg/100 mL. A standard EDs formula usually contains 2400 mg/L of D-glucuronolactone and 4000 mg/L of taurine [26,28,29]. Nevertheless, the mean average taurine content in EDs has progressively increased since the first commercialized formulations [30]. While ANSES reported a mean taurine content (mg/L) of 3800 [27], EFSA reported 3412 [29] and Health Canada reported a mean average of 4000 (range: 40–8000 mg/L) [31]. The mean D-glucuronolactone content (mg/L) was 1700 (range: 240–2400) but according to Health Canada, the D-glucuronolactone content may be up to 4800 [31].

Caffeine (1,3,7-trimethylxanthine) generates multisystemic effects not only in the central nervous system (CNS) but also in the respiratory, renal, endocrine, urinary, musculoskeletal and cardiovascular systems [32–34]. Caffeine, in the CNS, behaves as an antagonist of adenosine A1, A2A and A2B receptors, producing a mild excitatory effect [35–37]. Caffeine increases natriuresis and diuresis by an interaction with the A1 receptor [28] and inhibits phosphodiesterase, causing a smooth muscle relaxation [35,38,39]. A positive chronotropic and inotropic effect has been described at a cardiovascular level, as well as arrhythmias, tachycardias and an increase in blood pressure and heart rate [26,32,40]. In addition, caffeine is known for its potential to cause moderate physical dependence and tolerance. The EFSA associates intakes (mg/caffeine/kg b.w./day) of three with general effects (cardiovascular and hematological, neurological and psycho-behavioral) and of 1.4 with sleep disturbances (sleep onset latency and shorter duration) [35]. However, the Norwegian Scientific Committee for Food Safety [28] recently concluded that the benchmark of 3 mg caffeine/kg b.w./day may not necessarily protect against certain cardiac ailments. In any case, according to EFSA, general consumers (70 kg b.w.) should keep their caffeine ingestion under 400 mg/day [35].

The provision of information to consumers in Europe [41] includes labeling requirements for beverages with a high caffeine content (>150 mg/L), such as displaying *"High caffeine content. Not recommended for children or pregnant or breastfeeding women"* along with the caffeine amount in mg/100 mL. It is worth mentioning that some European brands [42] include *"Consume Moderately"* or similar wording on their labels and others follow a voluntary code where labels are committed to not promoting the combined use with alcoholic beverages [42,43].

One of the most recent risk communication actions on EDs has been promoted and executed by the Spanish Agency of Food Safety and Nutrition (AESAN) in 2022 [44]. As a risk management action, the AESAN, following a 2021 risk assessment scientific report [26], published a document in 2022 with recommendations on the consumption of EDs [44]. These recommendations remind athletes that EDs are not designed for rehydration and should not replace hydration and the recovery of metabolites by the conventional means such as water or, where appropriate, through isotonic drinks. They also say that the regular consumption of caffeine (100 mg/day) may cause a moderate physical dependence and tolerance, that an excessive caffeine consumption may have negative physiological effects and that EDs should not be combined with alcoholic beverages [44]. The AESAN has also recommended avoiding their consumption in case of children, adolescents, pregnant and breastfeeding women, people with hypertension, cardiovascular problems or with sleep disorders [44]. Finally, the AESAN risk communication campaign points out that EDs with sugars may contribute to exceeding the daily intake recommendations of simple sugars (the WHO recommendation: 50 g/day) since 250 mL of EDs may contain between 27.5 and 30 g of sugars and 500 mL of EDs between 55 and 60 g of sugars.

Although the dietary exposure to D-glucuronolactone is generally estimated to be low (1–2 mg/day) [29,36], the detection of unspecified renal lesions (renal papilla inflammation) in rats during the hazard identification of D-glucuronolactone raised concerns about the safety of including this ingredient in EDs [45]. The lowest no-observed-adverse-effect level (NOAEL) for these nephrotoxic effects was initially set at 300 mg/kg b.w./day, but based on the subsequent histopathological findings regarding renal inflammation, the NOAEL was finally set at 1000 mg/kg b.w./day [29].

Taurine (2-aminoethanesulfonic acid) is found in high concentrations in cardiac muscle and the CNS, although its levels decrease significantly with age. Taurine, unlike caffeine, behaves as an inhibitory neuromodulator. Its antioxidant and anti-inflammatory properties suggest its participation in several biological processes (the stabilization of the plasma membrane and bile salts, osmoregulation, calcium metabolism, skeletal muscle functionality and correct neuronal activity, among others) [46–48], but few studies have related dietary exposure with cardiovascular and neurological effects [49–52]. There are several dietary sources of taurine [36,46] that contribute to the estimated daily taurine intake (10–400 mg/day) [30] but, depending on the type of diet, the dietary intake may be lower (20–200 mg/day) [53]. In the case of omnivorous diets, the daily intake is estimated to be at 58 mg of taurine/day [29]. Based on the taurine hazard characterization, the EFSA established a daily reference intake of 1400 mg taurine/day for a 70 kg b.w. individual [29].

A taurine supplementation has been associated with a potential protective activity in aging brains and direct beneficial effects during nervous system toxicity episodes [54–57], but the EFSA states that a taurine dietary intake does not increase the taurine levels in the brain, ruling out the possibility of a stimulant effect on the CNS [29]. Therefore, a taurine supplementation may not be necessary in healthy consumers. Although Health Canada reported that acute taurine oral toxicity is low [58], and excess taurine may generate cognitive and behavioral effects in young adults [59].

Because an exposure to D-glucuronolactone and taurine has raised safety concerns, especially in high and chronic consumption scenarios [60], individual initiatives have been launched in different countries, such as Germany and Denmark [61], promoting the standardization of EDs with maximum caffeine levels at 32 mg/100 mL; taurine levels at 4000 mg/L; and glucuronolactone contents at 2400 mg/L [62].

Given this background, the objectives of the present assessment were to estimate the dietary exposures to caffeine, D-glucuronolactone and taurine derived from EDs in various consumption scenarios and for various consumer profiles, to characterize the potential health risks and to suggest some recommendations for risk management and communication.

2. Materials and Methods

The dietary exposure assessment (estimated daily intake, EDI) (1) of the three components under study was conducted by studying different volumes of ED containers marketed around the world (250, 333 and 500 mL) and the standard levels of caffeine (32 mg/100 mL), taurine (4000 mg/L) and D-glucuronolactone (2400 mg/L) in the above-mentioned commercial presentations. In addition, three consumption scenarios (250, 333 and 500 mL/day) and three consumer profiles based on body weight (40, 60 and 80 kg) were evaluated.

$$\text{EDI} = \text{C of caffeine/D-gluconolactone/taurine (mg/L)} \cdot \text{V of ED (L)} \quad (1)$$

C: concentration; V: volume.

A 1000 mL (1 L) consumption scenario was not considered as it was considered to be unusual among general consumers even though, according to Zucconi et al., 11% of all adult and 12% of all adolescent consumers of EDs were excessive consumers ingesting at least 1 L in a single ingestion [13].

The risk characterization for caffeine and taurine was performed by evaluating the caffeine and taurine estimated daily intakes (EDIs) with the established reference intakes for caffeine (intake > 1.4 mg/kg b.w./day leads to sleep disturbances; intake > 3 mg/kg b.w./day causes general adverse effects (cardiovascular and hematological, neurological and psycho-behavioral effects) [35] and taurine (1400 mg/day) [29].

In regard to D-glucuronolactone, the risk characterization was performed by calculating the margin of safety (MOS) using the no observed adverse effect level (NOAEL) and the estimated daily intake (EDI) (2) [63].

$$\text{MOS} = \frac{\text{NOAEL (mg/kg of body weight/day)}}{\text{EDI (mg/kg of body weight/day)}} \quad (2)$$

An acceptable value of the MOS for a NOAEL-based assessment extrapolated from an animal study is $\geq$100 (factor 10 for an extrapolation from animals to humans and a factor 10 for interindividual variation in humans). The D-gluconolactone NOAEL is set by EFSA at 1000 mg/kg b.w./day [29].

3. Results and Discussion

3.1. *Caffeine: Exposure Assessment and Risk Characterization from EDs*

Energy drinks are generally marketed worldwide in three standard volumes (250, 333 and 500 mL) and the most common caffeine content is 32 mg/100 mL. Considering these data, the estimated daily caffeine intakes for the three consumer profiles (40, 60 and 80 kg body weight) under evaluation are shown in Table 1.

Table 1. Caffeine: dietary exposure assessment and risk characterization when consuming 250, 333 and 500 mL of 32 mg caffeine/100 mL EDs.

	Volume of ED ingested (mL)		
	250 mL	333 mL	500 mL
	Total caffeine intake (mg)		
	80 mg	107 mg	160 mg
	Caffeine intake per kg of body weight (mg/kg b.w.)		
Body weight: 40 kg	2	2.7	4
Sleep disorders	X	X	X
General adverse effects on health	-	-	X
Body weight: 60 kg	1.3	1.8	2.6
Sleep disorders	-	X	X
General adverse effects on health	-	-	-
Body Weight: 80 kg	1.14	1.3	2
Sleep disorders	-	-	X
General adverse effects on health	-	-	-

X: caffeine intake is associated with health risks (either sleep disorders or general adverse effects); -: caffeine intake is not associated with the characterized risk (neither sleep disorders nor general adverse effects).

The caffeine estimated daily intakes (EDIs) from EDs ranged from 80 mg when 250 mL are consumed to 160 mg when 500 mL are ingested. These results are higher than those previously reported by Zucconi et al. and the Norwegian Ungkost 3 study [13,28]. According to Zucconi et al., the daily caffeine exposure was estimated at 22.4 mg (0.32 mg/kg b.w.) for adult European consumers and at 48.3 mg (0.7 mg/kg b.w.) for high chronic consumers. Likewise, a daily caffeine exposure was estimated at 23.5 mg (0.38 mg/kg b.w.) in European adolescents (10–18 years), increasing to 75.08 mg (1.18 mg/kg b.w.) in chronic high adolescent consumers [13]. In 2015, the mean average daily caffeine intakes in adults were estimated again, after observing a wide variability among EU Member States, obtaining a caffeine intake of 37–319 mg [35]. More recently the Norwegian Ungkost 3 study estimated the dietary caffeine exposure from Eds at 36.8 mg caffeine/day [28].

For a 40 kg person, daily caffeine intakes are estimated to be 2, 2.7 and 4 mg/kg b.w. when consuming 250, 333 and 500 mL, respectively. In the risk characterization, considering the limit values established by the EFSA for sleep disorders (1.4 mg/kg b.w./day), the authors conclude that any consumption equal to or higher than 250 mL will expose the consumer to the risk of sleep disorders. Similarly, intakes of 500 mL will expose the 40 kg b.w. consumer to levels over the 3 mg caffeine/kg b.w./day that the EFSA has correlated not only with sleeping disturbances but also with general adverse health effects [35].

For a 60 kg individual, a daily caffeine intake is estimated to reach 1.3, 1.8 and 2.6 mg/kg b.w. after consuming 250, 333 and 500 mL of EDs, respectively. Based on the EFSA health-based limit of 1.4 mg/kg b.w./day for sleep disorders, the risk characterization suggests limiting the consumption of EDs to 250 mL to avoid the risk of sleep disorders. However, the risk characterization concludes that any EDs consumption below 500 mL will keep one's caffeine intake below 3 mg caffeine/kg b.w./day, thereby avoiding the overall adverse health effects [35].

In the highest body weight scenario considered (80 kg), the daily estimated caffeine intakes are 1.14, 1.3 and 2 mg/kg b.w. after consuming 250, 333 and 500 mL of EDs, respectively. Based on the health-based limit of 1.4 mg/kg b.w./day for sleep disturbances, the risk characterization suggests limiting the consumption of EDs to 333 mL to avoid the risk of sleep disturbances. No overall adverse health effects are expected for any of the three consumption scenarios.

ED consumers undoubtedly have a total caffeine intake that exceeds that observed for non-EDs consumers [7]. As previously established by Ruiz and Scherr, Zucconi et al. and Ungkost 3 (Norwegian Ungkost 3 Study), the results here show a trend of an increased dietary caffeine exposure due to the increasing consumption of EDs [13,23,28]. Nevertheless, as reviewed by Verster and Koenig, caffeine intake is generally below the recommended levels [64]. However, the authors suggest enhancing the use of these consumption recommendations based on the upper intake limits proposed by the EFSA in the education, communication and management of the risks associated with EDs. All stakeholders should also be encouraged to contribute by applying education and communication strategies to minimize the risks associated with caffeine and to promote the moderate consumption of EDs considering the diversity of the consumers.

Table 2 suggests different ED consumption limits according to the different body weight profiles considered in this assessment. To prevent sleep disorders, the consumption of EDs should be limited to 175, 262.5 and 350 mL in consumers of a 40, 60 and 80 kg body weight, respectively. To prevent general adverse health effects, Eds formulated with 32 mg caffeine/100 mL should be limited to 375, 562.5 and 750 mL in consumers of a 40, 60 and 80 kg body weight, respectively.

Table 2. Maximum quantities of 32 mg caffeine/100 mL EDs to be consumed (ml) to prevent risks (sleep disturbances and/or general effects on health) derived from the caffeine content.

Body Weight (kg)					
40	60	80	40	60	80
Maximum quantity (ml) of EDs to be consumed to keep daily intake <1.4 mg caffeine/kg b.w. and avoid sleep disorders			Maximum quantity (ml) of EDs to be consumed to keep intake daily <3 mg caffeine/kg b.w. and avoid general adverse effects		
175 mL	262.5 mL	350 mL	375 mL	562.5 mL	750 mL

3.2. *D-glucuronolactone: Exposure Assessment and Risk Characterization from EDs*

Table 3 shows the estimated dietary intakes (EDI) of D-glucuronolactone from EDs formulated with 2400 mg/L. For the risk characterization of the dietary exposure to D-glucuronolactone from EDs, the margins of safety (MOS) were estimated considering the NOAEL of 1000 mg/kg b.w./day [29]. As mentioned above, an acceptable value of the MOS for an NOAEL-based assessment extrapolated from an animal study is $\geq$100.

Table 3. EDs formulated with 2400 mg D-glucuronolactone/L: exposure assessment and risk characterization.

		Consumption Scenarios	
EDs consumption (mL)	250	333	500
D-glucuronolactone intake (mg/day)	600	800	1200
Body weight (bw)		**D-glucuronolactone Intake by b.w. (mg/kg b.w.)**	
40 kg	15.0	20	30.0
60 kg	10.0	13.3	20.0
80 kg	7.5	10.0	15.0
Body weight (bw)		**D-glucuronolactone Margin of Safety (MOS)**	
40 kg	66.7	50	33.3
60 kg	100	75	50
80 kg	133.3	100	66.7

A dietary exposure to D-glucuronolactone from EDs ranges from 600 to 1200 mg depending on the volume of EDs with 2400 mg D-glucuronolactone/l consumed (250–500 mL). Considering the different body weight profiles proposed (40, 60 and 80 kg), a dietary exposure to D-glucuronolactone from EDs is estimated to vary from 7.5 to 30 mg/kg b.w.

Although the results here are higher than those previously reported for European populations by Zucconi et al.: adolescent (100.14 mg/day = 1.65 mg/kg b.w./day), adult (125.95 mg/day = 1.78 mg/kg b.w./day), chronic high adolescent EDs consumers (311.6 mg/day = 4.9 mg/kg b.w./day) and chronic high EDs consumers (268.84 mg/day = 3.9 mg/kg b.w./day). The results here are similar to those estimated for acute Spanish consumers by Zucconi et al.: adult 906.32 mg/day (12.87 mg/kg b.w./day) and 143 mg/day (2.02 mg/kg b.w./day) in acute and chronic use of EDs, respectively; adolescents 551.49 mg/day (9.56 mg/kg b.w./day); and 74.50 mg/day (1.27 mg/kg b.w./day) in an acute and chronic consumption, respectively [13]. It is not possible to compare the results of the present study with those published by the Norwegian Food Safety Agency [65] as this Agency estimated the mean average intake from Eds considering a 240 mg/L D-glucuronolactone content.

The risk characterization performed in the present study by estimating the margin of safety (MOS) suggests that the consumption of a high volume of EDs (up to 500 mL) reduces the MOS. Individuals weighing 60 and 80 kg would only present an MOS $\geq$100 when their consumption of Eds with 2400 mg of D-glucuronolactone/l is limited to 250 mL, although in the latter case this is also observed when their consumption is 333 mL in 80 kg individuals. These results do not support the EFSA statement based on the NOAEL established for the toxicological effects of D-glucuronolactone (1000 mg/kg b.w./day) which reported that dietary exposures at the levels present in EDs are not a health concern for a person of a 60 kg body weight, even when the chronic consumption of EDs is high (350 mL/day) [29]. Finally, an MOS <100 was estimated in all three consumption scenarios (250, 333 and 500 mL) for those individuals with low body weights (around 40 kg) so the health risks from the exposure to the D-glucuronolactone contents in EDs might be expected.

3.3. *Taurine: Exposure Assessment and Risk Characterization from EDs*

Considering a mean taurine content in EDs of 4000 mg/L, Table 4 shows the estimated taurine exposure under three EDs consumption scenarios (250, 333 and 500 mL) and three body weights (40, 60 and 80 kg b.w.). Along with a taurine exposure, the risk is characterized considering the reference EFSA intake for taurine set at 1400 mg/day [29,66].

Table 4. 4000 mg taurine/l EDs: exposure assessment (EDI).

	EDs Consumption Scenarios		
EDs volume (mL)	250	333	500
Taurine Intake (mg/day)	1000	1332	2000
Body weight (kg) and Reference intake (mg/kg b.w./day) [29]	**Taurine Estimated Dietary Intake (EDI) per b.w. (mg/kg b.w./day)**		
40 kg (35 mg/kg b.w./day)	25	33.3	50.0
60 kg (23.3 mg/kg b.w./day)	16.7	22.2	33.3
80 kg (17.5 mg/kg b.w./day)	12.5	16.7	25

A taurine exposure from EDs varies from 1000 to 2000 mg depending on the volume of the EDs consumed. The acute taurine exposure estimated in the assessment here (2000 mg/day) is similar to the acute taurine exposure previously assessed for the European population (1851 mg/day and 1809 mg/day for adults and adolescents, respectively) [13]. However, the intake estimates are higher than those previously reported for chronic consumers [13] not only for adult Europeans (271.9 mg/day (3.82 mg/kg b.w./day)–585.8 mg/day (8.49 mg/kg b.w./day)) but also for adolescents (283.9 mg taurine/day (4.6 mg/kg b.w./day)–924.3 mg taurine/day (14.5 mg/kg b.w./day)). The results are also higher than the mean daily taurine intakes estimated by the ANSES, 181 mg/day (3.02 mg/kg b.w./day; b.w. = 60 kg) for all consumers, 429 mg/day (7.5 mg/kg b.w./day; b.w. = 60 kg) for regular users; and 714 mg/day (53.57 mg/kg b.w./day; b.w. = 60 kg) for chronic users (P90)). The data here are at least five times higher than those reported by the EFSA for adults for Spain in 2013, where a daily taurine exposure from the consumption of EDs was estimated at 290 mg and 149 mg in adults and adolescents, respectively [13]. A possible explanation for this growing dietary exposure from EDs is, as mentioned above, the progressively increasing taurine content in EDs since the first commercialized formulations [30].

According to the present study, a daily EDs ingestion of 500 mL exposes the consumer to a daily dietary intake of 2000 mg of taurine, which exceeds the EFSA daily recommendation of 1400 mg taurine [29]. Considering the different body weight profiles and Eds as the only dietary source of taurine, the assessment here estimates that the taurine exposure from EDs varies between 12.5 mg/kg b.w./day for 80 kg and 50 mg/kg b.w./day for 40 kg.

Considering EDs as the only dietary source of taurine, the following risk characterization was assessed:

In 40 kg b.w. individuals, while the 250 and 333 mL consumption scenarios keep the taurine intake from EDs below the reference value established by the EFSA (35 mg/kg b.w/day), consuming 500 mL will expose the individual to intakes above the reference intake, posing a health risk that may require management and communication measures, such as those proposed above for caffeine.

In 60 kg b.w. individuals, the estimated dietary intake (EDI) ranges from 16.7 to 33.3 mg/kg b.w. Therefore, the 250 and 333 mL consumption scenarios will ensure that the consumer keeps the taurine intake below the 23.3 mg/kg b.w./day considered as the reference value.

In 80 kg b.w. consumers, the estimated dietary intake (EDI) when consuming 250 and 333 mL of EDs would be below the reference value of 17.5 mg/kg b.w./day and no risks are to be expected. However, as before, a 500 mL consumption will expose the consumer to exceeding the reference value and suffer the associated health risks.

Health Canada's health risk assessment concluded that two ED units (250 mL) could be safely consumed each day without negative health effects [58] because the acute oral toxicity of taurine is considered to be relatively low.

The results here are similar to those previously reported by the VKM taurine risk assessment from Eds and food supplements [65]. According to this agency, the dietary intakes in the chronic Eds intake model were all below the reference value and it was unlikely that a chronic taurine intake could cause adverse health effects. However, the abovementioned agency considered that a chronic high taurine intake from EDs could lead to health risks in young children (3 to <10 years) but not to children (10 to 14 years), adolescents (14 to <18 years) or adults [65].

Finally, it is worth mentioning that the uncertainty of the possible effects of a joint taurine and caffeine intake remains unclear, and this may influence a risk assessment as there is a lack of knowledge about the risks of a long-term chronic exposure.

3.4. Risk Management

The management of the risks derived from the dietary exposure to these three EDs active components would be strengthened if there was a legal framework for EDs at a European level with the setting of maximum limits for the active components and their possible combinations. The consumption of EDs and the results on health require a more detailed analysis and follow-up as consumption patterns and risk minimization depend on multiple factors, among which sociodemographic factors stand out [4,19]. Different authors and agencies highlight the need to regulate EDs, to limit and moderate their consumption in children and adolescents, to promote the communication of recommendations and risks associated with their consumption, among others [3,6,17,26,65].

The following recommendations stand out among the different strategies proposed to minimize the health risks associated with EDs: limiting and regulating direct marketing [6,17], raising awareness campaigns such as the one promoted by the AESAN in 2022 [44,67], educational programs on the risks of combining alcohol and energy drinks [1,67,68], having awareness and communication campaigns adapted to different genders and ages [69] and the promotion of the follow-up/monitoring of consumption trends [26,67].

Furthermore, in terms of risk management, the authors suggest following the quadruple helix model to enhance an active collaboration between risk managers and regulators with the industry and the community in order to optimize labeling, portion sizes and risk communication, among others. The volume of ED containers varies, reaching up to 500 mL in some cases, but Energy Drinks Europe (EDE) has committed, in its Code of Practice, to the production and marketing of containers with a net content of 250 mL as the main selling proposition [42]. Moving forward with this initiative and limiting/regulating the volume of marketed ED containers to a maximum of 333 mL would be an effective management action to minimize the risks associated with high intakes of EDs.

4. Conclusions

The growing concern for assessing the health risks associated with the consumption of EDs and the dietary exposure to their active components has led to the commitment of academia, government, industry and society to increase awareness, knowledge and monitoring. It is undoubtedly necessary to advance in the establishment of a legal framework for EDs in Europe that includes the setting of maximum contents of active ingredients, to monitor the dietary exposures to all the active components and not exclusively caffeine and to improve the information to consumers in collaboration with the industry and society at large.

Regarding labeling, there is much room for improvement, such as indicating the content of each of the ingredients, especially those that may pose a health risk, such as D-glucuronolactone and taurine. Smaller volume packaging should be encouraged because limiting this would contribute to moderating the exposure to the different active components. Furthermore, as stated in the report of the Scientific Committee of the AESAN [26], compliance with the industry's commitment to marketing packages containing no more than 250 mL is recommended to minimize exposure to the different active ingredients, some of which are psychoactive, and as well as studying the possibility of stopping the marketing of 500 mL packages.

Consumer recommendations on EDs should be included in risk communication and educational campaigns to increase public awareness and risk perception. EDs advertising and marketing should also be regulated.

Author Contributions: Conceptualization, C.R. and M.C.; methodology, C.R. and M.C.; investigation, C.R., M.C., R.M.G., M.J.G.-M., E.L.-G., F.J.M., M.V.M.-A., M.P.P. and E.B.; writing—original draft preparation, C.R., M.C., R.M.G., M.J.G.-M., E.L.-G., F.J.M., M.V.M.-A., M.P.P. and E.B.; writing—review and editing, C.R., M.C. and E.B.; funding acquisition, M.C. All authors have read and agreed to the published version of the manuscript.

Funding: This research was funded by UCM (Universidad Complutense de Madrid) ALIMNOVA Research Group ref: 951505.

Institutional Review Board Statement: Not applicable.

Informed Consent Statement: Not applicable.

Acknowledgments: This paper is related to the Report of the Scientific Committee of the Spanish Agency for Food Safety and Nutrition (AESAN) on the risks related to the consumption of energy drinks (Reference number: AESAN-2021-005 approved by the Scientific Committee in its plenary session on 17 February 2021). The authors are grateful to all the members of the Scientific Committee of AESAN (2019–2021) and AESAN staff from the NAOS Strategy and Sub directorate-General for Food Safety Promotion.

Conflicts of Interest: The authors declare no conflict of interest.

References

1. Flotta, D.; Micò, R.; Nobile, C.G.; Pileggi, C.; Bianco, A.; Pavia, M. Consumption of energy drinks, alcohol and alcohol-mixed energy drinks among Italian adolescents. *Clin. Exp. Res.* **2014**, *38*, 1654–1661. [CrossRef] [PubMed]
2. Nowak, D.; Jasionowski, A. Analysis of the Consumption of Caffeinated Energy Drinks among Polish Adolescents. *Int. J. Environ. Res. Public Health* **2015**, *12*, 7910–7921. [CrossRef] [PubMed]
3. Costa, B.M.; Hayley, A.; Miller, P. Adolescent energy drink consumption: An Australian perspective. *Appetite* **2016**, *105*, 638–642. [CrossRef] [PubMed]
4. Majori, S.; Pilati, S.; Gazzani, D.; Paiano, J.; Ferrari, S.; Sannino, A.; Checchin, E. Energy drink and ginseng consumption by Italian university students: A cross-sectional study. *J. Prev. Med. Hyg.* **2018**, *59*, E63–E74. [CrossRef] [PubMed]
5. Degirmenci, N.; Fossum, I.N.; Strand, T.A.; Vaktskjold, A.; Holten-Andersen, M.N. Consumption of energy drinks among adolescents in Norway: A cross-sectional study. *BMC Public Health* **2018**, *18*, 1391. [CrossRef] [PubMed]
6. Galimov, A.; Hanewinkel, R.; Hansen, J.; Unger, J.B.; Sussman, S.; Morgenstern, M. Energy drink consumption among German adolescents: Prevalence, correlates and predictors of initiation. *Appetite* **2019**, *139*, 172–179. [CrossRef]
7. Vercammen, K.A.; Koma, J.W.; Bleich, S.N. Trends in Energy Drink Consumption Among, U.S. Adolescents and Adults, 2003-2016. *Am. J. Prev. Med.* **2019**, *56*, 827–833. [CrossRef]
8. Silva-Maldonado, P.; Arias-Rico, J.; Romero-Palencia, A.; Román-Gutiérrez, A.D.; Ojeda-Ramírez, D.; Ramírez-Moreno, E. Consumption Patterns of Energy Drinks in Adolescents and Their Effects on Behavior and Mental Health: A Systematic Review. *J. Psychosoc. Nurs. Ment. Health Serv.* **2022**, *60*, 41–47. [CrossRef]
9. Nadeem, I.M.; Shanmugaraj, A.; Sakha, S.; Horner, N.S.; Ayeni, O.R.; Khan, M. Energy Drinks and Their Adverse Health Effects: A Systematic Review and Meta-analysis. *Sports Health* **2021**, *13*, 265–277. [CrossRef]
10. Tomanic, M.; Paunovic, K.; Lackovic, M.; Djurdjevic, K.; Nestorovic, M.; Jakovljevic, A.; Markovic, M. Energy Drinks and Sleep among Adolescents. *Nutrients* **2022**, *14*, 3813. [CrossRef]
11. Khouja, C.; Kneale, D.; Brunton, G.; Raine, G.; Stansfield, C.; Sowden, A.; Sutcliffe, K.; Thomas, J. Consumption and effects of caffeinated energy drinks in young people: An overview of systematic reviews and secondary analysis of UK data to inform policy. *BMJ Open* **2022**, *12*, e047746. [CrossRef] [PubMed]
12. European Food Safety Authority (EFSA). The food classification and description system FoodEx 2 (revision 2). *EFSA J.* **2015**, *12*, 804E. [CrossRef]
13. Zucconi, S.; Volpato, C.; Adinolfi, F.; Gandini, E.; Gentile, E.; Loi, A.; Fioriti, L. Gathering consumption data on specific consumer groups of energy drinks. *EFSA Support. Publ.* **2013**, *10*, 394E. [CrossRef]
14. Observatorio Español de las Drogas y las Adicciones (OEDA). Encuesta Sobre Uso de Drogas en Enseñanzas Secundarias en España (ESTUDES), 1994–2021. Available online: https://pnsd.sanidad.gob.es/profesionales/sistemasInformacion/sistemaInformacion/pdf/ESTUDES_2021_Informe_de_Resultados.pdf (accessed on 28 July 2022).
15. Mattioli, A.V.; Farinetti, A. Energy drinks and medical students: Bad drinking during COVID-19 quarantine. *Clin. Nutr. ESPEN* **2021**, *59*, 151429. [CrossRef] [PubMed]
16. Mattioli, A.V.; Sabatini, S. Changes in energy drink consumption during the COVID-19 quarantine. *Appl. Nurs. Res.* **2021**, *45*, 516–517. [CrossRef]
17. De Sanctis, V.; Soliman, N.; Soliman, A.T.; Elsedfy, H.; Di Maio, S.; El Kholy, M.; Fiscina, B. Caffeinated energy drink consumption among adolescents and potential health consequences associated with their use: A significant public health hazard. *Acta Biomed.* **2017**, *88*, 222–231.
18. Cruz Muñoz, V.; Urquizu Rovira, M.; Valls Ibañez, V.; Manresa Domínguez, J.M.; Ruiz Blanco, G.; Urquizu Rovira, M.; Toran, P. Consumo de bebidas refrescantes, deportivas y energéticas en adolescentes. Estudio BEENIS. *An. Pediatr.* **2020**, *93*, 242–250. [CrossRef]
19. Oliver Anglès, A.; Camprubí Condom, L.; Valero Coppin, O.; Oliván Abejar, J. Prevalencia y factores asociados al consumo de bebidas energéticas en jóvenes de la provincia de Barcelona. *Gac. Sanit.* **2020**, *35*, 30254–30257. [CrossRef]
20. Trapp, G.; Allen, K.; O'Sullivan, T.A.; Robinson, M.; Jacoby, P.; Oddy, W.H. Energy drink consumption is associated with anxiety in Australian young adult males. *Depresss Anxiety* **2014**, *31*, 420–428. [CrossRef]
21. Trapp, G.; Hurworth, M.; Christian, H.; Bromberg, M.; Howard, J.; McStay, C.; Ambrosini, G.; Martin, K.; Harray, A.; Cross, D.; et al. prevalence and pattern of energy drink intake among Australian adolescents. *J. Hum. Nutr. Diet.* **2021**, *34*, 300–304. [CrossRef]
22. Polak, K.; Dillon, P.; Koch, J.R.; Miller Jr, W.G.; Thacker, L.; Svikis, D. Energy drink use is associated with alcohol and substance use in eighth, tenth, and twelfth graders. *Prev. Med. Rep.* **2016**, *4*, 381–384. [CrossRef] [PubMed]
23. Ruiz, L.D.; Scherr, R.E. Risk of Energy Drink Consumption to Adolescent Health. *Am. J. Lifestyle Med.* **2019**, *13*, 22–25. [CrossRef]

24. Cofini, V.; Cecilia, M.R.; Di Giacomo, D.; Binkin, N.; Di Orio, F. Energy drinks consumption in Italian adolescents: Preliminary data of social, psychological and behavioral features. *Minerva Pediatr.* **2019**, *71*, 488–494. [CrossRef] [PubMed]
25. Higgins, J.P.; Tuttle, T.D.; Higgins, C.L. Energy beverages: Content and safety. *Mayo Clin. Proc.* **2010**, *85*, 1033–1041. [CrossRef] [PubMed]
26. Comité Científico AESAN (Grupo de Trabajo); Rubio, C.; Cámara, M.; Giner, R.M.; González, M.J.; López, E.; Morales, F.J.; Moreno, M.; Portillo, M.P. del Comité Científico de la Agencia Española de Seguridad Alimentaria y Nutrición (AESAN) sobre los riesgos asociados al consumo de bebidas energéticas. *Rev. Com. Científico AESAN* **2021**, *33*, 151–210.
27. French Agency for Food, Environmental and Occupational Health & Safety (ANSES). Opinion of the French Agency for Food, Environmental and Occupational Health & Safety on the Assessment of Risks Concerning the Consumption of So-Called "Energy Drinks". Available online: https://www.anses.fr/en/system/files/NUT2012sa0212EN.pdf (accessed on 5 August 2022).
28. Norwegian Scientific Committee for Food Safety (VKM). Risk assessment of energy drinks and caffeine. *VKM Rep.* **2019**, *1*, 1–277.
29. European Food Safety Authority (EFSA). The use of taurine and D-glucurono-γ-lactone as constituents of the so-called "energy" drinks. *EFSA J.* **2009**, *7*, 935. [CrossRef]
30. Shao, A.; Hathcock, J.N. Risk assessment for the amino acids taurine, L-glutamine and L-arginine. *Regul. Toxicol. Pharmacol.* **2008**, *50*, 376–399. [CrossRef]
31. Rotstein, J.; Barber, J.; Strowbridge, B.; Hayward, S.; Huang, R.; Godefroy, S.B. Energy Drinks: An Assessment of the Potential Health Risks in the Canadian Context. *Int. Food Risk Anal. J.* **2013**, *3*, 1–29. [CrossRef]
32. Pardo-Lozano, R.; Alvarez-García, Y.; Barral-Tafalla, D.; Farré-Albadejo, M. Cafeína: Un nutriente, un fármaco o una droga de abuso. *Adicciones* **2007**, *19*, 225–238. [CrossRef]
33. Soós, R.; Gyebrovszki, Á.; Tóth, Á.; Jeges, S.; Wilhelm, M. Effects of Caffeine and Caffeinated Beverages in Children, Adolescents and Young Adults: Short Review. *Int. J. Environ. Res. Public Health* **2021**, *18*, 12389. [CrossRef] [PubMed]
34. Da Costa, B.R.B.; El Haddad, L.P.; De Martinis, B.S. Caffeine content of energy drinks marketed in Brazil. *Drug Test. Anal.* **2022**, *14*, 1660–1664. [CrossRef] [PubMed]
35. European Food Safety Authority (EFSA). Scientific Opinion on the safety of caffeine. *EFSA J.* **2015**, *13*, 4102. [CrossRef]
36. Ehlers, A.; Marakis, G.; Lampen, A.; Hirsch-Ernst, K.I. Risk assessment of energy drinks with focus on cardiovascular parameters T and energy drink consumption in Europe. *Food Chem. Toxicol.* **2019**, *130*, 109–121. [CrossRef]
37. Aguiar Jr, A.S.; Speck, A.E.; Canas, P.M.; Cunha, R.A. Neuronal adenosine A2A receptors signal ergogenic effects of caffeine. *Sci. Rep.* **2020**, *10*, 13414. [CrossRef]
38. Ferré, S. An update on the mechanisms of the psychostimulant effects of caffeine. *J. Neurochem.* **2008**, *105*, 1067–1079. [CrossRef]
39. Wilson, C. The clinical toxicology of caffeine: A review and case study. *Toxicol. Rep.* **2018**, *5*, 1140–1152. [CrossRef]
40. Chou, T.M.; Benowitz, N.L. Caffeine and coffee: Effects on health and cardiovascular disease. *Comp. Biochem. Physiol. C. Pharmacol. Toxicol. Endocrinol.* **1994**, *109*, 173–189. [CrossRef]
41. Regulation (EU) N° 1169/2011 of the European Parliament and of the Council of 25 October 2011 on the Provision of Food Information to Consumers, Amending Regulations (EC) No 1924/2006 and (EC) N° 1925/2006 of the European Parliament and of the Council, and repealing Commission Directive 87/250/EEC, Council Directive 90/496/EEC, Commission Directive 1999/10/EC, Directive 2000/13/EC of the European Parliament and of the Council, Commission Directives 2002/67/EC and 2008/5/EC and Commission Regulation (EC) No 608/2004. Official Journal of the European Union L 304, 22 de noviembre de 2011, 18 a 63. Available online: https://eur-lex.europa.eu/LexUriServ/LexUriServ.do?uri=OJ:L:2011:304:0018:0063:en:PDF (accessed on 7 October 2022).
42. UNESDA Code for the Labelling and Marketing of Energy Drinks. Initially adopted by the UNESDA Board in May 2010 Updated in October 2016, November 2017 and December 2021. January 2022. Available online: https://www.unesda.eu/wp-content/uploads/2022/06/UNESDA-Code-for-the-Labelling-and-Marketing-of-Energy-Drinks_January-2022.pdf (accessed on 12 October 2022).
43. Code of Practice for the Marketing and Labelling of Energy Drinks (Adopted-BRUSSELS, December 9, 2014). Available online: https://www.energydrinkseurope.org/wp-content/uploads/2020/01/FINAL_EDE-Code-of-Practice_clean_250914.pdf (accessed on 6 February 2021).
44. Recomendaciones Sobre el Consumo de Bebidas Energéticas. Available online: https://www.aesan.gob.es/AECOSAN/docs/documentos/noticias/2022/recomendaciones_bebidas_energeticas.pdf (accessed on 7 October 2022).
45. Scientific Committee on Food (SCF). Opinion of the Scientific Committee on Food on Additional Information on "Energy" Drinks (Expressed on 5 March 2003). Available online: https://www.mast.is/static/files/Uploads/document/Skyrslur/opinionscientificcommitteeenergydr0503.pdf (accessed on 6 December 2021).
46. Brosnan, J.T.; Brosnan, M.E. The sulfur-containing amino acids: An overview. *J. Nutr.* **2006**, *136*, 1636S–1640S. [CrossRef]
47. Font, L.; Miguel, M.; Aragon, C.M. Behavioural consequences of the hypotaurineethanol interaction. *Pharmacol. Biochem. Behav.* **2001**, *70*, 333–339. [CrossRef]
48. Bkaily, G.; Jazzar, A.; Normand, A.; Simon, Y.; Al-Khoury, J.; Jacques, D. Taurine and cardiac disease: State of the art and perspectives. *Can. J. Physiol. Pharmacol.* **2020**, *98*, 67–73. [CrossRef]
49. Sirdah, M.M.; El-Agouza, I.M.; Abu Shahla, A.N. Possible ameliorative effect of taurine in the treatment of iron-deficiency anaemia in female university students of Gaza, Palestine. *Eur. J. Haematol.* **2002**, *69*, 236–242. [CrossRef]

50. Brons, C.; Spohr, C.; Storgaard, H.; Dyerberg, J.; Vaag, A. Effect of taurine treatment on insulin secretion and action, and on serum lipid levels in overweight men with a genetic predisposition for type II diabetes mellitus. *Eur. J. Clin. Nutr.* **2004**, *58*, 1239–1247. [CrossRef] [PubMed]
51. Spohr, C.; Brons, C.; Winther, K.; Dyerberg, J.; Vaag, A. No effect of taurine on platelet aggregation in men with a predisposition to type 2 diabetes mellitus. *Platelets* **2005**, *16*, 301–305. [CrossRef] [PubMed]
52. Gutiérrez-Hellín, J.; Varillas-Delgado, D. Energy Drinks and Sports Performance, Cardiovascular Risk, and Genetic Associations; Future Prospects. *Nutrients* **2021**, *13*, 715. [CrossRef] [PubMed]
53. Babu, K.; Zuckerman, M.D.; Cherkes, J.K.; Hack, J.B. First-onset seizure after use of an Energy Drink. *Pediatr. Emerg. Care* **2011**, *27*, 539–540. [CrossRef]
54. Lourenco, R.; Camilo, M.E. Taurine: A conditionally essential amino acid in humans? An overview in health and disease. *Nutr. Hosp.* **2002**, *17*, 262–270.
55. Schaffer, S.W.; Jong, C.J.; Ramila, K.C.; Azuma, J. Physiological roles of taurine in heart and muscle. *J. Biomed. Sci.* **2010**, *17*, S2–S8. [CrossRef]
56. Zhang, X.; Wang, X.; Zhang, J.; Pan, X.; Jiang, J.; Li, Y. Effects of taurine on alterations of neurobehavior and neurodevelopment key proteins expression in infant rats by exposure to hexabromocyclododecane. *Adv. Exp. Med. Biol.* **2017**, *975*, 119–130. [CrossRef]
57. Chen, C.; Xia, S.; He, J.; Lu, G.; Xie, Z.; Han, H. Roles of taurine in cognitive function of physiology, pathologies and toxication. *Life Sci.* **2019**, *231*, 116584. [CrossRef]
58. Health Canada's Proposed Approach to Managing Caffeinated Energy Drinks. Available online: https://www.canada.ca/content/dam/hc-sc/migration/hc-sc/fn-an/alt_formats/pdf/legislation/pol/energy-drinks-boissons-energisantes-eng.pdf (accessed on 21 July 2022).
59. Brown, J.; Villalona, Y.; Weimer, J.; Pickering Ludwig, C.; Breann, T.H.; Massie, L.; Marczinski, C.A.; Perdan Curran, C. Supplemental taurine during adolescence and early adulthood has sex-specific effects on cognition, behavior and neurotransmitter levels in C57BL/6J mice dependent on exposure window. *Neurotoxicol. Teratol.* **2020**, *79*, 106883. [CrossRef] [PubMed]
60. Jagim, A.R.; Harty, P.S.; Barakat, A.R.; Erickson, J.L.; Carvalho, V.; Khurelbaatar, C.; Camic, C.L.; Kerksick, C.M. Prevalence and Amounts of Common Ingredients Found in Energy Drinks and Shots. *Nutrients* **2022**, *14*, 314. [CrossRef] [PubMed]
61. Lovtidende, A. Bekendtgorelse om Tilsaetning af Visse Andre Stoffer End Vitaminer og Mineraler til Fodevarer. Udgivet den 13 August 2011, Nr 888, 12 August 2011. Available online: https://www.retsinformation.dk/eli/lta/2020/1697 (accessed on 20 September 2022).
62. Zweite Verordnung zur Änderung der Fruchtsaftverordnung und Anderer Lebensmittelrechtlicher Vorschriften vom 21. 2012. Available online: https://www.buzer.de/gesetz/10173/index.htm (accessed on 20 September 2022).
63. Repetto, M.; Sanz, P.; Jurado, C.; López-Artíguez, M.; Menéndez, M.; de la Pena, E. Glosario de Términos Toxicológicos IUPAC (Duffus y Cols. 1993). Available online: https://aetox.es/wp-content/uploads/old/glosater/glosater.aetox.pdf (accessed on 29 August 2022).
64. Verster, J.C.; Koenig, J. Caffeine intake and its sources: A review of national representative studies. *Crit. Rev. Food Sci. Nutr.* **2018**, *58*, 1250–1259. [CrossRef] [PubMed]
65. Risk Assessment of "Other Substances" —Taurine. Opinion of the Panel on Food Additives, Flavourings, Processing Aids, Materials in Contact with Food and Cosmetics of the Norwegian Scientific Committee for Food Safety. Available online: https://vkm.no/download/18.5387be10161937390293e0f/1518616535578/Risk%20assessment%20of%20other%20substances%20%E2%80%93%20Taurine.pdf (accessed on 6 February 2021).
66. Curran, C.P.; Marczinski, C.A. Taurine, caffeine, and energy drinks: Reviewing the risks to the adolescent brain. *Birth Defects Res.* **2017**, *109*, 1640–1648. [CrossRef]
67. Jackson, D.B.; Leal, W.E. Energy drink consumption and the perceived risk and disapproval of drugs: Monitoring the Future, 2010-2016. *Drug Alcohol Depend.* **2018**, *188*, 24–31. [CrossRef]
68. Frayon, S.; Wattelez, G.; Cherrier, S.; Cavaloc, Y.; Lerrant, Y.; Galy, O. Energy drink consumption in a pluri-ethnic population of adolescents in the Pacific. *PLoS ONE* **2019**, *14*, e0214420. [CrossRef]
69. Lebacq, T.; Desnouck, V.; Dujeu, M.; Holmberg, E.; Pedroni, C.; Castetbon, K. Determinants of energy drink consumption in adolescents: Identification of sex-specific patterns. *Public Health* **2020**, *185*, 182–188. [CrossRef]

nutrients

MDPI

Article

Development of the Cook-Ed™ Matrix to Guide Food and Cooking Skill Selection in Culinary Education Programs That Target Diet Quality and Health

Roberta C. Asher [1,2], Tammie Jakstas [1,2], Fiona Lavelle [3], Julia A. Wolfson [4,5,6], Anna Rose [1,2], Tamara Bucher [2,7], Moira Dean [3], Kerith Duncanson [2,8], Klazine van der Horst [9], Sonja Schonberg [9], Joyce Slater [10], Leanne Compton [11], Roslyn Giglia [12], Sandra Fordyce-Voorham [13], Clare E. Collins [1,2] and Vanessa A. Shrewsbury [1,2,*]

1 School of Health Sciences, College of Health, Medicine and Wellbeing, The University of Newcastle, Callaghan, NSW 2308, Australia; roberta.asher@uon.edu.au (R.C.A.); tammie.jakstas@uon.edu.au (T.J.); anna.rose@newcastle.edu.au (A.R.); clare.collins@newcastle.edu.au (C.E.C.)
2 Hunter Medical Research Institute, New Lambton Heights, NSW 2305, Australia; tamara.bucher@newcastle.edu.au (T.B.); kerith.duncanson@newcastle.edu.au (K.D.)
3 School of Biological Sciences, Institute for Global Food Security, Queen's University Belfast, Belfast BT9 5DL, UK; flavelle01@qub.ac.uk (F.L.); moira.dean@qub.ac.uk (M.D.)
4 Department of International Health, Johns Hopkins Bloomberg School of Public Health, Baltimore, MD 21205, USA; jwolfso7@jhu.edu
5 Department of Health Policy and Management, Johns Hopkins Bloomberg School of Public Health, Baltimore, MD 21205, USA
6 Department of Health Management and Policy, School of Public Health, University of Michigan, Ann Arbor, MI 48109, USA
7 School of Environmental and Life Sciences, College of Engineering, Science and Environment, The University of Newcastle, Callaghan, NSW 2308, Australia
8 School of Medicine and Public Health, College of Health Medicine and Wellbeing, The University of Newcastle, Callaghan, NSW 2308, Australia
9 School of Health Professions, Bern University of Applied Sciences, 3012 Bern, Switzerland; klazine.vanderhorst@bfh.ch (K.v.d.H.); sonja.schoenberg@bfh.ch (S.S.)
10 Department of Food and Human Sciences, Faculty of Agricultural and Food Sciences, University of Manitoba, Winnipeg, MB R3T 2N2, Canada; joyce.slater@umanitoba.ca
11 Victorian Curriculum and Assessment Authority, Melbourne, VIC 3000, Australia; leanne.compton@education.vic.gov.au
12 Foodbank Western Australia, Perth, WA 6105, Australia; roslyn.giglia@foodbankwa.org.au
13 Mentone Girls' Grammar School Melbourne, Melbourne, VIC 3194, Australia; sfordyce@mentonegirls.vic.edu.au
* Correspondence: vanessa.shrewsbury@newcastle.edu.au; Tel.: +61-4921-7860

Citation: Asher, R.C.; Jakstas, T.; Lavelle, F.; Wolfson, J.A.; Rose, A.; Bucher, T.; Dean, M.; Duncanson, K.; van der Horst, K.; Schonberg, S.; et al. Development of the Cook-Ed™ Matrix to Guide Food and Cooking Skill Selection in Culinary Education Programs That Target Diet Quality and Health. *Nutrients* **2022**, *14*, 1778. https://doi.org/10.3390/nu14091778

Academic Editor: Sheila Erin Fleischhacker

Received: 25 February 2022
Accepted: 18 April 2022
Published: 24 April 2022

Abstract: Culinary education programs are generally designed to improve participants' food and cooking skills, with or without consideration to influencing diet quality or health. No published methods exist to guide food and cooking skills' content priorities within culinary education programs that target improved diet quality and health. To address this gap, an international team of cooking and nutrition education experts developed the Cooking Education (Cook-Ed™) matrix. International food-based dietary guidelines were reviewed to determine common food groups. A six-section matrix was drafted including skill focus points for: (1) Kitchen safety, (2) Food safety, (3) General food skills, (4) Food group specific food skills, (5) General cooking skills, (6) Food group specific cooking skills. A modified e-Delphi method with three consultation rounds was used to reach consensus on the Cook-Ed™ matrix structure, skill focus points included, and their order. The final Cook-Ed™ matrix includes 117 skill focus points. The matrix guides program providers in selecting the most suitable skills to consider for their programs to improve dietary and health outcomes, while considering available resources, participant needs, and sustainable nutrition principles. Users can adapt the Cook-Ed™ matrix to regional food-based dietary guidelines and food cultures.

Keywords: food skills; cooking skills; education; culinary nutrition

1. Introduction

Cooking and food skills proficiency, and frequent consumption of home-prepared meals, are factors associated with higher diet quality, meaning dietary patterns more closely aligned with food-based dietary guidelines (FBDG) [1–6]. Many countries have created FBDGs to define dietary patterns associated with good health that also consider local cultural and geographical factors [7]. Across these country-specific FBDGs, the core nutrition principles consistently promote a dietary pattern with a high proportion and variety of plant-based whole foods such as vegetables, fruits, and wholegrains, with the addition of meat or meat alternatives, and often dairy or dairy alternatives [8–11]. However, the international literature indicates dietary intakes of most populations are not consistent with their nation's respective FBDGs [12].

Culinary education programs that teach food skills* and cooking skills* for domestic applications consider food agency* to varying degrees and are delivered in a range of settings across education and health sectors (* defined in Box 1) [13–17]. These programs commonly report positive outcomes such as improvements in diet quality [13,15,17–19], cooking confidence [3,13,17–19], and nutrition knowledge [13,17,18]. Culinary interventions that have incorporated food and cooking skills alongside gardening, physical activity, or shared meal experiences and preparation activities have demonstrated further positive outcomes [15,20]. Improving both food and cooking skill levels contribute to improvements in diet quality [3], with some evidence that food skills are a better predictor of diet quality compared with cooking skills [1,4]. Cooking skills may also play a role in preparing and consuming foods consistent with sustainable nutrition principles, as limited cooking skills for plant-based foods is reported as a barrier to reducing meat consumption [21]. Furthermore, improving food agency, which is associated with food and cooking skills, can lead to greater cooking frequency, including more frequent cooking from scratch, and higher intake of vegetables [22]. This evidence highlights the important role of culinary education programs in enhancing participants' food agency and both food and cooking skills.

However, not all studies report effects of culinary education on target health outcomes, and only one review in the field performed meta-analysis, finding no significant association between culinary education programs and anthropometric or cardiometabolic outcomes [15]. Research on the effects of culinary education programs has been limited by a range of factors including availability of valid tools for process and outcome evaluation, and the variable quality of other study design characteristics [3,13,15–19]. Culinary education research to date is further limited by insufficient reporting on the method of developing programs and how content is selected and prioritised [3,23]. Wolfson et al. reported that culinary education programs typically focus on "discrete mechanical tasks" [24], with little information provided about how program content and cooking tasks were selected for inclusion, and whether improving diet quality and health were considered [24]. There is a need for culinary education program developers to provide a rationale for food and cooking skill selection [24].

Box 1. Definitions.

Cooking skills: include food preparation techniques such as chopping, mixing, and heating [25,26] that may or may not require kitchen equipment. Cooking requires perceptual skills to understand how various foods react when manipulated and conceptual skills to understand how different food preparation techniques impact on the taste, colour, and texture of foods [25]. Food skills: are a distinct set of non-cooking skills where knowledge is applied to plan nutritious meals and snacks; select, acquire, and store ingredients; and dispose of food-related waste [27,28]. Food agency: is a framework for understanding the act of cooking within the myriad of factors that influence one's ability both to obtain cooking skills and execute those skills within the contexts of one's social, physical, and economic environments [24,29].

The Cooking Education (Cook-Ed™) model was published to assist culinary education program providers with the complex task of designing, implementing, and evaluating programs that specifically aim to improve diet and health [30]. During the development of the Cook-Ed™ model [30], a gap was identified in the availability of tools for culinary education program providers to assist them in selecting which food and cooking skills to teach within time-limited programs that aim to improve diet quality and health. Such a tool could help strengthen the evidence for food and cooking skill education programs, promote efficient use of program resources, and support development of programs to improve diet quality and health.

The current study addresses this gap through development of the Cook-Ed™ matrix to guide selection of food and cooking skills for inclusion in culinary education programs that target improved participant diet quality and health. This paper describes a modified e-Delphi process used to construct the matrix. The final Cook-Ed™ matrix is provided in Table 1, and this paper also discusses its potential applications as an applied tool that is highly recommended to be used within the context of applying the Cook-Ed™ model [30].

Table 1. The Cook-Ed^{TM} matrix to guide skill selection in culinary education programs that target improved diet quality and health.

	1. Kitchen safety skills		
1.1	Demonstrate familiarity with kitchen layout, equipment, and appliances		
1.2	Demonstrate awareness while working in the kitchen and clear communication practices when working with others		
1.3	Demonstrate appropriate personal hygiene		
1.4	Implement correct procedures to maintain clean kitchen space, equipment, and utensils		
1.5	Implement an ordered and functional workspace		
	2. Food safety skills		
2.1	Assess expiry information on packaged foods to select items for immediate use, or with sufficient storage life for pantry and future use		
2.2	Develop visual and olfactory senses to identify when food may be spoiled (no longer edible)		
2.3	Recognise key food allergens		
2.4	Apply correct transport, storage, and reheating food practices to minimise spoilage, microbial contamination, or cross-contamination		
2.5	Implement strategies to avoid cross-contamination when cooking		
2.6	Implement safe food preparation practices		
	3. General food skills applicable to all food groups listed below		
3.1	Review local nutrition recommendations, where provided, for different stages of life, gender, and health needs e.g., diabetes, hypertension	3.11	Assess food products using food label information and price to select most nutritious options that are compatible with sustainable practices and/or resources available
3.2	Investigate the nutrient profiles of each core food group, their functions, and roles	3.12	Identify sustainable food selection and preparation practices
3.3	Recognise and understand commonly used nutrition terms	3.13	Use ingredient substitutions for recipes when food items are unavailable or unsuitable
3.4	Recognise and understand commonly used culinary terms	3.14	Use leftover ingredients to make another meal/dish
3.5	Assess the need for variety to support a healthy dietary pattern	3.15	Implement culinary short-cuts to prepare a nutritious meal/dish when time is limited to suit skill level or reduce the work of cooking
3.6	Recognise culinary terms of measurement and apply common methods of conversion	3.16	Select suitable recipes for large group sizes, batch cooking for freezing, and/or for use in multiple meals
3.7	Prepare a dish/meal using a recipe	3.17	Prepare a meal with limited ingredients or resources
3.8	Plan a menu for a set period that meets household dietary needs, considering ecological footprint, available resources, and food budget	3.18	Develop planning and kitchen set up processes (mise en place) before meal preparation to enhance efficiency
3.9	Plan a grocery/shopping list based on a menu plan for a set period	3.19	Recognise correct reduce, reuse, and recycle processes of food and non-food kitchen waste
3.10	List common staple ingredients and describe appropriate storage methods for these foods		

Table 1. *Cont.*

4. Food group specific food skills				
Vegetables & Fruit	**Grains**	**Meat & Alternatives**	**Dairy & Alternatives**	**Extras**
4.1.1 Select in season unpackaged produce or minimally packaged produce or low sodium/low sugar packaged alternatives considering price, availability, and sustainable food practices 4.1.2 Identify veg or fruit with short vs. long storage life, purchase and use accordingly to promote diet variety and minimise wastage 4.1.3 Know when and how to clean/wash produce 4.1.4 Apply appropriate storage techniques for stage of ripeness and nutrient retention 4.1.5 Identify techniques and suitable uses for food that is bruised, imperfect, or approaching end of life but still safe for consumption 4.1.6 Identify ways to include different types of veg into snacks and each meal type of the day (e.g., B, L, D) 4.1.7 Modify recipes to include more veg	4.2.1 Identify and select wholegrain and wholegrain based products 4.2.2 Identify grain foods for multiple purposes and to increase wholegrain intake and variety 4.2.3 Know how to use when approaching end of life but still safe for consumption 4.2.4 Modify recipes to increase fibre	4.3.1 Identify and select minimally processed/wholefood meat alternatives to create a variety of plant-based meals 4.3.2 Identify and select lean meats, low sodium and minimally processed/wholefood meat, and meat alternatives 4.3.3 Select recipes that utilise a range of cooking techniques to prepare different cuts of meat, fish varieties, or alternatives considering budget, nutrition, and ecological footprint 4.3.4 Identify a variety of legumes and corresponding preparation and cooking methods 4.3.5 Identify and know how to select eggs or suitable egg alternatives for different purposes and know suitable recipe substitutions 4.3.6 Modify recipes to use lower salt and/or lower saturated fat meat and alternatives	4.4.1 Recognise core vs. extras/non-core dairy or alternatives products 4.4.2 Review the nutritional composition of plant-based milk alternatives to select the most suitable to meet nutritional needs and requirements 4.4.3 Select shelf stable varieties if access to fresh varieties or suitably healthier options is limited 4.4.4 Modify recipes to use lower salt and fat reduced products	4.5.1 Review packaging information to identify extra/non-core foods and/or ingredients and select better alternatives 4.5.2 Modify convenience foods to increase nutrition content 4.5.3 Modify recipes to use or incorporate more core group foods and to replace non-core food items
5. General cooking skills applicable to all food groups listed below				
5.1 Know what cooking methods are suitable to retain nutrients and flavour 5.2 Select healthier oils in suitable amounts to match recipe style 5.3 Develop dishes that add flavour using herbs, spices, and acidic foods as a way of minimising or as an alternative to salt 5.4 Create dishes without a recipe from available resources 5.5 Investigate what flavours, textures and foods complement each other				

Table 1. *Cont.*

6. Food group specific cooking skills				
Vegetables & Fruit	**Grains**	**Meat & Alternatives**	**Dairy & Alternatives**	**Extras**
6.1.1 Demonstrate how to properly wash or clean 6.1.2 Develop processes to use the complete food source (where appropriate) to increase food variety and reduce food waste 6.1.3 Peel (or not) 6.1.4 Pick/tear leaves 6.1.5 Slice, dice/cube $^{\mu}$ 6.1.6 Grate $^{\mu}$ 6.1.7 Boil and simmer 6.1.8 Microwave to retain nutrients 6.1.9 Pan fry/shallow fry, stir fry, sauté 6.1.10 Stew/slow cook 6.1.11 Blend to make a soup, puree, or sauce using available equipment $^{\mu}$ 6.1.12 Grill 6.1.13 Roast 6.1.14 Steam 6.1.15 Poach/Blanch 6.1.16 Prepare a variety of simple cold or hot veg dishes without a recipe 6.1.17 Identify required cooking times for individual veg or as part of a composite meal 6.1.18 Prepare a stock using saved veg peelings 6.1.19 Prepare a fruit-based sauce with no or minimal added sugar 6.1.20 Use a pressure cooker	6.2.1 Weigh and measure dry ingredients 6.2.2 Identify grains that need to soak and use appropriate timing 6.2.3 Microwave 6.2.4 Boil & simmer 6.2.5 Absorption method 6.2.6 Pan fry/shallow fry 6.2.7 Knead dough 6.2.8 Steam 6.2.9 Prepare wholegrain snacks and dishes for each meal of the day (e.g., B, L, D) 6.2.10 Prepare healthier baked products from scratch	6.3.1 Prepare legumes and minimally processed/wholefood alternatives 6.3.2 sup>· Slice, dice/cube $^{\mu}$ 6.3.3 Prepare meat cuts for cooking by trimming off excess fat $^{\mu}$ 6.3.4 Prepare meat or seafood-based stock using saved bones, skin, or fillet from fish, chicken, or beef 6.3.5 Prepare eggs 6.3.6 Preparing egg alternatives for different purposes 6.3.7 Pan fry, shallow fry, stir fry, sauté 6.3.8 Boil and simmer 6.3.9 Stew/slow cook 6.3.10 Grill 6.3.11 Steam 6.3.12 Poach 6.3.13 Blend to make a soup, puree, or sauce using available equipment 6.3.14 Roast 6.3.15 Cook meat, poultry, fish, legumes, and meat alternatives to correct temperature, safe for consumption and palatability 6.3.16 Prepare an egg-based (or egg alternatives) dish 6.3.17 Use nuts/seeds in a variety of dishes/snacks for non-allergic participants to increase nutrient value or as a suitable plant-protein substitute with other ingredients	6.4.1 Weigh and measure liquids, semi-solid and solid food 6.4.2 Grate $^{\mu}$ 6.4.3 Apply heat 6.4.4 Prepare healthier dairy or dairy alternatives-based sauces and dressings	6.5.1 Identify and prepare recipes where high saturated fat ingredients can be swapped for monounsaturated and polyunsaturated fat alternatives 6.5.2 Prepare a typical convenience food using core foods to increase nutritional content 6.5.3 Prepare a healthy beverage from fruit, veg, or dairy/alternatives ingredients 6.5.4 Prepare healthy snacks using a combination of nuts/seeds, grains, fruit, dairy/or alternatives

Table 1. *Cont.*

6. Food group specific cooking skills				
Vegetables & Fruit	**Grains**	**Meat & Alternatives**	**Dairy & Alternatives**	**Extras**
		6.3.18 Prepare healthier meat-based sauces from scratch 6.3.19 Prepare healthier marinades 6.3.20 Use a pressure cooker		

Abbreviations/key: All section headings and sub-headings appear as bolded text, B—breakfast, L—lunch, D—dinner, nutr—nutrient/nutritious/nutritional, w/out—without, info—information, veg—vegetables, vegetable. + 'Use only sometimes and in small amounts' and 'Use in small amounts' as per Australian Guide to Healthy Eating [8], µ include knife/sharps safety training

How to use the Cook-Ed™ matrix

The Cook-Ed™ matrix is a comprehensive table of skills for consideration in cooking education programs that aim to primarily improve diet quality and health. The skills represent those required to prepare basic food groups so that eating patterns align with common food-based dietary guidelines (FBDG) in a general population [31]. The Cook-Ed™ matrix could be adapted to different populations and different FBDGs.

Working across the matrix from left to right are common food groups. Working down each section, skill focus points are ordered in the Cook-Ed™ matrix in the sequence that aligns with typical food preparation i.e., acquiring, transporting, storing, preparing, cooking, disposing, re-purposing, or recycling food or its by-products. To tailor culinary education programs to the precise needs of specific groups, program developers are advised to use the Cook-Ed™ matrix with the Cook-Ed™ model [30] to identify which skills are most relevant and re-arrange the matrix based on factors that have been identified in the planning or evaluation stages of program development. This might include the dietary needs of the specific group or the program aims.

2. Materials and Methods

Matrix Construction

The Cook-Ed^{TM} matrix was developed collaboratively by authors in Australia, Canada, Switzerland, United States, and the United Kingdom with consideration to the findings of the global review of FBDGs by Herforth et al. [31] to enhance its international relevance. Here the three-step process of developing the matrix and its adaptability for international use is described.

- *Step 1. Developing the Structure of the Matrix*

The final version of the Cook-Ed^{TM} matrix (Table 1) included 117 skill focus points spread across six sections: (1) Kitchen safety skills, (2) Food safety skills, (3) General food skills, (4) Food group specific food skills, (5) General cooking skills, (6) Food group specific cooking skills. As the key function of the matrix is to assist with improving the diet quality and health outcomes of culinary education program participants, sections four and six of the matrix include skill focus points categorised by common food groups identified in Herforth et al.'s review [31].

Herforth et al.'s review reported that over 90 countries have FBDGs developed for general populations, with 78 countries also having a "food guide" with graphic representations. However, many had caveats around the use of the FBDGs, or separate guidelines for people at a different life stage or people classified as not 'healthy'. Across the food guides examined in the review, the most common food groups included: starchy staples, vegetables and fruits, protein sources (including meat, poultry, fish, eggs, legumes, nuts, and seeds), dairy and dairy alternatives, fats and oils, and foods and food components to limit. Therefore, columns within matrix sections four and six represent all of these food groups.

- *Step 2. Identifying and Mapping Culinary-Related Skills to Include in the Matrix*

Author RCA (a qualified chef, dietitian, and culinary nutrition researcher) reflected on her training and experience in kitchen and food safety, and reviewed consumer food safety guidelines [32] to draft the initial list of skill focus points in matrix sections one and two. Authors RCA and VAS (a dietitian and culinary nutrition researcher) then drafted a list of general food skill focus points, applicable to all food groups, in section three, and a list of food group-specific food skill focus points in section four based on food skills described by Fordyce-Voorham [27], McGowan et al. [3] and Lavelle et al. [33]. They also drafted a list of general cooking skill focus points in section five of the matrix and food group-specific cooking skill focus points in section six based on domestic cooking skills described by Raber et al. [34], McGowan et al. [3], Lavelle et al. [33], and Short [25,26]. In line with the purpose of the matrix, in sections three to six, only skills considered relevant to promoting diet quality and health were included. For example, healthier cooking methods such as steaming are included in the matrix, whereas less healthful methods such as deep frying are not included. Complex or specialised techniques that would not be necessary for domestic cooking e.g., sous vide, were also not included.

- *Step 3. Modified e-Delphi Process*

The modified e-Delphi process used in this study is shown in Figure 1. In each round, team members were asked to consider the study purpose when giving their responses. As per a traditional Delphi method, three structured feedback rounds were conducted collecting responses from all participants, blinded to each other's responses within each round. A cut off agreement rate of 75% [35–38] was required for decisions about the matrix structure, skill focus point inclusion, order, and wording to be implemented in the matrix presented in the following round and final matrix. The modified aspect of this e-Delphi process [39] was the addition of a structured collaborative meeting in between rounds two and three that provided the opportunity for all authors to participate and share ideas (non-blinded). Several key e-Delphi studies within the field of health and nutrition [36–39] were also used to inform the modified e-Delphi methodology used in this study. Round one of the modified e-Delphi took place in September 2019. Due to the disruption of the COVID-19 pandemic, the next two rounds were postponed and completed between August and October 2021.

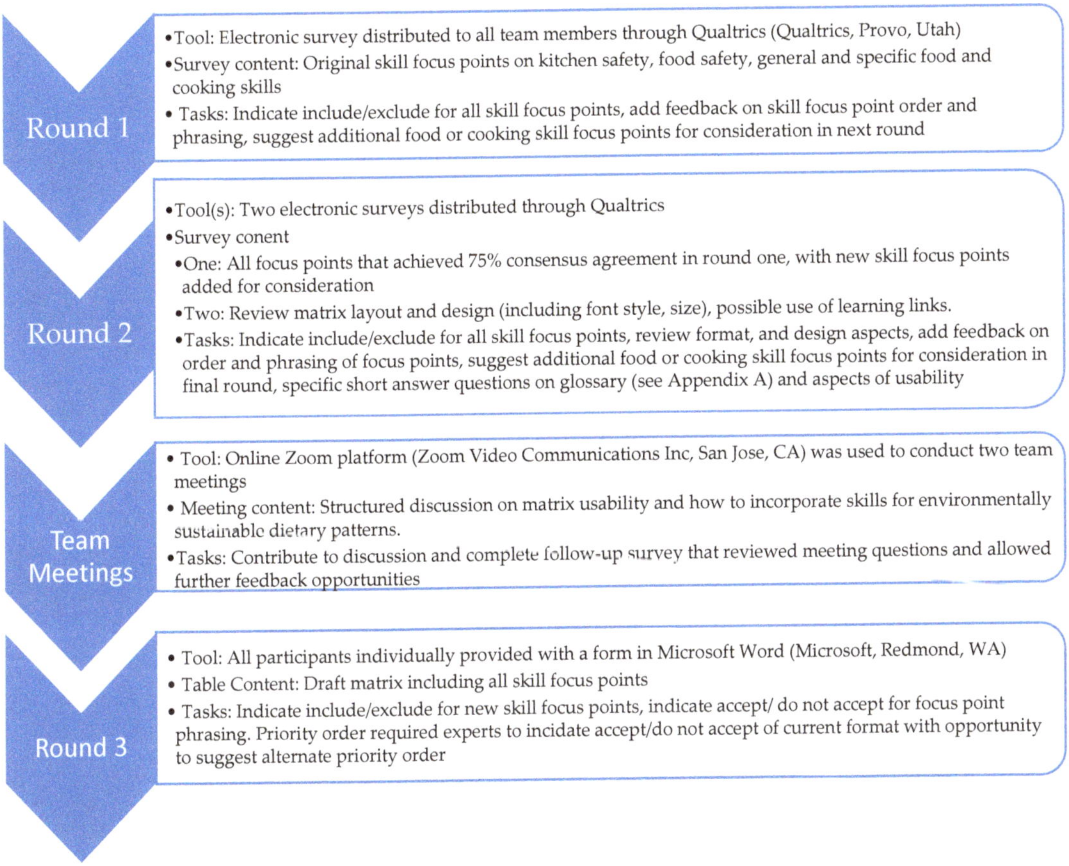

Figure 1. The modified e-Delphi process used in this study.

Round one involved nine authors as participants and a fellow researcher from the University of Newcastle who could not continue to contribute due to changing work commitments (see acknowledgements). Six additional colleagues and collaborators joined the team from round two through to completion. In total, 16 team members (all are authors of this paper) completed rounds two and three. Team members have extensive experience and training in one or more of the following fields: nutrition (CEC, LC, SFV, VAS), dietetics (CEC, JS, KD, RCA, RG, SS, TJ, VAS), commercial cookery (JAW, RCA), cooking and food skill (culinary) education research and/or program development (all authors), behavioural and consumer sciences (FL, KvdH, MD, TB), public health (CEC, JAW, JS), education and curriculum review (LC, SFV, TJ), and occupational therapy (AR).

Ethical considerations: Ethical approval was not needed for this research as the participants were the authors and acted in a consultation capacity.

3. Results

The final matrix includes 117 skill focus points, including 5 kitchen safety skills, 6 food safety skills, 19 general food skills, 24 food group-specific food skills, 5 general food and cooking skills, and 58 food group specific food and cooking skills (Table 1). Working down the matrix, each column lists the order in which the skills would typically be performed when preparing food i.e., acquiring, transporting, storing, preparing, cooking, disposing, repurposing, or recycling food or its by-products. A glossary of terms used in the matrix is provided in Appendix A.

3.1. Modified e-Delphi Consensus and Refinement of Food and Cooking Skill Focus Points

Table 2 details changes in the number of skill focus points in each section of the matrix during the modified e-Delphi process. Throughout the e-Delphi process, new skill focus points were created and some skill focus points were merged. There were 13 skill focus points that did not reach the ≥75% consensus required for inclusion, and these were removed. Skill focus points did not achieve consensus on the basis of: (1) skills were deemed as beyond what is required to achieve a healthy dietary pattern, (i.e., butterfly meats or prepare dough) or (2) concepts that required a high level of existing nutrition knowledge, which were therefore out of the scope of achieving a healthy dietary pattern in the general population (e.g., understanding the functional properties of foods). Comments made by the participants during round three of the modified e-Delphi further highlighted the need to refine skill focus points to contain a verb statement constructed as a learning objective. Using Blooms Taxonomy [40], the majority of skill focus points were rephrased as a learning objective with an embedded safety, food, or cooking skill.

Table 2. Kitchen safety, food safety, food skill, and cooking skill focus points: Selection and categorisation throughout modified e-Delphi rounds.

	Matrix Section	Food Group	Focus Points (n)			
Year			2019		2021	
e-Delphi Round			Original	1	2	3
	1. Kitchen Safety Skills		2	5	5	5
	2. Food Safety Skills		9	6	6	6
	3. General Food Skills		20	17	20	19
	4. Food Group Specific Food Skills	Vegetables	7	7	9	7
		Fruit	6	6	*	*
		Grains	4	5	5	4
		Meat and Alternatives	4	5	7	6
		Dairy and Alternatives	5	3	4	4
		Extras	2	3	3	3
	5. General Cooking Skills		5	5	6	5
	6. Food Group Specific Cooking Skills	Vegetables	20	20	21	20
		Fruit	9	8	*	*
		Grains	11	12	10	10
		Meat and Alternatives	23	22	20	20
		Dairy and Alternatives	7	6	4	4
		Extras	4	4	4	4
Total			138	134	124	117
Team members participating (n)			2	7	15	15
Tools used in e-Delphi round				Qualtrics Survey	Qualtrics Survey	Structured Table

* Fruit merged with Vegetables subgroup from round 2.

3.2. Modified e-Delphi Team Meetings

While the initial focus of the matrix was to identify food and cooking skills necessary to achieve a healthy dietary pattern, as discussions progressed, the importance of including food and cooking skills to support sustainable dietary patterns for human and planetary health emerged [41,42]. This resulted in existing skill focus points (Table 1) being reviewed to incorporate sustainable nutrition principles where practical and relevant, e.g., emphasising the importance of and practical ways of improving legume consumption (skill focus point 4.3.4), the concept of recycle, reuse, and reduce (3.19), and in developing processes to use the complete food source (6.1.2). These skill focus points were then reviewed in round three of the e-Delphi for inclusion or exclusion and optimal phrasing.

3.3. Using the Cook-Ed^{TM} Matrix Together with the Cook-Ed^{TM} Model to Determine Priority Food and Cooking Skills

Where applicable, food and cooking skills specific to each of the common food groups are outlined in sections four and six of the matrix to ensure the necessary skills required to select, prepare, and ultimately consume a wide variety of foods from each of these groups can be achieved. While the matrix can be used on its own as an applied programming tool to guide content and learning materials, it is highly recommended that program providers use it within the context of applying the Cook-Ed^{TM} model [30] (as shown in Figure 2). The Cook-Ed^{TM} model has been created to assist program providers in tailoring culinary education programs to the needs of specific groups and guide them through all steps of program creation from conception and development to evaluation [30]. The selection and structure of culinary education program activities, such as food and cooking skill instruction, should align with the program aims and objectives as well as participant's learning goals and needs [43,44]. Once program aims and objectives have been defined using the model (see Cook-Ed^{TM} model [30] Stage 4—"Develop program content and facilitation guides"), culinary education program providers can use the matrix (Table 1) to select and prioritise food and cooking skills to teach based on the needs and characteristics of the target audience and information gathered in program planning (see Cook-Ed^{TM} model [30] Stages 1 to 3—"Define the cooking-related need or problem", "Consider behavior change factors", and "Capacity assessment").

Health and safety principles should underpin food and cooking skill education programs to any audience and be a common thread integrated throughout the program. These are listed within section one and two of the Cook-Ed^{TM} matrix (Table 1). Throughout a cooking program, participants should receive appropriate information about health and safety, applicable to the demonstration kitchen and also the home setting where learned skills will be applied. This may include information on the safe handling of knives, electrical equipment, hot surfaces, slip or trip hazards in the kitchen, and appropriate kitchen attire. This is in addition to general food safety knowledge and practices to minimise microbial and other contamination of food.

Program providers without nutrition and dietetic expertise are encouraged to consult with such qualified professionals in the planning phases to ensure that program content aligns with current dietary advice and nutrition principles.

When determining skills to include, life stage, cognitive and motor skills of participants also need to be considered, e.g., culinary education programs for younger children need to teach food and cooking skills that are developmentally appropriate [45]. For people with cognitive and/or physical impairments, the demands of the skills selected need to consider an individual's capacity to perform the skill and the availability of helpful modifications (e.g., assistive technology). Consultation with an occupational therapist is suggested to support efficient and effective skill development and/or adaptation to the environment or activity to enable participant engagement.

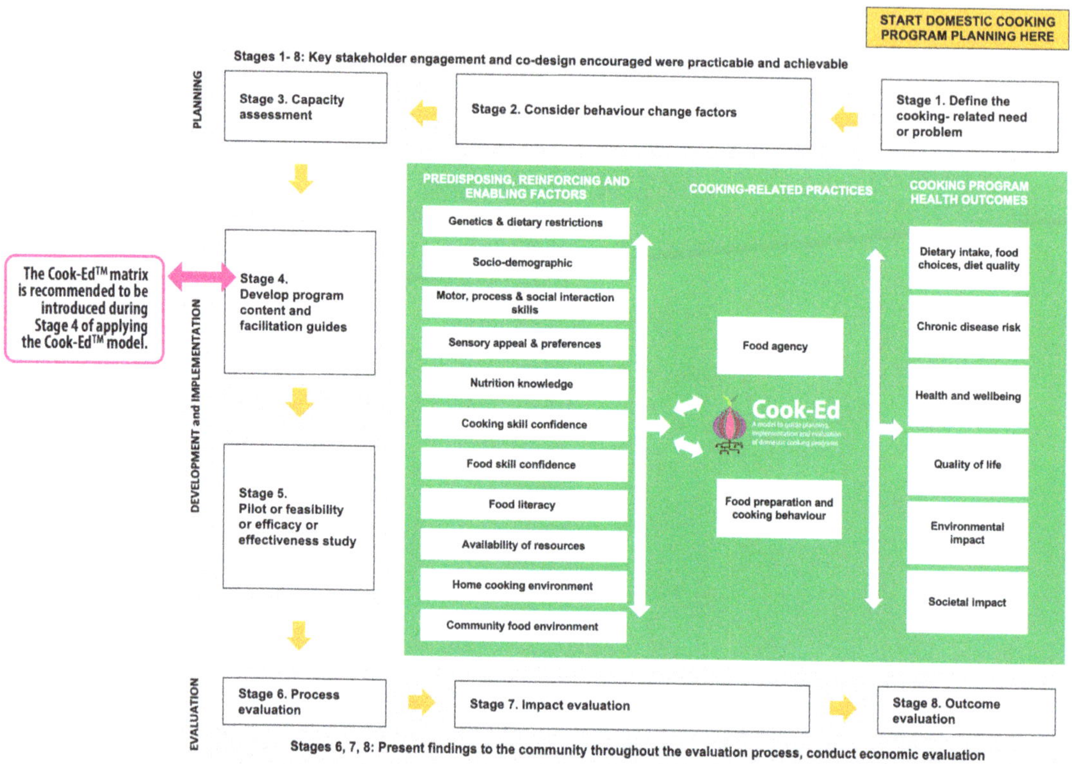

Figure 2. Illustration showing where to introduce the Cook-Ed^{TM} matrix when applying the Cook-Ed^{TM} model [30].

The Cook-Ed^{TM} matrix has been designed to support practical application of learning theory by program providers. The matrix assists with the selection of appropriate activities and can therefore support matching of both food and cooking skill development needs with the current skill levels of program participants. Evaluation data gathered may also be used to modify future programs in an iterative manner.

3.4. Consdering Appropriate Skill Level of Cook-Ed^{TM} Matrix Items

To enhance usability of the Cook-Ed^{TM} matrix, the concept of tiered learning opportunities (See Box 2) for some skill focus points was raised in the e-Delphi. For example, skills focus points could be further broken down into basic, intermediate, and advanced skills. The basic level is suitable to achieve a healthy dietary pattern, with intermediate and advanced levels offering enhanced skills to expand food and cooking skill development opportunities. This concept would allow program providers to select the level of the skill focus point that is best suited to the abilities and needs of their participants and adapt teaching as their skills increase, allowing them to build on skills previously acquired.

Box 2. Example of a tiered learning opportunity for skills focus point 6.3.1.

Original: prepare legumes, and minimally processed/whole food alternatives Basic: identify low/no sodium tin/canned legume varieties, drain, and rinse for use Advanced: purchase dried legumes and prepare using pressure cooker to reduce cooking time, freeze excess for use in other dishes.

4. Discussion

The Cook-Ed™ matrix is a comprehensive set of safety, food, and cooking skills specific to common food groups in FBDGs. To our knowledge, the matrix is the first tool available, generated through expert consensus, to guide researchers and culinary education program providers in selecting skills to improve diet and health outcomes. The skill focus points aim to promote development of skills required to achieve healthy dietary patterns that align with FBDGs for a general population and incorporate sustainable nutrition principles. It is recommended that the Cook-Ed™ matrix be used in the context of applying the Cook-Ed™ model [30], as illustrated in Figure 2, so that it guides culinary education program providers to select the most suitable skill focus points based on participants' available resources and needs.

Limitations of cooking research to date include weak study designs, a high degree of heterogeneity in outcome measures and study populations, and poor reporting of program development activities, including selection of program content [3,16–19]. When used together (Figure 2), the Cook-Ed™ model [30] and the Cook-Ed™ matrix (Table 1) provides researchers and culinary education program providers with resources to strengthen the evidence for culinary nutrition education programs and their influence on diet quality and health.

Consideration of other factors influencing cooking behaviour should be recognised. Healthy cooking behaviour is complex, and a myriad of personal, socioeconomic, cultural, and environmental factors can interact to influence cooking behaviour and diet quality [4,5]. Factors other than food and cooking skills, such as socio-demographic characteristics, nutrition knowledge, and psychological wellbeing are key influences on diet quality [4]. In a nationally representative sample of adults in the USA, Wolfson et al., [6] reported that cooking frequency does not influence diet quality equally across socio-economic groups, suggesting additional factors such as food provision may be more pertinent considerations for culinary nutrition education program providers when working with different groups. As recommended in the Cook-Ed™ model [30], conducting an assessment of these factors before developing program content, and iteratively through program implementation, can inform education sessions focused on highest priority skills. Examples of prioritising skills in a culinary nutrition education program after assessment of the target audience can be found in Table 3.

Table 3. Example of prioritising skills in a culinary nutrition education program.

Participant Context	Do not Prioritise	Do Prioritise
Limited access to fresh produce due to finances, availability, or capacity to safely store food	Preparation skills of mainly fresh vegetables and fruit Recipes with expensive ingredients, batch cooking for freezing, and/or for use in multiple meals	Food and cooking skills for frozen, canned, and/or identify long-storage shelf life vegetables (e.g., cabbage) Preparation of single portion meals using econonomical ingredients
No access to a blender	Blended soups, puree, or sauce	Soups or dips that remain texturally and visually appealing when mashed with a fork and served chunky Assess food products using food label information and price to select most nutritious soup, puree, or sauce options that are compatible with sustainable practices and/or resources available
Young children not yet able to use knives and hot cooking equipment independently	Meals and snacks that require extensive cutting with large sharp knives (e.g., pumpkin) and/or use of heat	Meal and snack assembly skillsSoft food items that can be easily cut with appropriate knives (e.g., banana, mushrooms)

Complimentary activities such as shared meal preparation, sitting down to a shared meal at the close of a practical session, and taste testing may be considered, and are frequently associated with, positive outcomes [46–49]. These can enrich culinary learning programs and enhance learning experiences by encouraging group discussion, family food preparation and meal planning discussion beyond the program and provide participants with opportunities to try new recipes and unfamiliar foods and flavours [46,48,49]. Developing an appreciation of new flavours, tastes and foods, and increased preference for fruit and vegetables can support dietary intakes that align more closely with FBDGs [46,48]. Similarly, program providers may consider other social and physical activities, such as gardening, grocery store tours, or physical activity sessions that can enhance program outcomes [15].

Incorporating sustainable nutrition principles was not an a priori aim of the matrix. However, it was an important consideration raised by participants during the e-Delphi process who recognize that culinary education researchers, program providers, and consumers all have a key role to play in achieving environmentally sustainable nutrition goals that can also be compatible with achieving higher dietary quality and favourable health outcomes [42,50]. Informed by the growing evidence on healthy diets from sustainable food systems, the e-Delphi participants acknowledged that foods consistent with sustainable nutrition principles (e.g., unprocessed plant-based food) can require greater time, effort, and skill to prepare, and they must taste good and be culturally appropriate [42,50]. With the current developments towards sustainable nutrition, the complexity of food skills to be taught in interventions is increasing substantially, and therefore sustainable nutrition principles were considered an important element to consider when developing skill focus points in the matrix.

The Cook-Ed™ matrix may have other applications beyond dedicated culinary education programs. For example, many of the food skill components of the matrix could be used to guide the content of nutrition education sessions in health-related programs (e.g., in chronic disease prevention or treatment programs reviewing local nutrition recommendations for different stages of life and health needs, or investigating the nutrient profiles of each core food group, their functions, and roles), which may not always have the facilities, resources, or time allocation to practically teach cooking skills). Other examples include learning to recognise key nutrition and culinary terms, planning a menu to meet personal and household needs, and accompanying shopping/grocery list. Furthermore, with the onset of the COVID-19 pandemic, a transition to virtual education modes to deliver culinary education programs has been more common with programs facilitated outside the traditional kitchen space [51,52].

A strength of this study is that the authors contributing to the development of the matrix are an international team, but it needs to be highlighted that this expertise is focused across countries with similar food and cooking cultural requirements. The Cook-Ed™ matrix has broad international relevance, but culinary education providers should consider the items in the matrix within the context of their own FBDGs, food and cooking culture and practices, and food availability and adapt the matrix accordingly. Additional food and cooking skills may need to be considered for the matrix to be applied to programs for other cultural groups and countries with eating patterns other than a Western diet. Similarly, additional food and cooking skills may need to be considered for non-domestic culinary education programs (e.g., commercial cookery programs), or programs where skills to improve diet quality and health are not the primary aim. A limitation of the matrix is that it is not a comprehensive list of all food and cooking skills that could be included in culinary programs

A further strength is that the design of the matrix and skill focus point selection process, via a modified e-Delphi process with three rounds, permitted independent and deep analysis to develop the final skill focus points shown in the matrix in Table 1. It is acknowledged that while the use of the Herforth et al review of FBDG provided a structured approach for linking the matrix learning objectives with dietary quality outcomes, the approach to incorporating sustainable nutrition principles was less structured [31].

5. Conclusions

The Cook-Ed™ matrix presented is an evidence-based applied tool to assist in the selection and prioritisation of food and cooking skills for inclusion in culinary nutrition education programs to improve diet quality and health of participants. The matrix can be used in a variety of global settings by adapting outcomes to meet country-specific FBDGs. By detailing the process of developing the matrix and publishing it here as a freely available tool in an open access journal, cooking program providers in a variety of settings will be able to use the Cook-Ed™ matrix as a program development tool. To assist with tracking the application and impact of the Cook-Ed™ matrix, we encourage users to acknowledge when and how the matrix was used in their projects. When used together with the Cook-Ed™ model [30], the Cook-Ed™ matrix supports program providers in selecting and prioritising food and cooking skills relevant to their participant group based on program goals, nutrition recommendations for different life stages, and participant skill development needs and preferences. Further research is needed to examine the application of the matrix as an applied tool to guide program content development across a wide range of settings and target groups.

Author Contributions: Conceptualization, V.A.S. and C.E.C.; methodology, R.C.A., T.J., C.E.C. and V.A.S.; formal analysis, T.J. and V.A.S.; investigation, R.C.A., T.J., F.L., J.A.W., A.R., T.B., M.D., K.D., K.v.d.H., S.S., J.S., L.C., R.G., S.F.-V., C.E.C. and V.A.S.; writing—original draft preparation, R.C.A., T.J., C.E.C. and V.A.S.; writing—review and editing, R.C.A., T.J., F.L., J.A.W., A.R., T.B., M.D., K.D., K.v.d.H., S.S., J.S., L.C., R.G., S.F.-V., V.A.S. and C.E.C.; supervision, V.A.S. and C.E.C. All authors have read and agreed to the published version of the manuscript.

Funding: R.C.A. and T.J. are supported by King and Amy O'Malley Trust postgraduate scholarships. V.A.S. is supported by a Hunter Medical Research Institute grant (HMRI Grant: 1664). T.B. is supported by the Australian Research Council (Grant G1901512). J.A.W. was supported by the National Institutes of Diabetes and Digestive and Kidney Diseases of the National Institutes of Health (Award #K01DK119166). CEC is supported by an NHMRC Investigator Grant (APP2009340).

Institutional Review Board Statement: Ethical review and approval were waived for this study, as the international experts acted in a consultation capacity and all are authors, or acknowledgment is noted for contributions.

Informed Consent Statement: Not applicable.

Data Availability Statement: The complete dataset generated from this study are available on request from the corresponding author.

Acknowledgments: Tracy Burrows (Participated in the first e-Delphi round), Grace Manning (Assisted with the matrix design and layout, Figure 2, and graphical abstract).

Conflicts of Interest: No author conflicts of interest or funding conflicts have been identified in the production of this research.

Appendix A

Table A1. Glossary of key terms within the Cook-Ed™ matrix.

Term	Definition
	Kitchen & Food Safety
Cross-contamination	Unintended movement of micro-organisms, contaminants, or allergens from between foods e.g., from raw food to cooked food [53].
Microbial contamination	Unintended introduction of potentially harmful microorganisms (e.g., bacteria, mould, fungi, yeast) into food.

Table A1. *Cont.*

Term	Definition
	Kitchen & Food Safety
Personal hygiene	The practice of maintaining a standard of cleanliness of one's body. Personal hygiene required for food preparation can include hand and body washing, cough and sneeze etiquette, maintenance of hair and nails, clothing.
	Food & Nutrition Terminology
Beans	A type of legume, examples include red kidney beans, black beans, borlotti beans.
Chickpeas	A type of legume.
Convenience food	Food that requires little preparation or cooking prior to consumption. Often refers to commercially prepared food such as TV dinners, ready-meals, frozen meals.
Cooking skills	Include a range of food preparation techniques such as chopping, mixing, and heating [25,26] that may or may not require kitchen equipment. Cooking requires perceptual skills to understand how various foods react when manipulated and conceptual skills to understand how different food preparation techniques impact on the taste, colour, and texture of foods [25].
Core foods	The Australian Dietary Guidelines definition "foods that form the basis of a healthy diet, based on or developed with reference to recommended daily intakes (RDIs)" [8].
Core food groups (within the Cook-Ed™ matrix)	Vegetables and Fruits, Grains, Meat and Alternatives (e.g., legumes, nuts, seeds, tofu), Dairy and Alternatives.
Dietary fibre	Edible part of plant food that resists digestion in the small intestine and may be fermented to varying degrees in the large intestine. Includes soluble and insoluble fibre and resistant starches.
Dietary pattern	Refers to the variety, amount, and combination of food and drinks in the diet and the frequency with which they are habitually consumed.
Fats & Oils	Edible fats and oils occurring naturally in food, used in food manufacturing or cooking. May also be referred to as dietary fat. Dietary fats can be classified as saturated fat, trans fat, polyunsaturated fat, and monounsaturated fat. Edible fats and oils typically contain a combination of the different dietary fat.
Food-based dietary guidelines	The Food and Agriculture Organization of the United Nations definition (also known as dietary guidelines) are intended to establish a basis for public food and nutrition, health and agricultural policies, and nutrition education programmes to foster healthy eating habits and lifestyles. They provide advice on foods, food groups, and dietary patterns to provide the required nutrients to the general public to promote overall health and prevent chronic diseases" [7].
Food skills	Include meal planning, shopping, budgeting, resourcefulness, and interpreting food labels and nutrition information panels [27,33]. Lavelle et al. 2019 used psychometric testing to delineate food skills as a distinct set of non-cooking skills that enable individuals to apply knowledge about food to then prepare meals and snacks that are nutritionally appropriate within the available resources [33].
Food waste	The Food and Agricultural Organization definition "the decrease in quantity or quality of food resulting from decisions and actions made by retailers, food service providers and consumers" [54].
Grains	Commonly referred to as cereals or cereal grains and which are the edible seeds of specific grasses [8].
Legumes	Plant in the Leguminosae (Fabeceae) family. The term legume may also be used to refer to the edible seed or pod (e.g., beans, lentils, peas, and chickpeas). Legumes come in a variety of shapes, sizes, and colours.
Lentils	A type of legume, examples include yellow lentils, brown lentils, red lentils.

Table A1. *Cont.*

Term	Definition
	Food & Nutrition Terminology
Meat alternatives	Can include a range of wholefood items such as nuts, seeds, legumes and mushrooms, or minimally processed foods made from combinations of these.
Menu plan	A detailed list of dishes and/or recipes for a specific meal, day, or week.
Minimally processed	NOVA classification definition "natural foods altered by methods that include removal of inedible or unwanted parts, and also processes that include drying, crushing, grinding, powdering, fractioning, filtering, roasting, boiling, non-alcoholic fermentation, pasteurisation, chilling, freezing, placing in containers, and vacuum packaging ... methods and processes ... designed to preserve natural foods, to make them suitable for storage, or else to make them safe or edible or more pleasant to consume" [55].
Non-core food	Foods that do not fit within the definition of 'core foods' (refer to core foods).
Non-core food group (within the Cook-Ed^{TM} matrix)	Extras (also called energy dense, nutrient poor foods, discretionary or junk).
Nutrient dense foods	A good source of essential macro and micronutrients.
Peas	A type of legume, examples include chickpeas, black-eyed peas, split peas.
Plant-based	A meal or dietary pattern that focuses on including mostly core foods that come from vegetable, fruit, nuts, seeds, legumes, and wholegrain groups.
Pulse	The edible, dried seed of a legume (e.g., beans, lentils, peas, chickpeas). The term legume is used to describe pulses within the matrix.
Processed products	Made by adding salt, oils, sugar or items used to prepare and/or season food. Using preservation methods such as canning, bottling, and in some cases using non-alcoholic fermentation processes [55].
Shelf life	The expected length of time a food will maintain its best quality [53].
Shelf stable	Does not require refrigeration.
Staple food	Food item(s) that are eaten frequently and form the basic components of a usual dietary pattern [53].
Storage life	Time in which a food item can be safely kept in the fridge, freezer, or pantry to maintain quality and remain edible.
Sustainable eating	Selecting foods that are healthful for the environment and that support human health.
Vegan	A meal or dietary pattern that includes only foods from plant-based origin.
Vegetarian	A meal or dish that focuses on including mostly core foods that come from vegetable, fruit, nuts, seeds, legumes, and wholegrain foods with variation that can include some dairy, seafood, and eggs.
Ultra-processed	NOVA classification definition "formulations of ingredients, mostly of exclusive industrial use, made by a series of industrial processes, many require sophisticated equipment and technology ... colours, flavours, emulsifiers and other additives ... to make the product palatable or hyper-palatable" [55].
	Culinary terms
Absorption method	Wholegrains like rice or quinoa, place in cool water, bring the water to the boil, simmer for a short period and then turn off heat and cover with pot lid for the remainder of the cooking time to allow grain to absorb liquid and finishing cooking for a drier, fluffy result.
Baking	Cook food in dry heat in an oven.
Blanch	To subject food to boiling water by plunging into boiling water and removing after a few seconds.

Table A1. *Cont.*

Term	Definition
	Culinary terms
Blend (puree)	Using a mini blender/stick blender/bar mix or hot blender (e.g., Thermomix^{TM}) to produce a finely mashed, smooth, or liquid consistency.
Boil	Cook food submerged in a boiling liquid, or food being cooked at boiling point.
Dice/cube	To cut even pieces in the rough shape of a dice or cube, size of dice/cube dependent upon the dish being prepared.
Grate	Using a vegetable/box grater, run the food item down and up or along the grater, being mindful of having the grater set securely on a cutting board or large plate/bowl and to keep fingers at a safe distance.
Grill	Cook food by radiant heat. May also be referred to as broiling or barbequing.
Pan fry	Cook food in a small amount of fat/oil. May also be referred to as shallow frying or sauté.
Poach	Cook food in a liquid that is below boiling point.
Roast	Cook food in dry heat in the presence of fat/oil.
Sauté	Cook food in a small amount of fat/oil. May also be referred to as pan frying or sauté or gently fry.
Scratch cooking	Cook food from raw or minimally processed ingredients.
Simmer	Cook food submerged in a liquid that is just below boiling point but bubbling.
Slice	To cut thin pieces either along or across the food item depending on the dish being prepared.
Stew/Slow cook	Cook food at a long temperature for an extended period of time in a sufficient amount of liquid; the food and cooking liquid are typically served together.
Steam	Cook food in steam/vapour.
Shallow fry	Cook food in a small amount of fat/oil. May also be referred to as pan frying or sauté.
Stir fry	Cook food in a small amount of oil, often at a high heat for a short period of time while stirring constantly. Stir frying is often performed in a wok (bowl shaped pan).

Key: the section headings and subheadings appear as bolded text

References

1. Lavelle, F.; Bucher, T.; Dean, M.; Brown, H.M.; Rollo, M.E.; Collins, C.E. Diet quality is more strongly related to food skills rather than cooking skills confidence: Results from a national cross-sectional survey. *Nutr. Diet.* **2020**, *77*, 112–120. [CrossRef] [PubMed]
2. Lavelle, F.; Spence, M.; Hollywood, L.; McGowan, L.; Surgenor, D.; McCloat, A.; Mooney, E.; Caraher, M.; Raats, M.; Dean, M. Learning cooking skills at different ages: A cross-sectional study. *Int. J. Behav. Nutr. Phys. Act.* **2016**, *13*, 119. [CrossRef] [PubMed]
3. McGowan, L.; Caraher, M.; Raats, M.; Lavelle, F.; Hollywood, L.; McDowell, D.; Spence, M.; McCloat, A.; Mooney, E.; Dean, M. Domestic cooking and food skills: A review. *Crit. Rev. Food Sci. Nutr.* **2017**, *57*, 2412–2431. [CrossRef] [PubMed]
4. McGowan, L.; Pot, G.K.; Stephen, A.M.; Lavelle, F.; Spence, M.; Raats, M.; Hollywood, L.; McDowell, D.; McCloat, A.; Mooney, E.; et al. The influence of socio-demographic, psychological and knowledge-related variables alongside perceived cooking and food skills abilities in the prediction of diet quality in adults: A nationally representative cross-sectional study. *Int. J. Behav. Nutr. Phys. Act.* **2016**, *13*, 111. [CrossRef]
5. Mills, S.; White, M.; Brown, H.; Wrieden, W.; Kwasnicka, D.; Halligan, J.; Robalino, S.; Adams, J. Health and social determinants and outcomes of home cooking: A systematic review of observational studies. *Appetite* **2017**, *111*, 116–134. [CrossRef]
6. Wolfson, J.A.; Leung, C.W.; Richardson, C.R. More frequent cooking at home is associated with higher Healthy Eating Index-2015 score. *Public Health Nutr.* **2020**, *23*, 2384–2394. [CrossRef]
7. Food and Agriculture Organization of the United Nations. Food-Based Dietary Guidelines. Available online: https://www.fao.org/nutrition/education/food-based-dietary-guidelines (accessed on 2 February 2022).
8. National Health and Medical Research Council. *Australian Dietary Guidelines*; National Health and Medical Research Council: Canberra, Australia, 2013.
9. Public Health England. *Government Dietary Recommendations*; Public Health: London, UK, 2016.

10. Swiss Society for Nutrition SGE. Swiss Food Pyramid. Available online: https://www.sge-ssn.ch/ich-und-du/essen-und-trinken/ausgewogen/schweizer-lebensmittelpyramide/ (accessed on 24 February 2022).
11. U.S. Department of Agriculture; U.S. Department of Health and Human Services. *Dietary Guidelines for Americans, 2020–2025*; U.S. Department of Agriculture: Washington, DC, USA, 2020.
12. GDP 2017 Diet Collaborators. Health effects of dietary risks in 195 countries, 1990–2017: A systematic analysis for the Global Burden of Disease Study 2017. *Lancet* **2019**, *393*, 1958–1972. [CrossRef]
13. Asher, R.C.; Shrewsbury, V.A.; Bucher, T.; Collins, C.E. Culinary medicine and culinary nutrition education for individuals with the capacity to influence health related behaviour change: A scoping review. *J. Hum. Nutr. Diet.* **2021**, *35*, 388–395. [CrossRef]
14. Downer, S.; Berkowitz, S.A.; Harlan, T.S.; Olstad, D.L.; Mozaffarian, D. Food is medicine: Actions to integrate food and nutrition into healthcare. *BMJ* **2020**, *369*, m2482. [CrossRef]
15. Hasan, B.; Thompson, W.G.; Almasri, J.; Wang, Z.; Lakis, S.; Prokop, L.J.; Hensrud, D.D.; Frie, K.S.; Wirtz, M.J.; Murad, A.L.; et al. The effect of culinary interventions (cooking classes) on dietary intake and behavioral change: A systematic review and evidence map. *BMC Nutr.* **2019**, *5*, 29. [CrossRef]
16. Hersch, D.; Perdue, L.; Ambroz, T.; Boucher, J.L. The Impact of Cooking Classes on Food-Related Preferences, Attitudes, and Behaviors of School-Aged Children: A Systematic Review of the Evidence, 2003–2014. *Prev. Chronic Dis.* **2014**, *11*, 140267. [CrossRef] [PubMed]
17. Taylor, R.M.; Wolfson, J.A.; Lavelle, F.; Dean, M.; Frawley, J.; Hutchesson, M.J.; Collins, C.E.; Shrewsbury, V.A. Impact of preconception, pregnancy, and postpartum culinary nutrition education interventions: A systematic review. *Nutr. Rev.* **2020**, *79*, 1186–1203. [CrossRef] [PubMed]
18. Reicks, M.; Kocher, M.; Reeder, J. Impact of Cooking and Home Food Preparation Interventions Among Adults: A Systematic Review (2011–2016). *J. Nutr. Educ. Behav.* **2018**, *50*, 148–172. [CrossRef]
19. Reicks, M.; Trofholz, A.C.; Stang, J.S.; Laska, M.N. Impact of Cooking and Home Food Preparation Interventions Among Adults: Outcomes and Implications for Future programs. *J. Nutr. Educ. Behav.* **2014**, *46*, 259–276. [CrossRef] [PubMed]
20. Farmer, N.; Touchton-Leonard, K.; Ross, A. Psychosocial Benefits of Cooking Interventions: A Systematic Review. *Health Educ. Behav.* **2018**, *45*, 167–180. [CrossRef] [PubMed]
21. Neff, R.A.; Edwards, D.; Palmer, A.; Ramsing, R.; Righter, A.; Wolfson, J. Reducing meat consumption in the USA: A nationally representative survey of attitudes and behaviours. *Public Health Nutr.* **2018**, *21*, 1835–1844. [CrossRef]
22. Wolfson, J.A.; Lahne, J.; Raj, M.; Insolera, N.; Lavelle, F.; Dean, M. Food Agency in the United States: Associations with Cooking Behavior and Dietary Intake. *Nutrients* **2020**, *12*, 877. [CrossRef]
23. Begley, A.; Gallegos, D.; Vidgen, H. Effectiveness of Australian cooking skill interventions. *Br. Food J.* **2017**, *119*, 973–991. [CrossRef]
24. Wolfson, J.A.; Bostic, S.; Lahne, J.; Morgan, C.; Henley, S.C.; Harvey, J.; Trubek, A. A comprehensive approach to understanding cooking behavior: Implications for research and practice. *Br. Food J.* **2017**, *119*, 1147–1158. [CrossRef]
25. Short, F. Domestic cooking skills: What are they? *J. Home Econ. Inst. Aust.* **2003**, *10*, 13–22.
26. Short, F. Domestic cooking practices and cooking skills: Findings from an English study. *Food Serv. Technol.* **2003**, *3*, 177–185. [CrossRef]
27. Fordyce-Voorham, S. Identification of Essential Food Skills for Skill-based Healthful Eating Programs in Secondary Schools. *J. Nutr. Educ. Behav.* **2011**, *43*, 116–122. [CrossRef]
28. Fordyce-Voorham, S. Essential food skills required in a skill-based healthy eating program. *J. Home Econ. Inst. Aust.* **2009**, *16*, 16–20.
29. Trubek, A.B.; Carabello, M.; Morgan, C.; Lahne, J. Empowered to cook: The crucial role of 'food agency' in making meals. *Appetite* **2017**, *116*, 297–305. [CrossRef] [PubMed]
30. Asher, R.C.; Jakstas, T.; Wolfson, J.A.; Rose, A.J.; Bucher, T.; Lavelle, F.; Dean, M.; Duncanson, K.; Innes, B.; Burrows, T.; et al. Cook-Ed(TM): A Model for Planning, Implementing and Evaluating Cooking Programs to Improve Diet and Health. *Nutrients* **2020**, *12*, 1011. [CrossRef]
31. Herforth, A.; Arimond, M.; Álvarez-Sánchez, C.; Coates, J.; Christianson, K.; Muehlhoff, E. A Global Review of Food-Based Dietary Guidelines. *Adv. Nutr.* **2019**, *10*, 590–605. [CrossRef]
32. NSW Government Food Authority. Safe Food, Clear Choices NSW Food Authority. Available online: https://www.foodauthority.nsw.gov.au/ (accessed on 21 July 2021).
33. Lavelle, F.; McGowan, L.; Hollywood, L.; Surgenor, D.; McCloat, A.; Mooney, E.; Caraher, M.; Raats, M.; Dean, M. The development and validation of measures to assess cooking skills and food skills. *Int. J. Behav. Nutr. Phys. Act.* **2017**, *14*, 118. [CrossRef]
34. Raber, M.; Chandra, J.; Upadhyaya, M.; Schick, V.; Strong, L.L.; Durand, C.; Sharma, S. An evidence-based conceptual framework of healthy cooking. *Prev. Med. Rep.* **2016**, *4*, 23–28. [CrossRef] [PubMed]
35. Dalkey, N.C. *The Dephi Method: An Experimental Study of Group Opinion*; Rand: Santa Monica, CA, USA, 1969.
36. Mete, R.; Kellett, J.; Bacon, R.; Shield, A.; Murray, K. The P.O.S.T Guidelines for Nutrition Blogs: A Modified e-Delphi Study. *J. Acad. Nutr. Diet.* **2021**, *121*, 1219–1230. [CrossRef]
37. Porter, J.; Charlton, K.; Tapsell, L.; Truby, H. Using the Delphi process to identify priorities for Dietetic research in Australia 2020–2030. *Nutr. Diet.* **2020**, *77*, 437–443. [CrossRef]

38. Trevelyan, E.G.; Robinson, P.N. Delphi methodology in health research: How to do it? *Eur. J. Integr. Med.* **2015**, *7*, 423–428. [CrossRef]
39. Hasson, F.; Keeney, S.; McKenna, H. Research guidelines for the Delphi survey technique. *J. Adv. Nurs.* **2000**, *32*, 1008–1015. [CrossRef]
40. Anderson, L.W.; Krathwohl, D.R. *A Taxonomy for Learning, Teaching, and Assessing: A Revision of Bloom's Taxonomy of Educational Objectives*; Longman: New York, NY, USA, 2001.
41. Papier, K.; Fensom, G.K.; Knuppel, A.; Appleby, P.N.; Tong, T.Y.N.; Schmidt, J.A.; Travis, R.C.; Key, T.J.; Perez-Cornago, A. Meat consumption and risk of 25 common conditions: Outcome-wide analyses in 475,000 men and women in the UK Biobank study. *BMC Med.* **2021**, *19*, 53. [CrossRef] [PubMed]
42. Willett, W.; Rockström, J.; Loken, B.; Springmann, M.; Lang, T.; Vermeulen, S.; Garnett, T.; Tilman, D.; DeClerck, F.; Wood, A.; et al. Food in the Anthropocene: The EAT-Lancet Commission on healthy diets from sustainable food systems. *Lancet* **2019**, *393*, 447–492. [CrossRef]
43. Case-Smith, J.; O'Brien, J.C. *Occupational Therapy for Children and Adolescents*; Elsevier: St. Louis, MO, USA, 2014.
44. Zoltan, B. *Vision, Perception, and Cognition: A Manual for the Evaluation and Treatment of the Adult with Acquired Brain Injury*, 4th ed.; SLACK: Thorofare, NJ, USA, 2007.
45. Dean, M.; O'Kane, C.; Issartel, J.; McCloat, A.; Mooney, E.; Gaul, D.; Wolfson, J.A.; Lavelle, F. Guidelines for designing age-appropriate cooking interventions for children: The development of evidence-based cooking skill recommendations for children, using a multidisciplinary approach. *Appetite* **2021**, *161*, 105125. [CrossRef] [PubMed]
46. Cunningham-Sabo, L.; Lohse, B. Impact of a school-based cooking curriculum for fourth-grade students on attitudes and behaviors is influenced by gender and prior cooking experience. *J. Nutr. Educ. Behav.* **2014**, *46*, 110–120. [CrossRef] [PubMed]
47. Fulkerson, J.A.; Rydell, S.; Kubik, M.Y.; Lytle, L.; Boutelle, K.; Story, M.; Neumark-Sztainer, D.; Dudovitz, B.; Garwick, A. Healthy Home Offerings via the Mealtime Environment (HOME): Feasibility, acceptability, and outcomes of a pilot study. *Obesity* **2010**, *18* (Suppl. 1), S69–S74. [CrossRef]
48. Herbert, J.; Flego, A.; Gibbs, L.; Waters, E.; Swinburn, B.; Reynolds, J.; Moodie, M. Wider impacts of a 10-week community cooking skills program—Jamie's Ministry of Food, Australia. *BMC Public Health* **2014**, *14*, 1161. [CrossRef]
49. West, E.G.; Lindberg, R.; Ball, K.; McNaughton, S.A. The Role of a Food Literacy Intervention in Promoting Food Security and Food Literacy-OzHarvest's NEST Program. *Nutrients* **2020**, *12*, 2197. [CrossRef]
50. von Koerber, K.; Bader, N.; Leitzmann, C. Wholesome Nutrition: An example for a sustainable diet. *Proc. Nutr. Soc.* **2017**, *76*, 34–41. [CrossRef]
51. Poulton, G.; Antono, A. A Taste of Virtual Culinary Medicine and Lifestyle Medicine-An Online Course for Medical Students. *Am. J. Lifestyle Med.* **2022**, *16*, 57–60. [CrossRef] [PubMed]
52. Silver, J.K.; Finkelstein, A.; Minezaki, K.; Parks, K.; Budd, M.A.; Tello, M.; Paganoni, S.; Tirosh, A.; Polak, R. The Impact of a Culinary Coaching Telemedicine Program on Home Cooking and Emotional Well-Being during the COVID-19 Pandemic. *Nutrients* **2021**, *13*, 2311. [CrossRef] [PubMed]
53. Burnett-Fell, B.; Stuchbury, K. *Food Technology in Action*, 2nd ed.; Jacaranda Press: Milton, Australia, 2000.
54. Food and Agriculture Organization of the United Nations. Food Loss and Food Waste. Available online: https://www.fao.org/food-loss-and-food-waste/ (accessed on 2 February 2022).
55. Monteiro, C.A.; Cannon, G.; Lawrence, M.; Costa Louzada, M.L.; Pereira Machado, P. *Ultra-Processed Foods, Diet Quality, and Health Using the NOVA Classification System*; FAO: Rome, Italy, 2019.

nutrients MDPI

Article

Modelling the Impact of Reducing Ultra-Processed Foods Based on the NOVA Classification in Australian Women of Reproductive Age

Nahal Habibi [1,2], Shalem Yiner-Lee Leemaqz [3] and Jessica Anne Grieger [1,2,*]

1 Robinson Research Institute, University of Adelaide, Adelaide, SA 5005, Australia; nahal.habibi@adelaide.edu.au
2 Adelaide Medical School, University of Adelaide, Adelaide, SA 5005, Australia
3 Flinders Health and Medical Research Institute, Flinders University, Adelaide, SA 5042, Australia; shalem.leemaqz@flinders.edu.au
* Correspondence: jessica.grieger@adelaide.edu.au

Abstract: Women of reproductive age have a high proportion of overweight/obesity and an overall poor nutritional intake and diet quality. Nutritional modelling is a method to forecast potential changes in nutrition composition that may offer feasible and realistic changes to dietary intake. This study uses simulation modelling to estimate feasible population improvements in dietary profile by reducing ultra-processed food (UPF) consumption in Australian women of reproductive age. The simulation used weighted data from the most recent 2011–2012 National Nutrition and Physical Activity Survey. A total of 2749 women aged 19–50 years was included, and 5740 foods were examined. The highest daily energy, saturated fat, and added sugar and sodium came from UPF. Reducing UPF by 50% decreased energy intake by 22%, and saturated fat, added sugar, sodium, and alcohol by 10–39%. Reducing UPF by 50% and increasing unprocessed or minimally processed foods by 25% led to a lower estimated reduction in energy and greater estimated reductions in saturated fat and sodium. Replacement of 50% UPF with 75% of unprocessed or minimally processed foods led to smaller estimated reductions in energy and nutrients. Our results provide insight as to the potential impact of population reductions in UPF, but also increasing intake of unprocessed or minimally processed foods, which may be the most feasible strategy for improved nutritional intake.

Keywords: dietary modelling; simulation modelling; reproductive age; women; ultra-processed food; discretionary nutrients; Australian Health Survey; NOVA classification

Citation: Habibi, N.; Leemaqz, S.Y.-L.; Grieger, J.A. Modelling the Impact of Reducing Ultra-Processed Foods Based on the NOVA Classification in Australian Women of Reproductive Age. *Nutrients* **2022**, *14*, 1518. https://doi.org/10.3390/nu14071518

Academic Editors: Clare Collins and George Moschonis

Received: 24 March 2022
Accepted: 4 April 2022
Published: 5 April 2022

1. Introduction

Reproductive life stages include the preconception, pregnancy, and postpartum period, and it typically refers to all women aged 15–49 years [1]. Women in this reproductive age group have demonstrated the greatest rise in the prevalence of obesity [2], with up to 1 kg annual weight gain from early adulthood to middle-age [3]. Whilst such weight gain is known to play an adverse role in maternal and offspring health during pregnancy [4,5], excessive weight gain before, during, and after pregnancy also posits heightened risk for early and future chronic disease risk such as type 2 diabetes and cardiovascular disease [6–8].

There is clear evidence indicating that women of reproductive age have poor diet quality and consumption patterns, reflected by a low intake of fruits and vegetables and higher intakes of discretionary foods containing added sugar, sodium, and saturated fat [9–14]. Furthermore, there is increasing concern that excess consumption of industrially processed foods is driving the increase in the prevalence of diet-related chronic diseases [15]. Such foods that, for example, include packaged instant soups and noodles, and pre-prepared meat, fish, and vegetables, are often made from cheap ingredients and additives, which are lower in nutritional quality and higher in energy density [16]. While most young and older consumers understand the term 'ultra-processed', and they can correctly classify items such as soft drinks, biscuits, and confectionary, they tend to mis-classify some more healthful foods such as milk, flour, meat, cheese, and bread [17,18], potentially contributing to lower intakes of these foods.

Intakes of ultra-processed foods (UPF) are increasing, with food surveys demonstrating around 27–60% total daily energy intake in adults from UPF [5,19–21], including 38.9% of total energy intake among Australian adults [22]. Limited studies have specifically examined UPF intake in women; intake of UPF was 33% in UK women aged 19–60 years [23], 51.2% of total daily energy intake in Brazilian women aged 21 to 24 years of age [24], and 59% in Korean women aged 19–64 years [25]. High intakes of UPF, equivalent to approximately 76% of total energy intake is associated with a 30% higher risk for obesity in Canadian adults [21], and in an adult French population a 10% increase in the proportion of UPF is associated with an approximate 10% higher risk for cardiovascular disease [26] and cancer [27]. In Australia, an increased dietary share of UPF was also associated with higher BMI [22], and an increased risk of inadequate intakes of nutrients critical to obesity and other non-communicable diseases [28].

Modelling studies use analytical methods that account for events over time and across populations and that are based on data drawn from a range of sources [29]. Within the Australian context, nutritional modelling has been used to forecast or predict changes in dietary intake quantity and/or composition that are needed to achieve certain targets, such as the Australian Dietary Guidelines [30], and that has demonstrated impactful population level reductions in salt and trans fatty acid intake, along with implementation of sodium and trans-fat reformulation programs [31]. Modelling taxes on saturated fat, salt, sugar, and sugar-sweetened beverages, and placing a subsidy on fruits and vegetables, estimated cost-savings for the Australian health sector [32], with more than 30,000 deaths from coronary heart disease, stroke and cancer predicted to be saved if UK dietary guidelines were met [33]. No studies have assessed the impact of theoretical changes to UPF consumption using Australian data. This is clearly of relevance, particularly in women of reproductive age, given their overall poor dietary quality, increasing rates of overweight and obesity, and that diet and lifestyle intervention studies are currently ineffective for consistent weight management or loss, particularly during pregnancy and post-partum [34]. In reproductive age women participating in the 2011–2013 Australian Health Survey, the aims of this study are to (1) describe the energy, macronutrient, and discretionary nutrient profile according to the NOVA food classification and their contribution to total daily energy intake; and (2) use simulation modelling to estimate feasible population improvements in dietary profile by reducing ultra-processed and processed food consumption. Outcomes from the modelling scenarios will enable the development of dietary interventions to improve diet quality and support body weight loss in these at-risk women.

2. Materials and Methods

2.1. Study Population

The data source for this study was the National Nutrition and Physical Activity Survey (NNPAS) 2011–2012, part of the 2011–2013 Australian Health Survey [35]. This survey studied a randomly selected, national sample (n = 12,153) of the Australian population using a complex, stratified, multistage probability cluster sampling design with selection of strata, households, and people within households. The current analysis used the food intake data from the first 24-h recall among reproductive aged women 19–50 years (n = 2749), and population weighted using sample weighting factors provided in the survey [35]. The Census and Statistics Act, 1905, provided the Australian Bureau of Statistics with the authority to conduct NNPAS, with all respondents providing written informed consent.

2.2. Dietary Data

AUSNUT 2011–2013 was the Food Standards Australian and New Zealand nutrient database [36] developed to enable food, dietary, supplement, and nutrient intake estimates to be made from the 2011–2013 Australian Health Survey [35]. The AUSNUT 2011–2013 database groups foods according to a major (2-digit), sub-major (3-digit), or minor (5-digit) food group. The 5-digit group then forms the basis of the survey ID (8-digit) assigned to each food, beverage, or ingredient, as previously described [37]. Weighted population averages for each unique 8-digit food code were obtained using SPSS software (version 25, IBM SPSS Inc., Chicago, IL, United States). Population intakes of food (grams), energy, macronutrients, and discretionary components (mean intake/day) were aggregated with the food data and nutrient values (per 100 g) from AUSNUT 2011–2013 [36] in Microsoft Excel (2019, Microsoft Corporation, Redmond, WA, USA).

Each food was allocated to one of the four NOVA food groups [38]. The NOVA system is a food classification based on the nature, extent, and purpose of industrial food processing, which classifies foods into four groups: unprocessed and minimally processed foods; processed culinary ingredients; processed foods; and ultra-processed foods (UPF) [39]. The NOVA food classification system was based on what was previously applied to all 5740 8-digit food and beverage items in AUSNUT 2011–2013 [37,40]. As such, results presented in the simulation models and the NOVA foods are slightly different from each other, as the NOVA system classifies each individual food item within a mixed food item to a NOVA group and is more granular, whereas in the modelling dataset, the entire food is allocated to either an unprocessed, processed, or minimally processed food group.

2.3. Dietary Scenarios

The first model strategy used a simulation model to reduce the gram weight of all UPF by 50% (Model 1). This strategy was chosen to demonstrate the effects of reducing predominantly discretionary/unhealthy food choices in the diet that are high in saturated fat, added sugars, and sodium, and that form around twice the recommended intake of discretionary choices in the Australian diet [41]. Whilst a simple reduction in UPF may appear a feasible option to reduce energy intake and discretionary nutrient profile, two supplementary strategies were tested; that is, in conjunction with reducing the weight of all UPF by 50% (Strategy 1, Model 1), the quantities of unprocessed or minimally processed foods were increased by 25% (Strategy 1, Model 2) and 75% (Strategy 1, Model 3). Unprocessed or minimally processed foods are typically fresh fruits and vegetables, grains (cereals), pasteurized full fat, low-fat, skimmed milk, and fermented milks, and meats, poultry, fish, and seafood. The reported intakes of these foods are typically suboptimal [28,41]; thus, it is important to examine the estimated impact of increasing intake of unprocessed and minimally processed foods with a concomitant reduction in UPF.

The second strategy was a simulation model to reduce all processed foods, which are typically processed meat and fish such as ham, bacon, and dried fish; cheeses made from milk, salt, and ferments; and unpackaged freshly made breads; and beer, cider, wine by 50%. The same strategies that were used for modelling UPF were also modelled for processed foods, that is, a simulation model to reduce all processed foods by 50% (Strategy 2, Model 1); and in conjunction with reducing all processed foods by 50%, intake of unprocessed and minimally processed foods were increased by 25% (Strategy 2, Model 2) and 75% (Strategy 2, Model 3).

2.4. Dietary Modelling

To investigate the impact of the different modelling scenarios below, the Microsoft Excel Solver add-in was used to manipulate baseline food and beverage quantity (grams). Nutrition modelling was undertaken at the population level, such that food group intakes were aggregated at the 8-digit food level (n = 4028 foods and beverages).

3. Results

3.1. Population Baseline Intakes

Women aged 19–50 years from the Australian Health Survey were included (n = 2749) and population weighted. Population mean daily intakes of energy, macronutrients, and key discretionary nutrients are reported in Table 1. Women consumed a mean 3.1 kg/d food, totalling a mean energy intake of 7388 kJ/d (1765 kcal/d). The percent energy from protein, carbohydrate, fat, saturated fat, and added sugars was a respective 16.9%, 45.0%, 32.6%, 12.4%, and 10.5%, with respective mean daily intakes of fibre and alcohol 19.8 g/d and 9.1 g/d.

Table 1. Mean population baseline intakes of Australian women aged 19–50 years, and according to the NOVA classification (n = 2749).

	Mean Baseline Intake	Intake from Ultra-Processed Foods (%)	Intake from Processed Foods (%)	Intake from Unprocessed or Minimally Processed Foods (%)	Intake from Processed Culinary Ingredients (%)
Quantity (g)	3112.6	548.9 (17.6)	175.3 (5.6)	2361.8 (75.9)	26.6 (0.9)
Energy (kJ) *	7388.2	3056.2 (41.4)	1093.0 (14.8)	2656.1 (36.0)	582.9 (7.9)
Protein (g)	74.6	20.8 (27.9)	10.9 (14.6)	42.7 (57.2)	0.2 (0.3)
Fat (g)	63.9	26.5 (41.5)	8.7 (13.6)	17.1 (26.8)	11.6 (18.2)
Carbohydrate (g)	198.7	97.1 (48.9)	20.8 (10.5)	71.5 (36.0)	9.3 (4.7)
Fibre (g)	19.8	6.3 (31.8)	2.4 (12.1)	11.1 (56.1)	0.0 (0.0)
Saturated Fat (g)	24.3	10.6 (43.6)	4.0 (16.5)	6.0 (24.7)	3.7 (15.2)
Added sugar (g)	46.2	36.8 (79.7)	1.4 (3.0)	0.2 (0.3)	7.9 (17.1)
Sodium (mg)	2142.3	1309.5 (61.1)	463.4 (21.6)	289.8 (13.5)	79.6 (3.7)
Alcohol (g)	9.1	1.8 (19.8)	7.3 (80.2)	0.0 (0.0)	0 (0.0)

* To convert kJ to kcal, divide by 4.1868.

Ultra-processed foods contributed 41.4% of total daily energy intake, with the included foods contributing to one fifth of daily grams of food consumed (Table 1). Women consumed the highest percentage of energy, total fat, carbohydrate, saturated fat, and added sugars and sodium from UPF, whereas the highest percentage of protein and fibre was from unprocessed or minimally processed food. The largest gram weight of food came from unprocessed or minimally processed foods, contributing around a third of total daily energy intake, and more than half of total protein and fibre intake. Processed foods contributed the highest amount of alcohol, 7.3 g/d, contributing 14.8% of energy, and 21.6% of sodium to the diet.

Table 2 shows the contribution of different foods and drinks to mean daily energy intake. Mass-produced packaged breads, pastries, buns, and cakes and fast foods dishes contributed the highest energy from UPF. Processed breads and beer and wine accounted for about half of the energy contribution from processed foods. Within the unprocessed or minimally processed foods category, around 6–8% percent of energy came from red meat and poultry, cereal grains and flours, and milk and plain yoghurt. Plant oil had the highest contribution to daily energy within the processed culinary ingredients group.

Table 2. Mean absolute and relative daily energy intake of Australian women aged 19–50 years, according to the NOVA food classification (n = 2749).

NOVA Food Groups	Energy (kJ)	Energy (kcal)	% of Total Energy Intake
Ultra-processed foods	3056.2	730.4	41.4
Mass-produced packaged breads	333.5	79.7	4.5
Pastries, buns, and cakes	292.3	69.9	4.0
Fast foods dishes [a]	286.7	68.5	3.9
Confectionery	247.9	59.2	3.4
Frozen and shelf stable ready meals [b]	237.4	56.7	3.2
Fruit drinks and iced teas	206.2	49.3	2.8
Breakfast cereals	190.4	45.5	2.6

Table 2. *Cont.*

NOVA Food Groups	Energy (kJ)	Energy (kcal)	% of Total Energy Intake
Biscuits	180.4	43.1	2.4
Carbonated soft drinks	171.7	41.0	2.3
Milk-based drinks	168.5	40.3	2.3
Sausage and other reconstituted meat products	163.5	39.1	2.2
Sauces, dressing, and gravies	157.7	37.7	2.1
Salty snacks	118.5	28.3	1.6
Ice cream, ice pops, and frozen yoghurts	101.7	24.3	1.4
Margarine and other spreads	91.3	21.8	1.2
Alcoholic distilled drinks	53.7	12.8	0.7
Other [c]	54.8	13.1	0.7
Processed foods	1093.0	261.2	14.8
Processed breads	427.0	102.1	5.8
Beer and wine	233.5	55.8	3.2
Cheese	220.2	52.6	3.0
Bacon and other salted, smoked, or canned meat or fish	84.0	20.1	1.1
Vegetables and other plant foods preserved in brine	36.2	8.7	0.5
Other [d]	92.1	22.0	1.2
Unprocessed or minimally processed foods	2656.1	634.8	36.0
Red meat and poultry	582.5	139.2	7.9
Cereal grains and flours	485.8	116.1	6.6
Milk and plain yoghurt	452.7	108.2	6.1
Fruits [e]	323.2	77.2	4.4
Vegetables	239.2	57.2	3.2
Pasta	204.8	48.9	2.8
Nuts and seeds	96.3	23.0	1.3
Potatoes and other tubers and roots	80.5	19.2	1.1
Eggs	71.7	17.1	1.0
Fish	62.1	14.8	0.8
Legumes	31.7	7.6	0.4
Other [f]	25.8	6.2	0.3
Processed culinary ingredients	582.9	139.3	7.9
Plant oils	269.6	64.4	3.6
Animal fats	164.3	39.3	2.2
Table sugar	125.6	30.0	1.7
Other [g]	23.4	5.6	0.3
Total	7388.2	1765.8	100.0

[a] Hamburger, pizza, and French fries from fast food places; [b] frozen lasagne, pizza, and other pastas and meals, and instant soups and noodles; [c] ultra-processed cheese, baby food, and baby formula; [d] salted or sugared nuts, seeds, and dried fruits; [e] fruits and freshly squeezed juices; [f] meat from other animals, teas, coffees, and dried spices; [g] honey, maple syrup (100%), and vinegar.

3.2. *Strategy 1*

3.2.1. Model 1: Reducing Ultra-Processed Foods by 50%

The impact of reducing UPF by 50% is shown in Figure 1 (green bars). Compared to population baseline intakes, halving the intake of UPF resulted in a theoretical 316 g lower intake of total food consumed, and a 1689 kJ (404 kcal) lower daily energy intake. Modelled intakes were lower for all discretionary components such as saturated fat, added sugar, and sodium by 20–40%, with a lower intake of alcohol by 10.0%. Halving the intake of UPF also reduced macronutrients by 15–30%.

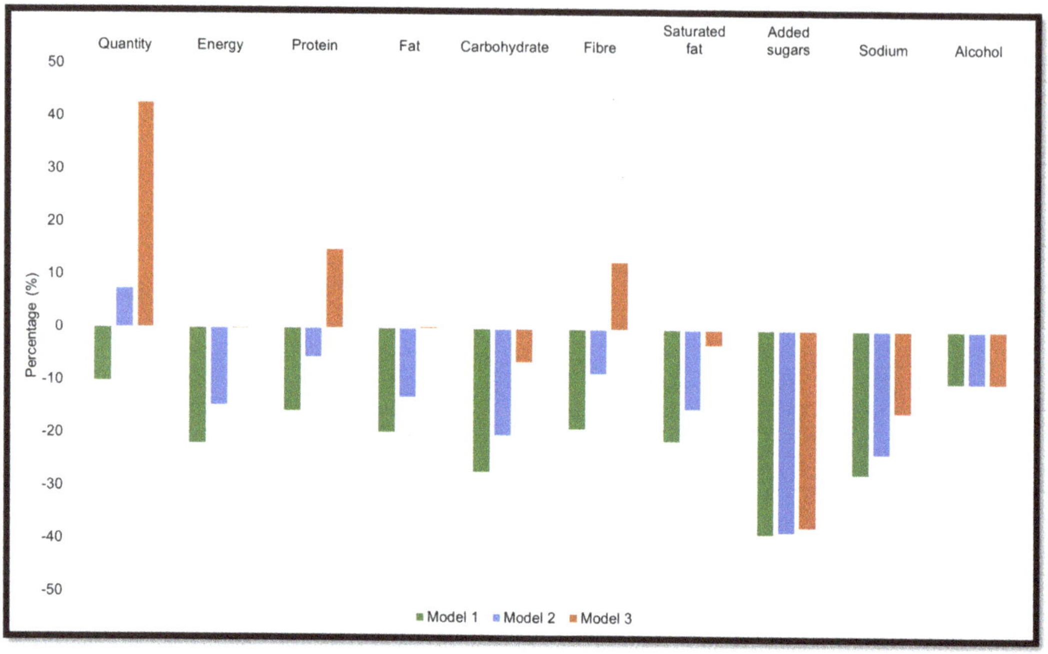

Figure 1. Estimated changes in population mean intakes of food (g), energy, macronutrients, and discretionary nutrients, according to Strategy 1 (3 different models). Results are presented as a percentage change relative to baseline intake. Model 1: Reducing ultra-processed foods by 50%. Model 2: Reducing ultra-processed foods by 50% with a 25% increase in unprocessed or minimally processed foods. Model 3: Reducing ultra-processed foods by 50% with a 75% increase in unprocessed or minimally processed foods.

3.2.2. Models 2: Reducing Ultra-Processed Foods by 50% and Increasing Unprocessed or Minimally Processed Foods by 25%

Figure 1 shows the impact of replacing 50% of UPF with 25% (blue bars) or 75% (orange bars) of unprocessed or minimally processed foods. Compared with the baseline intake, partial replacement by 25% reduced daily energy intake by 1131 kJ (270 kcal), while the quantity of all consumed foods increased by 231 g. This model also led to theoretical reductions in saturated fat (15.1%), added sugars (38.3%), sodium (23.4%), and alcohol (10.0%). Modelled food intakes were lower in protein, fat, carbohydrate, and fibre by 5.6%, 13.1%, 20.2%, and 8.4%, respectively.

3.2.3. Model 3: Reducing Ultra-Processed Foods by 50% and Increasing Unprocessed or Minimally Processed Foods by 75%

Partial replacement of UPF with 75% unprocessed or minimally processed foods resulted in a hypothetical increase in the quantity of food consumed by around 1.3 kg (Figure 1, orange bars). Energy intake was not shown to change (−16 kJ/d [3.8 kcal]), whereas protein and fibre increased (12–15%), and carbohydrate intake decreased (6.3%). Modelled intakes led to a reduction in all discretionary components, with the largest decrease in intakes of added sugars.

3.3. Strategy 2

3.3.1. Model 1: Reducing Processed Foods by 50%

Figure 2 (green bars) shows the theoretical changes in food consumed, energy, macronutrients, and discretionary nutrients by reducing processed foods by 50%. Compared to population baseline intakes, reducing processed foods reduced the intake of grams of food consumed (165 g), daily energy intake (913 kJ), and macronutrients (7–14%). Discretionary nutrients were reduced by 4–14%, except for alcohol with an estimated reduction of 40% (−3.6 g).

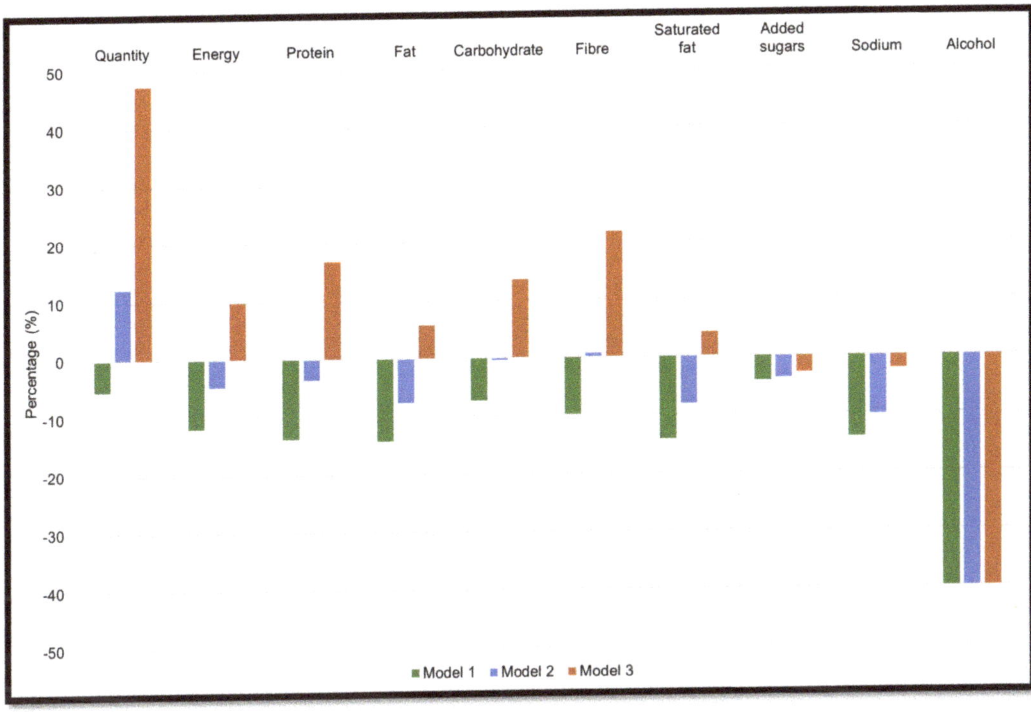

Figure 2. Estimated changes in population mean intakes of food (g), energy, macronutrients, and discretionary nutrients, according to Strategy 2 (3 different models). Results are presented as a percentage change relative to baseline intake. Model 1: Reducing processed foods by 50%. Model 2: Reducing processed foods by 50% with a 25% increase in unprocessed or minimally processed foods. Model 3: Reducing processed foods by 50% with a 75% increase in unprocessed or minimally processed foods.

3.3.2. Model 2: Reducing Processed Foods by 50% and Increasing Unprocessed or Minimally Processed Foods by 25%

Replacing 50% of processed foods with 25% of unprocessed or minimally processed foods led to estimated reductions in energy intake of 355 kJ (85 kcal), protein, fat, and carbohydrates by 0.4% to 7.6%, but an estimated 0.7% increase in fibre intake (Figure 2, blue bars). The estimated reduction in alcohol (40%) was the same to when there was no increase intake of unprocessed or minimally processed foods (Model 1), and the reduction in discretionary nutrients was similar (3.8% to 10.2%).

3.3.3. Model 3: Reducing Processed Foods by 50% and Increasing Unprocessed or Minimally Processed Foods by 75%

The impact of replacing 50% of processed foods with 75% of unprocessed or minimally processed foods is shown in Figure 2 (orange bars). The model led to a theoretical 1.5 kg higher intake of food consumed and 760 kJ (182 kcal) increase in energy intake in comparison with population baseline intakes. Macronutrients were estimated to increase by 6–17% and fibre by 4.5 g. The estimated reduction in alcohol remained the same at 40%, whether unprocessed or minimally processed foods were increased or not, but there were smaller estimated reductions in added sugars (2.9%), and sodium (2.3%), but an increase in saturated fat of 4.1% (1 g).

4. Discussion

This study describes the NOVA food classification and potential reductions in energy, macronutrients, and discretionary nutrients, following simulation modelling of processed and unprocessed foods. We extend our previous work demonstrating the overall low diet quality in reproductive age women from the same Australian Health survey [42], to now report that a high proportion of energy intake comes from UPF. Our modelling shows that halving intake of processed foods resulted in an estimated reduction in energy (11.9%), saturated fat (14.3%), added sugar (4.3%), sodium (14.1%), and alcohol (40.0%), whereas halving UPF resulted in a greater reduction in energy (22.0%) and discretionary components, namely saturated fat, added sugar, and sodium (21–39%) but not alcohol (10.0%).

The highest amount of total daily energy intake (41.4%, or 3 MJ of energy) was from UPF. Using the Australian Health Survey, older children and adolescents were reported to consume around 54% of total daily energy intake from UPF [28], and within the 2011–2013 Australian food composition database, the proportion of UPF was 38%, and unprocessed and minimally processed food was 36% [37]. Whilst many foods are incorporated into the UPF category, the fact that the contribution to energy intake is higher than that from unprocessed or minimally processed foods, at 36% (2.7 MJ), is concerning, given their link to obesity and non-communicable diseases [43]. Such high consumption may be partly due to their longer shelf life than fresh foods, affordability, appetizing and palatable qualities, and less effort and time required for preparation and cooking [44–46]. Furthermore, featuring inaccurate nutrition and health statements on UPF packaging may make them appear healthier than they really are [44–46]. Improved accuracy of food labels would allow consumers to better understand the nutritional content of foods and select more nutritious foods. While the Australian dietary guidelines do not currently incorporate NOVA food categories but instead describe discretionary choices [47], future and/or alternative guidelines may be warranted with a focus on level of processing.

The first simulation strategy, reducing UPF by 50%, demonstrated the largest theoretical reductions for all macronutrients as well as saturated fatty acids and sodium; however, reductions in added sugar and alcohol were similar in the energy compensation scenarios that included a 25% or 75% increase in unprocessed or minimally processed foods. Reducing UPF intake led to a proposed reduction in energy (~1700 kJ; 400 kcal), which would be equivalent to the energy of nearly three servings of discretionary choices [47], or several servings of foods within this category. For sustained weight loss, a continued energy restriction of between 2000 and 3000 kJ (500–750 kcal) is recommended [48]. However, it is evident that the practicality of reducing energy intake is rarely achieved over the longer term [49], and continuous energy restriction may be problematic, partly due to increases in the desire to eat [50], feelings of hunger [51], and cravings [52]. Thus, while reducing intakes of UPF offers a potential strategy with important reductions in discretionary nutrients, and which would contribute to improvements in lipid profile [53], the long term success of this strategy is likely hampered by other genetic [54], behavioural, and hormonal [55,56] factors that mitigate sustained weight loss efforts.

The most practical solution from this strategy is likely to be reducing UPF by 50% and increasing unprocessed or minimally processed foods by 25%. A smaller, albeit important, reduction in energy was apparent, along with considerable reductions of added sugar (17.8 g, ~4.5 teaspoons) and saturated fat (3.8 g, 15.1%). To implement this, one could eliminate 100 g French fries from the diet, eliminate 375 mL soft drink and two sweet biscuits, or reduce intake of bread and sweet pastries/buns by half. These foods could be replaced with any two of the following examples: $\frac{1}{2}$ cup vegetables, $\frac{1}{2}$ serving meat or nuts; one serving of fruit. This strategy could assist in weight management programs and potential future risk reduction of chronic diseases such as obesity and type 2 diabetes. A previous study in adults aged over 18 years, also using Australian Health Survey data, highlighted that substituting unhealthier/discretionary foods with a range of healthier foods lowered intakes of added sugars, sodium, and saturated fat and appeared the most feasible strategy for improving nutritional intake [57].

Processed foods contributed nearly 15% of total daily energy intake, of which processed breads contributed 5.8% and beer and wine contributed 3.2%. Reducing processed foods by 50% resulted in around half the reduction in energy from what was observed when UPF was reduced by 50%. Importantly, in this scenario there was a theoretical reduction in alcohol of 40% (3.6 g), or equivalent to just under a half of a standard alcoholic drink. Whilst this may seem small, at a population level, this has huge implications for pursuing a healthier lifestyle and lowering the burden on health services. There has been a continued increase in alcohol consumption among women of reproductive age, not only in Australia [58], but also in the USA [38] and worldwide [39]. This is a critical issue for women who are intending to become pregnant, as higher intakes of alcohol in the preconception period is associated with a longer time to conceive [59]. Similar to the first modelling strategy, incorporating 75% of unprocessed or minimally processed foods is likely to be the least feasible. A 1.5 kg increase in food volume was predicted, and although beneficial increases in protein and fibre were estimated, there were only small changes to discretionary nutrients. The potential benefits of reducing processed foods and increasing by 25% unprocessed and minimally professed foods is unclear. While a modest reduction in daily energy intake of 355 kJ was predicted, which could be helpful for women who opt for weight maintenance, the changes to discretionary nutrients were not remarkable, and the longer-term health outcomes of such a change is difficult to establish. For women who do not consume alcohol, benefits to reducing intake of processed foods, particularly lowering total fat, saturated fat, and sodium would be apparent; however, future studies could investigate such strategies in sub-groups of women.

Our study extends previous findings using the NOVA system, and which could be applied to intervention studies in women of reproductive age. The high proportion of energy from UPF that we report, and which is consistent with previous studies, further compels public health strategies to be developed to monitor the accuracy of food labels and inform women about nutrition risks of consuming these foods, but also the potential adverse reproductive health outcomes. Related, more than 8000 packaged foods in Australia bear a Health Star Rating, a nutrient-based front-of-pack labelling scheme [60]. Three-quarters of UPF display a Health Star Rating quality of $\geq$2.5, which is a 'pass' rating [61]. Thus, discerning between UPF and foods that are marketed as 'healthy' is another challenge. Women continue to be the regular supermarket shoppers, they more often shop with children who have a key influence on household purchasing behaviour, but they also shop hurriedly [62]. As such, there is little time to digest and interpret front of pack labels, and to make informed decisions. Globally, the availability of UPF is high. Trends in the purchase and sales of UPF demonstrate the greatest consumption in high-income countries, but they are increasing in lower- and middle-income countries [16]. Interestingly, Australian data show that the lowest household income quintile consumes less UPF [63]. However, this may reflect healthy diets being cheaper than non-healthy diets in general in Australia [64,65]; the cost of UPF vs. non-UPF is not currently available. Thus, while the proposed dietary scenarios may impact the family food cost, future research on the potential impact on food prices will be helpful. Lastly, lower socio-economic status is consistently associated with higher UPF consumption [19,63,66]. The lack of access to fresh foods and the predominance of convenience foods, particularly in low-resource settings [67,68], presents an ongoing challenge and complexity of the relationship between improving diet quality and decreasing UPF consumption. A multi system approach is clearly needed that supports improved knowledge on, and encourages the consumption of, unprocessed and minimally processed foods; minimizes structural barriers such as access to healthy foods; improves their affordability; and attends to minimizing gender inequalities and food insecurity.

This is the first study to explore the potential impact of reducing UPF in Australian diets. We developed the strategies based on the unmet need to improve diet quality in reproductive aged women, and to identify a potential feasible strategy that could be applied in an intervention setting. We considered various simulation models, including different options to not only reduce unhealthy food choices, but to allow for energy compensation through increasing healthier food choices. The use of systematically collected nutrition data in the Survey provides a convincing effect of the potential impact on energy and nutrient intake. A strength of this study was the use of individual-level dietary survey data taken from a nationally representative sample of Australian children and adults. However, the modelling conducted was only in women aged 19–50 years, thus reducing the generalizability of our findings, and whether such modelling outcomes differ across different regions and socio-demographics is unclear. Limitations also include the use of a single 24-h dietary recall and thus may not reflect usual intake and potential misclassification of the level of food processing from food composition databases [38]. Our modelling assumes that all reproductive age women will make the changes to their diet, but this is an unrealistic expectation. The models that include allowances for extra unprocessed and minimally processed foods account for some of this difficulty. Furthermore, the NOVA classification categorizes foods according to food processing and not nutritional content. The food composition database is not designed to categorize foods in this way, thus errors related to the classification of foods cannot be excluded. Finally, while we used the most recent population nutrition survey data, this was reported on 10 years ago, and food consumption patterns would have likely changed since then.

5. Conclusions

In conclusion, Australian women of reproductive age consume nearly half of the energy in their diets from UPF. Reducing UPF by 50% considerably lowers estimated energy intake and discretionary nutrients; however, incorporation of 25% of unprocessed or minimally processed foods may be the most feasible strategy for improved health over the longer term. Reducing processed foods offers an important health strategy, particularly for women who consume alcohol; however, the relevance to women who do not drink requires further investigation. Study results can contribute to the development of dietary interventions to improve health, including potential weight loss that utilizes a multi system approach that encourages increased education and behaviour change strategies.

Author Contributions: Conceptualization, J.A.G. and N.H.; Formal analysis, N.H. and S.Y.-L.L.; Methodology, J.A.G., N.H. and S.Y.-L.L.; Writing—original draft, N.H. and J.A.G.; Writing—review and editing, J.A.G., N.H. and S.Y.-L.L. All authors have read and agreed to the published version of the manuscript.

Funding: Funding support from the National Health and Medical Research Council (NHMRC) Ideas Grant (APP2000905) had no input into the results or outcomes of this research.

Institutional Review Board Statement: As this study is a secondary analysis of the National Nutrition and Physical Activity Survey, data that was collected as part of the 2011–2013 Australian Health Survey, no ethics was required.

Informed Consent Statement: The Census and Statistics Act, 1905 provided the Australian Bureau of Statistics with the authority to conduct NNPAS, with all respondents providing written informed consent.

Data Availability Statement: Data and material are available for data transparency.

Acknowledgments: We acknowledge the Australian Bureau of Statistics (ABS) for giving us access to the National Nutrition and Physical Activity Survey data. We would like to thank Carlos Monteiro and Priscila Machado for sharing the STATA codes for the NOVA food categories.

Conflicts of Interest: The authors declare no conflict of interest.

References

1. World Health Organisation (WHO). Reproductive Health Indicators. Reproductive Health and Research Guidelines for Their Generation, Interpretation and Analysis for Global Monitoring. 2006. Available online: http://apps.who.int/iris/bitstream/handle/10665/43185/924156315X_eng.pdf;jsessionid=13280E8CC5E65685D35F6AF1DA27B394?sequence=1 (accessed on 18 November 2021).
2. Ng, M.; Fleming, T.; Robinson, M.; Thomson, B.; Graetz, N.; Margono, C.; Mullany, E.C.; Biryukov, S.; Abbafati, C.; Abera, S.F.; et al. Global, regional, and national prevalence of overweight and obesity in children and adults during 1980-2013: A systematic analysis for the Global Burden of Disease Study 2013. *Lancet* **2014**, *384*, 766–781. [CrossRef]
3. Gomersall, S.R.; Dobson, A.J.; Brown, W.J. Weight Gain, Overweight, and Obesity: Determinants and Health Outcomes from the Australian Longitudinal Study on Women's Health. *Curr. Obes. Rep.* **2014**, *3*, 46–53. [CrossRef] [PubMed]
4. Grieger, J.A.; Hutchesson, M.J.; Cooray, S.D.; Bahri Khomami, M.; Zaman, S.; Segan, L.; Teede, H.; Moran, L.J. A review of maternal overweight and obesity and its impact on cardiometabolic outcomes during pregnancy and postpartum. *Ther. Adv. Reprod. Health* **2021**, *15*. [CrossRef] [PubMed]
5. Patro Golab, B.; Santos, S.; Voerman, E.; Lawlor, D.A.; Jaddoe, V.W.V.; Gaillard, R.; Authors, M.S.G. Influence of maternal obesity on the association between common pregnancy complications and risk of childhood obesity: An individual participant data meta-analysis. *Lancet Child Adolesc. Health* **2018**, *2*, 812–821. [CrossRef]
6. Jacob, C.M.; Baird, J.; Barker, M.; Cooper, C.; Hanson, M.; World Health Organization. The Importance of a Life Course Approach to Health: Chronic Disease Risk from Preconception through Adolescence and Adulthood. 2017. Available online: https://www.who.int/life-course/publications/life-course-approach-to-health.pdf (accessed on 18 November 2021).
7. Rooney, B.L.; Schauberger, C.W.; Mathiason, M.A. Impact of perinatal weight change on long-term obesity and obesity-related illnesses. *Obstet. Gynecol.* **2005**, *106*, 1349–1356. [CrossRef] [PubMed]
8. Linné, Y.; Dye, L.; Barkeling, B.; Rössner, S. Long-term weight development in women: A 15-year follow-up of the effects of pregnancy. *Obes. Res.* **2004**, *12*, 1166–1178. [CrossRef] [PubMed]
9. Blumfield, M.L.; Hure, A.J.; Macdonald-Wicks, L.K.; Patterson, A.J.; Smith, R.; Collins, C.E. Disparities exist between National food group recommendations and the dietary intakes of women. *BMC Womens Health* **2011**, *11*, 37. [CrossRef] [PubMed]
10. Martin, J.C.; Moran, L.J.; Teede, H.J.; Ranasinha, S.; Lombard, C.B.; Harrison, C.L. Exploring Diet Quality between Urban and Rural Dwelling Women of Reproductive Age. *Nutrients* **2017**, *9*, 586. [CrossRef]
11. Mishra, G.D.; Schoenaker, D.A.; Mihrshahi, S.; Dobson, A.J. How do women's diets compare with the new Australian dietary guidelines? *Public Health Nutr.* **2015**, *18*, 218–225. [CrossRef]
12. Bhandari, S.; Sayami, J.T.; Thapa, P.; Sayami, M.; Kandel, B.P.; Banjara, M.R. Dietary intake patterns and nutritional status of women of reproductive age in Nepal: Findings from a health survey. *Archives of Public Health* **2016**, *74*, 2. [CrossRef]
13. Devarshi, P.P.; Legette, L.L.; Grant, R.W.; Mitmesser, S.H. Total estimated usual nutrient intake and nutrient status biomarkers in women of childbearing age and women of menopausal age. *Am. J. Clin. Nutr.* **2021**, *113*, 1042–1052. [CrossRef]
14. Padmadas, S.S.; Dias, J.G.; Willekens, F.J. Disentangling women's responses on complex dietary intake patterns from an Indian cross-sectional survey: A latent class analysis. *Public Health Nutr.* **2006**, *9*, 204–211. [CrossRef]
15. Chen, X.; Zhang, Z.; Yang, H.; Qiu, P.; Wang, H.; Wang, F.; Zhao, Q.; Fang, J.; Nie, J. Consumption of ultra-processed foods and health outcomes: A systematic review of epidemiological studies. *Nutr. J.* **2020**, *19*, 86. [CrossRef]
16. Monteiro, C.A.; Moubarac, J.C.; Cannon, G.; Ng, S.W.; Popkin, B. Ultra-processed products are becoming dominant in the global food system. *Obes. Rev.* **2013**, *14* (Suppl. S2), 21–28. [CrossRef]
17. Aguirre, A.; Borneo, M.T.; El Khori, S.; Borneo, R. Exploring the understanding of the term "ultra-processed foods" by young consumers. *Food Res. Int.* **2019**, *115*, 535–540. [CrossRef]
18. Ares, G.; Vidal, L.; Allegue, G.; Gimenez, A.; Bandeira, E.; Moratorio, X.; Molina, V.; Curutchet, M.R. Consumers' conceptualization of ultra-processed foods. *Appetite* **2016**, *105*, 611–617. [CrossRef]
19. Adams, J.; White, M. Characterisation of UK diets according to degree of food processing and associations with socio-demographics and obesity: Cross-sectional analysis of UK National Diet and Nutrition Survey (2008–2012). *Int. J. Behav. Nutr. Phys. Act.* **2015**, *12*, 160. [CrossRef]
20. Cediel, G.; Reyes, M.; da Costa Louzada, M.L.; Martinez Steele, E.; Monteiro, C.A.; Corvalan, C.; Uauy, R. Ultra-processed foods and added sugars in the Chilean diet (2010). *Public Health Nutr* **2018**, *21*, 125–133. [CrossRef]
21. Nardocci, M.; Leclerc, B.S.; Louzada, M.L.; Monteiro, C.A.; Batal, M.; Moubarac, J.C. Consumption of ultra-processed foods and obesity in Canada. *Can. J. Public Health* **2019**, *110*, 4–14. [CrossRef]
22. Machado, P.P.; Steele, E.M.; Levy, R.B.; da Costa Louzada, M.L.; Rangan, A.; Woods, J.; Gill, T.; Scrinis, G.; Monteiro, C.A. Ultra-processed food consumption and obesity in the Australian adult population. *Nutr. Diabetes* **2020**, *10*, 39. [CrossRef]
23. Rauber, F.; Steele, E.M.; Louzada, M.; Millett, C.; Monteiro, C.A.; Levy, R.B. Ultra-processed food consumption and indicators of obesity in the United Kingdom population (2008–2016). *PLoS ONE* **2020**, *15*, e0232676. [CrossRef] [PubMed]
24. Bielemann, R.M.; Motta, J.V.S.; Minten, G.C.; Horta, B.L.; Gigante, D.P. Consumption of ultra-processed foods and their impact on the diet of young adults. *Rev. Saude Publica* **2015**, *49*, 28. [CrossRef] [PubMed]
25. Sung, H.; Park, J.M.; Oh, S.U.; Ha, K.; Joung, H. Consumption of Ultra-Processed Foods Increases the Likelihood of Having Obesity in Korean Women. *Nutrients* **2021**, *13*, 698. [CrossRef] [PubMed]

26. Srour, B.; Fezeu, L.K.; Kesse-Guyot, E.; Alles, B.; Mejean, C.; Andrianasolo, R.M.; Chazelas, E.; Deschasaux, M.; Hercberg, S.; Galan, P.; et al. Ultra-processed food intake and risk of cardiovascular disease: Prospective cohort study (NutriNet-Sante). *BMJ* **2019**, *365*, l1451. [CrossRef]
27. Fiolet, T.; Srour, B.; Sellem, L.; Kesse-Guyot, E.; Alles, B.; Mejean, C.; Deschasaux, M.; Fassier, P.; Latino-Martel, P.; Beslay, M.; et al. Consumption of ultra-processed foods and cancer risk: Results from NutriNet-Sante prospective cohort. *BMJ* **2018**, *360*, k322. [CrossRef]
28. Machado, P.P.; Steele, E.M.; Louzada, M.; Levy, R.B.; Rangan, A.; Woods, J.; Gill, T.; Scrinis, G.; Monteiro, C.A. Ultra-processed food consumption drives excessive free sugar intake among all age groups in Australia. *Eur. J. Nutr.* **2020**, *59*, 2783–2792. [CrossRef]
29. Weinstein, M.C.; O'Brien, B.; Hornberger, J.; Jackson, J.; Johannesson, M.; McCabe, C.; Luce, B.R. Principles of good practice for decision analytic modeling in health-care evaluation: Report of the ISPOR Task Force on Good Research Practices–Modeling Studies. *Value Health* **2003**, *6*, 9–17. [CrossRef]
30. Australian Government. Department of Health and Aging, and the National Health and Medical Research Council. A Modelling System to Inform the Revision of the Australian Guide to Healthy Eating. 2011. Available online: https://www.eatforhealth.gov.au/sites/default/files/files/public_consultation/n55a_dietary_guidelines_food_modelling_111216.pdf (accessed on 16 June 2021).
31. Heart Foundation. Rapid Review of the Evidence. Effectiveness of Food Reformulation as a Strategy to Improve Population Health. 2012. Available online: https://www.heartfoundation.org.au/getmedia/2bcb1637-1a86-48fc-bb6c-b243c4746272/RapidReview_FoodReformulation.pdf (accessed on 8 July 2021).
32. Cobiac, L.J.; Tam, K.; Veerman, L.; Blakely, T. Taxes and Subsidies for Improving Diet and Population Health in Australia: A Cost-Effectiveness Modelling Study. *PLoS Med.* **2017**, *14*, e1002232. [CrossRef]
33. Scarborough, P.; Nnoaham, K.E.; Clarke, D.; Capewell, S.; Rayner, M. Modelling the impact of a healthy diet on cardiovascular disease and cancer mortality. *J. Epidemiol. Community Health* **2012**, *66*, 420–426. [CrossRef]
34. Hutchesson, M.J.; de Jonge Mulock Houwer, M.; Brown, H.M.; Lim, S.; Moran, L.J.; Vincze, L.; Rollo, M.E.; Hollis, J.L. Supporting women of childbearing age in the prevention and treatment of overweight and obesity: A scoping review of randomized control trials of behavioral interventions. *BMC Womens Health* **2020**, *20*, 14. [CrossRef]
35. Australian Bureau of Statistics. ABS. Australian Health Survey: Users' Guide 2011–2013 Catalogue No. 4363.0.55.001. 2015. Available online: http://www.abs.gov.au/ausstats/abs@.nsf/Lookup/4363.0.55.001Chapter1002011-13 (accessed on 16 June 2021).
36. Food Standards Australia New Zealand. FSANZ. AUSNUT 2011–2013. Available online: http://www.foodstandards.gov.au/science/monitoringnutrients/ausnut/Pages/about.aspx (accessed on 8 July 2021).
37. O'Halloran, S.A.; Lacy, K.E.; Grimes, C.A.; Woods, J.; Campbell, K.J.; Nowson, C.A. A novel processed food classification system applied to Australian food composition databases. *J. Hum. Nutr. Diet.* **2017**, *30*, 534–541. [CrossRef]
38. Machado, P.P.; Steele, E.M.; Levy, R.B.; Sui, Z.; Rangan, A.; Woods, J.; Gill, T.; Scrinis, G.; Monteiro, C.A. Ultra-processed foods and recommended intake levels of nutrients linked to non-communicable diseases in Australia: Evidence from a nationally representative cross-sectional study. *BMJ Open* **2019**, *9*, e029544. [CrossRef]
39. Monteiro, C.A.; Cannon, G.; Levy, R.B.; Moubarac, J.C.; Louzada, M.L.; Rauber, F.; Khandpur, N.; Cediel, G.; Neri, D.; Martinez-Steele, E.; et al. Ultra-processed foods: What they are and how to identify them. *Public Health Nutr.* **2019**, *22*, 936–941. [CrossRef]
40. Moubarac, J.C.; Parra, D.C.; Cannon, G.; Monteiro, C.A. Food Classification Systems Based on Food Processing: Significance and Implications for Policies and Actions: A Systematic Literature Review and Assessment. *Curr. Obes. Rep.* **2014**, *3*, 256–272. [CrossRef]
41. Australian Institute of Health and Welfare. AIHW. Poor Diet. 2019. Available online: https://www.aihw.gov.au/reports/food-nutrition/poor-diet/contents/poor-diet-in-adults (accessed on 8 July 2021).
42. Habibi, N.; Livingstone, K.M.; Edwards, S.; Grieger, J.A. Do Older Women of Reproductive Age Have Better Diet Quality than Younger Women of Reproductive Age? *Nutrients* **2021**, *13*, 3830. [CrossRef]
43. Food and Agriculture Organization of the United Nations. Plates, Pyramids, Planet. Developments in National Healthy and Sustainable Dietary Guidelines: A State of Play Assessment. FAO/University of Oxford. Rome. 2016. Available online: https://www.fao.org/documents/card/en/c/d8dfeaf1-f859-4191-954f-e8e1388cd0b7/ (accessed on 24 September 2021).
44. Crimarco, A.; Landry, M.J.; Gardner, C.D. Ultra-processed Foods, Weight Gain, and Co-morbidity Risk. *Curr. Obes. Rep.* **2021**. [CrossRef]
45. Pulker, C.E.; Scott, J.A.; Pollard, C.M. Ultra-processed family foods in Australia: Nutrition claims, health claims and marketing techniques. *Public Health Nutr.* **2018**, *21*, 38–48. [CrossRef]
46. Forde, C.G. From perception to ingestion; the role of sensory properties in energy selection, eating behaviour and food intake. *Food Qual. Prefer.* **2018**, *66*, 171–177. [CrossRef]
47. Australian Government. National Health and Medical Research Council. Eat for Health. Discretionary Food and Drink Choices. 2017. Available online: https://www.eatforhealth.gov.au/food-essentials/discretionary-food-and-drink-choices (accessed on 16 June 2021).
48. Ryan, D.; Heaner, M. Guidelines (2013) for managing overweight and obesity in adults. Preface to the full report. *Obesity* **2014**, *22* (Suppl. S2), S1–S3. [CrossRef]
49. Greenway, F.L. Physiological adaptations to weight loss and factors favouring weight regain. *Int. J. Obes.* **2015**, *39*, 1188–1196. [CrossRef]

50. Gilbert, J.A.; Drapeau, V.; Astrup, A.; Tremblay, A. Relationship between diet-induced changes in body fat and appetite sensations in women. *Appetite* **2009**, *52*, 809–812. [CrossRef]
51. Sumithran, P.; Prendergast, L.A.; Delbridge, E.; Purcell, K.; Shulkes, A.; Kriketos, A.; Proietto, J. Long-term persistence of hormonal adaptations to weight loss. *N. Engl. J. Med.* **2011**, *365*, 1597–1604. [CrossRef]
52. Hill, A.J. The psychology of food craving. *Proc. Nutr. Soc.* **2007**, *66*, 277–285. [CrossRef]
53. Hasan, H.; Nayfeh, T.; Alzuabi, M.; Wang, Z.; Kuchkuntla, A.R.; Prokop, L.J.; Newman, C.B.; Murad, M.H.; Rajjo, T.I. Weight Loss and Serum Lipids in Overweight and Obese Adults: A Systematic Review and Meta-Analysis. *J. Clin. Endocrinol. Metab.* **2020**, *105*, 3695–3703. [CrossRef]
54. Xiang, L.; Wu, H.; Pan, A.; Patel, B.; Xiang, G.; Qi, L.; Kaplan, R.C.; Hu, F.; Wylie-Rosett, J.; Qi, Q. FTO genotype and weight loss in diet and lifestyle interventions: A systematic review and meta-analysis. *Am. J. Clin. Nutr.* **2016**, *103*, 1162–1170. [CrossRef]
55. Melby, C.L.; Paris, H.L.; Foright, R.M.; Peth, J. Attenuating the Biologic Drive for Weight Regain Following Weight Loss: Must What Goes Down Always Go Back Up? *Nutrients* **2017**, *9*, 468. [CrossRef]
56. Schwarz, N.A.; Rigby, B.R.; La Bounty, P.; Shelmadine, B.; Bowden, R.G. A review of weight control strategies and their effects on the regulation of hormonal balance. *J. Nutr. Metab.* **2011**, *2011*, 237932. [CrossRef]
57. Grieger, J.A.; Johnson, B.J.; Wycherley, T.P.; Golley, R.K. Comparing the Nutritional Impact of Dietary Strategies to Reduce Discretionary Choice Intake in the Australian Adult Population: A Simulation Modelling Study. *Nutrients* **2017**, *9*, 442. [CrossRef]
58. Australian Institute of Health and Welfare. AIHW. Australian Government. The Health of Australia's Females. 2019. Available online: https://www.aihw.gov.au/reports/men-women/female-health/contents/lifestyle-risk-factors/tobacco-smoking-alcohol-and-illicit-drugs (accessed on 24 September 2021).
59. Anwar, M.Y.; Marcus, M.; Taylor, K.C. The association between alcohol intake and fecundability during menstrual cycle phases. *Hum. Reprod.* **2021**, *36*, 2538–2548. [CrossRef]
60. Lawrence, M.A.; Dickie, S.; Woods, J.L. Do Nutrient-Based Front-of-Pack Labelling Schemes Support or Undermine Food-Based Dietary Guideline Recommendations? Lessons from the Australian Health Star Rating System. *Nutrients* **2018**, *10*, 32. [CrossRef]
61. Dickie, S.; Woods, J.L.; Lawrence, M. Analysing the use of the Australian Health Star Rating system by level of food processing. *Int. J. Behav. Nutr. Phys. Act.* **2018**, *15*, 128. [CrossRef] [PubMed]
62. Page, B.; Sharp, A.; Lockshin, L.; Sorensen, H. Parents and children in supermarkets: Incidence and influence. *J. Retail. Consum. Serv.* **2018**, *40*, 31–39. [CrossRef]
63. Marchese, L.; Livingstone, K.M.; Woods, J.L.; Wingrove, K.; Machado, P. Ultra-processed food consumption, socio-demographics and diet quality in Australian adults. *Public Health Nutr.* **2022**, *25*, 94–104. [CrossRef] [PubMed]
64. Lee, A.J.; Kane, S.; Herron, L.M.; Matsuyama, M.; Lewis, M. A tale of two cities: The cost, price-differential and affordability of current and healthy diets in Sydney and Canberra, Australia. *Int. J. Behav. Nutr. Phys. Act.* **2020**, *17*, 80. [CrossRef]
65. Lee, A.J.; Kane, S.; Ramsey, R.; Good, E.; Dick, M. Testing the price and affordability of healthy and current (unhealthy) diets and the potential impacts of policy change in Australia. *BMC Public Health* **2016**, *16*, 315. [CrossRef]
66. Baraldi, L.G.; Martinez Steele, E.; Canella, D.S.; Monteiro, C.A. Consumption of ultra-processed foods and associated sociodemographic factors in the USA between 2007 and 2012: Evidence from a nationally representative cross-sectional study. *BMJ Open* **2018**, *8*, e020574. [CrossRef]
67. Conde, W.L.; Monteiro, C.A. Nutrition transition and double burden of undernutrition and excess of weight in Brazil. *Am. J. Clin. Nutr.* **2014**, *100*, 1617S–1622S. [CrossRef]
68. Monteiro, C.A.; Levy, R.B.; Claro, R.M.; de Castro, I.R.; Cannon, G. Increasing consumption of ultra-processed foods and likely impact on human health: Evidence from Brazil. *Public Health Nutr.* **2011**, *14*, 5–13. [CrossRef]

nutrients

MDPI

Article

Absolute and Relative Agreement between the Current and Modified Brazilian Cardioprotective Nutritional Program Dietary Index (BALANCE DI) and the American Heart Association Healthy Diet Score (AHA-DS) in Post Myocardial Infarction Patients

Camila Weschenfelder [1], Philip Sapp [2], Terrence Riley [2], Kristina Petersen [3], Jacqueline Tereza da Silva [4], Angela Cristine Bersch-Ferreira [5], Rachel Helena Vieira Machado [5], Erlon Oliveira de Abreu-Silva [5], Lucas Ribeiro Silva [5], Bernardete Weber [5], Alexandre Schaan de Quadros [1], Penny Kris-Etherton [2] and Aline Marcadenti [1,5,*]

1. Graduate Program in Health Sciences (Cardiology), Instituto de Cardiologia do Rio Grande do Sul, Fundação Universitária de Cardiologia (IC/FUC), Princesa Isabel Avenue 395, Porto Alegre 90040-371, Brazil; camilawesche@gmail.com (C.W.); consult.asq@gmail.com (A.S.d.Q.)
2. Department of Nutritional Sciences, Pennsylvania State University, 110 Chandlee Laboratory, University Park, State College, PA 16802, USA; philip.sapp@psu.edu (P.S.); tmr359@psu.edu (T.R.); pmk3@psu.edu (P.K.-E.)
3. Department of Nutritional Sciences, Texas Tech University, Lubbock, TX 79409, USA; kristina.petersen@ttu.edu
4. Global Academy of Agriculture and Food Security, University of Edinburgh, Sir Alexander Robertson Building, Easter Bush Campus, Edinburgh EH25 9RG, UK; jacqueline.silva@ed.ac.uk
5. Hcor Research Institute, Hcor (IP-Hcor), Abílio Soares Street 250, São Paulo 04004-050, Brazil; abferreira@hcor.com.br (A.C.B.-F.); rhelena@hcor.com.br (R.H.V.M.); erlon@terra.com.br (E.O.d.A.-S.); luciribeiro@hcor.com.br (L.R.S.); bweber@hcor.com.br (B.W.)

* Correspondence: marcadenti.aline@gmail.com; Tel.: +55-11-3053-6611 (ext. 8220)

Citation: Weschenfelder, C.; Sapp, P.; Riley, T.; Petersen, K.; da Silva, J.T.; Bersch-Ferreira, A.C.; Machado, R.H.V.; de Abreu-Silva, E.O.; Silva, L.R.; Weber, B.; et al. Absolute and Relative Agreement between the Current and Modified Brazilian Cardioprotective Nutritional Program Dietary Index (BALANCE DI) and the American Heart Association Healthy Diet Score (AHA-DS) in Post Myocardial Infarction Patients. *Nutrients* **2022**, *14*, 1378. https://doi.org/10.3390/nu14071378

Academic Editors: Clare Collins, George Moschonis and Hayato Tada

Received: 10 February 2022
Accepted: 22 March 2022
Published: 25 March 2022

Abstract: The American Heart Association Diet Score (AHA-DS) defines the cardiovascular health, and the Brazilian Cardioprotective Nutritional Program Dietary Index (BALANCE DI) was designed to evaluate diet quality in secondary cardiovascular prevention settings. Our aim was to assess the absolute and relative agreement between both tools in Brazilian adults after a myocardial infarction (MI). In this cross-sectional study, 473 individuals were included and had their diet assessed by a 24 h food recall and a semi-quantitative Food Frequency Questionnaire. The weighted Kappa between BALANCE DI and primary AHA-DS was 0.66 (95% CI: 0.08–0.21), and between BALANCE DI and total AHA-DS was 0.70 (95% CI: 0.20–0.32). To improve the agreement between the tools, modifications were made to the BALANCE DI scoring system. The weighted Kappa between New BALANCE DI and primary AHA-DS was 0.77 (95% CI: 0.36–0.48), and between BALANCE DI and total AHA-DS was 0.76 (95% CI: 0.34–0.46). The mean bias observed between the New BALANCE DI as compared to the primary and total AHA-DS was −16% (−51 to 19) and −8% (−41 to 24), respectively. Our results suggest that the New BALANCE DI may be a useful tool to evaluate diet quality in post MI patients.

Keywords: dietary patterns; diet; healthy; myocardial infarction

1. Introduction

Ischemic heart disease (IHD) is the leading cause of death worldwide [1]. Myocardial infarction (MI) is a common manifestation of IHD and is the greatest cause of cardiovascular mortality in Brazil [2]. Diet is a modifiable risk factor for IHD [3,4]. Many epidemiologic studies and clinical trials have shown that a healthy dietary pattern is associated with primary and secondary prevention of cardiovascular disease (CVD) [5–8]. This evidence is the basis of current dietary recommendations for the prevention and treatment of CVD [9,10].

In the 2020 American Heart Association (AHA) Impact Goal, a healthy eating pattern consistent with the DASH (Dietary Approaches to Stop Hypertension) diet was recommended for cardiovascular health (CVH) [11]. This healthy eating pattern is the basis for the scoring system developed by the AHA to evaluate diet quality and define CVH. The AHA proposed dietary targets and a healthy diet score (AHA-DS) [12], which classifies the dietary pattern as ideal, intermediate, or poor. Few studies have evaluated the AHA-DS in patients after an MI [13].

The Brazilian Cardioprotective Nutritional Program (BALANCE) is a regional and feasible dietary pattern that was designed to improve diet quality in adults with atherosclerotic cardiovascular disease [14–16]. BALANCE is composed of four food groups represented by the three colors of the Brazilian flag (green, yellow, and blue represent recommended foods and red represents foods to avoid) [15]. To assess adherence to the BALANCE recommendations, the BALANCE DI was developed [17]. Thus, the BALANCE DI reflects adherence to a country-specific recommended dietary pattern. The BALANCE DI performs similarly to other diet quality indices regarding reliability and construct validity [17].

Although it can be used to assess diet quality in adults with IHD, it is unknown how BALANCE DI relates to CVH. This study was conducted to assess the absolute and relative agreement between the BALANCE DI and the AHA-DS in Brazilian adults after an MI (2 to 6 months after the event). Investigation of this country-specific diet quality index is needed because cultural adaption of recommended dietary patterns to the target population enhances adherence.

2. Materials and Methods

2.1. Study Design and Participants

This is a cross-sectional analysis of baseline data from the DICA-NUTS Study, for which a detailed protocol was previously published [18]. Briefly, DICA-NUTS is a 16-week, parallel, multicenter, randomized clinical trial (ClinicalTrials.gov NCT03728127) carried out in four regions of Brazil (Northeast, Southeast, South, and Midwest), from January 2019 to December 2021 [18]. The study included patients over 40 years old with diagnosed MI, either ST-Elevation MI (STEMI) or non-STEMI in the last 2 to 6 months. At baseline, participants completed questionnaires on sociodemographic, lifestyle, medical, and dietary intake. All data were collected by trained nutritionists [18]. Ethical approval for the analysis was provided by Research Ethics Committee of Instituto de Cardiologia do Rio Grande do Sul/Fundação Universitária de Cardiologia (IC/FUC) under number 5.115.455 (CAAE 52734921.0.0000.5333). All participants provided written informed consent.

2.2. Dietary Assessment

At baseline, participants completed one 24-h food recall (24hR) and a semi-quantitative Food Frequency Questionnaire (FFQ) [18]. Both tools were administered on the same day during the participant's first appointment. The FFQ collected data on their consumption over the previous 365 days. A photo album with standardized household measures or grams was used in both the 24hR and FFQ [18,19]. For the analysis of the 24hR, a computerized system (Sistema Vivanda de Alimentação®, São Paulo, Brazil) was used that prioritizes Brazilian nutrition composition tables [18].

2.2.1. BALANCE DI

The BALANCE DI was calculated based on the 24hR. The scoring system considers the four BALANCE food groups [17] (Supplemental Table S1). Foods are classified into each food group using the BALANCE recommendations tool that categorizes foods by caloric equivalents and the density of sodium, saturated fat, and cholesterol. For each food group, portions consumed were summed and scores were determined for individuals based on energy intake from the 24hR. The caloric ranges and recommended intake of food groups are described in Supplemental Table S2 [18].

Supplemental Table S3 summarizes the BALANCE DI score. Higher scores represent greater adherence to recommendations [17]. The scores were calculated as continuous variables and rounded to the nearest tenth decimal point.

2.2.2. AHA-DS

The AHA-DS for ideal, intermediate, and poor dietary patterns uses a binary scoring system [12]. The highest score of 10 is given for meeting or exceeding the AHA target, and the lowest score of zero is given for no intake of the following cardioprotective dietary factors, i.e., fruits and vegetables, fish and shellfish, whole grains, nuts, seeds, and legumes, or for high intake of foods/nutrients that should be limited (i.e., sodium, sugar-sweetened beverages, processed meats and saturated fat). Scores are determined on a continuous scale (rounded to the nearest whole number). The range of the primary AHA-DS is 0 to 50 (for 5 components: fruits and vegetables, fish and shellfish, whole grains, sodium, and sugar-sweetened beverages).

Three secondary components (nuts, seeds, and legumes; processed meats; and saturated fat) are included in the total AHA-DS. The range for the total AHA-DS is 0 to 80 (for 8 components: the 5 components for the primary score + the 3 components for the secondary score). For both the primary AHA-DS and the total AHA-DS, an ideal score is given for meeting ≥80% of the targets, an intermediate score corresponds to 40–79% of the targets, and a poor score corresponds to meeting <40% of the targets. The AHA scoring system is summarized in Supplemental Table S4.

AHA scores were determined using the available data from the FFQ and the 24hR. Data from the 24hR were used for components scored as servings per day (fruits and vegetables, whole grains, saturated fat, and sodium). Scores reported in servings per week (fish and shellfish, sugar sweetened beverages, nuts, seeds, legumes, and processed meats) were derived from the FFQ (in grams or mL). For legumes, reported intake in grams was transformed into cups/day according to the portions defined in the United States Department of Agriculture (USDA) FoodData Central database [20]. All mixed composition foods were scored using estimates of the amount contained within a mixed food item (i.e., the meat content of a hamburger was considered separately from the whole hamburger, including the bun and condiments). A full list of FFQ items and classifications can be found in the Supplemental Tables S5 and S6.

2.3. *Sociodemographic, Clinic, Lifestyle Variables and Biochemical Assessment*

Self-reported sociodemographic data were collected including: sex (male or female), age (years), marital status (single, married, divorced, widowed, stable union), education level (illiterate/incomplete elementary school, complete elementary school/incomplete middle school, complete middle school/incomplete high school, complete high school school/incomplete college degree, complete college degree) [18]. Clinical and lifestyle variables were smoking status (never smoked, ex-smoker, smoker) and comorbidities as determined by previous medical diagnosis such as Type 2 Diabetes Mellitus (T2DM), arterial hypertension, and dyslipidemia [18].

Anthropometrics were collected by a licensed nutritionist trained in study procedures as previously described [18]. Parameters collected were: weight (kg), height (m), waist circumference (WC (cm)), and body mass index (BMI (kg/m^2)). Physical activity was accessed in minutes per week using the International Physical Activity Questionnaire (IPAQ) [18,21].

Fasting blood samples were collected at the baseline visit. Plasma was analyzed for total cholesterol (TC (mmol/L)), high density lipoprotein cholesterol (HDL-C (mmol/L)), triglycerides (TG (mmol/L)), fasting glucose (FG (mmol/L)), fasting insulin (FI (mU/L)), glycated hemoglobin (HbA1c (%)), at the clinical analysis laboratories at each center using standardized techniques [18]. Additionally, low-density lipoprotein (LDL-C (mmol/L)) was calculated from Martin's mathematical formula [22].

2.4. Statistical Analysis

Statistical analyses were performed using SAS (version 9.4; SAS Institute, Cary, NC, USA). All variables were tested for normality (PROC UNIVARIATE) based on the distribution, normal probability plots (Q-Q plots), and skewness. For non-parametric data, natural log transformations were made prior to analysis. To enable direct comparison between the AHA-DS and the BALANCE DI, data from both indices were converted to a percentage of total score for each subject. Paired t-tests were used to assess mean bias of the BALANCE DI compared to the AHA-DS (standard reference). Pearson's correlations were used to assess the correlation between the two indices. Bland–Altman plots and weighted kappa were used to assess the agreement between the two indices. $p < 0.05$ was considered statistically significant.

3. Results

From 486 individuals included in the DICA-NUTS study, a total of 473 were included in this analysis; 13 patients were excluded from the analysis due to missing dietary data at the baseline visit. The average age was 59 ± 9.4 years and 72% were male. The mean BMI was 28.5 ± 4.3 kg/m^2. At the baseline visit, lipid parameters were within normal limits. The average blood glucose was 6.41 mmol/L (±2.46 mmol/L), HbA1c was 6.33% (±1.4%), and insulin was within normal limits. Table 1 summarizes the characteristics of the study participants.

Table 1. Demographic, clinical, lifestyle, laboratory, and dietary intake characteristics of participants (n = 473).

Characteristic	Mean ± SD, Median (IQR) or *n* (%)
Age (years)	60 ± 9.4
Sex	
Female	135 (28)
Male	344 (72)
Days after MI	108 ± 36.3
Marital status	
Single	79 (16)
Married	276 (58)
Divorced	59 (12)
Widowed	33 (7)
Common Law Marriage	32 (7)
Education Level	
Illiterate/incomplete elementary school	99 (21)
Complete elementary school/incomplete middle school	87 (18)
Complete middle school/incomplete high school	65 (14)
Complete high school school/incomplete college degree	142 (30)
Complete college degree	84 (17)
Smoking	
No	172 (36)
Ex-smoker	255 (53)
Smoker	50 (11)

Table 1. *Cont.*

Characteristic	Mean ± SD, Median (IQR) or *n* (%)
T2DM *	134 (28)
Hypertension *	313 (65)
Dyslipidemia *	195 (41)
BMI (kg/m^2)	28.5 ± 4.3
Weight (kg)	78.2 ± 15.1
WC (cm)	97.9 ± 11.5
WHR	0.9 ± 0.08
Level of Physical Activity (according to IPAQ **)	
High	127 (27)
Moderate	266 (56)
Low	82 (17)
Dietary intake ***	
Energy (Kcal)	1616 ± 624
Carbohydrates (% energy)	52 ± 14
Proteins (% energy)	20 ± 10.1
Fat (% energy)	31 ± 14.2
SFA (% energy)	10.6 ± 5.5
PUFA (% energy)	7.3 ± 4.4
MUFA (% energy)	9.5 ± 5
Dietary Fiber (g)	20.7 ± 8.1
Sodium (mg)	3131 ± 1656
Biochemical data	
TC (mmol/L)	4.08 ± 1.39
LDL-C (mmol/L)	2.2 ± 1.13
HDL-C (mmol/L)	1.09 ± 0.49
TG (mmol/L)	1.5 (0.5–8.39)
Glucose (mmol/L)	6.41 ±2.46
HbA1c (%)	6.33 ±1.4
Insulin (UI/mL)	10.2 (0.1–200)

* Determined by previous medical diagnosis; ** High: vigorous-intensity activity on at least 3 days and accumulating at least 1500 MET-minutes/week OR 7 or more days of any combination of walking, moderate- or vigorous- intensity activities accumulating at least 3000 MET-minutes/week; Moderate: 3 or more days of vigorous-intensity activity of at least 20 min per day OR 5 or more days of moderate-intensity activity and/or walking of at least 3 min per day OR 5 or more days of any combination of walking, moderate-intensity or vigorous-intensity activities achieving a minimum of at least 600 MET-min/week; Low: no activity is reported OR some activity is reported but not enough to meet Categories 2 or 3; *** Based on 24hR. T2DM: Type 2 Diabetes Mellitus; BMI: body mass index; WC: waist circumference; WHR: waist to hip ratio; IPAQ: International Physical Activity Questionnaire; SFA: saturated fatty acids; PUFA: polyunsaturated fatty acids; MUFA: monounsaturated fatty acids; TC: total cholesterol; LDL-C: low density lipoprotein cholesterol; HDL-C: high density lipoprotein cholesterol; TG: triglycerides; HbA1c: glycated hemoglobin.

Diet quality was assessed 108 days ± 36.3 days following MI. Dietary intake according to the 24hR is described in Table 1. Mean energy intake was 1616 ± 624 kcals and sodium intake was 3131.8 ± 1656 mg. Adherence to the primary and total AHA-DS was 59 ± 17% and 51 ± 14%, respectively, which is consistent with an intermediate diet score. Mean adherence to the BALANCE DI was 43 ± 18.7%.

Comparison between the AHA-DS and the BALANCE DI showed weak to moderate correlations (Table S7). When comparing the BALANCE DI with the primary AHA-DS, 23% of the cohort was ranked in the same quintile by both indices (weighted Kappa was 0.66 (95% CI: 0.08–0.21), Table S8. Partial agreement (±1 quintile) was 24% and gross misclassification (±4 quintiles) was 5.1%. When comparing the BALANCE DI with the total AHA-DS, the exact agreement was 28%, the partial (±1 quintile) was 22% and gross misclassification (±4 quintiles) was 1.5% (weighted Kappa 0.70, 95% CI: 0.20–0.32).

To improve the agreement between the BALANCE DI and the AHA-DS, modifications were made to the BALANCE DI scoring system (Table 2). The modifications we made to the BALANCE DI were to improve the agreement with the AHA-DS components "fruits and vegetables" (extracted from the green group) and "whole grains" (extracted from the yellow group). When both components were extracted from the BALANCE DI green and yellow food groups, the index needed to be rescored and we assumed that 50% needed to be composed of fruits and vegetables and whole grains, respectively. Additionally, when whole grains consumption exceeded the recommendation for the yellow group, a score of 0 was given since one of the principles of the BALANCE DI is energy prescription. The scoring system for the blue and red groups were unchanged.

Table 2. Scoring system for the New BALANCE DI.

BALANCE Groups	**Recommendation (Portions/d)**	**Energy Requirements (kcal/d)**					
		1400	**1600**	**1800**	**2000**	**2200**	**2400**
Green	Original	9	11	11	12	14	16
	Fruits and vegetables	4.5	5.5	5.5	6	7	8
	Proportionally scored	0–4.5	0–5.5	0–5.5	0–6	0–7	0–8
	Score 10	>4.5	>5.5	>5.5	>6	>7	>8
Yellow	Original	6	7	9	10	11	13
	Whole grains	3	3.5	4	5	5.5	6.5
	Proportionally scored	0–3	0–3.5	0–4.5	0–5	0–5.5	0–6.5
	Score 10	>3	>3.5	>4.5	>5	>5.5	>6.5
	Score 0	>6	>7	>9	>10	>11	>13
Blue	Original	2	2	3	3	4	4
Red	Original	0	0	0	0	0	0

New BALANCE DI: New Brazilian Cardioprotective Nutritional Program Dietary Index; BALANCE: Brazilian Cardioprotective Nutritional Program.

The correlations between the New BALANCE DI and the AHA-DS were improved, as shown in Table S9. The New BALANCE DI ranked 35% of the cohort in the same quintile as the AHA-DS (weighted Kappa 0.77 (95% CI: 0.36–0.48). Partial (±1 quintile) was 24% and gross misclassification (±4 quintiles) was 0.6% (Table S10) When comparing the New BALANCE DI with the total AHA-DS, the exact quintile agreement was 36%, the partial quintile agreement (±1 quintile) was 25% and the gross misclassification (±4 quintiles) was 0.4% (weighted Kappa 0.76 (95% CI: 0.34–0.46). Figure 1 shows the Bland–Altman plots for the primary and secondary AHA-DS versus the BALANCE DI (Panel A and B) and the New BALANCE DI (Panel C and D). Proportional bias was observed when comparing the total AHA score with the BALANCE DI (Panel B) and the new BALANCE DI (Panel D) such that bias was greater for those with higher diet quality.

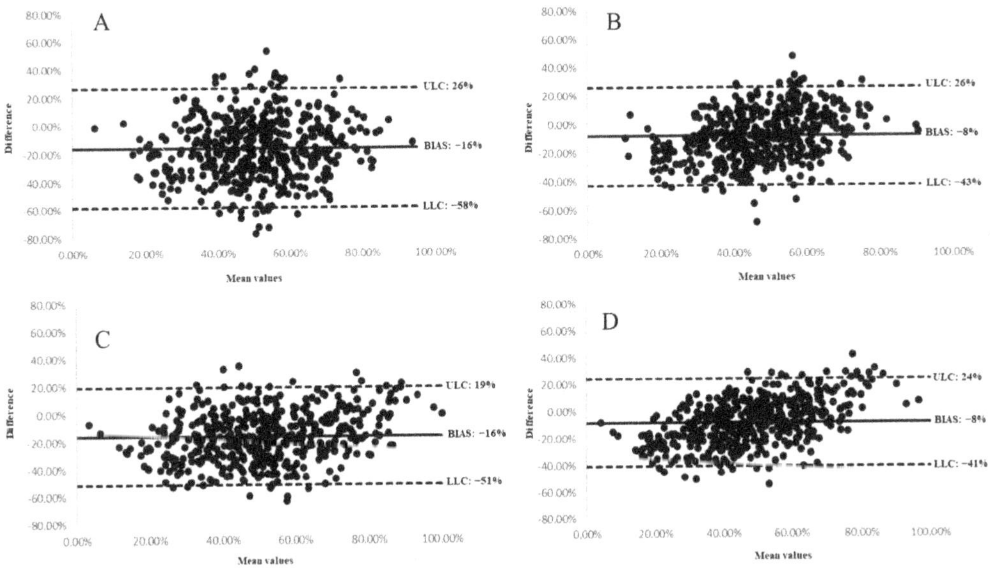

Figure 1. Bland-Altman plots between the BALANCE DI, the New BALANCE DI and both primary and secondary AHA-DS for determining overall diet quality of patients after myocardial infarction (n = 473). (**A**) BALANCE DI and primary AHA-DS; (**B**) BALANCE DI and total AHA-DS; (**C**) New BALANCE DI and primary AHA-DS; (**D**) New BALANCE DI and total AHA-DS. The solid line represents the mean difference between the two instruments, and the dotted lines represent the minimum and maximum differences between the scores. ULC: upper limit of concordance; LLC: lower limit of concordance.

4. Discussion

This study aimed to assess the strength of the relationship and degree of agreement between the BALANCE DI and the AHA-DS in post MI patients in Brazil to evaluate the BALANCE DI as a tool for CVH assessment. The BALANCE DI and the primary AHA-DS were weakly correlated (r = 0.28), which improved modestly when correlating the total AHA-DS (r = 0.46). Similarly, measures of agreement were fair between quintiles of the BALANCE DI and AHA-DS (23%) or the total AHA-DS (28%). Bland–Altman analysis showed that the BALANCE DI was on average higher than both the primary and total AHA-DS with large limits of agreement in both cases. However, some evidence of proportional bias was present whereby bias varied by diet quality.

In general, for dietary index development and/or comparisons, different approaches are used. We used a more comprehensive score, specific for measuring CVH, as a comparator. However, studies that use another tool as the reference for the development of a new index are scarce in the literature. Antonio et al. [23], when comparing the Healthy Eating Index (HEI) and the Diabetes Healthy Eating Index (DHEI) among T2DM patients, reported mean bias of 17 points. These results are similar to ours since comparisons between both the BALANCE and the New BALANCE DI with the primary AHA-DS demonstrate a difference of 16 points. In healthy individuals, comparisons between the agreement of five indexes that measure adherence to a Mediterranean dietary pattern showed a moderate–fair concordance among indexes evaluated by Cohen's Kappa coefficient, except for the Mediterranean diet score (MDS) and alternative Mediterranean diet (aMED) with a 0.56 (95% CI 0.55–0.59) and 0.67 (95% CI 0.66–0.68) using linear and quadratic weighting, respectively [24]. The authors attributed the disagreement between the indexes to the lack of common criteria to develop the indexes, the type of foods or nutrients considered, the variability of the methods used to construct them, and the dependence or independence of the scores from the study sample, factors that might also explain our results.

Low agreement between the tools may be due to the distinct methods of food classifications between tools. The BALANCE-DI measures adherence to a healthy dietary pattern composed of food groups, that differ from the AHA-DS food groups. For example, the BALANCE DI green group is composed of vegetables, fruits, beans and legumes, and low-fat milk whereas the AHA-DS considers these food groups separately (fruits and vegetables, and legumes are scored as different components). Additionally, in contrast with the AHA-DS, that specifically recommends whole grains, the BALANCE DI yellow group is composed of both refined grains and whole grains.

Modifications to the BALANCE DI focused only on including fruits and vegetables in the green group and removing refined grains from the yellow group improved the correlation with the AHA-DS. However, Bland–Altman analyses showed a wide limit of agreement for the New Balance DI. These results suggest that the New BALANCE DI may be limited in its use for diet assessment of individuals, but may be suitable for use in cohorts of patients post MI. This approach to modifying diet assessment tools may be a useful model for the modification of other culturally specific diet quality assessment tools.

High diet quality has been associated with better prognosis for secondary cardiovascular prevention [25,26]. To evaluate the relationship between diet quality and mortality among MI survivors, Li et al. [25] included 4098 participants that were free of CVD, stroke or cancer at the time of enrollment and survived a first MI during the follow up. Comparing the extreme quintiles of the post-MI Alternative Healthy Eating Index (AHEI) 2010 (excluding the alcohol component), the adjusted HR associated were 0.73 (95% CI: 0.58–0.93) for all-cause mortality and 0.81 (95% CI: 0.64–1.04) for cardiovascular mortality. In a prospective cohort study [26] of 31,546 individuals with prior CVD or DM, higher diet quality was associated with a lower risk of recurrent or new CVD events in people receiving drug therapy for secondary prevention (HR 0.78; 95% CI 0.71–0.87, top versus lowest quintile of modified AHEI; p for trend <0.001). The study estimated that at least 20% of CVD recurrence could be avoided by adhering to a healthy diet.

However, few studies have assessed diet quality in patients after an MI, especially with instruments designed specifically for this population. We used a validated Brazilian dietary index to determine adherence to a healthy dietary pattern based on the current national guidelines for secondary CVD prevention [17]. Our study showed relatively poor adherence (43 $\pm$ 18.7%) to the BALANCE dietary eating patterns. The association between the BALANCE DI and CVD-related outcomes has not been assessed. The AHA-DS, a validated diet quality assessment tool associated with CVD outcomes, showed that overall diet quality in this sample of 473 post-MI patients was consistent with an intermediate diet score. Previous studies with large samples, but in different populations, reported similar findings. Among 33,932 US [27] and 37,803 Europeans [28], the AHA-DS from both samples was consistent with an intermediate score. Conversely, Mok et al. [13] found that 50.8% of the 1277 participants from the ARIC study (aged 45–64 years old) who developed an MI had a poor diet score [13]. The timepoint at which diet assessment occurs may explain the difference between our findings and those of Mok et al. [13], who collected dietary data prior to the event; we collected data from our sample post-MI. Dietary habits are reportedly altered after a coronary event to align more closely with diet recommendations [29].

A healthy diet is part of The Life's Simple 7 (LS7) metrics proposed by the AHA for the CVH definition [11]. Besides diet, smoking, physical activity, body mass index, total cholesterol, blood pressure and blood glucose are characterized as being ideal, intermediate, or poor. The achievement of a greater number of ideal metrics is associated with a lower risk of incident CVD [30–33], including IHD [33], and closer adherence to optimal levels of the 7 CVH metrics is associated with better prognosis after an MI [13]. Thus, the AHA-DS was used in this study for comparison because meeting the AHA recommendations for healthy eating supports cardiovascular risk reduction.

This study has several strengths. We investigated diet quality in patients up to 6 months after an MI and most studies are conducted later. However, the first months after the infarction might be a window of opportunity to improve dietary habits and consequently diet quality. Another strength of our study is the use and modification of a Brazilian DI that measures adherence to a recommended dietary pattern for this population. The New BALANCE DI aligns with the AHA-DS for CVH. Our study has shown that a DI that is based on a culturally unique dietary pattern can be adapted in alignment with the AHA-DS and used to assess diet quality in patients with IHD. Further research is needed to assess the ease of use of the New BALANCE DI in clinical settings.

Our study has several limitations as well. First, the BALANCE DI uses 24hR, whereas our analysis used both the 24hR and the FFQ for scoring the AHA-DS. This was because the AHA-DS considers weekly intake for some components. Thus, our results might reflect differences in the dietary assessment tools used. Second, instead of classifying the AHA-DS components "fruits and vegetables" in cups/day and "whole grains" in oz-equivalent-servings/day, we used the number of portions used for the BALANCE DI scoring, which could have influenced our results, since the BALANCE DI portions are based on caloric equivalents and conversion to household measurements could have resulted in some errors in assessing adherence to current recommendations. Third, the agreement between the BALANCE DI, the New BALANCE DI and the AHA-DS seems to be proportional to diet quality, which is difficult to correct for and suggests additional modifications are needed to the BALANCE DI.

5. Conclusions

In post-MI Brazilian adults, the BALANCE DI and the AHA-DS showed limited agreement. Our results suggest that the New BALANCE DI may be used to assess diet quality in cohorts of post MI patients. Further studies are needed to assess the association between the New BALANCE DI with CVH in a primary prevention setting and in patients with established IHD to evaluate its effectiveness in predicting future events.

Supplementary Materials: The following supporting information can be downloaded at: https://www.mdpi.com/article/10.3390/nu14071378/s1. Table S1: BALANCE food group composition; Table S2: BALANCE caloric ranges and recommended intake of food groups; Table S3: Scoring criteria for the BALANCE DI; Table S4: AHA Dietary Targets and Healthy Diet Score for Defining Cardiovascular Health; Table S5: Foods items from the FFQ and mean cup for the scoring system for AHA-DS components measured in cups/day; Table S6: Foods from the FFQ for the scoring system for AHA-DS components measured in g/week, oz/week, and oz-equivalent servings/day; Table S7: Pearson correlations and mean differences between the AHA-DS and the BALANCE DI; Table S8: Weighted kappa on quintile rankings of agreement between the BALANCE DI, the primary and the total AHA-DS; Table S9: Pearson correlations and mean differences between the AHA-DS and the New BALANCE DI; Table S10: Weighted kappa on quintile rankings of agreement between the New BALANCE DI, the primary and the total AHA-DS. See [12,17,18,20,34].

Author Contributions: Conceptualization, A.M. and C.W.; methodology, A.M., P.K.-E. and K.P.; formal analysis, P.S.; investigation, C.W.; writing—original draft preparation, C.W.; writing—review and editing, P.S., T.R., K.P., J.T.d.S., A.C.B.-F., R.H.V.M., E.O.d.A.-S., L.R.S., A.S.d.Q., P.K.-E. and A.M.; supervision, K.P., P.K.-E. and A.M.; project administration, A.M. and R.H.V.M.; funding acquisition, A.M. and B.W. All authors have read and agreed to the published version of the manuscript.

Funding: This research was funded by Coordenação de Aperfeiçoamento de Pessoal de Nível Superior-Brasil (CAPES)-Finance Code 001; by Hcor as part of the "Hospitais de Excelência a Serviço do SUS", in partnership with the Programa de Apoio ao Desenvolvimento Institucional do Sistema Único de Saúde (PROADI-SUS) and Brazilian Ministry of Health; and by Instituto de Cardiologia do Rio Grande do Sul/Fundação Universitária de Cardiologia (IC/FUC). The APC was funded by Instituto de Cardiologia do Rio Grande do Sul/Fundação Universitária de Cardiologia (IC/FUC).

Institutional Review Board Statement: The study was conducted according to the guidelines of the Declaration of Helsinki and approved by the Institutional Review Board (or Ethics Committee) of

Instituto de Cardiologia do Rio Grande do Sul/Fundação Universitária de Cardiologia (IC/FUC) under number 5.115.455 (CAAE 52734921.0.0000.5333) on 19 November 2021.

Informed Consent Statement: Informed consent was obtained from all subjects involved in the study.

Data Availability Statement: The data presented in this study are available on request from the corresponding author. The data are not publicly available because DICA-NUTS trial is not published yet.

Acknowledgments: Authors would like to acknowledge the Department of Science and Technology/Brazilian Ministry of Health (DECIT/MS) and the following investigation sites: Hcor, Instituto de Cardiologia/Fundação Universitária de Cardiologia (IC/FUC), Hospital de Clínicas de Porto Alegre/Universidade Federal do Rio Grande do Sul (HCPA-UFRGS), Hospital de Clínicas/Universidade Federal de Goiás (HC-UFG/EBSERH), Universidade Federal do Rio Grande do Norte (UFRN), Universidade Federal de Alagoas (UFAL), Universidade Federal do Maranhão (UFMA), Complexo Hospital de Clínicas/Universidade Federal do Paraná (HC-UFPR), and Instituto Nacional de Cardiologia (INC).

Conflicts of Interest: The authors declare no conflict of interest.

References

1. World Health Organization (WHO). Available online: https://www.who.int/news-room/fact-sheets/detail/the-top-10-causes-of-death (accessed on 19 January 2022).
2. Siqueira, C.A.D.S.; de Souza, D.L.B. Reduction of mortality and predictions for acute myocardial infarction, stroke, and heart failure in Brazil until 2030. *Sci. Rep.* **2020**, *10*, 17856. [CrossRef] [PubMed]
3. Aune, D.; Giovannucci, E.; Boffetta, P.; Fadnes, L.T.; Keum, N.; Norat, T.; Greenwood, D.C.; Riboli, E.; Vatten, L.J.; Tonstad, S. Fruit and vegetable intake and the risk of cardiovascular disease, total cancer and all-cause mortality-a systematic review and dose-response meta-analysis of prospective studies. *Int. J. Epidemiol.* **2017**, *4*, 1029–1056. [CrossRef]
4. Aune, D.; Keum, N.; Giovannucci, E.; Fadnes, L.T.; Boffetta, P.; Greenwood, D.C.; Tonstad, S.; Vatten, L.J.; Riboli, E.; Norat, T. Whole grain consumption and risk of cardiovascular disease, cancer, and all cause and cause specific mortality: Systematic review and dose-response meta-analysis of prospective studies. *BMJ* **2016**, *353*, i2716. [CrossRef] [PubMed]
5. Rosato, V.; Temple, N.J.; La Vecchia, C.; Castellan, G.; Tavani, A.; Guercio, V. Mediterranean diet and cardiovascular disease: A systematic review and meta-analysis of observational studies. *Eur. J. Nutr.* **2019**, *58*, 173–191. [CrossRef] [PubMed]
6. Filippou, C.D.; Tsioufis, C.P.; Thomopoulos, C.G.; Mihas, C.C.; Dimitriadis, K.S.; Sotiropoulou, L.I.; Chrysochoou, C.A.; Nihoyannopoulos, P.I.; Tousoulis, D.M. Dietary Approaches to Stop Hypertension (DASH) Diet and Blood Pressure Reduction in Adults with and without Hypertension: A Systematic Review and Meta-Analysis of Randomized Controlled Trials. *Adv. Nutr.* **2020**, *11*, 1150–1160. [CrossRef] [PubMed]
7. Dinu, M.; Abbate, R.; Gensini, G.F.; Casini, A.; Sofi, F. Vegetarian, vegan diets and multiple health outcomes: A systematic review with meta-analysis of observational studies. *Crit. Rev. Food Sci. Nutr.* **2017**, *57*, 3640–3649. [CrossRef] [PubMed]
8. Shan, Z.; Li, Y.; Baden, M.Y.; Bhupathiraju, S.N.; Wang, D.D.; Sun, Q.; Rexrode, K.M.; Rimm, E.B.; Qi, L.; Willett, W.C.; et al. Association Between Healthy Eating Patterns and Risk of Cardiovascular Disease. *JAMA Intern. Med.* **2020**, *180*, 1090–1100. [CrossRef]
9. Smith, S.C., Jr.; Benjamin, E.J.; Bonow, R.O.; Braun, L.T.; Creager, M.A.; Franklin, B.A.; Gibbons, R.J.; Grundy, S.M.; Hiratzka, L.F.; Jones, D.W.; et al. AHA/ACCF Secondary Prevention and Risk Reduction Therapy for Patients with Coronary and other Atherosclerotic Vascular Disease: 2011 update: A guideline from the American Heart Association and American College of Cardiology Foundation. *Circulation* **2011**, *124*, 2458–2473.
10. Piegas, L.S.; Timerman, A.; Feitosa, G.S.; Nicolau, J.C.; Mattos, L.A.P.; Andrade, M.D.; Avezum, A.; Feldman, A.; De Carvalho, A.C.C.; Sousa, A.C.S.; et al. V Diretriz Da Sociedade Brasileira de Cardiologia sobre Tratamento so Infarto Agudo do Miocárdio com Supradesnível do Segmento St. *Arq. Bras. Cardiol.* **2015**, *105*, 1–105. [CrossRef]
11. Lloyd-Jones, D.M.; Hong, Y.; Labarthe, D.; Mozaffarian, D.; Appel, L.J.; Van Horn, L.; Greenlund, K.; Daniels, S.; Nichol, G.; Tomaselli, G.F.; et al. Defining and setting national goals for cardiovascular health promotion and disease reduction: The American Heart Association's strategic Impact Goal through 2020 and beyond. *Circulation* **2010**, *121*, 586–613. [CrossRef]
12. Virani, S.S.; Alonso, A.; Benjamin, E.J.; Bittencourt, M.S.; Callaway, C.W.; Carson, A.P.; Chamberlain, A.M.; Chang, A.R.; Cheng, S.; Delling, F.N.; et al. Heart Disease and Stroke Statistics-2020 Update: A Report from the American Heart Association. *Circulation* **2020**, *141*, e139–e596. [CrossRef]
13. Mok, Y.; Sang, Y.; Ballew, S.H.; Rebholz, C.M.; Rosamond, W.D.; Heiss, G.; Folsom, A.R.; Coresh, J.; Matsushita, K. American Heart Association's Life's Simple 7 at Middle Age and Prognosis After Myocardial Infarction in Later Life. *J. Am. Heart Assoc.* **2018**, *7*, e007658. [CrossRef]
14. Weber, B.; Galante, A.P.; Bersch-Ferreira, A.C.; Torreglosa, C.R.; Carvalho, V.O.; Victor, E.; Espírito-Santo, J.A.; Ross-Fernandes, M.B.; Soares, R.M.; Costa, R.P.; et al. Effects of Brazilian Cardioprotective Diet Program on risk factors in patients with coronary heart disease: A Brazilian Cardioprotective Diet randomized pilot trial. *Clinics* **2012**, *67*, 1407–1414. [CrossRef]

15. Weber, B.; Bersch-Ferreira, Â.C.; Torreglosa, C.R.; Ross-Fernandes, M.B.; da Silva, J.T.; Galante, A.P.; Lara, E.; Costa, R.P.; Soares, R.M.; Cavalcanti, A.B.; et al. The Brazilian Cardioprotective Nutritional Program to reduce events and risk factors in secondary prevention for cardiovascular disease: Study protocol (The BALANCE Program Trial). *Am. Heart J.* **2016**, *171*, 73–81.e812. [CrossRef]
16. Weber, B.; Bersch-Ferreira, Â.C.; Torreglosa, C.R.; Marcadenti, A.; Lara, E.S.; da Silva, J.T.; Costa, R.P.; Santos, R.; Berwanger, O.; Bosquetti, R.; et al. Implementation of a Brazilian Cardioprotective Nutritional (BALANCE) Program for improvement on quality of diet and secondary prevention of cardiovascular events: A randomized, multicenter trial. *Am. Heart J.* **2019**, *215*, 187–197. [CrossRef]
17. Tereza da Silva, J.; Bersch-Ferreira, Â.C.; Torreglosa, C.R.; Weber, B.; Levy, R.B. Development of a dietary index based on the Brazilian Cardioprotective Nutritional Program (BALANCE). *Nutr. J.* **2018**, *4*, 17–49. [CrossRef]
18. Marcadenti, A.; Weber, B.; Bersch-Ferreira, A.C.; Machado, R.; Torreglosa, C.R.; de Sousa Lara, E.M.; da Silva, L.R.; Santos, R.; Miyada, D.; Sady, E.; et al. Effects of a Brazilian cardioprotective diet and nuts on cardiometabolic parameters after myocardial infarction: Study protocol for a randomized controlled clinical trial. *Trials* **2021**, *22*, 582. [CrossRef]
19. Pérez Rodrigo, C.; Aranceta, J.; Salvador, G.; Varela-Moreiras, G. Food frequency questionnaires. *Nutr. Hosp.* **2015**, *31*, 49–56. [CrossRef]
20. United States Department of Agriculture (USDA). Available online: http://www.usda.gov (accessed on 1 November 2021).
21. Matsudo, S.; Araújo, T.; Matsudo, V.; Andrade, D.; Andrade, E.; Oliveira, L.C.; Braggion, G. International physical activity questionnaire (IPAQ): Study of validity and reability in Brazil. *Rev. Bras. Ativ. Fís. Saúde* **2001**, *6*, 5–18. [CrossRef]
22. Martin, S.S.; Blaha, M.J.; Elshazly, M.B.; Toth, P.P.; Kwiterovich, P.O.; Blumenthal, R.S.; Jones, S.R. Comparison of a novel method vs the Friedewald equation for estimating low-density lipoprotein cholesterol levels from the standard lipid profile. *JAMA* **2013**, *310*, 2061–2068. [CrossRef]
23. Antonio, J.P.; da Rosa, V.C.; Sarmento, R.A.; de Almeida, J.C. Diet quality and therapeutic targets in patients with type 2 diabetes: Evaluation of concordance between dietary indexes. *Nutr. J.* **2017**, *16*, 74. [CrossRef]
24. Olmedo-Requena, R.; González-Donquiles, C.; Dávila-Batista, V.; Romaguera, D.; Castelló, A.; Molina de la Torre, A.J.; Amiano, P.; Dierssen-Sotos, T.; Guevara, M.; Fernández-Tardón, G.; et al. Agreement among Mediterranean Diet Pattern Adherence Indexes: MCC-Spain Study. *Nutrients* **2019**, *11*, 488. [CrossRef]
25. Li, S.; Chiuve, S.E.; Flint, A.; Pai, J.K.; Forman, J.P.; Hu, F.B.; Willett, W.C.; Mukamal, K.J.; Rimm, E.B. Better diet quality and decreased mortality among myocardial infarction survivors. *JAMA Intern. Med.* **2013**, *173*, 1808–1818. [CrossRef]
26. Dehghan, M.; Mente, A.; Teo, K.K.; Gao, P.; Sleight, P.; Dagenais, G.; Avezum, A.; Probstfield, J.L.; Dans, T.; Yusuf, S.; et al. Relationship between healthy diet and risk of cardiovascular disease among patients on drug therapies for secondary prevention: A prospective cohort study of 31 546 high-risk individuals from 40 countries. *Circulation* **2012**, *126*, 2705–2712. [CrossRef]
27. Rehm, C.D.; Peñalvo, J.L.; Afshin, A.; Mozaffarian, D. Dietary Intake among US Adults, 1999–2012. *JAMA* **2016**, *315*, 2542–2553. [CrossRef]
28. Uijl, A.; Koudstaal, S.; Vaartjes, I.; Boer, J.M.A.; Verschuren, W.M.M.; van der Schouw, Y.T.; Asselbergs, F.W.; Hoes, A.W.; Sluijs, I. Risk for Heart Failure: The Opportunity for Prevention with the American Heart Association's Life's Simple 7. *JACC Heart Fail.* **2019**, *7*, 637–647. [CrossRef]
29. Wallström, P.; Mattisson, I.; Tydén, P.; Berglund, G.; Janzon, L. Dietary habits after myocardial infarction-results from a cross-sectional study. *J. Intern. Med.* **2005**, *257*, 329–337. [CrossRef]
30. Ramírez-Vélez, R.; Saavedra, J.M.; Lobelo, F.; Celis-Morales, C.A.; Pozo-Cruz, B.D.; García-Hermoso, A. Ideal Cardiovascular Health and Incident Cardiovascular Disease among Adults: A Systematic Review and Meta-analysis. *Mayo Clin. Proc.* **2018**, *93*, 1589–1599. [CrossRef]
31. Guo, L.; Zhang, S. Association between ideal cardiovascular health metrics and risk of cardiovascular events or mortality: A meta-analysis of prospective studies. *Clin. Cardiol.* **2017**, *40*, 1339–1346. [CrossRef]
32. Folsom, A.R.; Yatsuya, H.; Nettleton, J.A.; Lutsey, P.L.; Cushman, M.; Rosamond, W.D.; ARIC Study Investigators. Community prevalence of ideal cardiovascular health, by the American Heart Association definition, and relationship with cardiovascular disease incidence. *J. Am. Coll. Cardiol.* **2011**, *57*, 1690–1696. [CrossRef]
33. Gaye, B.; Tafflet, M.; Arveiler, D.; Montaye, M.; Wagner, A.; Ruidavets, J.B.; Kee, F.; Evans, A.; Amouyel, P.; Ferrieres, J.; et al. Ideal Cardiovascular Health and Incident Cardiovascular Disease: Heterogeneity Across Event Subtypes and Mediating Effect of Blood Biomarkers: The PRIME Study. *J. Am. Heart Assoc.* **2017**, *6*, e006389. [CrossRef] [PubMed]
34. *Tabela Brasileira de Composição de Alimentos*, 4th ed.; NEPA-UNICAMP: Campinas, Brazil, 2011.

nutrients

MDPI

Article

Innovation as a Factor Increasing Fruit Consumption: The Case of Poland

Dagmara Stangierska [1], Iwona Kowalczuk [2,*], Katarzyna Widera [3], Dawid Olewnicki [1] and Piotr Latocha [4]

1 Department of Pomology and Horticulture Economics, Institute of Horticulture Sciences, Warsaw University of Life Sciences—SGGW, Nowoursynowska 166, 02-787 Warszawa, Poland; dagmara_stangierska@sggw.edu (D.S.); dawid_olewnicki@sggw.edu.pl (D.O.)
2 Department of Food Market and Consumer Research, Institute of Human Nutrition Sciences, Warsaw University of Life Sciences—SGGW, Nowoursynowska 159C, 02-776 Warsaw, Poland
3 Department of Economics, Finance, Regional and International Research, Faculty of Economics and Management, Opole University of Technology, Prószkowska 76, 45-758 Opole, Poland; k.widera@po.edu.pl
4 Department of Environmental Protection and Dendrology, Institute of Horticulture Sciences, Warsaw University of Life Sciences—SGGW, Nowoursynowska 166, 02-787 Warsaw, Poland; piotr_latocha@sggw.edu.pl
* Correspondence: iwona_kowalczuk@sggw.edu.pl

Abstract: Due to the low level of fruit consumption in relation to dietary recommendations in many European countries, including Poland, multidirectional actions should be taken to increase the consumption of these products. One of the ideas could be the introduction of innovative products. The main goal of the study is to determine the relationship between consumer propensity to purchase innovative products and the frequency of consumption of fruits and their preserves of consumers. The research sample consisted of 600 respondents who declared to consume fruit and were responsible for food shopping in their households. The results obtained indicate that consumers with a higher propensity to purchase innovative products consumed fruit and fruit preserves more. In addition, statistically significant differences were found between innovators and non-innovators in terms of income, expenditures on fruit purchases, places where fruit and fruit preserves were purchased and product characteristics that determined the purchase decision. The logistic regression results indicate that a higher frequency of supermarket/hypermarket and online shopping, a higher weekly spending on fruit and a greater importance attributed to the biodegradability of the packaging increased the favorability of innovation relatively to fruit products (by 23.8%, 31.4%, 32.7% and 21.6%, respectively). The relationships found may have important implications for both private and public stakeholders in the fruit and vegetable sector.

Keywords: innovation; consumer behavior; fruit market

Citation: Stangierska, D.; Kowalczuk, I.; Widera, K.; Olewnicki, D.; Latocha, P. Innovation as a Factor Increasing Fruit Consumption: The Case of Poland. *Nutrients* **2022**, *14*, 1246. https://doi.org/10.3390/nu14061246

Academic Editors: Clare Collins and George Moschonis

Received: 9 February 2022
Accepted: 7 March 2022
Published: 16 March 2022

1. Introduction

There is a close correlation between the innovative activity of enterprises and consumers; innovative enterprises (firms that implement innovations), by introducing new or improved products into the market, pique consumers' interest with their offer, whereas innovative consumers (consumers willing to purchase innovative products), by exerting pressure on companies, motivate them to create innovative solutions [1,2]. The results of studies conducted in recent years on consumer innovation in the food market suggest that product innovation (new or an improved version of previous goods) in a particular market sector can stimulate consumer buying behavior for all products in that sector [3]. This raises the question of whether consumers can be encouraged to increase their consumption of health-beneficial products through innovation, thereby motivating them to behave in line with dietary recommendations. This paper attempts to clarify this issue by analyzing the example of fruit and fruit preserves.

Producers of fruit and fruit preserves offer many diverse, innovative solutions. They fit into the innovation categories selected by XTC World Innovation, such as pleasure, health, physical, convenience and ethics, which reflect consumer expectations regarding the directions for developing the market offer [3].

New varieties of fruit are introduced to the market, with unusual form, flavor and higher nutritional value than traditional fruit [4,5]. The market offer is diversified by visually appealing fruit mixes [5], as well as tasty and convenient fruit snacks [6]. Consumers looking for healthy solutions are offered fruit and preserves sourced with ecological cultivation [7], as well as fruit preserves enriched with additional nutrients [8]. Innovation also applies to packaging, such as the so-called active packaging, which keeps the fruit fresh, nutritious and appealing for longer, while making it more convenient to store and consume the product [9]. An important motivation for producers to constantly search for innovations in the agriculture–food market is the high market failure rate of new products, which is mainly due to the consumers' lack of acceptance of such products [10].

According to researchers studying the issue of innovation in the consumer goods market, both today and in recent decades, the key to the effective commercialization of an innovative offer is recognizing the consumers' needs and their reaction to new products, as well as characterizing the recipients of the new products [11]. Over the years, many concepts of the innovation process have been proposed [12,13]. One of the most prominent theories explaining this matter is Rogers' model [14]. Rogers identifies five recipient groups based on their openness to innovation, namely, innovators, early adopters, early majority, late majority and laggards, with the corresponding shares in the overall population of 1.5%, 13.5%, 34%, 34% and 16%. In order to learn about consumer behaviors towards market innovations, researchers typically conduct a purchase-intention study and analyze opinions on new products [15], while, when characterizing consumer innovation, socio-demographic and psychographic features are analyzed [16]. As for the socio-demographic features, it has been proven that the innovation level is affected by age (younger consumers are more innovative) [17,18], level of education [19,20], income [19,21] and country of origin [22]. The innovation level is also conditioned by features such as openness to new experiences, curiosity and susceptibility to external influence [16,23], including media [24,25] and influencers [26]. Research on consumer innovation in the fruit market has shown that young and middle-aged consumers with higher education and income are more open to new products. It has also been shown that innovations following the trends of health and ethics (environment-friendly innovations) receive the most attention from recipients [27].

Actions to promote a healthy lifestyle and prevent diseases in most European countries focus on initiatives oriented at increasing the consumption of fruits and vegetables among various consumer groups [28]. A diet rich in fruit and vegetables is widely recommended due to the health benefits of these products [29]. Numerous research studies have proven that consuming fruit and fruit preserves is beneficial to the prevention of some chronic diseases [30], including type 2 diabetes [31], obesity [32], cardiovascular diseases [33], hypertension [34], various types of cancer [35,36] asthma [37], depression [38] and cognitive disorders [39]. In addition to having a positive effect on the health of individuals and the general population, switching to a plant-based diet can also have a significant impact on the environment by reducing the carbon footprint [40]. According to experts, eating at least 400 g of fruits and vegetables per day can have the most beneficial effects for personal well-being and the planet [41,42]. However, despite many initiatives to promote healthy lifestyles, the populations of less than half of the WHO member states consume fruits and vegetables according to the WHO recommendations [43,44]; Poland also belongs to this group.

According to Statistics Poland, in 2020, the consumption was merely 46.3 kg/year [45], which amounts to 127 g per day (293 g, including vegetables). This is only 73% of the daily consumption recommended by the WHO [46]. According to the Eurostat data from 2019, only 62.5% of Poles eat fruit at least once per day (EU average—67%) and women consume fruit more often than men do (72.9% and 56.4%, respectively) [47].

Considering the too-low fruit consumption (in relation to dietary recommendations) both in Poland and other countries and the potential relationship, not yet confirmed by existing studies, between consumer tendencies for innovative behaviors relative to the fruit market and their consumption of these products, this research study was undertaken to determine the following:

- Consumer structures based on affinity for innovation in the fruit and fruit preserve market;
- Characteristics of consumers with varying tendencies for innovative behaviors;
- Correlation between the consumer tendency to buy innovative fruit and fruit preserve products and the level of consumption of these products and expenses incurred to purchase them;
- Features of an innovative offer and means to distribute it that would stimulate consumer interest in the innovative offer.

2. Materials and Methods

2.1. Study Design and Participants

The paper is based on the results of a questionnaire research study conducted with the CAWI method by a professional research company, BioStat; this methodological choice guaranteed the ethical standards necessary for the execution of the study. The ethical aspects followed throughout the study ensured the continued safety of participants, as well as the integrity of the accumulated data. A brief description of the study and its aim, and the declaration of anonymity and confidentiality were given to the participants before the start of the questionnaire. Respondents did not provide their names nor contact information (including the IP address) and could finish the survey at any stage. The answers were saved only when participants clicked the "submit" button after filling in the questionnaire.

The online survey was conducted in full observance of the national and international regulations compliant with the Declaration of Helsinki (2000). The personal information and data of the participants were anonymous, according to the General Data Protection Regulation of the European Parliament (GDPR 679/2016). The survey did not require approval by the ethics committee because of the anonymous nature of the online survey and impossibility of tracking sensitive personal data.

Study participants were recruited among the people registered with the respondent panel of the BioStat research company. Respondents were non-randomly selected for the study—they were adults who declared to eat fruit at least once per month and were responsible or co-responsible for buying fruits and fruit preserves in their household. Ultimately, the criteria assumed for selection were met by 600 people.

2.2. Questionnaire

The research study was conducted with the use of an original questionnaire. In order to specify questions and clarify any ambiguities, prior to the study proper, a pilot study was carried out; the questionnaire was distributed to a group of 30 people, together with a form allowing respondents to assess the questionnaire layout, comprehension of the questions asked and relevance of the questions for the goal of the study. The questionnaire was constructed using E. Rogers' scale [14] and the scales developed for nutrition research validated and approved by the Scientific Research Committee of the Polish Academy of Sciences (KomPAN®)Warsaw, Poland [48].

According to the assumed goal of the study and the formulated research problems, the survey questionnaire included questions regarding the following:

- Reactions of the respondents to innovative products in the fruit market (answers on a scale of 1–5, where 1—"I buy new products immediately after they show up on the market"; 2—"I buy new products relatively quickly, though after some consideration"; 3—"I buy new products when some of my acquaintances have tried them and given

positive opinions"; 4—"I buy new products when most of my acquaintances have tried them and given positive opinions"; and 5—"I am reluctant to buy new products");
- Frequency of eating fruits and preserves (answers on a scale of 1–7: 1—never; 2—less often than once a month; 3—1–3 times per month; 4—once a week; 5—several times a week; 6—once a day; and 7—several times a day);
- Places for buying fruits and fruit preserves (answers on a scale of 1–6: 1—never; 2—less than once per month; 3—1–3 times per month; 4—once a week; 5—several times a week; and 6—once a day);
- Weekly expenses on fruits and fruit preserves (single choice question with 5 ranges of expenses incurred);
- Factors conditioning purchase decisions in the fruit market (position scale 1–7: 1—definitely irrelevant factor; 7—definitely relevant factor);
- Respondents' characteristics (accounting for gender, age, place of residence, education and income).

2.3. Characteristic of Respondents

In terms of gender, the sample consisted of 52% women and 48% men. The age structure of the studied group was: 18–19 years old—18.3%; 30–44 years old—29.5%; 45–59 years old—23.3%; 55 and older—28.3%. Nearly 40% of the respondents lived in rural areas, 32% in towns of under 100,000 people, 16.8% in towns with 100–500 thousand residents and 11.3% in cities with a population larger than 500,000 people. In terms of education, the largest group was people with secondary education (34.7%); a total of 29.2% of the respondents had completed vocational education, 28.3% had completed higher education and only 7.8% had completed primary education. Among the respondents, most lived in households of 3–4 people (55.3%). The analysis of the economic situation of the respondents showed that nearly half (48.8%) of them had a monthly income of PLN 1500–3000 per person, while 20% made less than PLN 1500; a total of 14.8% of the respondents had an income in the range of PLN 3001–4500 and 10.8% earned more than PLN 4500 per person per month (Table 1).

Table 1. Sample characteristics (%).

Gender				
Female			Male	
52.00			48.00	
Age				
18–29	30–44	45–59	Over 55	
18.33	29.50	23.33	28.33	
Place of Residence				
Rural areas	Towns, up to 100,000 residents	Towns, 100,000–500,000 residents	Cities, over 500,000 residents	
39.83	32.00	16.84	11.33	
Education				
Primary	Vocational	Secondary	Higher	
7.83	29.17	34.67	28.33	
Number of People in the Household				
1–2	3–4	5 and more		
29.83	55.33	14.84		
Per Capita Income PLN (EUR) *				
Under 1500 (332.6)	1500–3000 (332.7–665.2)	3001–4500 (665.3–997.8)	4501–6000 (997.9–1330.4)	Over 6000 (1330.5)
20.17	48.83	14.83	6.17	4.67

* As of 19 January 2022 [49].

2.4. Statistical Analyses

Based on the questions in the survey, the variables to be subjected to a later analysis were identified. The rank scale (qualitative) of most of the variables accepted for the study determined the choice of adequate statistical tests. The only quantitative variable did not show a normal distribution. Thus, non-parametric Pearson χ^2 and Mann–Whitney U tests were used in the analysis. The statistical significance of differences between selected groups of respondents was tested with the Mann–Whitney U test, whereas the statistical dependence between variables was assessed with the χ^2 test. Descriptive statistics included calculations of relative frequencies (the number of categories of variables expressed as a percentage) and mean, median, minimum and maximum values of the examined variables. The assumed minimum level of significance for all statistical tests was 0.05.

All factors differentiating at the established level of significance between the behaviors of innovators and non-innovators were included as potential independent variables in the logistic regression model. Finally, the model presented below only includes those independent variables whose structural parameters met the condition of statistical significance.

The interpretation of the results (odds ratio) of the logistic regression analysis consisted of determining by what percentage the likelihood of changing consumer behavior shifted with the changes in the value of a specific independent variable.

All calculations were made using the Statistica 14.1 statistical packageunder statsoft license available for university employees.

3. Results

3.1. Respondents' Innovation in the Fruit and Preserve Market

In the studied population, 13.0% of the respondents declared to buy new fruits and preserves immediately after they showed up on the market (innovators); a total of 44.8% responded that they purchased new products relatively quickly, though after some consideration (early adopters); a total of 23.0% of the respondents said they bought novelties after some of their acquaintances had tried them and given positive opinions (early majority); a total of 9.8% of the questioned people purchased new products after most of their acquaintances had tried them and given positive opinions (late majority); and 9.0% declared reluctance to buy new products (laggards). Upon projecting the acquired data onto Rogers' model of distribution [14], the studied population was found to consist mostly of innovators and early adopters, with a significantly lower percentage of those consumer groups who were less enthusiastic or downright skeptical towards innovative products (Figure 1).

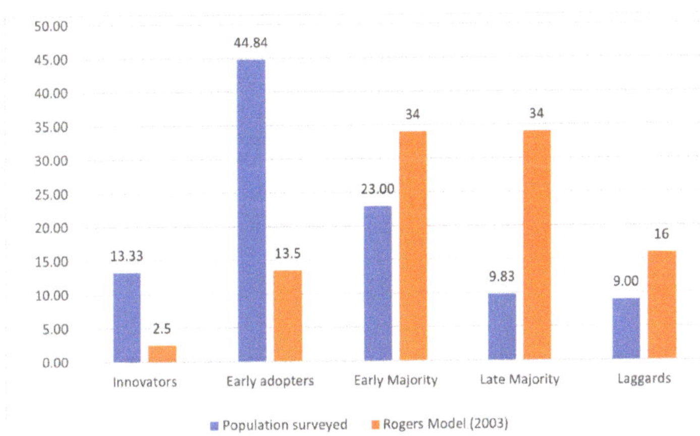

Figure 1. Comparison of the studied population's distribution with Rogers' model, accounting for innovation level (%).

Considering the acquired results, for the purpose of further analyses, the studied population was divided into two groups based on innovation level, the group of innovators, including innovators and early adopters (n = 349, 58.2%); and the group of non-innovators, consisting of early majority, late majority and laggards (n = 251, 41.8%).

3.2. Comparative Characteristics of Innovators and Non-Innovators Accounting for Demographic, Social and Economic Features

The conducted analyses showed no statistically significant correlations between consumer groups with different affinities for innovative behaviors and their gender, age, place of residence, number of people in the household or education level.

In the case of income, a larger percentage of innovators than non-innovators declared earnings in the ranges of PLN 1501–3000 and PLN 3000–4500, whereas nearly twice as many non-innovators compared with innovators declared earning less than PLN 1500. The value of the χ^2 = 14.2845 test statistics and the value of p = 0.0064 assigned to it indicated a statistically significant correlation in terms of the income levels of innovators and non-innovators. Higher income meant a higher percentage of people with affinity for innovation (Table 2).

Table 2. Characteristics of innovators and non-innovators accounting for demographic, social and economic features.

Variable	Innovators (349)	Non-Innovators (251)	Statistic	*p*-Value
	Age (years)			
Average (median)	46 (45.8)	47 (46.10)	Z = −0.2671 *	0.7893
	Gender (%)			
Female	50.14	54.58	χ^2 = 1.1523	0.2831
Male	46.86	45.42		
	Place of Residence (%)			
Rural areas	40.97	38.24	χ^2 = 0.8133	0.8463
Towns, up to 100,000 residents	30.95	33.47		
Towns, 100,000–500,000 residents	16.33	17.53		
Cities, over 500,000 residents	11.75	10.76		
	Education (%)			
Primary	6.30	9.96	χ^2 = 7.1373	0.0677
Vocational	32.66	24.30		
Secondary	34.67	34.66		
Higher	26.36	31.08		
	Number of People in the Household (%)			
1–2	29.23	30.68	χ^2 = 1.4869	0.4755
3–4	54.44	56.57		
5 and more	16.33	12.75		
	Monthly Per Capita Income (%)			
Under PLN 1500 (332.6 EUR)	16.92	28.89	χ^2 = 14.2845	0.0064
1501–3000 (332.7–665.2 EUR)	51.96	48.44		
3001–4500 (665.3–997.8 EUR)	18.13	12.89		
4500–6000 (997.9–1330.4 EUR)	8.16	4.44		
Over PLN 6000 (1330.5 EUR)	4.83	5.33		

* Z-statistics and the corresponding *p*-values refer to the comparison of the medians with a non-parametric Mann–Whitney U test.

3.3. Frequency of Consuming Fruit and Fruit Preserves of Innovators and Non-Innovators

Both the innovators and those respondents who were less willing to purchase innovative products most often consumed fruit juices (means of 4.87 and 4.48, respectively) and fresh fruit (4.66 and 4.34). Much less popular among both groups were products such as dried fruit (3.21 and 2.90), fruit and vegetable juices (3.12 and 2.80) and canned fruit (3.04 and 2.59), while the least frequently consumed products, among both innovators and non-innovators, were frozen fruit (2.67 and 2.44), fruit mousses (2.96 and 2.39), fruit/fruit and vegetable salads (2.90 and 2.37), fruit chips (2.54 and 2.02) and freeze-dried fruit (2.12 and 1.69). For all the product categories analyzed, the innovators exhibited a higher level of consumption (Figure 2; detailed data are provided in Appendix A, Table A1).

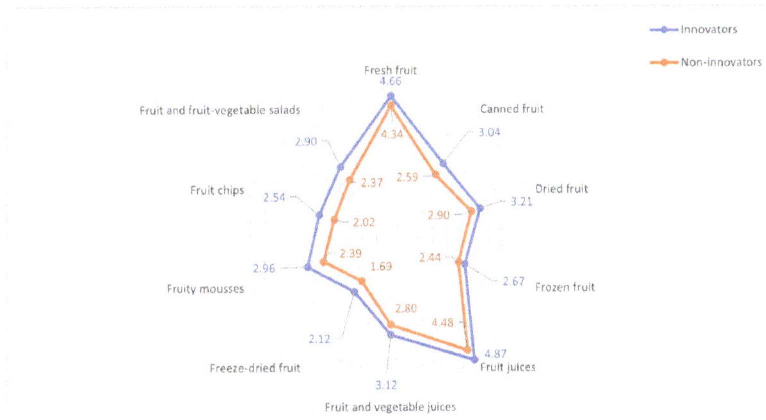

Figure 2. Frequency (On a scale of 1–7: 1—never; 2—less often than once a month; 3—1–3 times a month; 4—once a week; 5—several times a week; 6—once a day; 7—several times a day)of consuming fruits and fruit preserves of innovators and non-innovators.

Regarding fresh fruit and traditional fruit preserves (juices, dried fruit, frozen fruit), differences in the frequency of consumption of these products were statistically significant at $p < 0.05$, whereas in regard to modern fruit preserves (fruit mousses, salads, fruit chips and freeze-dried fruit), they were significant at $p < 0.001$ (Table 3).

Table 3. Variation in frequency of consuming fruits and fruit preserves for innovators and non-innovators.

	Variable	Z-Statistic *	*p*-Value *
	Fresh fruit	3.1742	0.0015
Traditional fruit preserves	Dried fruit	2.9140	0.0036
	Frozen fruit	2.6022	0.0093
	Fruit juices	3.2152	0.0013
	Fruit and vegetable juices	2.6848	0.0073
Modern fruit preserves	Freeze-dried fruit	4.6026	0.0000
	Canned fruit	4.3668	0.0000
	Fruit mousses	5.4274	0.0000
	Fruit chips	5.0225	0.0000
	Fruit and fruit-vegetable salads	4.7406	0.0000

* Z-statistics and the corresponding *p*-values refer to the comparison of the medians with a non-parametric Mann–Whitney U test.

3.4. Expenses for Purchasing Fruit Incurred by Innovators and Non-Innovators

The majority of innovators (57.6%) declared spending more than PLN 41 (EUR 8.9) per week on fruit, whereas 62.9% of non-innovators spent less than that (Figure 3). The value of the Mann–Whitney U test (5.1779; $p = 0.0000$) indicated a statistically significant difference in expenses on fruit incurred by innovators and non-innovators.

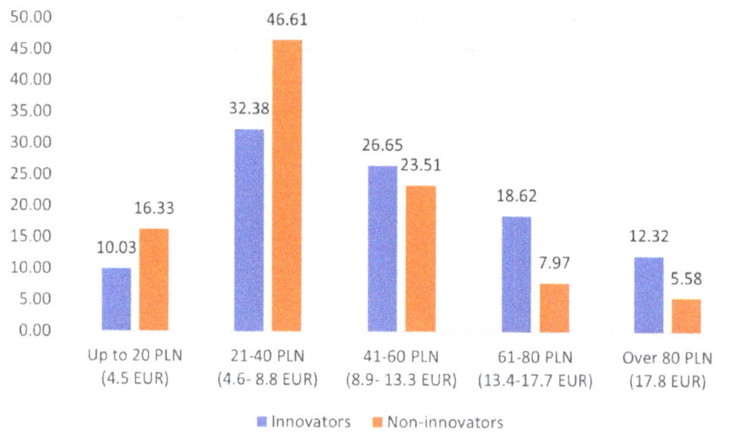

Figure 3. Weekly expenses on fruits and fruit preserves by innovators and non-innovators.

3.5. Places for Innovators and Non-Innovators to Purchase Fruits and Fruit Preserves

Both innovators and non-innovators most frequently bought their fruit at discount stores (means of 3.98 and 3.96, respectively) and supermarkets/hypermarkets (3.45 and 3.06). Less popular places for purchasing included convenience stores (3.21 and 3.01), marketplaces (2.96 and 2.76) and local grocery stores, while the least frequently used sources of fruits were street stalls (2.01 and 1.7) and online shopping (1.58 and 1.29) (Figure 4; detailed data are provided in Appendix A, Table A2).

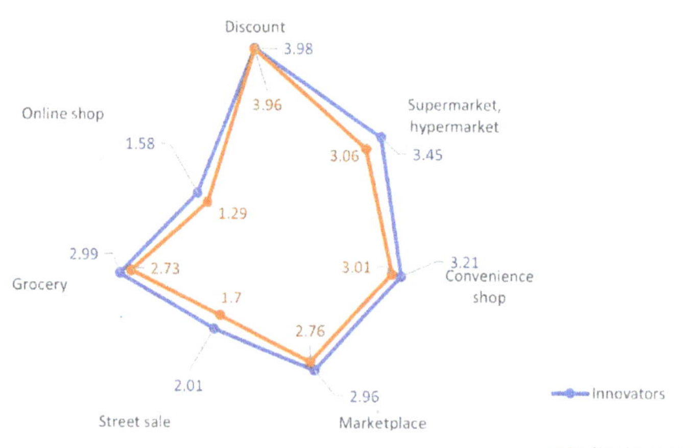

Figure 4. Frequency (On a scale of 1–6: 1—never; 2—less than once a month; 3—1–3 times per month; 4—once a week; 5—several times a week; 6—once a day) of purchasing fruit and fruit preserves at selected places of purchase of innovators and non-innovators.

Statistically significant differences between innovators and non-innovators in the frequency of purchasing from the analyzed sources were found in the case of supermarkets/hypermarkets and online shops ($p < 0.001$), while for the local grocery stores, street stalls and marketplaces, the level of statistical significance of the differences was less than 0.05. No differences were found among the consumer groups in the frequency of buying at discount stores and convenience stores (Table 4).

Table 4. Variations in the frequency of buying fruits and fruit preserves from selected sources for innovators and non-innovators.

Variable	Z-Statistic *	*p*-Value *
Discount	0.0843	0.9328
Supermarket, hypermarket	4.1529	0.0000
Convenience store	1.7903	0.0734
Marketplaces	2.0570	0.0397
Street stall	2.8337	0.0046
Grocery store	2.7099	0.0067
Online shop	3.7700	0.0000

* Z-statistics and the corresponding *p*-values refer to the comparison of the medians with a non-parametric Mann–Whitney U test.

3.6. Relevance of Selected Features of Fruits and Fruit Preserves for Innovators and Non-Innovators

Consumers with both high and low innovation levels considered the following features to be the most relevant in their choice of fruit and fruit preserves: freshness (means of 6.40 and 6.61, respectively), taste preferences (5.95 and 6.12) and appearance (5.93 and 6.17). Less important factors included the following: habits (5.20 and 5.45), price (4.90 and 5.24), information on the packaging (4.83 and 4.51), packaging size (4.61 and 4.56), country of origin (4.35 and 4.03) and biodegradability of the packaging (4.09 and 3.50) (Figure 5; detailed data are provided in Appendix A, Table A3).

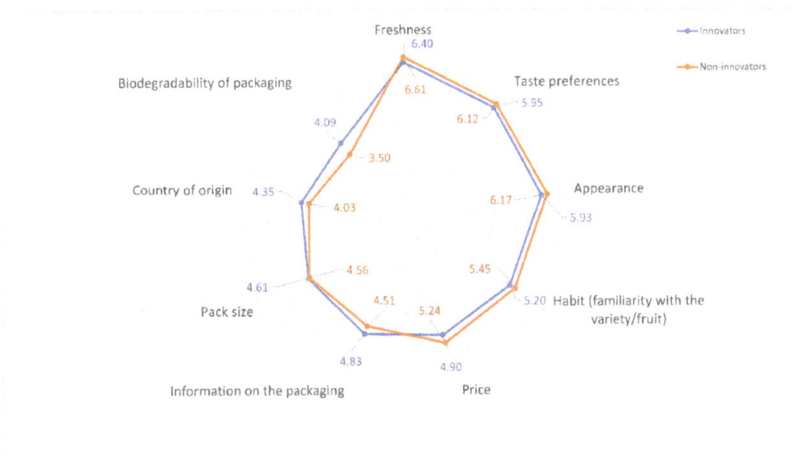

Figure 5. Significance (On a scale of 1–7: 1—definitely irrelevant factor; 7—definitely relevant factor) of selected features of fruits and fruit preserves for innovators and non-innovators.

The innovators, with statistical significance, found features of fruits and fruit preserves such as biodegradability of the packaging ($p < 0.001$), information on the packaging

($p < 0.05$) and country of origin of the products ($p < 0.05$) to be the most relevant, whereas for non-innovators, the importance of price ($p < 0.05$) and habits of consuming specific types of fruit ($p < 0.05$) was higher (Table 5).

Table 5. Variations in significance of selected features of fruit and fruit preserves for innovators and non-innovators.

Variable	Z-Statistic *	*p*-Value *
Price	−2.6263	0.0086
Appearance	−1.8090	0.0705
Freshness	−1.4786	0.1393
Taste preferences	−0.6476	0.5172
Country of origin	2.0305	0.0423
Packaging size	0.0781	0.9378
Information on the packaging	2.3897	0.0169
Biodegradability of the packaging	4.0720	0.0000
Habits (familiarity with the variety/fruit)	−2.1706	0.0300

* Z-statistics and the corresponding *p*-values refer to the comparison of the medians with a non-parametric Mann–Whitney U test.

3.7. Using Logistic Regression to Analyze the Factors Determining Consumer Innovation

Among the factors stimulating consumer affinity for innovation in the fruit and fruit preserve market accounted for in the regression analysis, statistically significant differences ($p < 0.05$) were found in the case of six of the analyzed independent variables, such as frequency of making purchases in supermarkets/hypermarkets (1) and via the Internet (2); level of weekly expenses on fruit (3); importance of the price (4); biodegradability of the packaging (5); and habits (6) of buying fruits and fruit preserves.

The results of the regression show that a higher frequency of buying at supermarkets/hypermarkets and online increased the chance for a consumer to have an affinity for innovative solutions in the fruit and fruit preserve market by 23.8% and 31.4%, respectively. Higher weekly expenses on fruit resulted in innovation being increased by 32.7% and greater importance of biodegradability of the packaging increased affinity for innovation by 21.6%. On the other hand, a greater importance of price in purchasing fruit and preserves resulted in the chance for innovation to be decreased by 11.8%, whereas a greater significance of habits reduced affinity for innovation by 19.7% (Table 6).

Table 6. Values of logistic regression model coefficients.

Variable	Coefficient	Odds Ratio	Standard Error	*t*-Stat. (593)	*p*-Value
Frequency of buying at super-/hypermarkets	0.213	1.238	0.081	2.639	0.009
Frequency of buying online	0.273	1.314	0.119	2.294	0.022
Expenses on fruit	0.283	1.327	0.084	3.366	0.001
Importance of price in buying fruit	−0.126	0.882	0.060	−2.094	0.037
Importance of biodegradability of the packaging in buying fruit	0.196	1.216	0.053	3.698	0.000
Importance of habits in buying fruit	−0.220	0.803	0.072	−3.041	0.002
Constant	−0.42				

4. Discussion

The problem of low fruit and vegetable consumption in comparison with dietary recommendations concerns more than a half of the WHO countries, mainly Eastern Europe [43]. Considering the nutritional value of these products, their protective effects against various chronic diseases and the fact that a diet rich in vegetables and fruit has a beneficial effect on the environment, many countries are undertaking intervention activities, mainly of educational [43] and marketing nature, but also within the scope of the so-called nudge interventions [50]. Such activities are also undertaken in Poland. However, they do not solve the problem, so other methods for stimulating consumer interest in the consumption of these products should be searched for. In the undertaken research study, it was decided to check whether innovation, in its broadest sense, could constitute such a method.

One of the assumed objectives of the study was to determine the consumer structure based on affinity for innovation in the fruit and preserve market. The obtained results indicate that the distribution of the studied population differed from the Rogers' model distribution in this matter; a much larger percentage of innovators (13.33% and 2.50%, respectively) and early adopters (44.84% and 13.50%) were found, as well as significantly fewer consumers exhibiting the behaviors of early majority (23% and 34%, respectively), late majority (9.83% and 34%) and laggards (9% and 16%). Previous research on this issue also proves a greater consumer affinity for innovative behaviors in the food market [51]; moreover, Gonera et al. [52] have found a higher degree of innovation among consumers with high acceptance of plant-based products. Winger and Wall [53] explain the greater consumer affinity for innovation in the food market with lower risk being related to purchasing innovative products. The risk level related to purchasing decisions regarding new products depends, among other factors, on the extent to which they differ from what is familiar to the consumer [54]; since the majority of food innovations are incremental changes (continuous innovations), the innovative offer does not differ dramatically from traditional products, which lowers the risk and increases the consumer willingness to purchase.

By analyzing the socio-demographic profile of innovators and non-innovators, as opposed to other research studies [17–20], no differences between the two groups were found in regard to age, sex, education, place of residence or number of people in the household. However, a statistically significant influence of income on the respondents' innovation level was discovered, confirmed by other research studies, both on Polish consumers [51] and other nationalities [19].

The crucial issue in the conducted study was to determine the differences in the frequency of consuming fruit and preserves between innovators and non-innovators. The obtained results show that all the analyzed product categories were consumed by innovators more frequently, with statistical significance. The most obvious explanation of the fact that innovators consumed fruit and preserves more often is the higher income declared by the members of this group, as well as the correlation between income level and volume of fruit and preserve consumption, which has been proven in earlier research [55,56]. However, in explaining this correlation, it can be assumed with high probability that affinity for innovative behaviors goes hand in hand with seeking information on new products, consequently obtaining knowledge about properties of fruits and preserves, their nutritional value and health benefits (this thesis has been proven in a study on ecological food) [57]. As a result, an innovative consumer becomes convinced that consuming fruit and preserves is useful, which, according to the theory of planned behavior [58], is one of the factors determining their buying intentions and decisions to purchase. The more frequent consumption of fruit and preserves, as well as the higher income declared by the innovators, resulted in them spending more on fruit.

An analysis of the variation in innovators' and non-innovators' preferred places for purchasing fruit and preserves only showed statistically significant differences in the case of supermarkets/hypermarkets and online shopping; innovators declared using both of these forms of distribution more often. In relation to both of these places of purchase, the identified difference can be explained by a relatively larger offer of innovative fruit and preserves than in other stores; in the case of supermarkets/hypermarkets this would be the result of a broad selection of products on offer [59], whereas in the case of online stores, of a highly specialized offer [60,61]. Moreover, in the big-box stores, the presence of other customers enhances the bandwagon effect and reduces social risk [62], which might cause the innovative offer to garner more attention. Online stores, on the other hand, allow one to obtain information about the purchased products, which is important for innovative consumers [63,64] and, at the same time, caters to their openness to new experiences and their aspiration to take advantage of innovative solutions in different areas of activity [16].

Both the consumers with high and low levels of innovation found the following factors the most important in selecting fruits and preserves: freshness, preference for taste and appearance. The importance of these factors in selecting food products has also been found in other studies [65–71]. Previous studies on the consumer-preferred characteristics of fruits and processed fruits have also found the importance of other characteristics of these products, such as health benefits, attractiveness and uniqueness (for tropical fruits), [72], health benefits and convenience (for dried fruits) [73], composition and origin (for canned fruits) [74] or naturalness (for fruit juices) [75]. Differences between innovators and non-innovators in evaluating the importance of determinants for selecting fruits and preserves were found in the case of factors such as biodegradability of the packaging, information included on the packaging and country of origin, which were more important to the innovators; price and habits were more important to non-innovators. More innovative consumers have also been found to value environment-friendly and healthy solutions in the study by Samoggi and Nicolodi [27]. This correlation can be justified by a (psychologically conditioned) greater openness of this consumer group to innovative solutions [16], as well as greater awareness of the benefits coming with those. Moreover, current research suggests that, in the case of fresh fruit, biodegradability of the packaging enhances the innovative image of a product and positively affects its selection [76,77]. As for innovators paying attention to the information on the packaging and the product's country of origin, these can be linked to a greater affinity for seeking knowledge about purchased goods, which is characteristic of this consumer group [78]. When it comes to those features of fruits and preserves that are more important to non-innovators, the greater significance of price should be attributed to those with lower incomes in this consumer group and the resulting limitations regarding the selection of purchased products [79], whereas sticking to buying habits is considered to be a typical feature of consumers reluctant to adopt innovative behaviors [16,80].

5. Strengths, Limitations and Future Research

The obtained results can be important both for the enterprises of the fruit–vegetable sector and for the institutions and organizations dealing with nutrition. Studying consumer behaviors and expectations in regard to innovative products can be helpful to create marketing strategies for such products and positively affect their adaptation and diffusion, eventually contributing to a greater consumption of fruit and fruit preserves.

The weakness of this study could be the relatively small sample group, though the criteria for its selection (consuming fruit and preserves at least once per month and being responsible for buying these products for the household) could be seen as an explanation of the final number of participants of the study. The research study was indubitably limited by the fact that the sample consisted exclusively of Polish consumers, which calls for confirming the observed correlations with studies in other countries. It would also be advisable to make future research more detailed by analyzing more factors that potentially differentiate consumer behaviors, or by focusing the analysis on specific types of products. It should also be noted that market behaviors of consumers eating fruit less often than once per month also need to be studied; this was omitted in this research study.

6. Conclusions

The results of the study show that consumers with greater affinity for purchasing innovative products ate fruit and fruit preserves more often. Differences were found between innovators and non-innovators in terms of income, expenses incurred for buying fruits and places for purchasing fruit and fruit preserves, as well as product features determining the decision to buy.

The regression analysis showed that selling innovative products through modern channels of distribution, using biodegradable packaging and rationalizing the prices of the innovative offer showed to be the most promising factors in terms of affecting the increase in consumer affinity for innovative behaviors.

Author Contributions: Conceptualization, D.S. and I.K.; methodology, D.S., P.L. and D.O.; software, D.S. and K.W.; formal analysis, D.S. and K.W.; investigation, D.S., I.K., P.L. and D.O.; resources, D.S., I.K., P.L. and D.O.; data curation, D.S. and K.W.; writing—original draft preparation, I.K. and D.S. writing—review and editing, I.K., D.S., P.L. and K.W.; visualization, D.S. and K.W.; supervision, P.L.; project administration, P.L.; funding acquisition, P.L. All authors have read and agreed to the published version of the manuscript.

Funding: This research study was funded by "Innovation Incubator+", project no. 513-01-040900-P00064-04, implemented under the Intelligent Development Operational Program 2014-2020 (Faculty of Horticulture, Biotechnology and Landscape Architecture; contractor—P.L.).

Institutional Review Board Statement: Ethical review and approval were waived for this study due to the full anonymity and voluntariness of participation in the survey, as well as the fact that the survey was conducted by a certified company that adheres to ethical standards.

Informed Consent Statement: Informed consent was obtained from all subjects involved in the study.

Data Availability Statement: The authors confirm that the datasets analyzed during the study are available from the corresponding author upon reasonable request.

Conflicts of Interest: The authors declare no conflict of interest.

Appendix A

Table A1. Frequency * of consuming fruits and fruit preserves of innovators and non-innovators.

	Variable	Innovators	Non-Innovators
	Fresh fruit	4.66	4.34
Traditional fruit preserves	Dried fruit	3.21	2.90
	Frozen fruit	2.67	2.43
	Fruit juices	4.87	4.48
	Fruit and vegetable juices	3.12	2.80
Modern fruit preserves	Freeze-dried fruit	2.12	1.69
	Canned fruit	3.04	2.59
	Fruit mousses	2.96	2.39
	Fruit chips	2.54	2.02
	Fruit and fruit-vegetable salads	2.90	2.37

* On a scale of 1–7: 1—never; 2—less often than once a month; 3—1–3 times a month; 4—once a week; 5—several times a week; 6—once a day; 7—several times a day.

Table A2. Frequency * of purchasing fruit and fruit preserves at selected places of purchase of innovators and non-innovators.

Variable	Innovators	Non-Innovators
Discount	3.98	3.96
Supermarket, hypermarket	3.45	3.06
Convenience store	3.21	3.01
Marketplaces	2.96	2.76
Street stall	2.01	1.70
Grocery store	2.99	2.73
Online shop	1.58	1.26

* On a scale of 1-6: 1—never; 2—less than once a month; 3—1–3 times per month; 4—once a week; 5—several times a week; 6—once a day.

Table A3. Significance * of selected features of fruits and fruit preserves for innovators and non-innovators.

Variable	Innovators	Non-Innovators
Price	4.89	5.23
Appearance	5.35	5.27
Freshness	5.93	6.17
Taste preferences	6.39	6.61
Country of origin	5.95	6.12
Packaging size	4.52	4.29
Information on the packaging	4.35	4.03
Biodegradability of the packaging	4.61	4.56
Habits (familiarity with the variety/fruit)	4.83	4.51

* On a scale of 1–7: 1—definitely irrelevant factor; 7—definitely relevant factor.

References

1. Biraghi, S.; Gambetti, R.; Pace, S. Between tribes and markets: The emergence of a liquid consumer-entrepreneurship. *J. Bus. Res.* **2018**, *92*, 392–402. [CrossRef]
2. Martin, D.M.; Schouten, J.W. Consumption-Driven Market Emergence. *J. Consum. Res.* **2014**, *40*, 855–870. [CrossRef]
3. Figiel, S.; Kufel-Gajda, J. Trends in Food Product Innovations and the Level of Economic Development. *Econ. Environ. Stud.* **2017**, *17*, 429–446. [CrossRef]
4. Latocha, P. The Nutritional and Health Benefits of Kiwiberry (Actinidia arguta)—A Review. *Plant Foods Hum. Nutr.* **2017**, *72*, 325–334. [CrossRef] [PubMed]
5. Zanetti, M.; Samoggia, A.; Young, J. Fruit Sector Strategic Management: An Exploration of Agro-food Chain Actors' Perception of Market Sustainability of Apple Innovation. *Sustainability* **2020**, *12*, 6542. [CrossRef]
6. Kowalska, H.; Marzec, A.; Domian, E.; Kowalska, J.; Ciurzyńska, A.; Galus, S. Edible coatings as osmotic dehydration pretreatment in nutrient-enhanced fruit or vegetable snacks development: A review. *Compr. Rev. Food Sci. Food Saf.* **2021**, *20*, 5641–5674. [CrossRef] [PubMed]
7. Jarczok-Guzy, M. Obstacles to the development of the organic food market in Poland and the possible directions of growth. *Food Sci. Nutr.* **2018**, *6*, 1462–1472. [CrossRef] [PubMed]
8. Žuntar, I.; Petric, Z.; Bursać Kovačević, D.; Putnik, P. Safety of Probiotics: Functional Fruit Beverages and Nutraceuticals. *Foods* **2020**, *9*, 947. [CrossRef] [PubMed]
9. Pace, B.; Cefola, M. Innovative Preservation Technology for the Fresh Fruit and Vegetables. *Foods* **2021**, *10*, 719. [CrossRef] [PubMed]
10. Dijksterhuis, G. New product failure: Five potential sources discussed. *Trends Food Sci. Technol.* **2016**, *50*, 243–248. [CrossRef]
11. Rothwell, R. Innovation and re-innovation: A role for the user. *J. Mark. Manag.* **1986**, *2*, 109–123. [CrossRef]
12. Buijs, J. Modelling Product Innovation Processes, from Linear Logic to Circular Chaos. *Creat. Innov. Manag.* **2003**, *12*, 76–93. [CrossRef]
13. Cunha, M.P.E.; Gomes, J.F.S. Order and Disorder in Product Innovation Models. *Creat. Innov. Manag.* **2003**, *12*, 174–187. [CrossRef]

14. Rogers, E. *The Diffusion of Innovations*, 5th ed.; The Free Press: New York, NY, USA, 2003.
15. Lassar, W.M.; Manolis, C.; Lassar, S.S. The relationship between consumer innovativeness, personal characteristics, and online banking adoption. *Int. J. Bank Mark.* **2005**, *23*, 176–199. [CrossRef]
16. Arts, J.W.C.; Frambach, R.T.; Bijmolt, T.H.A. Generalizations on consumer innovation adoption: A meta-analysis on drivers of intention and behavior. *Int. J. Res. Mark.* **2011**, *28*, 134–144. [CrossRef]
17. Barrena-Figueroa, R.; Garcia-Lopez-de-Meneses, T. The effect of consumer innovativeness in the acceptance of a new food product. An application for the coffee market in Spain. *Span. J. Agric. Res.* **2013**, *11*, 578. [CrossRef]
18. Capitanio, F.; Coppola, A.; Pascucci, S. Indications for drivers of innovation in the food sector. *Br. Food J.* **2009**, *111*, 820–838. [CrossRef]
19. Sanjuán-López, A.I.; Philippidis, G.; Resano-Ezcaray, H. How useful is acceptability to explain economic value? An application on the introduction of innovative saffron products into commercial markets. *Food Qual. Prefer.* **2011**, *22*, 255–263. [CrossRef]
20. Rodríguez-Entrena, M.; Salazar-Ordóñez, M. Influence of scientific–technical literacy on consumers' behavioural intentions regarding new food. *Appetite* **2013**, *60*, 193–202. [CrossRef] [PubMed]
21. Loizou, E.; Michailidis, A.; Chatzitheodoridis, F. Investigating the drivers that influence the adoption of differentiated food products. *Br. Food J.* **2013**, *115*, 917–935. [CrossRef]
22. Onwezen, M.C.; Bartels, J. Which perceived characteristics make product innovations appealing to the consumer? A study on the acceptance of fruit innovations using cross-cultural consumer segmentation. *Appetite* **2011**, *57*, 50–58. [CrossRef] [PubMed]
23. Joachim, V.; Spieth, P.; Heidenreich, S. Active innovation resistance: An empirical study on functional and psychological barriers to innovation adoption in different contexts. *Ind. Mark. Manag.* **2018**, *71*, 95–107. [CrossRef]
24. Bieberstein, A.; Roosen, J.; Marette, S.; Blanchemanche, S.; Vandermoere, F. Consumer choices for nano-food and nano-packaging in France and Germany. *Eur. Rev. Agric. Econ.* **2013**, *40*, 73–94. [CrossRef]
25. Cousins, J.; O'Gorman, K.; Stierand, M. Molecular gastronomy: Cuisine innovation or modern day alchemy? *Int. J. Contemp. Hosp. Manag.* **2010**, *22*, 399–415. [CrossRef]
26. Svejenova, S.; Mazza, C.; Planellas, M. Cooking up change in haute cuisine: Ferran Adrià as an institutional entrepreneur. *J. Organ. Behav.* **2007**, *28*, 539–561. [CrossRef]
27. Samoggia, A.; Nicolodi, S. Consumer's Perception of Fruit Innovation. *J. Int. Food Agribus. Mark.* **2017**, *29*, 92–108. [CrossRef]
28. Elmadfa, I. 2. Outlook. In *European Nutrition and Health Report*; Forum of Nutrition; Karger Medical and Scientific Publishers: Basel, Switzerland, 2009; Volume 62, pp. 12–13.
29. Slavin, J.L.; Lloyd, B. Health Benefits of Fruits and Vegetables. *Adv. Nutr.* **2012**, *3*, 506–516. [CrossRef] [PubMed]
30. Fardet, A.; Richonnet, C.; Mazur, A. Association between consumption of fruit or processed fruit and chronic diseases and their risk factors: A systematic review of meta-analyses. *Nutr. Rev.* **2019**, *77*, 376–387. [CrossRef] [PubMed]
31. Mamluk, L.; O'Doherty, M.G.; Orfanos, P.; Saitakis, G.; Woodside, J.V.; Liao, L.M.; Sinha, R.; Boffetta, P.; Trichopoulou, A.; Kee, F. Fruit and vegetable intake and risk of incident of type 2 diabetes: Results from the consortium on health and ageing network of cohorts in Europe and the United States (CHANCES). *Eur. J. Clin. Nutr.* **2017**, *71*, 83–91. [CrossRef] [PubMed]
32. Schwingshackl, L.; Hoffmann, G.; Kalle-Uhlmann, T.; Arregui, M.; Buijsse, B.; Boeing, H. Fruit and Vegetable Consumption and Changes in Anthropometric Variables in Adult Populations: A Systematic Review and Meta-Analysis of Prospective Cohort Studies. *PLoS ONE* **2015**, *10*, e0140846. [CrossRef] [PubMed]
33. He, F.J.; Nowson, C.A.; Lucas, M.; MacGregor, G.A. Increased consumption of fruit and vegetables is related to a reduced risk of coronary heart disease: Meta-analysis of cohort studies. *J. Hum. Hypertens.* **2007**, *21*, 717–728. [CrossRef] [PubMed]
34. Li, B.; Li, F.; Wang, L.; Zhang, D. Fruit and Vegetables Consumption and Risk of Hypertension: A Meta-Analysis. *J. Clin. Hypertens.* **2016**, *18*, 468–476. [CrossRef] [PubMed]
35. Wang, T.; Cai, H.; Sasazuki, S.; Tsugane, S.; Zheng, W.; Cho, E.R.; Jee, S.H.; Michel, A.; Pawlita, M.; Xiang, Y.-B.; et al. Fruit and vegetable consumption, Helicobacter pylori antibodies, and gastric cancer risk: A pooled analysis of prospective studies in China, Japan, and Korea. *Int. J. Cancer* **2017**, *140*, 591–599. [CrossRef] [PubMed]
36. Vieira, A.R.; Abar, L.; Vingeliene, S.; Chan, D.S.M.; Aune, D.; Navarro-Rosenblatt, D.; Stevens, C.; Greenwood, D.; Norat, T. Fruits, vegetables and lung cancer risk: A systematic review and meta-analysis. *Ann. Oncol.* **2016**, *27*, 81–96. [CrossRef]
37. Hosseini, B.; Berthon, B.S.; Wark, P.; Wood, L.G. Effects of Fruit and Vegetable Consumption on Risk of Asthma, Wheezing and Immune Responses: A Systematic Review and Meta-Analysis. *Nutrients* **2017**, *9*, 341. [CrossRef] [PubMed]
38. Liu, X.; Yan, Y.; Li, F.; Zhang, D. Fruit and vegetable consumption and the risk of depression: A meta-analysis. *Nutrition* **2016**, *32*, 296–302. [CrossRef] [PubMed]
39. Jiang, X.; Huang, J.; Song, D.; Deng, R.; Wei, J.; Zhang, Z. Increased Consumption of Fruit and Vegetables Is Related to a Reduced Risk of Cognitive Impairment and Dementia: Meta-Analysis. *Front. Aging Neurosci.* **2017**, *9*, 18. [CrossRef] [PubMed]
40. Mason-D'Croz, D.; Bogard, J.R.; Sulser, T.B.; Cenacchi, N.; Dunston, S.; Herrero, M.; Wiebe, K. Gaps between fruit and vegetable production, demand, and recommended consumption at global and national levels: An integrated modelling study. *Lancet Planet. Heal.* **2019**, *3*, e318–e329. [CrossRef]
41. Willett, W.; Rockström, J.; Loken, B.; Springmann, M.; Lang, T.; Vermeulen, S.; Garnett, T.; Tilman, D.; DeClerck, F.; Wood, A.; et al. Food in the Anthropocene: The EAT–Lancet Commission on healthy diets from sustainable food systems. *Lancet* **2019**, *393*, 447–492. [CrossRef]
42. WHO. *Promoting Fruit and Vegetable Consumption around the World*; WHO: Geneva, Switzerland, 2021.

43. Stea, T.H.; Nordheim, O.; Bere, E.; Stornes, P.; Eikemo, T.A. Fruit and vegetable consumption in Europe according to gender, educational attainment and regional affiliation—A cross-sectional study in 21 European countries. *PLoS ONE* **2020**, *15*, e0232521. [CrossRef] [PubMed]
44. Dreher, M. Whole Fruits and Fruit Fiber Emerging Health Effects. *Nutrients* **2018**, *10*, 1833. [CrossRef] [PubMed]
45. Central Statistical Office. *Statistical Yaerbook of the Republic of Poland in 2020*; Central Statistical Office: Warsaw, Poland, 2021.
46. WHO. *Diet, Nutrition and the Prevention of Chronic Diseases. Research Report*; WHO Technical Report Series; WHO: Geneva, Switzerland, 2003.
47. Daily Consumption of Fruit and Vegetables by Sex, Age and Educational Attainment Level. Available online: https://ec.europa.eu/eurostat/databrowser/view/HLTH_EHIS_FV3E__custom_1588514/default/table?lang=en (accessed on 20 January 2022).
48. Jezewska-Zychowicz, M.; Gawecki, J.; Wadolowska, L.; Czarnocinska, J.; Galinski, G.; Kollajtis Dolowy, A.; Roszkowski, W.; Wawrzyniak, A.; Przybylowicz, K.; Stasiewicz, B.; et al. KomPAN® Dietary Habits and Nutrition Beliefs Questionnaire for people 15–65 years old, version 1.1.—Interviewer administered questionnaire. In *KomPAN® Dietary Habits and Nutrition Beliefs Questionnaire and the Manual for Developing of Nutritional Data*; Gawecki, J., Ed.; The Committee of Human Nutrition, Polish Academy of Science: Warsaw, Poland, 2020; pp. 4–21.
49. Narodowy Bank Polski Exchange Rates. Available online: https://www.nbp.pl/ (accessed on 19 January 2022).
50. Gonçalves, D.; Coelho, P.; Martinez, L.F.; Monteiro, P. Nudging Consumers toward Healthier Food Choices: A Field Study on the Effect of Social Norms. *Sustainability* **2021**, *13*, 1660. [CrossRef]
51. Sajdakowska, M.; Jankowski, P.; Gutkowska, K.; Guzek, D.; Żakowska-Biemans, S.; Ozimek, I. Consumer acceptance of innovations in food: A survey among Polish consumers. *J. Consum. Behav.* **2018**, *17*, 253–267. [CrossRef]
52. Gonera, A.; Svanes, E.; Bugge, A.B.; Hatlebakk, M.M.; Prexl, K.-M.; Ueland, Ø. Moving Consumers along the Innovation Adoption Curve: A New Approach to Accelerate the Shift toward a More Sustainable Diet. *Sustainability* **2021**, *13*, 4477. [CrossRef]
53. Winger, R.; Wall, G. *Food Product Innovation*; Food and Agriculture Organization of the United Nations: Rome, Italy, 2006.
54. Albertsen, L.; Wiedmann, K.-P.; Schmidt, S. The impact of innovation-related perception on consumer acceptance of food innovations—Development of an integrated framework of the consumer acceptance process. *Food Qual. Prefer.* **2020**, *84*, 103958. [CrossRef]
55. Lallukka, T.; Pitkäniemi, J.; Rahkonen, O.; Roos, E.; Laaksonen, M.; Lahelma, E. The association of income with fresh fruit and vegetable consumption at different levels of education. *Eur. J. Clin. Nutr.* **2010**, *64*, 324–327. [CrossRef] [PubMed]
56. Moran, A.; Thorndike, A.; Franckle, R.; Boulos, R.; Doran, H.; Fulay, A.; Greene, J.; Blue, D.; Block, J.P.; Rimm, E.B.; et al. Financial Incentives Increase Purchases Of Fruit And Vegetables Among Lower-Income Households With Children. *Health Aff.* **2019**, *38*, 1557–1566. [CrossRef] [PubMed]
57. Li, L.; Wang, Z.; Li, Y.; Liao, A. Consumer innovativeness and organic food adoption: The mediation effects of consumer knowledge and attitudes. *Sustain. Prod. Consum.* **2021**, *28*, 1465–1474. [CrossRef]
58. Ajzen, I.; Fishbein, M. *Understanding Attitudes and Predicting Social Behavior*; Prentice Hall: Englewood Cliffs, NJ, USA, 1980.
59. Fornari, E.; Grandi, S.; Menegatti, M.; Fornari, D. Discounters versus Supermarkets and Hypermarkets: What drives store-switching? *Int. Rev. Retail. Distrib. Consum. Res.* **2020**, *30*, 555–574. [CrossRef]
60. Barska, A.; Wojciechowska-Solis, J. E-Consumers and Local Food Products: A Perspective for Developing Online Shopping for Local Goods in Poland. *Sustainability* **2020**, *12*, 4958. [CrossRef]
61. Nguyen, T.T.H.; Nguyen, N.; Nguyen, T.B.L.; Phan, T.T.H.; Bui, L.P.; Moon, H.C. Investigating Consumer Attitude and Intention towards Online Food Purchasing in an Emerging Economy: An Extended TAM Approach. *Foods* **2019**, *8*, 576. [CrossRef] [PubMed]
62. Kleijnen, M.; Lee, N.; Wetzels, M. An exploration of consumer resistance to innovation and its antecedents. *J. Econ. Psychol.* **2009**, *30*, 344–357. [CrossRef]
63. Fernandez, M.A.; Raine, K.D. Digital Food Retail: Public Health Opportunities. *Nutrients* **2021**, *13*, 3789. [CrossRef] [PubMed]
64. Liu, C.-F.; Lin, C.-H. Online Food Shopping: A Conceptual Analysis for Research Propositions. *Front. Psychol.* **2020**, *11*, 583768. [CrossRef] [PubMed]
65. Steptoe, A.; Pollard, T.M.; Wardle, J. Development of a Measure of the Motives Underlying the Selection of Food: The Food Choice Questionnaire. *Appetite* **1995**, *25*, 267–284. [CrossRef] [PubMed]
66. Đorđević, Đ.; Buchtová, H. Factors influencing sushi meal as representative of non-traditional meal: Consumption among Czech consumers. *Acta Aliment.* **2017**, *46*, 76–83. [CrossRef]
67. Appleton, K.; Dinnella, C.; Spinelli, S.; Morizet, D.; Saulais, L.; Hemingway, A.; Monteleone, E.; Depezay, L.; Perez-Cueto, F.; Hartwell, H. Consumption of a High Quantity and a Wide Variety of Vegetables Are Predicted by Different Food Choice Motives in Older Adults from France, Italy and the UK. *Nutrients* **2017**, *9*, 923. [CrossRef]
68. Wongprawmas, R.; Mora, C.; Pellegrini, N.; Guiné, R.P.F.; Carini, E.; Sogari, G.; Vittadini, E. Food Choice Determinants and Perceptions of a Healthy Diet among Italian Consumers. *Foods* **2021**, *10*, 318. [CrossRef] [PubMed]
69. Almli, V.L.; Næs, T.; Enderli, G.; Sulmont-Rossé, C.; Issanchou, S.; Hersleth, M. Consumers' acceptance of innovations in traditional cheese. A comparative study in France and Norway. *Appetite* **2011**, *57*, 110–120. [CrossRef] [PubMed]
70. Ariyawardana, A.; Govindasamy, R.; Lisle, A. Capturing the consumer value: The case of red lentils. *Br. Food J.* **2015**, *117*, 1032–1042. [CrossRef]
71. Iop, S.C.F.; Teixeira, E.; Deliza, R. Consumer research: Extrinsic variables in food studies. *Br. Food J.* **2006**, *108*, 894–903. [CrossRef]

72. Sabbe, S.; Verbeke, W.; Van Damme, P. Familiarity and purchasing intention of Belgian consumers for fresh and processed tropical fruit products. *Br. Food J.* **2008**, *110*, 805–818. [CrossRef]
73. Sijtsema, S.J.; Jesionkowska, K.; Symoneaux, R.; Konopacka, D.; Snoek, H. Perceptions of the health and convenience characteristics of fresh and dried fruits. *LWT—Food Sci. Technol.* **2012**, *49*, 275–281. [CrossRef]
74. Ion, R.A. Fruits and Vegetables Market in Romania: Better Understand Consumers' Preferences. In *Agrarian Economy and Rural Development—Realities and Perspectives for Romania*; 6th Edition of the International Symposium, November 2015; ICEADR: Bucharest, Romania, 2015; pp. 426–433.
75. Bonilla, T. Analysis of Consumer Preferences Toward 100% Fruit Juice Packages and Labels. Master's Thesis, Louisiana State University and Agricultural and Mechanical College, Baton Rouge, LA, USA, 2010.
76. Campbell, B.L.; Mhlanga, S.; Lesschaeve, I. Consumer preferences for peach attributes: Market segmentation analysis and implications for new marketing strategies. *Agric. Resour. Econ. Rev.* **2013**, *42*, 518–541. [CrossRef]
77. Arboretti Giancristofaro, R.; Bordignon, P. Consumer preferences in food packaging: CUB models and conjoint analysis. *Br. Food J.* **2016**, *118*, 527–540. [CrossRef]
78. Migliore, G.; Farina, V.; Tinervia, S.; Matranga, G.; Schifani, G. Consumer interest towards tropical fruit: Factors affecting avocado fruit consumption in Italy. *Agric. Food Econ.* **2017**, *5*, 24. [CrossRef]
79. Ryu, J.P.; Shin, J.T.; Kim, J.; Kim, Y.W. Consumer preference for edible insect-containing cookies determined by conjoint analysis: An exploratory study of Korean consumers. *Entomol. Res.* **2017**, *47*, 74–83. [CrossRef]
80. Talke, K.; Heidenreich, S. How to Overcome Pro-Change Bias: Incorporating Passive and Active Innovation Resistance in Innovation Decision Models. *J. Prod. Innov. Manag.* **2014**, *31*, 894–907. [CrossRef]

nutrients

MDPI

Article

Adherence to the Japanese Food Guide: The Association between Three Scoring Systems and Cardiometabolic Risks in Japanese Adolescents

Masayuki Okuda [1,*], Aya Fujiwara [2,3] and Satoshi Sasaki [3]

1 Graduate School of Sciences and Technology for Innovation, Yamaguchi University, 1-1-1 Minami-Kogushi, Ube 755-8505, Japan
2 Department of Nutritional Epidemiology and Shokuiku, The National Institutes of Biomedical Innovation, Health and Nutrition, 1-23-1 Toyama, Shinjuku-ku, Tokyo 162-8636, Japan; fujiwaraay@nibiohn.go.jp
3 Department of Social and Preventive Epidemiology, Graduate School of Medicine and School of Public Health, The University of Tokyo, 7-3-1 Hongo, Bunkyo-ku, Tokyo 113-0033, Japan; stssasak@m.u-tokyo.ac.jp
* Correspondence: okuda@yamaguchi-u.ac.jp; Tel.: +81-836-22-2231

Abstract: The Japanese Food Guide Spinning Top (JFGST) indicates optimal intake of five food groups (grain, fish and meat, vegetables, milk, and fruits) and sugar and confectionaries. We aimed to investigate whether adherence to the JFGST in 8th grade junior high school students (n = 3162) was associated with cardiometabolic risks and how different scorings of the JFGST influenced the associations. Metabolic risks were assessed from anthropometrics, blood pressure measurements, and blood glucose and lipid profile measurements. Three types of scoring adherent to the JFGST were analyzed (10 points were given for each item with optimal intake; range: 0–60): the original scoring (ORG scoring); first modified scoring, which had no upper limits for vegetables and fruits (MOD1 scoring); and MOD2 scoring without upper limits for five dishes (MOD2 scoring). The MOD2 scoring was positively associated with dietary fiber, potassium, calcium, and vitamins. All types of scorings were associated with low glucose levels ($p \leq 0.001$); the MOD2 scoring was associated with low systolic blood pressure ($p = 0.001$) and low cardiometabolic risk ($p = 0.003$). Our findings suggest that Japanese adolescents adherent to the JFGST had low cardiometabolic risks and should not fall below lower limits for intake of the abovementioned five food groups.

Keywords: adolescents; blood pressure; cardiometabolic risks; diet quality; energy-providing nutrients; fasting plasma glucose level; Japan Food Guide Spinning Top; Shokuiku

Citation: Okuda, M.; Fujiwara, A.; Sasaki, S. Adherence to the Japanese Food Guide: The Association between Three Scoring Systems and Cardiometabolic Risks in Japanese Adolescents. *Nutrients* **2022**, *14*, 43. https://doi.org/10.3390/nu14010043

Academic Editors: Clare Collins and George Moschonis

Received: 2 December 2021
Accepted: 20 December 2021
Published: 23 December 2021

1. Introduction

Numerous dietary indices, including modifications and variants, have been proposed to assess overall diet quality representing nutrient recommendations, healthy dietary habits, and dietary variety [1]. People consume a combination of several foods containing various nutrients that are interrelated metabolically and functionally in one sitting. Dietary indices have been reported to be associated with health outcomes, such as total mortality and cardiovascular diseases [2]. Most dietary indices are based on dietary guidelines and food guides in the US, such as the Healthy Eating Index and the Diet Quality Index [3,4], or on a Mediterranean diet pattern, such as the Mediterranean Diet Score and the Mediterranean Diet Quality Index for children and adolescents [5,6]. Dietary patterns in these countries are different from those of Japan. Fat and carbohydrate in food supply accounted for 37.7–43.8% and 43.3–48.7% of the total energy, respectively, in 2017 in North America, Western Europe, and Australia. In contrast, the proportions of these nutritional components were 29.8–30.3% and 56.7–57.3%, respectively, in 2017–2019 in Japan [7]. Japanese people may consume less fat and more carbohydrates than people in countries where the aforementioned dietary indices are used. The longevity and relatively low morbidity of cardiovascular diseases in Japan are attributed to the Japanese diet. Appropriate dietary indices associated with

Japanese health should be used to assess Japanese dietary patterns. Since high carbohydrate intake is considered a feature of the Japanese diet [8], a diet index comprising energy-providing nutrients could be applied to achieve health-promoting benefits.

The Japanese Food Guide Spinning Top (JFGST) was developed in 2005 as an educational tool to promote healthy behavior in Japanese people [9]. It was based on the Dietary Guidelines for Japanese and the Dietary Reference Intakes for Japanese, which take into account the Japanese culture, that is, considering carbohydrate intake. The JFGST is applicable for individuals aged 6 years or older on the assumption that they adhere to their estimated energy requirements. The JFGST is expected to be available in food and nutrition education ("Shokuiku") campaign.

JFGST-based scoring has been used to assess diet quality in several reports. Adherence to the JFGST showed beneficial associations with the scores on mortality, metabolic risk factors, depression, and sleep [10–20]. However, scoring methods based on the JFGST vary among reports, that is, with or without upper limits of the recommended range of food groups [10–12]; with additional scoring items, such as energy [10,11], sodium intake [12], and red/white meat [11]; and using continuous points [12] or discrete points after rounding to whole numbers [16]. Different scoring methods may influence associations with health outcomes in different ways.

The original JFGST comprises five food groups with upper and lower limits using discrete points, and two items with upper limits, including sugar and confectionaries, and alcohol beverages. However, it does not include items on energy, sodium, or red and white meat [9]. Since there were few habitual consumers of alcohol beverages in Japanese adolescents (0.5–1.8%) [21], six items, including five food groups and sugar and confectionaries, are appropriate. Meanwhile, achieving dietary and nutritional balance is an essential goal of the JFGST [9]. In the Dietary Reference Intakes for Japanese, items with defined upper limits for preventing lifestyle-related diseases are sodium and saturated fatty acids [22]. However, these could not determine the upper limits of vegetable dishes, fish and meat dishes, milk, and fruits. Oba et al. used the original lower and upper limits of the JFGST [10], Kurotani et al. removed the upper limits for vegetable dishes and fruits [11], and Kuriyama et al. did not use the upper limits for five food groups [12]. While only the score without the upper limits was associated with favorable nutrient intake patterns in Japanese women [12], all three scoring systems showed inverse associations with mortality [10,11] and metabolic risk factors [15,17]. In addition, there are no reports that the scores were coincidentally calculated with or without upper limits of the food groups to assess the associations with metabolic factors except for one study on adults, which showed that both scorings had unexpected associations with serum cholesterols and glycosylated hemoglobin [17].

Previous reports based on the JFGST targeted adult population [10–18,20], except for one study that analyzed a population aged < 6 years [19], which is not a target age population of the JFGST. However, there are no reports for adolescents. Therefore, the association between metabolic risk factors and the scoring system in adolescents is still unknown. The aim of the study was to investigate the association between diet quality score of adherence to the JFGST, representing a feature of Japanese diet, and metabolic risk factors in Japanese adolescents. We examined three scoring systems to clarify the different factors that influence the associations between the scores and cardiometabolic risk factors.

2. Materials and Methods

2.1. Participants

This study was part of the Shunan Child Cohort Study described in detail elsewhere [23–25]. The participants were 8th-grade junior high school students from 17 junior high schools in Shunan City, Japan. From 6805 students attending any of the schools between 2006 and 2010, 6226 students participated in this study with their guardians' consent. We excluded those with missing variables; with physician-diagnosed diseases; who had taken breakfast before blood extraction; with high plasma glucose, triglyceride, or low-density lipoprotein cholesterol levels due to possible postprandial values, or familial hypercholesterolemia; and with implausible energy intake (Figure 1). Overall, we analyzed the data of 3162 participants.

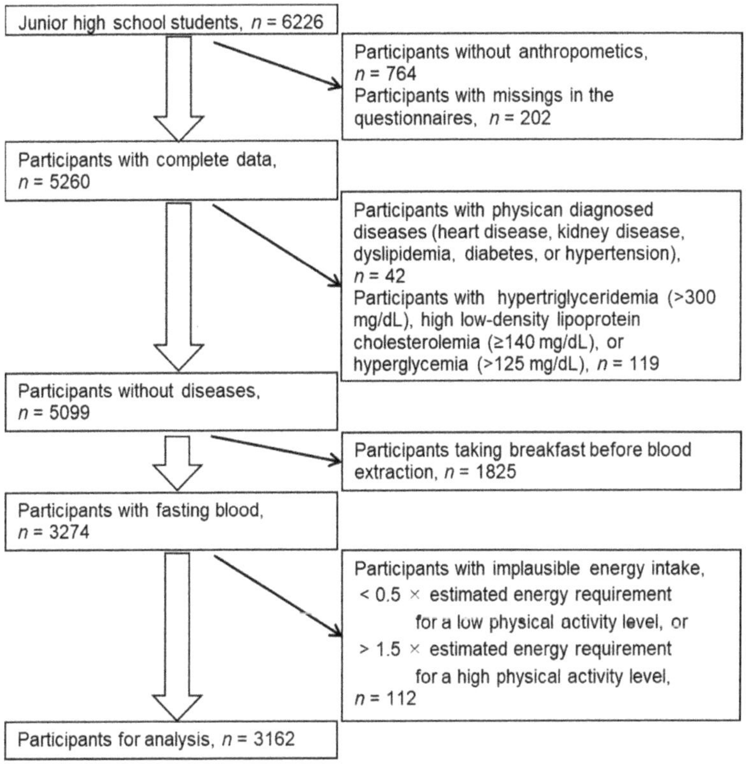

Figure 1. Selection of participants for analysis.

2.2. Dietary Assessment

Foods and nutrients were assessed using a brief-type self-administered diet history questionnaire for youths (BDHQ15y). The BDHQ15y, which assesses the consumption frequency of 63 selected food items and 17 dietary behaviors in the previous month, is a modification of the BDHQ for adults. The correlation coefficients between the estimates from the single BDHQ for adults and 16-day dietary records were 0.17–0.66 (Spearman correlation) for cereals, sugar and confectionaries, vegetables, potatoes, fruits, fish, meat, egg, dairy products, and non-alcoholic beverages [26]; 0.35–0.64 (Pearson correlation) for protein, fat, and carbohydrate; 0.44–0.66 (Pearson correlation) for sodium, potassium, calcium, magnesium, and iron; and 0.42–0.63 (Pearson correlation) for beta-carotene equivalent, and vitamin C [27]. Spearman correlation coefficients with corresponding biomarkers in adolescents were 0.26–0.31 for serum carotenoids; 0.22–0.48 for red blood corpuscle marine omega-3 polyunsaturated fatty acids [28]; 0.11–0.30 for urinary nitrogen [29]; and 0.05 for sodium; 0.11 for potassium; and 0.10 for the sodium-to-potassium ratio [30]. Plausible responders were considered to have energy intake ≥0.5 and ≤1.5 times of age- and sex-specific estimated energy requirements for low and high physical activity levels (PALs), respectively [31]. Intake of nutrients and food was adjusted using an energy density method [32]. As we could not determine the PAL of the participants, individual intake was standardized assuming energy intake equal to age- and sex-specific estimated energy requirements for moderate PAL.

Diet quality was assessed from five food dish groups (grain dishes, vegetable dishes, fish and meat dishes, milk, and fruits) and sugar and confectionaries based on the JFGST (Supplementary Table S1) [9,33]. The original score was calculated from the standardized energy-adjusted nutrient and food intake based on the serving standards of the JFGST scoring system. For five dishes, one serving (SV) corresponded to 40 g of carbohydrate for grains, 70 g of vegetables for vegetable dishes, 6 g of protein for fish and meat, 100 mg of calcium for milk, and 100 g of fruits for fruits. The number of servings was rounded to whole numbers as follows: if the value obtained was between 0.67 and <1.5, it was counted as one serving; any value between 1.5 and <2.5 was rounded off to two servings; and any value between 2.5 and <3.5 was rounded off to three servings. The rounding-off manner applies to the succeeding values (i.e., 3.5 to <4.5 and so on). The maximum point per dish was 10. When the intake was lower or higher than the optimum, a point was calculated as SV/lower limit of the optimum × 10 or 10 − (SV − the upper limit)/upper limit × 10, respectively (Supplementary Table S1). When the calculated point was less than zero, zero point was given. Optimum intake of sugar and confectionaries, which are not counted in SV, was <200 kcal giving 10 points, and points for ≥200 kcal were calculated (corresponding energy − 200)/200 × 10. When the calculated point was less than zero, zero point was given. The first modified score (MOD1 score) was the same as the original score (ORG score), except that no upper limits were set for vegetable dishes and fruits according to Kurotani et al. [10,11]. The second modified score (MOD2 score) had no upper limits for the five dishes according to Kuriyama et al. [12]. The scores of three scoring methods ranged from 0 to 60, with higher values indicating higher adherence to the JFGST.

2.3. Cardiometabolic Risk Factors

School nurses measured the participants' body height and weight near 0.1 cm and 0.1 kg, respectively. Body mass index (BMI; kg/m^2) was calculated as the weight divided by the square of height. The standard deviation score of BMI (zBMI) was calculated based on the Japanese reference in 2000 [34] using the Lambda–Mu–Sigma method [35]. Blood pressure (BP) was measured twice using auto-sphygmomanometers (HEM-707, HEM-757, or HEM-780, OMRON, Kyoto, Japan) after 5 min of sitting. Mean systolic and diastolic blood pressure (SBP and DBP, respectively) measurements were used. The participants were asked to fast 10–12 h before the blood extraction. Triglyceride (TG), low-density and high-density lipoprotein serum cholesterol (LDL-C and HDL-C, respectively), and plasma glucose levels were measured from blood specimens. Cardiometabolic risks were defined based on the definition of the International Diabetes Federation (32): zBMI ≥ 1; TG ≥ 150 mg/dL; LDL-C ≥ 120 mg/dL; HDL-C < 40 mg/dL; fasting plasma glucose ≥ 100 mg/dL; and SBP ≥ 130 mmHg and/or DBP ≥ 85 mmHg. Cardiometabolic risks were summed up as a metabolic syndrome score (MS score) ranging from 0 to 6.

2.4. Confounding Factors

The lifestyle questionnaire assessed movement behavior and household information. Sports activity (>2 times/week or not), TV watching (>2 h/d or not), sleep duration (h), number of siblings (1, 2, or ≥3), and single parent (yes or no) were used as possible confounders.

2.5. Statistical Analysis

Unless specified, variables are expressed as mean ± standard deviation or count (%). After checking for normality using quantile–quantile plots, the JFGST score points and triglyceride levels are expressed as median (minimum, maximum). Scores were categorized based on quintile levels (the lowest Q1 to the highest Q5). The median of energy-adjusted food and nutrient intake (% of total energy intake for energy-providing nutrients and amount per 1000 kcal for remaining nutrients and food groups) in each category and the ratio of intake in Q5:Q1 (%) were calculated to examine the contribution of foods and nutrients to the score. Non-parametric trend tests for food and nutrients across Q1 to

Q5 were performed using the Jonckheere–Terpstra test for two-sided monotonic trends. Gaussian linear regression models were used to examine the association between the score and individual cardiometabolic risks. When the triglyceride level was used as a dependent variable, it was natural log transformed. Poisson regression models were used for the MS score because it had a skewed distribution of zero (Table 1); the effect on the dependent variable was an exponential function of a coefficient. Coefficients of both regression models were calculated as an effect of 10 points of score. R version 4.0.3 (R Foundation for Statistical Computing) was used [36], and the significance level was set at $p = 0.05$.

Table 1. Characteristics of the analyzed participants ($n = 3162$).

Characteristics	Value
Age, years	13.6 ± 0.3
Body mass index (BMI), kg/m^2	19.2 ± 2.6
z-score of BMI	−0.2 ± 0.9
Triglyceride, mg/dL	52 (15, 249)
LDL-C, mg/dL	88.1 ± 19
HDL-C, mg/dL	67.7 ± 13.9
Fasting plasma glucose, mg/dL	90 ± 5.8
Systolic blood pressure, mmHg	114.2 ± 11.6
Diastolic blood pressure, mmHg	68.1 ± 8.7
Energy intake, kcal/day	2220 ± 632
Sex	
Male	1627 (51.5)
Female	1535 (48.5)
MS score	
0	2298 (72.7)
1	684 (21.6)
2	150 (4.7)
3, or 4	30 (1.0)

Data are expressed as mean ± standard deviation, median (minimum, maximum), or count (%). LDL-C, low-density lipoprotein cholesterol; HDL-C, high-density lipoprotein cholesterol. The MS score (metabolic syndrome score) is the clustering of cardiometabolic risks.

3. Results

The mean age of the participants was 13.6 ± 0.3 years, and the average BMI was 19.2 ± 2.6 kg/m^2 (Table 1). Of 3162 participants, 27.3% had one or more cardiometabolic risk factors.

For many students, the servings of fish and meat dishes and milk were over the upper limits (70.2% and 52.3%, respectively), and some of them had zero points for these dishes (11.7% and 41.1% of total participants, respectively; Supplementary Figures S1–S3). Therefore, the median points for fish and meat dishes and milk using the scoring with the upper limits (6.7 and 5 points, respectively) increased when using the scoring without the upper limits (10 and 10 points, respectively; Table 2). For less than 10% of the students, the points for grain dishes (3.4%), vegetable dishes (9.7%), and fruits (4.3%) were above the upper limits. The points for these dishes were similar regardless of whether the upper limits were applied or not. The median JFGST scores were 32 (minimum: 6.7, maximum: 58.3) using the ORG scoring, 33 (3.7, 58.8) using the MOD1 scoring with no upper limits for vegetable dishes and fruits, and 40.9 (15, 60) using the MOD2 scoring with no upper limits for all dishes except for sugar and confectionaries.

Table 2. Diet quality scoring based on the Japanese Food Guide Spinning Top for adolescents ($n = 3162$).

	Applying Both Upper and Lower Limits			Applying Only the Lower Limits			Applying Only the Upper Limits		
	Median	Min.	Max.	Median	Min.	Max.	Median	Min.	Max.
Grains	8.3	2	10	8.3	2	10	—	—	—
Vegetables	6.7	0	10	6.7	0	10	—	—	—
Fish and meat	6.7	0	10	10	0	10	—	—	—
Milk	5	0	10	10	0	10	—	—	—
Fruits	5	0	10	5	0	10	—	—	—
Sugar and confectionaries	—	—	—	—	—	—	0	0	10

Min., minimum; Max., maximum.

Using the MOD2 scoring, the higher the total score, the higher the median intake of fish and meat, fish, and milk (Q5:Q1 ratios, 122–282%), whereas other scorings showed opposite trends of the medians across the quintile categories in these food groups (Q5:Q1 ratios, 62–83%; Table 3). In addition, the MOD2 scoring had higher Q5:Q1 ratios for vegetables and fruits than other scorings. In terms of nutrients, protein, sodium, and calcium intake showed opposite trends of the medians across the quintile categories in the MOD2 scoring and other scorings (Table 4); the higher score of the MOD2 scoring, the higher median intake of protein, sodium, and calcium. Beneficial health nutrients, such as dietary fiber, potassium, β-carotene equivalents, and vitamin C, had larger differences between the lowest and the highest score categories (Q1 and Q5) in the MOD2 scoring (Q5:Q1 ratios, 141–229%). Saturated fatty acids showed similar trends across the three types of scorings; Q5:Q1 ratios in the ORG and MOD1 scores were 72%, and that in the MOD2 score was 87%.

Table 3. Median intake of food groups among quintile categories of the diet quality scores.

	ORG Score				MOD1 Score				MOD2 Score			
	Q1	Q3	Q5	Q5:Q1	Q1	Q3	Q5	Q5:Q1	Q1	Q3	Q5	Q5:Q1
Grain, g/1000 kcal	167	215	253	152%	170	213	251	148%	193	209	231	120%
Vegetable, g/1000 kcal	96	113	136	141%	93	113	142	153%	78	109	155	198%
Fish and meat, g/1000 kcal	125	107	104	83%	125	107	104	84%	102	107	125	122%
Fish, g/1000 kcal	31	26	24	80%	30	26	25	83%	23	27	30	132%
Meat, g/1000 kcal	39	33	31	80%	39	33	31	80%	36	32	36	101%
Milk, g/1000 kcal	132	92	82	62%	133	91	82	62%	44	102	124	282%
Fruits, g/1000 kcal	14	21	34	248%	13	22	37	281%	12	26	39	340%
Sugar and confectionaries, g/1000 kcal	119	92	62	52%	119	93	60	50%	133	97	46	35%

ORG score, original score. MOD1 (first modified) score was calculated as scores with no upper limits for vegetable dishes and fruits. MOD2 (second modified) score was calculated as scores with no upper limits for all dishes except for sugar and confectionaries. Jonckheere–Terpstra tests were used to test the trend across the quintile categories of the scores, and all trends were significant ($p < 0.001$), except for the trend of meat intake across the MOD2 score ($p = 0.874$).

The scores of the three scorings were significantly associated with low glucose levels (all $p < 0.001$; Table 5). The Akaike's information criterion was the lowest in the model with the MOD2 score as a dependent variable. Only the MOD2 scoring was significantly associated with low SBP (−0.81 mmHg per 10 points of the score; $p = 0.001$). The MS score was also significantly associated with the MOD2 scoring ($p = 0.003$); an increase in the score by 10 points was related to 0.89 ($e^{-0.12}$) times in the number of risks.

Table 4. Median intake of nutrients among quintile categories of the diet quality scores.

	ORG Score				MOD1 Score				MOD2 Score			
	Q1	Q3	Q5	Q5:Q1	Q1	Q3	Q5	Q5:Q1	Q1	Q3	Q5	Q5:Q1
Protein, % of total energy intake	14.8	13.8	13.5	91%	14.7	13.8	13.6	92%	13.0	14.3	15.3	118%
Fat, % of total energy intake	34.0	30.2	27.1	80%	34.2	30.1	27.1	79%	32.0	29.6	28.6	89%
SFA, % of total energy intake	11.1	9.5	8.1	72%	11.2	9.4	8.1	72%	10.0	9.3	8.7	87%
Carbohydrate, % of total energy intake	49.2	54.1	57.8	117%	49.1	54.2	57.9	118%	53.4	54.6	54.6	102%
Dietary fiber, g/1000 kcal	4.7	5.3	5.9	125%	4.6	5.2	6.1	131%	4.4	5.8	6.3	142%
Sodium, mg/1000 kcal	1918	1807	1755	92%	1902	1799	1774	93%	1761	1843	1919	109%
Potassium, mg/1000 kcal	1172	1161	1203	103%	1150	1163	1231	107%	985	1255	1386	141%
Na/K ratio	2.8	2.7	2.5	92%	2.8	2.7	2.5	89%	3.1	2.5	2.4	78%
Calcium, mg/1000 kcal	380	326	292	77%	375	325	295	79%	260	345	374	144%
Magnesium, mg/1000 kcal	119	117	123	104%	117	117	124	106%	105	127	137	131%
Iron, mg/1000 kcal	3.8	3.7	3.8	101%	3.7	3.6	3.9	103%	3.4	3.9	4.2	121%
β carotene equivalents, μg/1000 kcal	1067	1291	1578	148%	1025	1275	1687	165%	829	1528	1896	229%
Vitamin C, mg/1000 kcal	44	51	61	140%	42	51	64	152%	38	59	68	176%
Energy, kcal	2044	2130	2184	107%	2057	2127	2171	106%	2062	2149	2016	98%

ORG score, original score. MOD1 (first modified) score was calculated as scores with no upper limits for vegetable dishes and fruits. MOD2 (second modified) score was calculated as scores with no upper limits for all dishes except for sugar and confectionaries. Jonckheere–Terpstra tests were used to test the trend across the quintile categories of the scores, and all trends were significant ($p < 0.001$), except for the trend of iron intake across the ORG score ($p = 0.413$) and energy intake across the MOD2 score ($p = 0.130$).

Table 5. Regression analysis of the effect of 10-point scores on cardiometabolic risks.

	ORG Score				MOD1 Score				MOD2 Score			
	β	SE	*p*	AIC	β	SE	*p*	AIC	β	SE	*p*	AIC
zBMI [1]	−0.03	0.02	0.141	8456.6	−0.03	0.02	0.133	8457	−0.01	0.02	0.641	8459
ln (TG, mg/dL) [1]	0.01	0.01	0.207	3601	0.01	0.01	0.249	3601	−0.01	0.01	0.285	3601
LDL-C, mg/DL [1]	−0.59	0.44	0.172	27,559	−0.58	0.43	0.173	27,559	−0.45	0.44	0.305	27,559
HDL-C, mg/dL [1]	−0.49	0.30	0.106	25,285	−0.57	0.30	0.057	25,284	−0.16	0.31	0.603	25,287
Glucose, mg/dL [1]	−0.46	0.13	<0.001	19,949	−0.45	0.13	<0.001	19,949	−0.50	0.13	<0.001	19,947
SBP, mmHg [1]	−0.09	0.25	0.710	24,120	−0.12	0.25	0.633	24,120	−0.81	0.25	0.001	24,110
DBP, mmHg [1]	−0.02	0.20	0.936	22,542	−0.01	0.19	0.963	22,542	−0.24	0.20	0.235	22,541
ln (MS score) [2]	−0.06	0.04	0.110	4264	−0.07	0.04	0.085	4264	−0.12	0.04	0.003	4258

[1] Analyzed using the linear model. [2] Analyzed using the Poisson model, with the number of cardiometabolic risks as a dependent variable. Both regression models were adjusted for age, sex, zBMI, sports activity, TV watching, sleep duration, number of siblings, and single parent. Models for zBMI as a dependent variable were adjusted for age, sex, sports activity, TV watching, sleep duration, number of siblings, and single parent. SE, standard error of a coefficient estimate (β); AIC, Akaike's information criteria; zBMI, z-score of body mass index; TG, triglyceride; LDL-C and HDL-C, low- and high-density lipoprotein cholesterol, respectively; SBP and DBP; systolic and diastolic blood pressure, respectively. The MS score is the clustering of cardiometabolic risks.

4. Discussion

We examined three scoring types of dietary quality based on the JFGST. The contribution of each food group to the total score and the trends of nutrients and foods across the quintile categories were similar between the original and the first modified (ORG, and MOD1) scoring with no upper limits for vegetable dishes and fruits. In contrast, the contribution of fish and meat dishes and milk to the score was high in the MOD2 scoring with no upper limits for all dishes except for sugar and confectionaries. In addition, the MOD2 scoring and other scorings showed opposite trends for protein, sodium, and calcium intake, and the MOD2 scoring could differentiate the variance in dietary fiber, potassium, and vitamins compared with other scorings. All the three scoring types were significantly associated with the fasting glucose level. Notably, the MOD2 score was significantly negatively associated with SBP and the MS score.

Based on the data from the National Health and Nutrition Survey Japan, the modified score without upper limits for five dishes was negatively associated with SBP in adults ≥20 years old of both sexes and with waist circumference in women [17]. In this study, only the modified score without upper limits for five dishes (MOD2 score) was associated with SBP and metabolic syndrome. However, in a study of female dietetic students aged

18–22 years, the score was negatively associated with waist circumference and low-density lipoprotein cholesterol but was not associated with SBP [15]. Thus, the associations noted in female dietetic students were different from those in adolescents. A systematic review of diet quality indices developed for other countries showed associations with a reduced risk of cardiovascular disease and its risk factors [2]. Diet quality indices based on the JFGST were related to low all-cause and cerebrovascular disease mortality [10,11]. In adolescents, diet quality adherence to the JFGST may imply an association with low cardiometabolic risks. In particular, the MOD2 scoring without the upper limits for five dishes is a suitable index for high intake of dietary fiber, minerals, vitamins, fish, vegetables, fruits, and milk.

The higher the participants' MOD2 score points without upper limits for the five dishes, the higher their sodium intake, whereas using other scoring methods, the lower the sodium intake. Similar to other food frequency questionnaires, the BDHQ is vulnerable to measurement errors and is weak in estimating nutrients from foods that have not been investigated. Although sodium intake estimated from the BDHQ was barely associated with urinary sodium excretion as an intake biomarker, the sodium-to-potassium ratio from the BDHQ was significantly associated with the urinary ratio [30]. Furthermore, the sodium-to-potassium ratio was more closely associated with blood pressure than sodium intake in previous studies in youths [37,38]. In this study, the range of the sodium-to-potassium ratio across quintile categories was the widest in the scoring without upper limits for the five dishes. Thus, the association between the scoring without upper limits for five dishes and SBP, as well as the MS score, may be attributed to the sodium-to-potassium ratio.

Among the tentative dietary goals of preventing life-style related diseases, tentative dietary goals for sodium, saturated fatty acids, and a balance of energy-providing nutrients have upper limits of intake. Trends of saturated fatty acids across the quintile categories were similar among the three types of scorings, but the ORG and MOD1 score showed higher saturated fatty acids in the lowest categories than the MOD2 score did; this may reflect that the participants with intake above the optimum had low score points due to upper limits. However, the ORG and MOD1 scores did not show significant associations with cardiometabolic risk factors except for plasma glucose. The intake of two energy-providing nutrients (carbohydrates and protein) corresponds to servings of grain and fish and meat dishes in the JFGST. Two of the three energy-providing nutrients (fat being the third) can determine the nutritional balance. The tentative dietary goals for the energy-providing nutrients for the prevention of lifestyle-related diseases are 13–20% for protein, 20–30% for fat, and 50–65% for carbohydrate according to the Dietary Reference Intakes for Japanese, 2020 [22]. Fat intake in the lowest categories of the three scores was above the tentative goals, but fat intake across the quintile categories was similar among the three scorings. The apparent difference in the trends across the quintile categories among the three scores was protein, although total protein is not considered a pivotal determinant of the nutritional balance for the tentative dietary goals to prevent lifestyle-related diseases [22]. Thus, nutrients other than those providing energy may determine the association between the score and cardiometabolic risks. A rice grain dish is the main staple of the Japanese diet [8,39], but this may not be a main source of health benefits.

The ORG scores with upper limits for vegetable dishes and fruits, and the MOD1 scores without upper limits had similar points for these food groups and dietary nutrient patterns. This means that the proportion of participants with vegetable and fruit intake above the upper limits was low; thus, this population could not ascertain the beneficial effects of vegetable and fruit intake in the JFGST scoring. The Health Japan 21 (the second term) program recommends a mean daily intake of vegetables ≥350 g, which represents a notable increase from 282 g in 2010. In addition, it aims to reduce the proportion of individuals who consume fruits <100 g from 61.4% in 2010 to 30% [22]. The MOD2 scoring, which showed large differences of vegetables and fruits between the lowest and highest scores, was negatively associated with metabolic risks. The MOD2 scoring results suggest limited evidence to support an intervention to increase adolescents' consumption of vegetables and fruits from their current intake. However, rather than focusing on a single food group, such as vegetables and fruits, consuming a healthy balance of food should be considered for Japanese adolescents.

Similar to previous dietary indices associated with cardiovascular diseases rather than cancers [1,2], the JFGST was associated with cardiometabolic risk factors. The JFGST was developed in consideration of the concept of Japanese culture. Japanese terms for dishes are derived from ichiju-sansai, a common formula of Japanese cuisine, Washoku. Grain dishes, shushoku, are the main staples; fish and meat dishes, shusai, are the main dishes; and vegetable dishes, fukusai, are the side dishes [40]. The concept of Japanese dishes is disseminated through homemaking classes and nutrition education at school. The JFGST is a food-based index unlike most of other existing dietary indices [41]. The Healthy Eating Index, the Diet Quality Index, and the Mediterranean Diet Quality Score use foods and nutrients together as scoring items [3–5]. The Mediterranean Diet Quality Index for children and adolescents uses food intake and dietary habits, but this scoring may be influenced by culture [6]. When using the JFGST as a health promotion and education tool, adolescents can easily understand their suitable dish servings. For effective nutrition education, the dietary index should be suited to the background of the target population.

In contrast to the scoring items, the JFGST scoring uses a combination of nutrient and food intake; the servings of grain dishes, fish and meat dishes, and milk were calculated from nutrient amount, but the servings of vegetable dishes and fruits were from the food amount. It is unknown whether servings that adolescents have in mind coincide with those of the JFGST scoring. Dietary indices have three objectives: to measure absolute diet quality, to evaluate adherence to dietary guidelines, and to guide health promotion [41]. According to the third objective, Japanese youths should be educated on favorable dietary habits to ensure longevity and low mortality. Practical use of existing dietary indices for health promotion should be addressed [1,2], and the JFGST should be adopted for nutrition education interventions.

This study had some limitations. The cross-sectional design of this study could not explain temporal causality between the scores and cardiometabolic risk factors, but the participants might not have known their own cardiovascular parameter levels before answering the BDHQ15y. The design could also not explore the effect on risks appearing in later life, such as cardiovascular mortality, cancer incidence, frailty, and dementia related to healthy life expectancy. Social norms regarding a healthy diet may contribute to a reporting bias, but this may attenuate observable associations. The BDHQ15y has weaknesses, similar to other frequent food questionnaires. Intrinsic measurement errors and biases of the BDHQ15y may attenuate or mask the true associations between the score and cardiovascular risk. Nevertheless, the associations found in this study could help adolescents whose diets are assessed using the BDHQ15y to review and modify their own dietary habits with the JFGST score. Another limitation is that the study location was limited to a small part of Japan, meaning that the data collection could not capture all Japanese dietary patterns.

5. Conclusions

We showed for the first time that Japanese adolescents adherent to the JFGST had low cardiovascular risk. However, only the modified JFGST scoring system with no upper limits for five food groups (grain dishes, fish and meat dishes, vegetable dishes, milk, and fruits) was beneficial in alleviating cardiovascular risks; this indicates that adolescents should not fall below the lower limits for intake of the abovementioned five food groups. The JFGST can be used for adolescent health education.

Supplementary Materials: The following are available online at https://www.mdpi.com/article/10.3390/nu14010043/s1, Table S1: Food groups in the Japanese Food Guide Spinning Top and their optimal ranges, Figure S1: Histogram and scores for grain and vegetable dishes, Figure S2: Histogram and scores for fish and meat dishes and milk, Figure S3: Histogram and scores for fruits, and sugar and confectionaries.

Author Contributions: M.O., A.F. and S.S. contributed to the conception of the study. M.O. contributed to the study design. M.O. organized the database. S.S. calculated the food and nutrient intake from the BDHQ. M.O. performed statistical analyses. M.O. wrote the first draft of this manuscript. All authors contributed to manuscript revision. All authors have read and agreed to the published version of the manuscript.

Funding: This study was funded by the Japan Society for the Promotion of Science (grant numbers JP18K10085 and JP21K10497).

Institutional Review Board Statement: The study was conducted according to the guidelines of the Declaration of Helsinki, and all procedures involving human subjects were approved by the Institutional Review Board of Yamaguchi University Hospital (H17-14-2).

Informed Consent Statement: Complying with the Japanese ethical guideline, informed assent was obtained from all participants 13 and 14 years old, and written informed consent was obtained from the guardians of all participants.

Data Availability Statement: The raw data supporting the conclusions of this article will be made available by the corresponding author without undue reservation.

Acknowledgments: We appreciate the collaboration of the health center, the education board, and schools of Shunan City. We thank the study participants and their guardians. We would also like to thank Ichiro Kunitsugu, Shin-ichi Sugiyama, and Norikazu Yoshitake for their help with the survey.

Conflicts of Interest: The authors declare that the research was conducted in the absence of any commercial or financial relationships that could be construed as a potential conflict of interest.

References

1. Kant, A.K. Dietary patterns and health outcomes. *J. Am. Diet. Assoc.* **2004**, *104*, 615–635. [CrossRef]
2. Wirt, A.; Collins, C.E. Diet quality—What is it and does it matter? *Public Health Nutr.* **2009**, *12*, 2473–2492. [CrossRef] [PubMed]
3. Patterson, R.E.; Haines, P.S.; Popkin, B.M. Diet quality index: Capturing a multidimensional behavior. *J. Am. Diet Assoc.* **1994**, *94*, 57–64. [CrossRef]
4. Krebs-Smith, S.M.; Pannucci, T.E.; Subar, A.F.; Kirkpatrick, S.I.; Lerman, J.L.; Tooze, J.A.; Wilson, M.M.; Reedy, J. Update of the Healthy Eating Index: HEI-2015. *J. Acad. Nutr. Diet.* **2018**, *118*, 1591–1602. [CrossRef] [PubMed]
5. Trichopoulou, A.; Kouris-Blazos, A.; Wahlqvist, M.L.; Gnardellis, C.; Lagiou, P.; Polychronopoulos, E.; Vassilakou, T.; Lipworth, L.; Trichopoulos, D. Diet and overall survival in elderly people. *BMJ* **1995**, *311*, 1457–1460. [CrossRef]
6. Serra-Majem, L.; Ribas, L.; Garcia, A.; Perez-Rodrigo, C.; Aranceta, J. Nutrient adequacy and Mediterranean Diet in Spanish school children and adolescents. *Eur. J. Clin. Nutr.* **2003**, *57* (Suppl. S1), S35–S39. [CrossRef] [PubMed]
7. Ministry of Agriculture Forestry and Fisheries. Food Supply and Demand Table. 2019. Available online: https://www.maff.go.jp/j/zyukyu/fbs/ (accessed on 15 October 2021).
8. Suzuki, N.; Goto, Y.; Ota, H.; Kito, K.; Mano, F.; Joo, E.; Ikeda, K.; Inagaki, N.; Nakayama, T. Characteristics of the Japanese diet described in epidemiologic publications: A qualitative systematic review. *J. Nutr. Sci. Vitaminol.* **2018**, *64*, 129–137. [CrossRef]
9. Yoshiike, N.; Hayashi, F.; Takemi, Y.; Mizoguchi, K.; Seino, F. A new food guide in Japan: The Japanese food guide Spinning Top. *Nutr. Rev.* **2007**, *65*, 149–154. [CrossRef]
10. Oba, S.; Nagata, C.; Nakamura, K.; Fujii, K.; Kawachi, T.; Takatsuka, N.; Shimizu, H. Diet based on the Japanese Food Guide Spinning Top and subsequent mortality among men and women in a general Japanese population. *J. Am. Diet. Assoc.* **2009**, *109*, 1540–1547. [CrossRef]
11. Kurotani, K.; Akter, S.; Kashino, I.; Goto, A.; Mizoue, T.; Noda, M.; Sasazuki, S.; Sawada, N.; Tsugane, S.; Japan Public Health Center Based Prospective Study Group. Quality of diet and mortality among Japanese men and women: Japan Public Health Center based prospective study. *BMJ* **2016**, *352*, i1209. [CrossRef]
12. Kuriyama, N.; Murakami, K.; Livingstone, M.B.E.; Okubo, H.; Kobayashi, S.; Suga, H.; Sasaki, S. Development of a food-based diet quality score for Japanese: Associations of the score with nutrient intakes in young, middle-aged and older Japanese women. *J. Nutr. Sci.* **2016**, *5*, e41. [CrossRef] [PubMed]
13. Sakai, H.; Murakami, K.; Kobayashi, S.; Suga, H.; Sasaki, S. Food-based diet quality score in relation to depressive symptoms in young and middle-aged Japanese women. *Br. J. Nutr.* **2017**, *117*, 1674–1681. [CrossRef] [PubMed]
14. Okubo, R.; Matsuoka, Y.J.; Sawada, N.; Mimura, M.; Kurotani, K.; Nozaki, S.; Shikimoto, R.; Tsugane, S. Diet quality and depression risk in a Japanese population: The Japan Public Health Center (JPHC)-based Prospective Study. *Sci. Rep.* **2019**, *9*, 7150. [CrossRef] [PubMed]
15. Nishimura, T.; Murakami, K.; Livingstone, M.B.; Sasaki, S.; Uenishi, K. Adherence to the food-based Japanese dietary guidelines in relation to metabolic risk factors in young Japanese women. *Br. J. Nutr.* **2015**, *114*, 645–653. [CrossRef]

16. Nanri, A.; Nagai, C.; Kochi, T.; Eguchi, M.; Kabe, I.; Mizoue, T. Diet quality and depressive symptoms among workers. *Clin. Nutr.* **2020**, *39*, 1951–1957. [CrossRef]
17. Murakami, K.; Livingstone, M.B.E.; Sasaki, S. Diet quality scores in relation to metabolic risk factors in Japanese adults: A cross-sectional analysis from the 2012 National Health and Nutrition Survey, Japan. *Eur. J. Nutr.* **2019**, *58*, 2037–2050. [CrossRef]
18. Yamamoto, K.; Ota, M.; Minematsu, A.; Motokawa, K.; Yokoyama, Y.; Yano, T.; Watanabe, Y.; Yoshizaki, T. Association between adherence to the Japanese Food Guide Spinning Top and sleep quality in college students. *Nutrients* **2018**, *10*, 1996. [CrossRef]
19. Shinsugi, C.; Tani, Y.; Kurotani, K.; Takimoto, H.; Ochi, M.; Fujiwara, T. Change in growth and diet quality among preschool children in Tokyo, Japan. *Nutrients* **2020**, *12*, 1290. [CrossRef]
20. Hashimoto, A.; Murakami, K.; Kobayashi, S.; Suga, H.; Sasaki, S. Associations of education with overall diet quality are explained by different food groups in middle-aged and old Japanese women. *J. Epidemiol.* **2021**, *31*, 280–286. [CrossRef]
21. Osaki, Y.; Minowa, M.; Suzuki, K.; Wada, K. Nationwide survey on alcohol use among junior and senior high school students in Japan. *Jpn. J. Public Health* **1999**, *46*, 883–893.
22. Minister of Health Labour and Welfare. Health Japan 21 (The Second Term). Available online: https://www.mhlw.go.jp/stf/seisakunitsuite/bunya/kenkou_iryou/kenkou/kenkounippon21.html (accessed on 25 October 2021).
23. Shinozaki, K.; Okuda, M.; Sasaki, S.; Kunitsugu, I.; Shigeta, M. Dietary fiber consumption decreases the risks of overweight and hypercholesterolemia in Japanese children. *Ann. Nutr. Metab.* **2015**, *67*, 58–64. [CrossRef]
24. Okuda, M.; Fujiwara, A.; Sasaki, S. Added and free sugars intake and metabolic biomarkers in Japanese adolescents. *Nutrients* **2020**, *12*, 2046. [CrossRef] [PubMed]
25. Okuda, M.; Fujiwara, A.; Sasaki, S. Composition of dietary fatty acids and health risks in Japanese youths. *Nutrients* **2021**, *13*, 426. [CrossRef]
26. Kobayashi, S.; Murakami, K.; Sasaki, S.; Okubo, H.; Hirota, N.; Notsu, A.; Fukui, M.; Date, C. Comparison of relative validity for food group intake estimated by comprehensive and brief-type self-administered diet history questionnaires against 16-day dietary records in Japanese adults. *Public Health Nutr.* **2011**, *14*, 1200–1211. [CrossRef] [PubMed]
27. Kobayashi, S.; Honda, S.; Murakami, K.; Sasaki, S.; Okubo, H.; Hirota, N.; Notsu, A.; Fukui, M.; Date, C. Both comprehensive and brief self-administered diet history questionnaires satisfactorily rank nutrient intakes in Japanese adults. *J. Epidemiol.* **2012**, *22*, 151–159. [CrossRef] [PubMed]
28. Okuda, M.; Sasaki, S.; Bando, N.; Hashimoto, M.; Kunitsugu, I.; Sugiyama, S.; Terao, J.; Hobara, T. Carotenoid, tocopherol, and fatty acid biomarkers and dietary intake estimated by using a brief self-administered diet history questionnaire for older Japanese children and adolescents. *J. Nutr. Sci. Vitaminol.* **2009**, *55*, 231–241. [CrossRef] [PubMed]
29. Okuda, M.; Asakura, K.; Sasaki, S. Protein intake estimated from brief-type self-administered diet history questionnaire and urinary urea nitrogen level in adolescents. *Nutrients* **2019**, *11*, 319. [CrossRef]
30. Okuda, M.; Sasaki, S. Assessment of foods associated with sodium and potassium intake in Japanese youths using the brief-type self-administered diet history questionnaire. *Nutrients* **2021**, *13*, 2345. [CrossRef] [PubMed]
31. Sasaki, S.; Katagiri, A.; Tsuji, T.; Shimoda, T.; Amano, K. Self-reported rate of eating correlates with body mass index in 18-y-old Japanese women. *Int. J. Obes. Relat. Metab. Disord.* **2003**, *27*, 1405–1410. [CrossRef] [PubMed]
32. Willet, W. *Nutritional Epidemiology*, 3rd ed.; Oxford University Press: New York, NY, USA, 2013; ISBN 978-0-19-975403-8.
33. Ministry of Health Laboror and Wealfare. Report on Utilization of Dietary Reference Intakes for Japanese. Available online: https://www.mhlw.go.jp/shingi/2010/03/s0331-9.html (accessed on 25 October 2021).
34. Kato, N.; Takimoto, H.; Sudo, N. The cubic functions for spline smoothed L, S and M values for BMI reference data of Japanese children. *Clin. Pediatr. Endocrinol.* **2011**, *20*, 47–49. [CrossRef]
35. Cole, T.J.; Green, P.J. Smoothing reference centile curves: The LMS method and penalized likelihood. *Stat. Med.* **1992**, *11*, 1305–1319. [CrossRef] [PubMed]
36. R Core Team. R: A Language and Environment for Statistical Computing. Available online: https://www.R-project.org/ (accessed on 1 December 2020).
37. Geleijnse, J.M.; Grobbee, D.E.; Hofman, A. Sodium and potassium intake and blood pressure change in childhood. *BMJ* **1990**, *300*, 899–902. [CrossRef] [PubMed]
38. Buendia, J.R.; Bradlee, M.L.; Daniels, S.R.; Singer, M.R.; Moore, L.L. Longitudinal effects of dietary sodium and potassium on blood pressure in adolescent girls. *JAMA Pediatr.* **2015**, *169*, 560–568. [CrossRef] [PubMed]
39. Ministry of Agriculture Forestry and Fisheries. Washoku: Traditional Dietary Cultures of the Japanese. Available online: https://www.maff.go.jp/e/data/publish/attach/pdf/index-20.pdf (accessed on 15 October 2021).
40. Ministry of Agriculture Forestry and Fisheries. The Washoku Way Japan's Nuanced Approach to Food. Available online: https://www.maff.go.jp/j/shokusan/gaisyoku/pamphlet/ (accessed on 15 December 2021).
41. Waijers, P.M.; Feskens, E.J.; Ocke, M.C. A critical review of predefined diet quality scores. *Br. J. Nutr.* **2007**, *97*, 219–231. [CrossRef] [PubMed]

nutrients

MDPI

Article

A Comparison of Diet Quality in a Sample of Rural and Urban Australian Adults

Rebekah Pullen [1], Katherine Kent [1,2], Matthew J. Sharman [1], Tracy L. Schumacher [3,4,*,†] and Leanne J. Brown [3,4,*,†]

1 School of Health Sciences, University of Tasmania, Launceston, TAS 7250, Australia; rebekah.pullen@utas.edu.au (R.P.); K.Kent@westernsyndey.edu.au (K.K.); matt.sharman@utas.edu.au (M.J.S.)
2 School of Health Sciences, Western Sydney University, Campbelltown, NSW 2560, Australia
3 Department of Rural Health, The University of Newcastle, Tamworth, NSW 2340, Australia
4 Hunter Medical Research Institute, New Lambton Heights, NSW 2305, Australia
* Correspondence: tracy.schumacher@newcastle.edu.au (T.L.S.); leanne.brown@newcastle.edu.au (L.J.B.); Tel.: +61-(26)-7553540 (L.J.B.)
† These authors share an equal seniorship.

Abstract: The diet quality of rural Australians is under researched. Characterising disparities in diet quality between rural and urban populations may inform targeted interventions in at- risk groups. A cross-sectional study aimed to determine the relationship between diet quality, rurality and sociodemographic characteristics in a sample of Australian adults. Participants were recruited at rural and regional events between 2017 and 2020, in New South Wales, Australia. Diet quality was measured using the Healthy Eating Quiz or Australian Eating Survey to generate an Australian Recommended Food Score (ARFS). ARFS was compared by rurality and sociodemographic characteristics using multivariate regression. Participants (n = 247; 53% female) had a mean ± SD ARFS of 34.5 ± 9.0. There was no significant effect of rurality on ARFS (β-coefficient = −0.4; 95%CI −3.0, 2.3). Compared to participants aged 18–30 years, higher ARFS was evident for those aged 31–50 (β = 5.4; 95%CI 0.3, 10.4), 51–70 (β = 4.4; 95%CI 0.3, 8.5) and >71 years (β = 6.5; 95% CI 1.6–11.4). Compared to those living alone, participants living with a partner (β = 5.2; 95%CI 2.0, 8.4) and families with children (β = 5.6; 95%CI 1.4, 9.8) had significantly higher ARFS. ARFS was significantly lower with each additional self-reported chronic health condition (β = −1.4; 95%CI −2.3, −0.4). Our results indicate that diet quality as defined by the ARFS was classified as 'getting there' and that age, living arrangements and chronic health conditions, but not rurality, influenced diet quality in a sample of Australian adults.

Keywords: Australian dietary guidelines; Australian recommended food score; diet quality; diet variety; rural

Citation: Pullen, R.; Kent, K.; Sharman, M.J.; Schumacher, T.L.; Brown, L.J. A Comparison of Diet Quality in a Sample of Rural and Urban Australian Adults. *Nutrients* **2021**, *13*, 4130. https://doi.org/10.3390/nu13114130

Academic Editor: Rosa Casas

Received: 22 October 2021
Accepted: 15 November 2021
Published: 18 November 2021

1. Introduction

Chronic diseases such as heart disease, stroke and type 2 diabetes are currently the leading cause of mortality and morbidity worldwide and have been described as the greatest public health challenge of the 21st century [1]. In 2018, 38% of the burden of disease in Australia was attributed to modifiable risk factors, with dietary risk factors directly accounting for 5.4% of the total burden of disease [2]. Worldwide, specific dietary risk factors for the development of diet-related disease have been identified as low consumption of fruits, vegetables and wholegrains, together with rising consumption of sodium and saturated fats [3–8].

In 2018, approximately 29% of the Australian population lived in rural or remote locations [9]. People living in rural and remote locations have shorter lives and experience disproportionately higher levels of chronic diet-related disease such as coronary heart disease, stroke, chronic kidney disease and type 2 diabetes when compared to their metropolitan counterparts [9–12]. Rural Australians experience many sociodemographic precursors to poor diet quality such as low education, low income and high unemployment [11,13]. Other factors that influence health outcomes in rural settings are location specific, including reduced access to health services combined with lower health literacy, and the relatively higher cost of, and poorer access to, fresh foods [14–17].

Evidence has demonstrated that components of food work synergistically, influencing the risk of developing chronic diseases [18,19]. As a consequence, nutrition research has moved away from the traditional approach of investigating single nutrient or specific foods when investigating diet and its relationship to disease towards analysing the patterns in which foods are consumed in a whole-of-diet context [18,20,21]. Dietary patterns research describes the consumption of nutrients, foods and food groups as well as examining the variation, diversity, frequency and quality of foods in the diet [20]. Recent definitions of diet quality incorporate the concepts of diversity, adequacy, proportionality and moderation, with the primary objective being a balance between each [21–23]. These concepts have informed the Australian Dietary Guidelines (ADG) and accompanying resources such as the Australian Guide to Healthy Eating (AGHE). The ADG identifies an evidence-based, optimal dietary pattern and presents the types and amounts of foods that Australians are recommended to eat for health and wellbeing. It consists of five core food groups representing similar nutrients within each, and advocates that a variety of foods should be consumed from the five food groups each day. One measure of diet quality is compliance with the ADG, which has been shown to reduce risk factors associated with the development of chronic diseases such as cardiovascular disease, obesity and hypertension [21,24,25].

Diet quality can be measured using two approaches: data-driven posteriori methods or a priori methods such as dietary quality indices (DQI) [8,21,26]. Higher DQI scores reflect closer adherence to dietary guidelines and therefore higher diet quality. In Australia, Indigenous Australians, those living with disabilities, the unemployed, single-parent households and people living in rural and remote communities have been identified as particularly vulnerable to poor diet quality and therefore at increased risk of chronic diet-related disease [9]. Investigations into diet quality of rural and remote Australians remains under prioritised [12]. For example, between 2000 and 2014, 184 (1.1%) of the total 16,651 National Health and Medical Research Council (NHMRC)-funded projects were defined as relating to Australian rural health research [12]. This, together with methodological challenges, has led to the under representation of these populations in dietary research, and has meant that the full breadth and interaction between determinants affecting dietary status have yet to be fully characterised [11,12].

Despite the under representation of rural and remote-dwelling adults, Australian national survey data identified a trend consistent across rural areas, with only 1 in 10 individuals meeting the ADG recommendations for fruits and vegetables [11], a further indication of the need for research and intervention. In order to prioritise this population in public health policy, studies investigating the sociodemographic and dietary characteristics of this population are urgently required. Therefore, the aim of this study is to determine the relationship between diet quality, rurality and sociodemographic characteristics in a sample of Australian adults recruited from rural and regional events.

2. Materials and Methods

The 'Changing Health Actions at Rural and reGional Events in 20 minutes' (CHAaRGE:20) project was conducted to determine the health status of participants attending rural and regional events using opportunistic face-to-face engagement in health-related activities. Ethics approval was obtained from the University of Newcastle Human Research Ethics Committee (H2017-10979).

2.1. Participants and Recruitment

Between 2017 and 2020, participants were recruited from Tamworth Country Music Festival (TCMF) (Tamworth, NSW, Australia) and AgQuip Field Day (AgQuip) (Gunnedah, NSW, Australia). These events were selected due to a high proportion of attendees being from rural locations. Participants were eligible for participation if they were over the age of 18 years and were not under the influence of drugs or alcohol. They were required to have proficient use of English and basic literacy level. Recruitment was achieved through convenience sampling methods such as volunteers handing out flyers, banner advertisements, media and word of mouth. Interested participants were provided a verbal and written summary outlining the project aims, specific measures being collected and participant-required tasks. Participants were offered individualised feedback about their health assessment results from a qualified dietitian. Written consent was obtained for all participants.

2.2. Measures

Participants answered survey questions relating to demographics and self-reported health conditions. Anthropometric measures were taken by trained researchers or student volunteers. The Healthy Eating Quiz (HEQ) [27] was completed on a tablet or laptop either before or after anthropometric measures to optimise waiting time in 2017. Given the time burden for answering the HEQ, this option was changed to the voluntary completion of the Australian Eating Survey (AES) [28] in January 2018. This survey was disseminated via email and completed in participants' own time, following the event. Study data were stored using REDCap electronic data capture, hosted at Hunter Medical Research Institute [29,30]. AES was collected by SurveyMonkey for the TCMF in 2018, prior to being collected by REDCap for AgQuip in 2018.

2.3. Dietary Assessment

The Australian Recommended Food Score (ARFS) is a validated dietary index modelled on diet variety from within and between food groups, as described in the Australian Dietary Guidelines (ADG) [28,31–33]. The ADG has five core food groups, which are organised according to their similar nutrient profiles. The HEQ consists of a validated subset of 70 questions from which the ARFS is derived [28,33]. Eight subscales within the HEQ reflect the core food groups of the ADG. The subscales are composed of 20 questions dedicated to vegetables, 12 to fruit, 7 to meat, 6 to plant-based protein foods, 12 to breads and cereals, 10 to dairy foods and 1 to water [33]. Calculation of relevant points from each subscale provided a total ARFS score (range 0–73) and subscale scores for diet variety. An ARFS score can be categorised into four groups: 'needs work' (<33), 'getting there' (33–38), 'excellent' (39–46) or 'outstanding' (47+). However, very high ARFS may indicate energy intake that is excessive to need. The ARFS has been demonstrated to be a reliable and valid measure of diet quality [28,32]. The higher the score on the ARFS, the greater the variety of nutrient-dense foods consumed and therefore the greater the diet quality [34]. The ARFS is also able to be derived from the Australian Eating Survey (AES), a more comprehensive food frequency questionnaire, which is inclusive of other foods, including discretionary foods [32].

2.4. Anthropometric Characteristics

Height and weight were measured using a Biospace BSM370 Automatic BMI Scale Stadiometer. Where multiple height and weight values were present, they were summed and divided for an average to enhance accuracy. BMI was calculated from measurements of participants' height and weight (weight (kg)/height (m^2), then categorised into "normal weight" (18.5–24.99 kg/m^2), "overweight" (25.0–29.99 kg/m^2) and "obese" (Obese I: 30.0 to 34.99 kg/m^2, Obese II: 35.0 to 39.99 kg/m^2, Obese III: 40.0 kg/m^2), as defined by the World Health Organisation [35].

2.5. Sociodemographic Characteristics

Participants self-reported living circumstances, household income, highest level of education completed, smoking status and diagnosed chronic health conditions. Participants reported having diagnosed chronic health conditions by answering the question: *"Have you EVER been told by a doctor or health professional that you have any of these conditions? Tick any that apply"*. Respondents selected any appropriate chronic condition from a list of predefined conditions that have been associated in the literature to be prevalent in rural populations [9,11]. The variables of age education, household income and living arrangements were collapsed due to low cell counts for data analysis. Age categories were reduced from sixteen levels (18–25; 26–30; 31–35; 36–40; 41–45; 46–50; 51–55; 56–60; 61–65; 66–70; 71–75; 75–80; 81–85; older than 85; under 18 years; don't wish to answer) to four (18–30; 31–50; 51–70; >71). Education categories were reduced from eight levels (less than year 10, Year 10 or 11, Year 12; Trade or Vocation; University or graduate degree; Postgraduate degree or higher; None of the above; I don't wish to answer) to four (Year 12 and less; Certificate or Diploma; University). Household income categories were reduced from fourteen levels (No in-come; Pension; AUD 1–6293; AUD 6240–15,999; AUD 16,000–25,999; AUD 26,000–36,399; AUD 36,400–51,999; AUD 52,000–77,999; AUD 78,000–103,999; AUD 104,000–129,999; AUD 130,000–155,000; >AUD 156,000; I do not know; I do not wish to answer) to six (No income; Pension; AUD 1–51,999; AUD 52,000–103,000; >AUD 104,000; I don't know). Living arrangements categories was collapsed from seven levels (living alone; partner/spouse; own children; someone else's children; parents; other adults; I don't wish to answer) to four (living alone; partner/spouse only; single/partnered with children; parents and other).

Self-reported chronic health conditions for each individual were summed and used to calculate the average number of chronic health conditions for the sample. Individual conditions with related aetiology were listed together to form an overarching condition classification. Circulatory conditions incorporated cardiovascular disease (CVD), heart disease (HD), high blood pressure (HTN) and high blood cholesterol. Chronic mental health included anxiety, depression, schizophrenia and any other diagnosed mental health condition. Musculoskeletal conditions included back problems, osteoporosis and rheumatoid arthritis and any other related diagnosed conditions. Respiratory conditions included asthma, chronic obstructive pulmonary disease COPD and any other diagnosed lung-related condition. Rurality was calculated according to ARIA+ scores [36] using post codes into major cities, inner regional, outer regional, remote and very remote categories. These categories were then collapsed into major cities and regional and remote. ARIA+ was used as it is a recognised standard measure of rurality. It was selected over other measures due to its sensitivity and is considered to be the most stable measure over time as it is based on road distance travelled for locality to service centres rather than factors of population density [36,37]. The use of ARIA+ allows for the capacity to conduct comparisons between population-based Australian Bureau of Statistics survey results and present and future variations in this study.

2.6. Statistical Analysis

Statistical analysis was conducted using IBM SPSS Statistics for Windows, version 26.0 (IBM Corp. Armonk, NY, USA). Power calculations were conducted [38]. A true detectable difference of 3.48 in ARFS can be found in a sample of 246 participants, based on a standard deviation of 9.7 [33], an alpha value of 0.5 and a beta of 0.8, and 1:1 ratio in each group. The demographic characteristics of the included sample were compared to those excluded from analysis to determine whether those providing dietary data were reflective of the whole cohort, using Chi Square tests. Continuous data were tested for normal distribution by visual methods of a histogram, quantile-quantile plot (QQ-plot) and formally tested using Shapiro–Wilk. Any variables that had p values greater than $p = 0.05$ in the Shapiro–Wilk test were reported as median and interquartile range. Data that were normally distributed were reported as means and standard deviations. Univariate tests assessed the differences in mean ARFS scores according to levels within sociodemographic variables. For the multivariate regression, respondents nominating survey answers *"I don't know"* or *"I don't wish to answer"* for variables with this option were coded as missing. Assumptions of linearity, homoscedasticity and independence were tested visually by means of scatter plots and box plots. Two outliers were identified; however, they were retained, as both outlier ARFS were within a justifiable range, and sensitivity tests indicated no change in univariate and multivariate linear regression models. All variables included in the analysis satisfied the assumption of equal variance, demonstrating properties of homogeneity. The significance level for inclusion of those variables investigated in univariate regression in the further multivariate linear regression model was set to $p \leq 0.20$. Rurality was included in the regression (regardless of p value) due to the relationship with the research question and strong links in the literature to diet variety [10,16,39–41].

3. Results

In this study, 638 participants were surveyed between 2018 and 2020. Of these, 391 participants had missing total and/or subscale ARFS and were therefore excluded. Participants who provided complete dietary data allowing a total ARFS to be calculated were significantly more likely to be female, with an income of up to AUD 51,000, aged between 51 and 70 years of age and have an education level of year 12 or under. Sociodemographic characteristics of the study sample are reported in Table 1. Within the total sample, the majority were female (52.6%) and lived in regional and remote locations (77.9%), with a large proportion classified as overweight (39.6%). The largest proportion of study participants had an education level of year 12 and under (45.7%), and 30.4% of participants reported income between AUD 1–51,999. Most (52.0%) lived with a spouse/partner only, while 17.5% lived with a partner/spouse and children. Of the total sample, 29.1% had previously smoked.

Table 1. Total number and percentage for sociodemographic characteristics in a sample of Australian adults.

		Male		**Female**		**Total**	
		n **- 117**		***n*** **= 130**		***n*** **= 247**	
Characteristics	**Levels**	***n*** **(100%)**		***n*** **(100%)**		***n*** **(100%)**	
Age (years)	18–30	20	(17.1%)	24	(18.5%)	44	(17.8%)
	31–50	16	(13.7%)	24	(18.5%)	40	(16.2%)
	51–70	57	(48.7%)	68	(52.3%)	125	(50.6%)
	>71	24	(20.5%)	14	(10.8%)	38	(15.4%)
Rurality	Major cities	27	(23.1%)	30	(23.1%)	57	(23.1%)
	Regional/remote	90	(76.9%)	100	(76.9%)	190	(77.9%)
Education	≤Year 12	53 [1]	(45.7%) [1]	59 [2]	(45.7%) [2]	112 [3]	(45.7%) [3]
	Cert [a]/Dip [b]	30 [1]	(25.9%) [1]	35 [2]	(27.1%) [2]	65 [3]	(26.5%) [3]
	University	33 [1]	(28.4%) [1]	35 [2]	(27.1%) [2]	68 [3]	(27.8%) [3]
HH [c] inc [d] (pa) [e]	No income	9	(7.7%)	7	(5.4%)	16	(6.5%)
	Pension	5	(4.3%)	5	(3.8%)	10	(4.0%)
	AUD 1–51,999	32	(27.4%)	43	(33.1%)	75	(30.4%)
	AUD 52,000–103,999	28	(23.9%)	27	(20.8%)	55	(22.3%)
	AUD > 104,000	22	(18.8%)	17	(13.1%)	39	(15.8%)
	Do not know [f]	21	(17.9%)	31	(23.8%)	52	(21.1%)
Living arrgmt [g]	Live alone	15	(12.8%)	23 [4]	(17.8%) [4]	38 [5]	(15.4%) [5]
	PR [h]/Spouse only	69	(59.0%)	59 [4]	(45.7%) [4]	128 [5]	(52.0%) [5]
	Single/PR [h] (CH [i])	18	(15.4%)	25 [4]	(19.4%) [4]	43 [5]	(17.5%) [5]
	Parent/other	15	(12.8%)	22 [4]	(17.1%) [4]	37 [5]	(15.0%) [5]
Smoking status	Yes	44	(37.6%)	28	(21.5%)	72	(29.1%)
	No	73	(62.4%)	102	(78.5%)	175	(70.9%)

[a] Cert = certificate. [b] Dip = diploma. [c] HH = household. [d] inc = income. [e] pa = per annum. [f] Combined with do not wish to answer. [g] arrgmt = arrangements. [h] PR = partner/partnered. [i] CH = children. [1] Education n = 116 males. [2] Education n = 129 females. [3] Total n = 245 for education. [4] Living arrangements n = 129 females. [5] Total n = 246 for living arrangements.

Diagnosed chronic health conditions by gender are reported in Table 2. The most prevalent chronic health conditions were circulatory conditions (27.7%), musculoskeletal conditions (23.7%) and overweight and obesity (21.2%) overall. For males, the most prevalent conditions were circulatory conditions (26.0%), overweight and obesity (21.7%) and musculoskeletal conditions (22.6%). The data highlight that more than a quarter of women in this sample had circulatory conditions (27.6%), musculoskeletal conditions (24.6%), were overweight or obese (20.8%) or had chronic mental health conditions (18.5%), which was higher compared to males. The average number of summed chronic health conditions for the total sample was 1.2 (±1.2), which was similar for both males and females.

Table 2. Descriptive statistics of anthropometric characteristics, chronic health conditions and categories of BMI in the study sample of Australian adults.

	Female		Male		Total	
	n = 130		n = 117		n = 247	
Characteristics	**Median**	**(IQR)**	**Median**	**(IQR)**	**Median**	**(IQR) ***
Height (cm)	163 *	(6.5) *	176.8 *	(6.6) *	169.5 *	(9.5) *
Weight (kg)	70.2	(22.6)	88.9	(18.7)	79.7	(24.3)
Waist circumference (cm)	84.9	(19.9)	98.9	(19.3)	92.0	(22.2)
BMI (kg/m^2)	n	(100%)	n	(100%)	n	(100%)
Normal	22 [1]	(18.8%) [1]	50	(39.1%)	72 [2]	(29.4%) [2]
Overweight	56 [1]	(47.9%) [1]	41	(32.0%)	97 [2]	(39.6%) [2]
Obese	39 [1]	(33.3%) [1]	37	(28.9%)	76 [2]	(31.0%) [2]
Number and proportions of chronic health conditions						
0	43	(33.1%)	48 [3]	(41.7%) [3]	91 [4]	(36.8%) [4]
1	45	(34.6%)	35 [3]	(30.4%) [3]	80 [4]	(32.4%) [4]
2	22	(16.9%)	17 [3]	(14.8%) [3]	39 [4]	(15.8%) [4]
3	14	(10.8%)	5 [3]	5(4.3%) [3]	19 [4]	(7.7%) [4]
4	4	(3.1%)	9 [3]	9(7.7%) [3]	13 [4]	(5.3%) [4]
5	2	(1.5%)	1 [3]	1(0.9%) [3]	3 [4]	(1.2%) [4]
Individual diagnosed Chronic health conditions						
Circulatory conditions	36	(27.6%)	31 [5]	(26.0%) [5]	67 [6]	(27.3%) [6]
Chronic kidney or renal disease	1	(0.8%)	2 [5]	(1.7%) [5]	3 [6]	(1.2%) [6]
Diabetes (type 1, type 2 or gestational)	9	(6.9%)	8 [5]	(7.0%) [5]	17 [6]	(6.9%) [6]
Overweight or obesity	27	(20.8%)	25 [5]	(21.7%) [5]	52 [6]	(21.2%) [6]
Cancer (any)	6	(4.6%)	10 [5]	(8.7%) [5]	16 [6]	(6.5%) [6]
Chronic mental health conditions [a]	24	(18.5%)	10 [5]	(8.7%) [5]	34 [6]	(13.9%) [6]
Musculoskeletal conditions [b]	32	(24.6%)	26 [5]	(22.6%) [5]	58 [6]	(23.7%) [6]
Respiratory conditions [c]	22	(16.9%)	14 [5]	(12.2%) [5]	36 [6]	(14.7%) [6]
None of the above	49	(33.1%)	43 [5]	(42.6%) [5]	92 [6]	(37.6%) [6]

[a] Including: anxiety, depression, schizophrenia or other mental chronic health condition. [b] Including: back problems, osteoarthritis, rheumatoid arthritis. [c] Including: asthma, COPD or any other lung condition. * Mean and standard deviation are reported for height. [1] BMI n = 128 for females. [2] Total n = 245 for BMI. [3] Number and proportion of chronic conditions n = 115 for males. [4] Number and proportion of chronic conditions n = 245. [5] Individual diagnosed chronic health conditions n = 115 for males. [6] Individual diagnosed chronic health conditions n = 245.

Total ARFS and ARFS subscales are reported in Table 3. Overall, the mean total ARFS was classified as *"getting there"* (34.5%) (Table 3). Females reported higher (35.5) mean total ARFS compared to males (33.4) (Table 3). When compared to males, females reported higher ARFS in subscale categories of vegetables (13.9), fruit (5.7), meat alternatives (2.3), grains (5.1), dairy (4.1) and water (0.7) (Table 3). Males reported higher subscale ARFS for the categories of meat (3.2) and extras (0.9) (Table 3). The ARFS for the total sample, as well as by gender in all subscale categories, except for vegetables, extras and water, was reported as being below half of their associated maximum score (Table 3).

Table 3. Total Australian Recommended Food Score (ARFS), subscales, reference ranges, mean and standard deviation for a sample Australian adults categorised by gender.

ARFS Subscales	Reference Range	TOTAL		Male		Female	
		Mean	(SD)	Mean	(SD)	Mean	(SD)
		(*n* = 247)		(*n* = 117)		(*n* = 130)	
Total	0–73	34.5	(9.0)	33.4	(8.9)	35.5	(9.2)
Vegetables	0–21	13.5	(4.2)	13	(4.2)	13.9	(4.1)
Fruit	0–12	5.5	(2.7)	5.3	(2.7)	5.7	(2.7)
Meat	0–7	3.1	(1.5)	3.2	(1.5)	3.0	(1.4)
Meat alternatives	0–6	2.2	(1.3)	2.0	(1.2)	2.3	(1.3)
Grains	0–13	5.0	(2.2)	4.9	(2.2)	5.1	(2.1)
Dairy	0–11	3.9	(1.8)	3.7	(1.7)	4.1	(1.9)
Extras	0–1	0.8	(0.8)	0.9	(0.8)	0.8	(0.7)
Water	0–2	0.6	(0.5)	0.6	(0.5)	0.7	(0.5)

Results of the multivariate linear regression for the effect of sociodemographic categories on total ARFS are reported in Table 4. Age, living arrangements and number of health conditions were retained for multiple regression analysis due to $p < 0.20$. No effect of rurality on ARFS was found in the multivariate analysis. Significant differences in total ARFS for all levels of age were found when compared to the reference group of 18–30 years old. The largest difference was detected for the 31–50 and 71 > age groups with a difference in ARFS of 5.4; $p = 0.037$ and 6.5; $p = 0.010$, respectively. Mean differences in ARFS were detected between all levels of living arrangements, demonstrating increased total ARFS for all levels when compared to the reference group living alone (Table 4). For every additional diagnosed health condition, the ARFS was reduced by −1.4; $p = 0.004$. The final model had an adjusted R square of 0.077, $p < 0.001$.

Table 4. Multivariate linear regression demonstrating the association between socio demographic variables and total ARFS.

Characteristics	Levels	Multivariate		(R^2 0.077, $p \leq 0.001$)	
		β Coefficient	SE [a]	95% CI [b]	*p*
Rurality	Major cities (*n* = 57)	Reference Category		-	-
	Regional/remote (*n* = 190)	−0.4	1.4	(−3.0, 2.3)	0.790
Age (years)	18–30 (*n* = 44)	Reference Category		-	-
	31-50 (*n* = 40)	5.4	2.6	(0.3, 10.4)	0.037 *
	51–70 (*n* = 125)	4.4	2.1	(0.3, 8.5)	0.035 *
	71 > (*n* = 38)	6.5	2.5	(1.6, 11.4)	0.010 *
Living arrgmt [c]	Alone (*n* = 38)	Reference Category		-	-
	PR [d]/Spouse only (*n* = 128)	5.2	1.6	(2.0, 8.4)	<0.002 *
	Single/PR [d] (CH) [e] (*n* = 43)	5.6	2.1	(1.4, 9.8)	0.008 *
	Parents/other (*n* = 37)	5.8	2.4	(1.1, 10.5)	0.016 *
Number of chronic health conditions	Continuous variable (*n* = 245)	−1.4	0.5	(−2.3, −0.4)	0.004 *

[a] SE = standard Error. [b] CI = confidence interval. [c] arrgmt = arrangements. [d] PR = partner/partnered. [e] CH = children. * = significance < p 0.20.

4. Discussion

This study investigated the relationship between sociodemographic characteristics and diet quality using the Australian Recommended Food Score (ARFS) in a sample of rural and urban Australian adults. The average ARFS was categorised as *"getting there"*, indicating a need to improve diet quality. Rurality had no significant effect on diet quality in this sample. Analysis of other sociodemographic characteristics showed living arrangements and the number of diagnosed chronic health conditions had the strongest associations with diet quality, where living alone and having multiple chronic health conditions were associated with poorer diet quality. Our study examined many of the same sociodemographic characteristics as previous studies [28,33,39,41–49] and observed similar findings showing a lack of relationship between diet quality, gender, socioeconomic status and education.

The literature has shown that adherence to the ADG within the Australian population is poor, resulting in low diet quality [45,50,51]. The mean diet quality score in our study (34.5 ± 9.0) was comparable with another study of Australian adults which found a mean total diet score of 34.1 using the ARFS from the HEQ [33]. Further, two Australian studies also with adult samples using the ARFS from the AES found a mean diet quality score of 33 ± 8.8 [32] and median score of 36 [28]. In this study, the diet quality score of "*getting there*" was driven by low individual scores for all the ARFS subscales. This finding is consistent with both national and international studies across a variety of diet quality indices, which show that low diet quality is driven by low scores across most, if not all, food groups [33,40–45,48,52,53].

While our study did not demonstrate a relationship between diet quality in rural and urban dwelling adults, this may be due to the limited sample size of our study. However, some literature has demonstrated that rural populations experience many of the sociodemographic precursors to poor diet quality such as low income, low education attainment and limited access to fresh foods, which could negatively affect diet quality [11,16,54]. Importantly, two recent systematic reviews highlight the scarcity of studies surrounding rural populations [6,55], limiting comparisons to our data. In a sample of older Australian adults using the DGI-2013 (score range 0–130), one study found that men but not women from rural areas had significantly lower total diet quality scores (80.1) compared to their urban counterparts (83.0). The authors concluded that rural-related disadvantage was the mediator of poor diet quality scores [41]. A second study in women of reproductive age found no difference between total diet quality scores between urban (84.8) and rural (83.9) women using the DGI. Unlike the present study, it found that rural women had a significantly higher component score for meat and meat alternatives [55]. The inconsistent effect of rurality on diet quality indicates that differences in diet quality may be driven by differences in rural food environments in different regions and, therefore, that multi-site trials comparing multiple rural populations should be a consideration for future research.

There are only a few Australian studies investigating living arrangements as a sociodemographic variable influencing diet quality, particularly in rural populations [33,56–59]. Studies investigating the effect of living arrangements of diet quality have focused predominantly on ageing populations. An international systematic review of the relationship between living arrangements and diet found that a number of studies consistently identified that living alone led to lower fruit and vegetable intake and lower adherence to dietary recommendations [60]. The determinants of low diet quality in those living alone are complex. Demographic characteristics influence the likelihood of a person living alone, including gender, socio-economic status and age, which may influence the relationship between living alone and low diet quality [60]. Psychosocial drivers of poor diet quality may affect those living alone, including decreased motivation and enjoyment of cooking, which increases the consumption of pre-packaged processed meals that are high in sodium, sugar and trans/saturated fats [61,62]. A lack of support for and encouragement for maintaining adherence with dietary recommendations has also been recognised as a difference experienced between those living alone and those living with others [63]. Similarly, one study demonstrated that those living in arrangements reflecting cohabitation or marriage-like arrangements have a higher adherence to dietary recommendations; this could be due to more regular and formalised shopping and eating habits [60,64,65], as well as social facilitation [63]. An Australian study exploring sociodemographic characteristics on diet quality in a sample of adults responding to the HEQ, incorporated a measure of meal sharing as a possible determinant of diet quality [33]. The results support the present study's finding that, when controlling for age, sex and socioeconomic status, diet quality increases in line with the number of people whom a person shares meals with as opposed to those who eat meals alone [33].

Given the association between diet and disease, and considering the increased prevalence of multimorbidity [10], it is surprising that there are so few studies, particularly in rural populations, investigating the effect of the presence of chronic health conditions on diet quality. In the present study, we found that, for every additional diagnosed chronic health condition in an individual, total diet quality score decreased. Previous research indicates that even small decreases in total diet quality scores are associated with increased all-cause and specific-cause mortality. For example, an American study [66] found that an increase in diet quality score up to or above the 20th percentile in their population group over 12 years was significantly associated with a reduction in total mortality of between 8 and 17%, as well as significantly lowering the risk of death from cardiovascular disease. In contrast, their results also suggested that decreases in diet quality over a 12-year timeframe, when compared to no change, were associated with an increase in total mortality between 6 and 12% [66]. Interestingly, the study suggests that an increase of 22 of the 110 available points within the Alternative Healthy Eating Index (AHEI) over a 12-year period could reduce risk of death by 20%, which could be achieved by increasing intake of nuts and legumes from 0 to 1 serving per day and reducing red or processed meats by 1.5 servings per day [66]. An Australian study [25] using the Total Diet Score (TDS) (range 0–20) found that those who had diets that closely adhered to the Australian Dietary Guidelines, as reflected by higher diet quality scores, had a 21% reduced risk of all-cause mortality and 23% decreased risk of cardiovascular mortality. This study found that, with every increase in the standard deviation of TDS (1 SD = 2.19 units of TDS), there was an 8% decrease in risk of all-cause mortality [25]. Further to this, another American study [67] exploring the relationship between four disease risk factors on diet quality found that those with one or none of the clinical risk factors had significantly higher total diet quality score (55.7 out of a possible 100), as measured by the Healthy Eating Index-2015, when compared with those who had all four risk factors. Those with all four risk factors had a significantly lower diet quality score of (51.1). Australian studies have explored the relationship between health and diet in terms of specific disease outcomes, mortality and relative risk or self-reported perception of health rather than the number of diagnosed chronic health conditions [45,46]. Studies that have measured the effect of perceived health status on diet quality found those who had a greater self-perceived health status demonstrated higher total diet quality scores [45,49].

A major strength of the present study was the use of validated food frequency methods in the assessment of dietary intake, which are able to accurately capture usual dietary intake, including temporal changes in eating patterns; as this is a limitation of the existing literature on dietary intakes in rural populations [54]. Additionally, relative to the published literature, there was a strong representation of rural and regional participants, demonstrating that engaging rural adults in settings where they work, live and play is key to increasing participation rates of rural people in research activities. Previously, the literature has identified this population as underrepresented and hard to access, and as such, recruitment at rural and regional events should be considered as a strategy for future research. TCMF and AgQuip provide examples of annual rural and regional events that are important pillars of rural and regional communities. These events are hosted at local community venues and possible to attend free of charge, which supports their use in research aiming to sample a diverse rural and regional population. However, the limitations of this include potentially under-representing some groups who do not attend these events. For example, our study may have over-represented the 'walking well' who are able to attend community-based health promotion activities and who have an interest in health or nutrition, meaning that those with chronic conditions and poor diet may have been underrepresented. Supporting this, our study found significant differences in age, gender, income and education within the CHAaRGE:20 study sample for those people who completed the comprehensive dietary assessment versus those who did not, potentially limiting the generalisability of our results. While successful in recruiting a high proportion of rural and regional-dwelling participants, our study also demonstrates the complexity of sampling in rural and remote communities and presents some important considerations for future diet quality studies. Another limitation of our study is that it was likely underpowered in detecting an effect of rurality on diet quality in this sample, as recruiting was suspended due to the COVID-19 pandemic. Further, in our study, there was a high prevalence (21.1%) of respondents not wishing to disclose income. This could have produced misleading results and ignored the contribution of income in diet quality. Further research in a larger sample size from multiple rural and remote regions would support stratifying diet quality results according to all levels of rurality (regional, rural, remote and very remote populations), which would enhance the sensitivity of our analyses. Additionally, future research may consider not grouping health conditions into predefined groups, so a more thorough exploration between diet quality and health outcomes can be prioritised.

5. Conclusions

This present study suggested that the diet quality in our sample of rural and urban Australian adults was classified as *"getting there"*, and that rurality did not influence diet quality in this sample. It highlighted that living alone may be a primary driver of diet quality and this sociodemographic characteristic should be investigated further in future research. Additionally, multimorbidity was associated with reduced diet quality, suggesting that efforts must be made to assist Australian adults living with chronic diseases to improve their diet quality, potentially improving their health outcomes. Further studies of diet quality that specifically represent the diverse experiences of Australians living in rural or remote locations are required.

Author Contributions: Conceptualization, T.L.S. and L.J.B.; methodology, T.L.S. and L.J.B.; software, R.P.; formal analysis, R.P.; investigation, T.L.S. and L.J.B.; resources, T.L.S. and L.J.B.; data curation, R.P.; writing—original draft preparation, R.P.; writing—review and editing, R.P., K.K., M.J.S., T.L.S. and L.J.B.; visualization, R.P., K.K., M.J.S., T.L.S. and L.J.B.; supervision, M.J.S. and K.K.; project administration, T.L.S. and L.J.B.; funding acquisition, T.L.S. and L.J.B. All authors have read and agreed to the published version of the manuscript.

Funding: The Article Processing Charge was funded by School of Health Sciences, University of Tasmania.

Institutional Review Board Statement: This study was conducted according to the guidelines of the Declaration of Helsinki, and approved by the University of Newcastle Human Research Ethics Committee (H2017-10979, 2017).

Informed Consent Statement: Informed consent was obtained from all subjects involved in the study.

Data Availability Statement: The data presented in this study may be available on request from the Chief Investigator Associate Professor Leanne Brown. The data are not publicly available due to privacy.

Acknowledgments: The author thanks Denis Visentin for his support during analysis of data.

Conflicts of Interest: The authors declare no conflict of interest.

References

1. Kraemer, K.; Cordaro, J.; Fanzo, J.; Gibney, M.; Kennedy, E.; Labrique, A.; Steffen, J.; Eggersdorfer, M. Diet and non-communicable diseases: An urgent need for new paradigms. In *Good Nutrition: Perspectives for the 21st Century*; Basel: New York, NY, USA, 2016; pp. 105–118. ISBN 978-3-318-05964-9.
2. Australian Institute of Health and Welfare. Australian Burden of Disease Study 2018: Key Findings. Available online: https://www.aihw.gov.au/getmedia/d2a1886d-c673-44aa-9eb6-857e9696fd83/aihw-bod-30.pdf.aspx?inline=true (accessed on 28 September 2021).

3. Murray, C.J.; Aravkin, A.Y.; Zheng, P.; Abbafati, C.; Abbas, K.M.; Abbasi-Kangevari, M.; Abd-Allah, F.; Abdelalim, A.; Abdollahi, M.; Abdollahpour, I. Global burden of 87 risk factors in 204 countries and territories, 1990–2019: A systematic analysis for the Global Burden of Disease Study 2019. *Lancet* **2020**, *396*, 1223–1249. [CrossRef]
4. Willey, J.; Wakefield, M.; Silver, H.J. Exploring the Diets of Adults with Obesity and Type II Diabetes from Nine Diverse Countries: Dietary Intakes, Patterns, and Quality. *Nutrients* **2020**, *12*, 2027. [CrossRef] [PubMed]
5. Fernstrom, M.H.; Reed, K.A.; Rahavi, E.B.; Dooher, C.C. Communication strategies to help reduce the prevalence of non-communicable diseases: Proceedings from the inaugural IFIC Foundation Global Diet and Physical Activity Communications Summit. *Nutr. Rev.* **2012**, *70*, 301–310. [CrossRef]
6. Alston, L.; Partridge, S.R. Limited dietary interventions in rural Australian communities: A systematic review. *Nutr. Diet* **2021**, *78*, 57–68. [CrossRef] [PubMed]
7. Afshin, A.; Sur, P.J.; Fay, K.A.; Cornaby, L.; Ferrara, G.; Salama, J.S.; Mullany, E.C.; Abate, K.H.; Abbafati, C.; Abebe, Z. Health effects of dietary risks in 195 countries, 1990–2017: A systematic analysis for the Global Burden of Disease Study 2017. *Lancet* **2019**, *393*, 1958–1972. [CrossRef]
8. Schulze, M.B.; Martínez-González, M.A.; Fung, T.T.; Lichtenstein, A.H.; Forouhi, N.G. Food based dietary patterns and chronic disease prevention. *BMJ* **2018**, *361*, k2396. [CrossRef]
9. Australian Institute of Health and Welfare. Australia's Health 2018. Available online: https://www.aihw.gov.au/reports/australias-health/australias-health-2018/contents/table-of-contents (accessed on 11 April 2021).
10. Australian Institute of Health and Welfare. Australian Burden of Disease Study—Impact and Causes of Illness and Death in Australia 2015. Available online: https://www.aihw.gov.au/getmedia/c076f42f-61ea-4348-9c0a-d996353e838f/aihw-bod-22.pdf.aspx?inline=true (accessed on 4 April 2021).
11. Australian Institute of Health and Welfare. Rural and Remote Health. Available online: https://www.aihw.gov.au/reports/rural-remote-australians/rural-remote-health/contents/health-status-and-outcomes (accessed on 2 February 2021).
12. Barclay, L.; Phillips, A.; Lyle, D. Rural and remote health research: Does the investment match the need? *AJRH* **2018**, *26*, 74–79. [CrossRef] [PubMed]
13. Brooke, F. Food Security and Health in Rural and Remote Australia. Available online: https://apo.org.au/sites/default/files/resource-files/2016-11/apo-nid70483.pdf (accessed on 2 February 2021).
14. Burns, C.M.; Gibbon, P.; Boak, R.; Baudinette, S.; Dunbar, J.A. Food cost and availability in a rural setting in Australia. *Rural Remote Health* **2004**, *4*, 311. [CrossRef]
15. Burgis-Kasthala, S.; Slimings, C.; Smith, M.; Elmitt, N.; Moore, M. Social and community networks influence dietary attitudes in regional New South Wales, Australia. *Rural Remote Health* **2019**, *19*, 5328. [CrossRef]
16. Whelan, J.; Millar, L.; Bell, C.; Russell, C.; Grainger, F.; Allender, S.; Love, P. You can't find healthy food in the bush: Poor accessibility, availability and adequacy of food in rural Australia. *Int. J. Environ. Res. Public Health* **2018**, *15*, 2316. [CrossRef]
17. Alston, L.; Jacobs, J.; Allender, S.; Nichols, M. A comparison of the modelled impacts on CVD mortality if attainment of public health recommendations was achieved in metropolitan and rural Australia. *Public Health Nutr.* **2020**, *23*, 339–347. [CrossRef]
18. Jacobs, D.R., Jr.; Steffen, L.M. Nutrients, foods, and dietary patterns as exposures in research: A framework for food synergy. *Am. J. Clin. Nutr.* **2003**, *78*, 508s–513s. [CrossRef] [PubMed]
19. Tapsell, L.C.; Neale, E.P.; Satija, A.; Hu, F.B. Foods, nutrients, and dietary patterns: Interconnections and implications for dietary guidelines. *Adv. Nutr.* **2016**, *7*, 445–454. [CrossRef] [PubMed]
20. Cespedes, E.M.; Hu, F.B. Dietary patterns: From nutritional epidemiologic analysis to national guidelines. *AJCN* **2015**, *101*, 899–900. [CrossRef]
21. Hu, F.B. Dietary pattern analysis: A new direction in nutritional epidemiology. *Curr. Opin. Lipidol.* **2002**, *13*, 3–9. [CrossRef] [PubMed]
22. Guerrero, M.L.P.; Pérez-Rodríguez, F.; Hueda, M. Diet quality indices for nutrition assessment: Types and applications. In *Functional Food-Improve Health through Adequate Food*; IntechOpen: London, UK, 2017; pp. 283–308. [CrossRef]
23. Alkerwi, A. Diet quality concept. *Nutrition* **2014**, *30*, 613–618. [CrossRef]
24. Reedy, J.; Krebs-Smith, S.M.; Miller, P.E.; Liese, A.D.; Kahle, L.L.; Park, Y.; Subar, A.F. Higher diet quality is associated with decreased risk of all-cause, cardiovascular disease, and cancer mortality among older adults. *J. Nutr.* **2014**, *144*, 881–889. [CrossRef]
25. Russell, J.; Flood, V.; Rochtchina, E.; Gopinath, B.; Allman-Farinelli, M.; Bauman, A.; Mitchell, P. Adherence to dietary guidelines and 15-year risk of all-cause mortality. *Br. J. Nutr.* **2013**, *109*, 547–555. [CrossRef]
26. Panagiotakos, D. α-Priori versus α-posterior methods in dietary pattern analysis: A review in nutrition epidemiology. *Nutr. Bull.* **2008**, *33*, 311–315. [CrossRef]
27. University of Newcastle. Healthy Eating Quiz. Available online: https://healthyeatingquiz.com.au/ (accessed on 5 May 2021).
28. Collins, C.E.; Burrows, T.L.; Rollo, M.E.; Boggess, M.M.; Watson, J.F.; Guest, M.; Duncanson, K.; Pezdirc, K.; Hutchesson, M.J. The comparative validity and reproducibility of a diet quality index for adults: The Australian recommended food score. *Nutrients* **2015**, *7*, 785–798. [CrossRef]
29. Harris, P.A.; Taylor, R.; Thielke, R.; Payne, J.; Gonzalez, N.; Conde, J.G. Research electronic data capture (REDCap)—A metadata-driven methodology and workflow process for providing translational research informatics support. *J. Biomed. Inform.* **2009**, *42*, 377–381. [CrossRef] [PubMed]

30. Harris, P.A.; Taylor, R.; Minor, B.L.; Elliott, V.; Fernandez, M.; O'Neal, L.; McLeod, L.; Delacqua, G.; Delacqua, F.; Kirby, J.; et al. The REDCap consortium: Building an international community of software platform partners. *J. Biomed. Inform.* **2019**, *95*, 103208. [CrossRef] [PubMed]
31. National Health and Medical Research Council. Australian Dietary Guidelines—Providing the Scientific Evidence for Healthier Australian Diets. Available online: https://www.nhmrc.gov.au/adg (accessed on 29 April 2021).
32. Ashton, L.; Williams, R.; Wood, L.; Schumacher, T.; Burrows, T.; Rollo, M.; Pezdirc, K.; Callister, R.; Collins, C. Comparison of australian recommended food score (ARFS) and plasma carotenoid concentrations: A validation study in adults. *Nutrients* **2017**, *9*, 888. [CrossRef]
33. Williams, R.L.; Rollo, M.E.; Schumacher, T.; Collins, C.E. Diet quality scores of australian adults who have completed the healthy eating quiz. *Nutrients* **2017**, *9*, 880. [CrossRef] [PubMed]
34. Aljadani, H.M.; Sibbritt, D.; Patterson, A.; Collins, C. The Australian Recommended Food Score did not predict weight gain in middle-aged Australian women during six years of follow-up. *Aust. N. Z. J. Public Health* **2013**, *37*, 322–328. [CrossRef] [PubMed]
35. World Health Organisation. Body Mass Index—BMI. Available online: https://www.euro.who.int/en/health-topics/disease-prevention/nutrition/a-healthy-lifestyle/body-mass-index-bmi (accessed on 29 April 2021).
36. Australian Institute of Health and Welfare. Rural, Regional and Remote Health—A Guide to Remoteness Classifications. Available online: https://www.ruralhealth.org.au/sites/default/files/other-bodies/other-bodies-04-03-01.pdf (accessed on 3 March 2021).
37. McGrail, M.R.; Humphreys, J.S. Geographical classifications to guide rural health policy in Australia. *Aust. N. Z. Health Policy* **2009**, *6*, 1–7. [CrossRef]
38. Dupont, W.D.; Plummer, W.D., Jr. Power and sample size calculations: A review and computer program. *Control. Clin. Trials* **1990**, *11*, 116–128. [CrossRef]
39. Thorpe, M.G.; Milte, C.M.; Crawford, D.; McNaughton, S.A. Education and lifestyle predict change in dietary patterns and diet quality of adults 55 years and over. *Nutr. J.* **2019**, *18*, 67. [CrossRef]
40. National Rural Health Alliance. Food Security and Health in Rural and Remote Australia. Available online: https://www.agrifutures.com.au/wp-content/uploads/publications/16-053.pdf (accessed on 5 May 2021).
41. Thorpe, M.G.; Milte, C.M.; Crawford, D.; McNaughton, S.A. A revised Australian dietary guideline index and its association with key sociodemographic factors, health behaviors and body mass index in peri-retirement aged adults. *Nutrients* **2016**, *8*, 160. [CrossRef]
42. Arabshahi, S.; Lahmann, P.H.; Williams, G.M.; Marks, G.C.; van der Pols, J.C. Longitudinal change in diet quality in australian adults varies by demographic, socio-economic, and lifestyle characteristics. *J. Nutr.* **2011**, *141*, 1871–1879. [CrossRef]
43. Grech, A.; Sui, Z.; Siu, H.Y.; Zheng, M.; Allman-Farinelli, M.; Rangan, A. Socio-Demographic Determinants of Diet Quality in Australian Adults Using the Validated Healthy Eating Index for Australian Adults (HEIFA-2013). *Healthcare* **2017**, *5*, 7. [CrossRef] [PubMed]
44. Baldwin, J.N.; Forder, P.M.; Haslam, R.L.; Hure, A.J.; Loxton, D.J.; Patterson, A.J.; Collins, C.E. Change in Diet Quality over 12 Years in the 1946–1951 Cohort of the Australian Longitudinal Study on Women's Health. *Nutrients* **2020**, *12*, 147. [CrossRef]
45. McNaughton, S.A.; Ball, K.; Crawford, D.; Mishra, G.D. An index of diet and eating patterns is a valid measure of diet quality in an Australian population. *J. Nutr.* **2008**, *138*, 86–93. [CrossRef]
46. Zarrin, R.; Ibiebele, T.I.; Marks, G.C. Development and validity assessment of a diet quality index for Australians. *Asia Pac. J. Clin. Nutr.* **2013**, *22*, 177–187. [PubMed]
47. Backholer, K.; Spencer, E.; Gearon, E.; Magliano, D.J.; McNaughton, S.A.; Shaw, J.E.; Peeters, A. The association between socio-economic position and diet quality in Australian adults. *Public Health Nutr.* **2016**, *19*, 477–485. [CrossRef] [PubMed]
48. Hendrie, G.A.; Baird, D.; Golley, R.K.; Noakes, M. The CSIRO healthy diet score: An online survey to estimate compliance with the Australian dietary guidelines. *Nutrients* **2017**, *9*, 47. [CrossRef] [PubMed]
49. Bivoltsis, A.; Trapp, G.S.A.; Knuiman, M.; Hooper, P.; Ambrosini, G.L. Can a simple dietary index derived from a sub-set of questionnaire items assess diet quality in a sample of australian adults? *Nutrients* **2018**, *10*, 486. [CrossRef]
50. Australian Institute of Health and Welfare. Poor Diet. Available online: https://www.aihw.gov.au/getmedia/f30d2eb2-b6e7-43cc-aba4-74802ad78f6a/Poor-diet.pdf.aspx?inline=true (accessed on 18 May 2021).
51. Nichols, T.; Craike, M.; Thevios, I.; Calder, R. Nutrition Policy in Australia: Adopting a Harm Minimisation Approach. Available online: https://www.vu.edu.au/sites/default/files/nutrition-policy-australia-harm-minimsation-approach-policy-evidence-brief.pdf (accessed on 18 May 2021).
52. Arabshahi, S.; van der Pols, J.C.; Williams, G.M.; Marks, G.C.; Lahmann, P.H. Diet quality and change in anthropometric measures: 15-year longitudinal study in Australian adults. *Br. J. Nutr.* **2012**, *107*, 1376–1385. [CrossRef]
53. Imamura, F.; Micha, R.; Khatibzadeh, S.; Fahimi, S.; Shi, P.; Powles, J.; Mozaffarian, D.; Global Burden of Diseases, N.; Chronic Diseases Expert, G. Dietary quality among men and women in 187 countries in 1990 and 2010: A systematic assessment. *Lancet Glob. Health* **2015**, *3*, e132–e142. [CrossRef]
54. Alston, L.; Walker, T.; Kent, K. Characterizing Dietary Intakes in Rural Australian Adults: A Systematic Literature Review. *Nutrients* **2020**, *12*, 3515. [CrossRef]
55. Martin, J.C.; Moran, L.J.; Teede, H.J.; Ranasinha, S.; Lombard, C.B.; Harrison, C.L. Exploring diet quality between urban and rural dwelling women of reproductive age. *Nutrients* **2017**, *9*, 586. [CrossRef] [PubMed]

56. Hunter, W.; McNaughton, S.; Crawford, D.; Ball, K. Does food planning mediate the association between living arrangements and fruit and vegetable consumption among women aged 40 years and older? *Appetite* **2010**, *54*, 533–537. [CrossRef] [PubMed]
57. Williams, L.; Ball, K.; Crawford, D. Why do some socioeconomically disadvantaged women eat better than others? An investigation of the personal, social and environmental correlates of fruit and vegetable consumption. *Appetite* **2010**, *55*, 441–446. [CrossRef] [PubMed]
58. Temple, J.B. Household factors associated with older Australian's purchasing a varied diet: Results from household expenditure data. *Nutr. Diet* **2006**, *63*, 28–35. [CrossRef]
59. Ball, K.; Mishra, G.D.; Thane, C.W.; Hodge, A. How well do Australian women comply with dietary guidelines? *Public Health Nutr.* **2004**, *7*, 443–452. [CrossRef] [PubMed]
60. Hanna, K.L.; Collins, P.F. Relationship between living alone and food and nutrient intake. *Nutr. Rev.* **2015**, *73*, 594–611. [CrossRef] [PubMed]
61. Dunford, E.K.; Ni Mhurchu, C.; Huang, L.; Vandevijvere, S.; Swinburn, B.; Pravst, I.; Tolentino-Mayo, L.; Reyes, M.; L'Abbé, M.; Neal, B.C. A comparison of the healthiness of packaged foods and beverages from 12 countries using the Health Star Rating nutrient profiling system, 2013–2018. *Obes. Rev.* **2019**, *20*, 107–115. [CrossRef] [PubMed]
62. Machado, P.P.; Steele, E.M.; Levy, R.B.; Sui, Z.; Rangan, A.; Woods, J.; Gill, T.; Scrinis, G.; Monteiro, C.A. Ultra-processed foods and recommended intake levels of nutrients linked to non-communicable diseases in Australia: Evidence from a nationally representative cross-sectional study. *BMJ Open* **2019**, *9*, e029544. [CrossRef]
63. Higgs, S.; Ruddock, H. Social influences on eating. In *Handbook of Eating and Drinking: Interdisciplinary Perspectives*; Springer: Berlin/Heidelberg, Germany, 2020; pp. 277–291.
64. Elstgeest, L.E.M.; Mishra, G.D.; Dobson, A.J. Transitions in Living Arrangements Are Associated with Changes in Dietary Patterns in Young Women. *J. Nutr.* **2012**, *142*, 1561–1567. [CrossRef]
65. Roos, E.; Lahelma, E.; Virtanen, M.; Prättälä, R.; Pietinen, P. Gender, socioeconomic status and family status as determinants of food behaviour. *Soc. Sci. Med.* **1998**, *46*, 1519–1529. [CrossRef]
66. Sotos-Prieto, M.; Bhupathiraju, S.N.; Mattei, J.; Fung, T.T.; Li, Y.; Pan, A.; Willett, W.C.; Rimm, E.B.; Hu, F.B. Association of changes in diet quality with total and cause-specific mortality. *N. Engl. J. Med.* **2017**, *377*, 143–153. [CrossRef] [PubMed]
67. Fanelli, S.M.; Jonnalagadda, S.S.; Pisegna, J.L.; Kelly, O.J.; Krok-Schoen, J.L.; Taylor, C.A. Poorer Diet Quality Observed Among US Adults with a Greater Number of Clinical Chronic Disease Risk Factors. *J. PrimCare Community Health* **2020**, *11*, 2150132720945898. [CrossRef] [PubMed]

nutrients

MDPI

Article

Do Older Women of Reproductive Age Have Better Diet Quality than Younger Women of Reproductive Age?

Nahal Habibi [1,2], Katherine M. Livingstone [3], Suzanne Edwards [4] and Jessica A. Grieger [1,2,*]

1 Robinson Research Institute, University of Adelaide, Adelaide, SA 5005, Australia; nahal.habibi@adelaide.edu.au
2 Adelaide Medical School, University of Adelaide, Adelaide, SA 5005, Australia
3 Institute for Physical Activity and Nutrition, School of Exercise and Nutrition Sciences, Deakin University, Geelong, VIC 3220, Australia; k.livingstone@deakin.edu.au
4 Adelaide Health Technology Assessment (AHTA), University of Adelaide, Adelaide, SA 5005, Australia; suzanne.edwards@adelaide.edu.au
* Correspondence: jessica.grieger@adelaide.edu.au

Abstract: There is increasing recognition of the importance of nutrition for reproductive health, but little is known regarding the diet quality of younger vs. older reproductive aged women, and how their intakes relate to dietary recommendations. The purpose of the study was to examine the diets of younger (19–35 years old) compared to older (35–50 years old) reproductive aged women, and how they align with dietary recommendations. Women aged 19–50 years from the 2011–13 Australian National Nutrition and Physical Activity Survey were included (n = 2323). Dietary intakes were assessed by a single 24-h dietary recall and were compared to (i) Australian Dietary Guidelines; (ii) Acceptable Macronutrient Distribution for protein, carbohydrates, and fat; and (iii) Dietary Guideline Index (DGI). Regression analyses comparing younger and older women against recommendations were undertaken, with confounders determined a priori. There was no difference between older and younger women in meeting food group recommendations, with 26% of all women meeting recommendations for fruit, and meat and alternatives, and <20% meeting recommendations for vegetables and alternatives, grains, and dairy. Although there was no difference between older and younger women in total DGI score (mean (SE) 75.6 (1.7) vs. 74.5 (2.5), $p > 0.05$), older women had higher component scores in limiting saturated fat, consuming low-fat milk, and limiting adding salt during cooking. Continued health promotion for women of reproductive age should be a key priority to improve their own health and that of future generations.

Keywords: Australia; dietary guidelines; dietary guideline index; dietary intake; nutrients; reproductive age; women; nutrition survey

Citation: Habibi, N.; Livingstone, K.M.; Edwards, S.; Grieger, J.A. Do Older Women of Reproductive Age Have Better Diet Quality than Younger Women of Reproductive Age? *Nutrients* **2021**, *13*, 3830. https://doi.org/10.3390/nu13113830

Academic Editor: Clare Collins

Received: 25 August 2021
Accepted: 23 October 2021
Published: 27 October 2021

1. Introduction

Over the last several decades, worldwide fertility rates have declined across all age groups, with largest decreases occurring in women younger than 35 years, whereas those aged 35 years and over effectively plateauing since 1995 [1]. Childbearing over 35 years of age is increasingly common in Australia [2], with around 20% of births in women aged 35 years and over [3].

There is increasing recognition of the importance of nutrition for reproductive health [4]. Observational studies have consistently shown associations between poorer food choices or unhealthier dietary patterns and higher risk for infertility [5–7], gestational diabetes (reviewed in [8,9]) and preterm birth [10], but also contributing to poorer outcomes for the offspring, including increased risk for low birth weight [11], child allergy [12], and child adiposity [13].

Reproductive life stages include the preconception period, pregnancy and postpartum. Across any of the specific stages, studies have demonstrated inadequate dietary quality [14–17]. However, little is known about food intake during childbearing years and whether this differs between younger and older age groups. Data from the Australian Longitudinal Study on Women's Health (n = 18,226) found that the majority of women (aged 31–36 years or 50–55 years), tended to consume intakes below the Australian recommended daily servings for all food groups, except for fruit intake, among pregnant women aged 31–36 years [18]. Women aged 25 to 30 years who had given birth in the last 12 months also reported to have greater median daily servings of breads and cereals, vegetables, dairy, meat and extras (i.e., foods outside of the core/basic five food groups) compared to women not trying to, or women who were recently pregnant [19]. Data from NHANES women aged 15–65 years (n = 6894), found that irrespective of age, more than half of the women were at risk of nutrient inadequacy, with insufficient intakes from food for vitamin D, vitamin E, magnesium, vitamin A, calcium, and vitamin C [20]. While compliance with dietary guidelines provides insight into dietary habits and population intakes, assessing diet quality within populations provides a holistic assessment of food intake and nutrient adequacy. Few studies however have reported on this in women of reproductive age. A small study in Australian women reported no difference in total diet quality between urban and rural women of reproductive age, aged between 18–50 years [21].

Reproductive aged women are in a critical life stage and have distinct and specific nutritional needs. They play diverse roles including planning or transitioning during pregnancies [22], being a role model to their children [4], and they are more likely to prepare meals for their family [5]. Women of reproductive age contribute to the highest rise in obesity prevalence [23], and also have increasing prevalence of other chronic disease–related risk factors such as diabetes, high cholesterol, and asthma [24]. Yet, we have little understanding regarding the diet quality of these women, nor how their intakes relate to dietary recommendations. We hypothesise that older women will be more likely to meet dietary recommendations and have better diet quality than younger women. The aim of this study is to examine how the diets of younger and older reproductive aged women participating in the 2011–13 Australian Health Survey compare with current food group recommendations and with the Dietary Guideline Index (DGI), as a means to understand overall diet quality. A secondary aim is to explore whether the younger and older age women who have children, have different diet quality compared to women without children.

2. Materials and Methods

2.1. Data and Study Population

Data was used from a sub-set of women participating in the 2011–13 Australian Health Survey: the Australian National Nutrition and Physical Activity Survey (NNPAS) [25]. In the NNPAS, a total of 14,363 private dwellings were selected in the sample (reduced to an actual sample of 12,366 dwellings after sample loss in the field stage), in which 77.0% were fully or adequately responding households to the first interview (n = 9519). Inclusion criteria for the current study was females aged 19 to 50 years and currently menstruating (n = 2323). Women were excluded if they were pregnant or breastfeeding as nutritional requirements are generally higher for these women (n = 228) [26], or if they were current or post-menopausal (n = 1993). Women were split into two groups: younger women aged 19 to 35 years, and women of advanced age, >35–50 years. The Census and Statistics Act, 1905 provided the Australian Bureau of Statistics with the authority to conduct NNPAS, with all respondents providing written informed consent.

Sociodemographic variables including age, country of birth (Australia; main English-speaking countries [Canada, Ireland, New Zealand, South Africa, UK, USA]; other), household type (person living alone; couple only; couple family with children; one parent family with children; unrelated persons aged 15+ only, all other households), education, and anthropometric data (height, weight) were collected by trained interviewers. Socioeconomic status was based on the Index of Relative Socio-Economic Disadvantage (IRSD). The IRSD ranks Australian areas according to relative socioeconomic disadvantage, obtained from four indices of disadvantage including low income, low educational achievement, high unemployment, and jobs in relatively unskilled occupations [25]. Smoking status was defined as daily, weekly or less than weekly current smoker, ex-smoker or never smoked. Physical activity was reported as whether individuals met the minimum recommendation of moderate intensity of physical activity for 150 min during the last week [27]. Supplement intake, and food and beverage intake data were collected using a 24-h recall, as described below.

2.2. *Dietary Intake*

In the survey, 2 × 24-h dietary recalls were administered by trained and experienced interviewers using the Automated Multiple-Pass Method (AMPM), to collect dietary information for food, beverages, and supplements. The AMPM method is an automated questionnaire to help respondents maximise responses regarding their prior food intake [28]. A Food Model Booklet was used to assist respondents to select the most appropriate amount consumed for each food and beverage. For the current analysis, only dietary data from the first day of collection was included since a single day's intake is sufficient to estimate population mean intake [29], and because Friday and Saturday intakes were under-represented due to the lower number of recalls performed on Saturdays and Sundays.

2.3. *Australian Dietary Recommendations*

The Australian Dietary Guidelines recommend food and beverage choices from the five core food groups and to limit discretionary choices [30]. Dietary intake of core food groups including vegetables and legumes/beans, fruits, grains, meat and alternatives (meat and poultry, fish, eggs, tofu, nuts and seeds and legumes/beans) and dairy in servings/day, and discretionary nutrients such as free sugars (% daily energy intake), sodium (mg/day), saturated fatty acids (SFA) (% daily energy intake), and alcohol (g/day) were obtained from the 24 hr recall and examined against the Australian Guide to Healthy Eating (AGHE) [30]. The AGHE defines types and amounts of foods that adult women should consume in order to meet dietary intakes. Macronutrient recommendations were based on the Acceptable Macronutrient Distribution (AMDR) for protein, carbohydrates, and fat [31]. The AMDR describes the acceptable percentage of energy from protein, carbohydrates, and fat as 15–25%, 45–65%, and 20–35% of total daily energy, respectively.

2.4. *Dietary Guidelines Index*

The DGI is a food-based score designed to reflect the diet quality of subjects according to compliance with the 2013 ADG for Australian adults [30]. The dietary intakes gathered from the 24-h recall and brief questionnaire were scored based on recommended dietary components (food variety, fruit, vegetables, cereals, meat and alternatives, dairy and alternatives, and fluid intake) and discretionary nutrients (SFA, unsaturated fat, added salt, extra sugar, and alcohol). The DGI used in the present study was based on the DGI-2013 [32], and adapted from a food frequency questionnaires, for use in the present 24-h recall [33]. The score of each item was calculated out of 10, such that a score of zero indicated that the guideline was not met. Where there was age- or sex-specific dietary recommendations provided by the ADG, cut-offs were used to acquire the maximum score for each component. For recommended dietary components, scores were calculated proportionally to the maximum scoring criteria. Scoring of discretionary foods, saturated and unsaturated fat, salt, sugar, and alcohol was either 0 or 10. The DGI scores ranged from 0 to 130 with a higher score indicating better diet quality.

2.5. *Statistical Analyses*

Throughout the analysis of this study (for both descriptive and inferential statistics) Survey weightings that were calibrated against population benchmarks (i.e., age, sex and area of usual residence) were used to account for the complex survey design [25,34]. Both base weight and 60 replicate weights have been incorporated into all estimations.

Population characteristics and dietary intakes were reported as *n* (%), mean (standard error, SE), and median (interquartile range, IQR). Binary and ordinal logistic regressions were used to determine the likelihood of meeting dietary recommendations between the younger and older age groups, both in unadjusted and adjusted models. A directed acyclic graph was used to determine covariates in the adjusted analyses, which included BMI, country of birth, household type, level of education (postgraduate degree/diploma/certificate, graduate degree, certificate, or school qualification or lower), SEIFA, smoking status, alcohol (except when it was the outcome), physical activity and supplements use. Adjusted linear regression was performed to assess the mean difference between age groups for total and sub-component DGI score outcomes. Separate unadjusted and adjusted binary and ordinal logistic models were undertaken for the interaction between age categories (binary) and child in household (yes/no) to examine relationships with the meeting of dietary recommendations. Similar interactions were included in adjusted linear models with total and sub-component DGI score outcomes. All data were analysed using the statistical software SAS 9.4 (SAS Institute Inc., Cary, NC, USA).

3. Results

3.1. Participant Characteristics

Table 1 shows the demographic characteristics of the 2323 reproductive age women participating in the Australian Health Survey, Nutrition and Physical Activity, 2011–13. The mean (SE) age of the women was 33.9 (1.2) years and majority (71.1%) were born in Australia. Half of the women (49.1%) were aged 19 to 35 years with a mean (SE) age and BMI of 26.7 (0.8) years and 25.2 (0.8) kg/m^2, respectively. The mean (SE) age and BMI of the older women (35 to 50 y) was 42.6 (0.5) years and 27.2 (0.7) kg/m^2, respectively. A higher percentage of the older women tended to have overweight or obesity, and reported to live as a couple with children (Table 1).

Table 1. Characteristics of reproductive age women participating in the Australian Health Survey, Nutrition and Physical Activity, 2011–12.

Characteristics		Frequency (%) or Mean (SE)		
		Total Population, *n* = 2323	**19–35 Years, *n* = 1141**	**35–50 Years, *n* = 1182**
Age (year)		33.9 (1.2) [1]	26.7 (0.8) [1]	42.6 (0.5) [1]
BMI (kg/m^2)		*n* = 1988	*n* = 1017	*n* = 971
		26.1 (0.4) [1]	25.2 (0.8) [1]	27.2 (0.7) [1]
	Underweight	51 (3.1)	42 (4.6)	9 (1.3)
	Normal weight	946 (50.5)	522 (55.9)	424 (43.5)
	Overweight	508 (24.2)	231 (20.5)	277 (28.9)
	Obesity	483 (22.2)	222 (19.0)	261 (26.4)
Country of birth	Australia	1706 (71.1)	860 (73.5)	846 (68.3)
	Main English-speaking countries [2]	224 (10.4)	93 (8.2)	131 (13.0)
	Other	393 (18.5)	188 (18.3)	205 (18.7)
Household type	Person living alone	323 (7.2)	139 (6.1)	184 (8.6)
	Couple only	338 (13.6)	221 (17.4)	117 (9.0)
	Couple family with children	965 (51.4)	397 (43.9)	568 (60.5)
	One parent family with children	445 (12.8)	199 (12.3)	246 (13.4)
	All other households [3]	252 (14.9)	185 (20.3)	67 (8.5)
Level of education		*n* = 2300	*n* = 1132	*n* = 1168
	Postgraduate degree (Diploma/Certificate)	233 (9.2)	86 (7.3)	147 (11.4)
	Graduate degree	831 (36.5)	412 (36.1)	419 (36.9)
	Certificate	510 (24.0)	285 (27.8)	225 (19.4)
	School qualification or lower	726 (30.3)	349 (28.8)	377 (32.3)

Table 1. *Cont.*

Characteristics		Frequency (%) or Mean (SE)		
		Total Population, n = 2323	19–35 Years, n = 1141	35–50 Years, n = 1182
SEIFA 2011—IRSD [4]	Quintile 1	418 (17.3)	233 (19.6)	185 (14.5)
	Quintile 2	420 (17.6)	218 (18.6)	202 (16.3)
	Quintile 3	476 (21.6)	237 (23.0)	239 (19.9)
	Quintile 4	416 (18.6)	182 (16.0)	234 (21.8)
	Quintile 5	593 (24.9)	271 (22.8)	322 (27.4)
Smoking status	Current smoker, daily	442 (16.5)	226 (18.1)	216 (14.6)
	Current smoker, weekly [5]	41 (1.4)	25 (1.7)	16 (1.1)
	Current smoker, less than weekly	18 (1.1)	15 (1.6)	3 (0.4)
	Ex-smoker	535 (22.4)	189 (16.2)	346 (29.8)
	Never smoked	1287 (58.6)	686 (62.4)	601 (54.1)
Meeting minimum physical activity requirement [6]		n = 2312	n = 1136	n = 1176
	Yes	1236 (53.6)	626 (55.7)	610 (51.1)
	No	1076 (46.4)	510 (44.3)	566 (48.9)
Supplement use	Yes	714 (28.9)	295 (25.5)	419 (33.1)
	No	1609 (71.1)	846 (74.5)	763 (66.9)

[1] Represents mean (SE); [2] Canada, Ireland, New Zealand, South Africa, United Kingdom and the United States of America; [3] All other households include Unrelated persons aged 15+ only and all other households, [4] Index of Relative Socio-Economic Disadvantage; [5] At least once a week but not daily; [6] Meeting the recommendation of physical activity for 150 min during the last week.

3.2. Food Intake Compared to AGHE Recommendations among All Women and by Age Group

Figure 1 displays the percentage of women meeting the AGHE recommended food group servings. Majority of women did not meet the minimum requirement for any of the five food groups. The highest percentage of women meeting recommendations was for meat and alternatives, and for fruit, at 26.9% and 26.2%, respectively. This was equivalent to a median (IQR) daily intake of meat and alternatives, and fruit, of 1.5 (0.7, 2.6) and 0.9 (0.0, 2.0) servings/day, respectively (Table 2). The lowest percentage of women who met recommendation was for vegetables (14.6%), equivalent to 2.1 (1.0, 3.7) servings/day (Table 2). Recommendations for grains and dairy was met by a respective 17.5% and 14.0%, of women. No significant differences were found between younger and older women in meeting AGHE recommendations (Table 3).

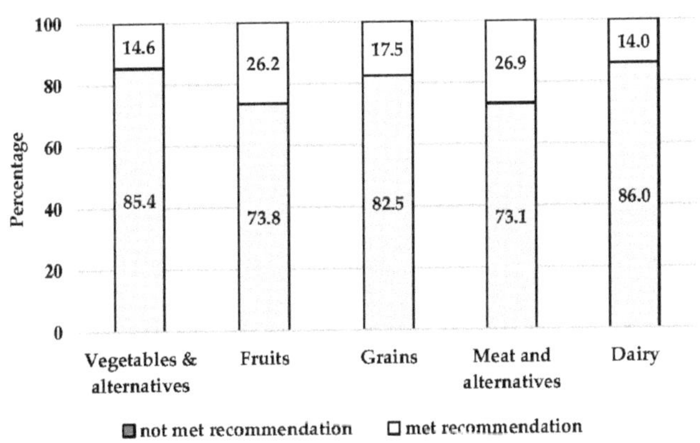

Figure 1. Adherence to food group recommendations in all reproductive age women (n = 2323). Australian Guide to Healthy Eating recommendations for vegetables & alternatives (≥5 servings), fruits (≥2 servings), grains (≥6 servings), meat and alternatives (≥2.5 servings), and dairy (≥2.5 servings).

Table 2. Food group intakes for the whole population and by age group.

		Daily Servings, Median (IQR)		
		Total Population, n = 2323	**19–35 Years, n = 1141**	**35–50 Years, n = 1182**
Food groups (serving/d)	Vegetables & alternatives	2.1 (1.0, 3.7)	1.9 (1.0, 3.7)	2.1 (1.0, 3.8)
	Fruits	0.9 (0.0, 2.0)	0.9 (0.0, 2.0)	0.9 (0.0, 2.0)
	Grains	3.4 (2.1, 5.1)	3.4 (2.2, 5.2)	3.4 (1.9, 5.1)
	Meat & alternatives	1.5 (0.7, 2.6)	1.5 (0.6, 2.5)	1.6 (0.8, 2.7)
	Dairy	1.1 (0.4, 1.9)	1.1 (0.4, 1.9)	1.1 (0.5, 1.9)
Macronutrients percentage (%)	Carbohydrate	44.7 (37.2, 51.3)	45.3 (38.4, 52.1)	43.6 (35.0, 50.1)
	Protein	17.7 (13.9, 21.5)	17.0 (13.5, 21.1)	18.2 (14.5, 22.1)
	Fat	31.4 (25.5, 37.0)	31.5 (25.6, 37.4)	31.2 (25.4, 36.6)
Discretionary choices	Percentage of energy from SFA	11.9 (8.7, 15.3)	12.2 (8.7, 15.3)	11.5 (8.5, 15.2)
	Percentage of energy from free sugars [1]	8.9 (4.7, 14.6)	9.9 (5.6, 15.8)	7.6 (4.0, 13.2)
	Sodium (mg/d)	1889.6 (1287.0, 2725.7)	1948.3 (1296.4, 2815.9)	1828.0 (1265.8, 2581.5)
	Alcohol (g/d)	0.0 (0.0, 0.1)	0.0 (0.0, 0.0)	0.0 (0.0, 13.6)
Dietary Guideline Index (total score)		76.3 (65.9, 85.8)	75.0 (64.4, 85.6)	77.5 (67.6, 86,1)

[1] Free sugars include added sugars, sugar component of honey, fruit juice and fruit juice concentrates, based on the definition by the World Health Organization.

Table 3. Odds ratios for adherence to AGHE and AMDR recommendations [1].

	Reference	Unadjusted OR (95% CI)	Adjusted [2] OR (95% CI)
Vegetables & alternatives	<5 servings/day	1.00 (0.49, 2.04)	1.16 (0.28, 4.81)
Fruits	<2 servings/day	1.01 (0.63, 1.64)	1.16 (0.68, 1.96)
Grains	<6 servings/day	0.99 (0.33, 2.97)	1.02 (0.30, 3.44)
Meat & alternatives	<2.5 servings/day	0.88 (0.57, 1.35)	0.87 (0.51, 1.48)
Dairy	<2.5 servings/day	0.81 (0.43, 1.52)	0.70 (0.25, 1.98)
Alcohol	<40 g/day	1.92 (0.54, 6.71)	2.32 (0.45, 11.96)
Sugar	<10% daily energy intake [3]	0.62 (0.25, 1.53)	0.69 (0.33, 1.44)
Sodium	<2000 mg/day	0.81 (0.48, 1.37)	0.82 (0.44, 1.52)
SFA	<10% daily energy intake	0.81 (0.48, 1.37)	0.82 (0.44, 1.52)
Carbohydrate	<45%	1.32 (0.80, 2.15)	1.13 (0.61, 2.08)
Protein	<15%	0.78 (0.50, 1.20)	0.75 (0.44, 1.28)
Fat	<20%	1.07 (0.70, 1.63)	1.07 (0.63, 1.82)

[1] Reference was 35–50 years compared to 19–35 years; all statistical differences between groups in unadjusted and adjusted analyses were $p > 0.05$, [2] Adjusted for country of birth, household type, level of education, SEIFA, smoking status, alcohol (except when it was the outcome), BMI, physical activity and supplements use, [3] based on World Health Organization definition.

3.3. Food Intakes Compared to AMDR Recommendations in All Women and by Age Group

The percentage of women meeting the AMDR is shown in Figure 2. Just over half of all women were within the AMDR for protein and fat and just under half were within the AMDR for carbohydrates. A third of women (31.5%) consumed less than the AMDR for protein but a third (32.9%) consumed higher than the AMDR for fat. There was no difference between younger and older women in meeting AMDR recommendations (Table 3).

3.4. Diet Quality and DGI Component Scores in All Women and by Age Group

Scores for both total DGI and its subcomponents are shown in Table 4. There was no significant difference for DGI total score between younger and older women. Compared to younger women, older women had higher DGI scores in limiting saturated fat, consuming low-fat milk, and limiting adding salt during cooking (Table 4).

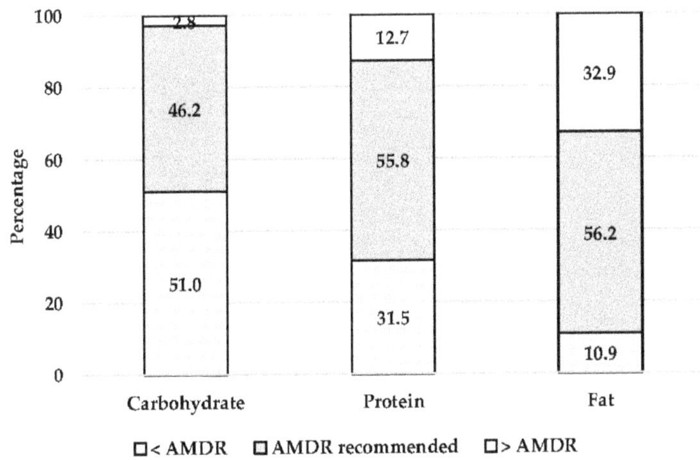

Figure 2. Percentage of daily energy from macronutrients in all reproductive age women (n = 2323). Acceptable macronutrient distribution range (AMDR) for carbohydrate (45–65%), protein (15–25%) and fat (20–35%).

Table 4. Dietary Guideline Index (DGI) and its components, by age groups (n = 2323).

DGI	Mean (SE)		Mean Difference (SE) [1,2]	*p*-Value
	19–35 Years (n = 1141)	35–50 Years (n = 1182)		
DGI (total score)	74.5 (2.5)	75.6 (1.7)	−0.54 (1.99)	0.79
DGI sub-components				
1. Food variety	1.9 (0.1)	2.3 (0.1)	−0.26 (0.27)	0.33
2. Vegetables	4.2 (0.2)	4.4 (0.3)	0.00 (0.49)	0.99
3. Fruit	4.8 (0.4)	4.8 (0.3)	0.12 (0.63)	0.84
4. Cereal (total)	3.6 (0.4)	3.3 (0.2)	0.15 (0.63)	0.80
4a. Serves per day	2.3 (0.2)	2.1 (0.2)	0.17 (0.37)	0.65
4b. Mostly wholegrain	1.2 (0.2)	1.2 (0.2)	−0.01 (0.31)	0.97
5. Meat and Alternatives (total)	7.0 (0.2)	7.3 (0.1)	−0.24 (0.33)	0.47
5a. Serves per day	2.5 (0.1)	2.8 (0.1)	−0.20 (0.20)	0.31
5b. Mostly lean	4.5 (0.1)	4.5 (0.1)	−0.03 (0.25)	0.89
6. Dairy and alternatives	4.9 (0.4)	5.0 (0.2)	−0.17 (0.41)	0.67
7. Fluid intake (total)	8.4 (0.1)	8.6 (0.2)	−0.17 (0.23)	0.44
7a. Serves per day	3.9 (0.1)	4.2 (0.2)	−0.24 (0.21)	0.26
7b. Mostly water	4.5 (0.1)	4.5 (0.1)	0.06 (0.11)	0.54
8. Limit discretionary foods	3.4 (0.7)	3.8 (0.3)	−0.55 (0.73)	0.45
9. Limit saturated fat (total)	7.8 (0.3)	8.5 (0.2)	−0.69 (0.33)	0.04
9a. Mostly trimmed meat	4.4 (0.1)	4.4 (0.1)	−0.07 (0.21)	0.74
9b. Mostly low-fat milk	3.4 (0.3)	4.0 (0.1)	−0.62 (0.28)	0.03
10. Moderate unsaturated-fat	7.9 (0.4)	7.6 (0.5)	0.36 (1.05)	0.73
11. Limit added salt (total)	5.9 (0.2)	6.1 (0.4)	−0.28 (0.32)	0.38
11a. During cooking	2.2 (0.2)	2.7 (0.3)	−0.47 (0.21)	0.03
11b. Added at the table	3.6 (0.1)	3.4 (0.2)	0.19 (0.22)	0.40
12. Limit extra sugar	6.2 (0.5)	6.8 (0.3)	−0.50 (0.56)	0.37
13. Limit alcohol	9.4 (0.3)	8.9 (0.2)	0.57 (0.45)	0.58

[1] Reference was 35–50 years, [2] Adjusted for country of birth, household type, level of education, SEIFA, smoking status, alcohol (except for when it was the outcome), BMI, physical activity and supplements use.

3.5. Sub Group Analyses in Women with and without Children

For women in any age group, there was no difference in meeting the AGHE food group serving recommendations, AMDR guidelines, or DGI score, if women had children or not (Supplementary Tables S1 and S2).

4. Discussion

Using the largest and most-recent Australian National Nutrition and Physical Activity Survey, our results do not support our hypothesis that older women are more likely to meet dietary recommendations or have better diet quality than younger women of reproductive age. There was also no difference in meeting dietary recommendations whether women had children or not. Our study reiterates the overall inadequate diet quality of women in Australia, but extends previous studies showing that older women, or women who have children, have no superior diets compared to younger women or those without children.

Our findings are not unique to the Australian population of reproductive aged women. Studies in women from low income [35,36] and high income [37] countries have reported similar findings with low consumption of fruits and vegetables, and higher intakes of junk foods and discretionary choices. Compared to data collected from earlier Australian surveys, in 4349 women aged 18–46 years from the Australian Resilience for Eating and Activity Despite Inequality study, >90% failed to meet the recommended guidelines for vegetables, grains, lean meat and alternatives, and dairy foods [38]. Data from the Australian Longitudinal Study on Women's Health (2001 to 2009) revealed that <2% of women aged 31–36 years or 50–55 years, met the Australian Dietary Guidelines recommendation of five daily servings of vegetables; and for women aged 31–36 years, less than one-third met recommendations for fruit and meat and alternatives [18]. The current analysis from the 2011 Australian Health Survey, reveals only 15% of women consumed adequate vegetable intake, with similar proportions of women still not meeting fruit, or meat and alternative groups compared to the Australian Longitudinal Study on Women's Health. Thus, little progress has been made among reproductive age women meeting nutrition recommendations, and substantial changes to their dietary intake are needed to meet these.

Novel to our study is that we reveal consistency in the proportion of younger and older women meeting dietary guidelines, and no superior diet quality in older women, apart from scoring higher for some components of the DGI including limiting saturated fat, higher consumption of low fat milk, and lower added salt during cooking. Although limiting both saturated fat and added salt is recommended in the Australian Dietary Guidelines [30], and low fat milk is recommended to lower saturated fat intake [30], the extent to which these sub components contribute to overall diet quality cannot be established from the data. Nevertheless, the demonstration that older women are not consuming better quality diets is intriguing. There are clear links between advancing age and reproductive health. Physiologically, older women have diminished ovarian reserve [39] and shorter menstrual cycles [40], which impact fertility. More older women are entering pregnancy than what they were decades ago [41], frequently with higher body weight and a greater number of pre-existing conditions [42], which associate with poor reproductive health outcomes [42]. Older women also have higher rates of numerous risk factors for chronic diseases [24]. Given that many women are unaware of the importance of lifestyle choices when planning a pregnancy [43,44], and that there are a number of perceived barriers relating to dietary behaviours [45], action is required to increase women's awareness and uptake of lifestyle advice and support [46].

Unique to our study is the report of no evidence of meeting dietary recommendations whether younger or older women had children or not. This has not been clearly assessed in previous studies. Parental influences play a large role in child feeding practices by deciding which foods are available and in what quantity [47,48]. Family eating habits have the greatest influence over young children's diets [49], and one study showed that dietary indicators of mothers was a strong predictor of children's dietary quality [50]. Although there is a large volume of research demonstrating the relationship between mothers' and children's food restraint and eating behaviours [51,52], no studies were found comparing dietary recommendations or quality between women with or without children. Our results reinforce the need for increased education to women and families to encourage healthy eating habits, as they are clear role models to their children. Our research also posits the need for research to examine relationships between mother-child diets.

Strengths of this study include the large nationally representative sample, generalisable to the broader Australian population of reproductive age women, and detailed sociodemographic and diet data. Specifically, the national survey collected food intake data in line with current Australian dietary recommendations, thereby providing easier translation of results. The systematic data collection methods employed within the Australian Health Survey allowed us to include appropriate confounding factors, reducing information bias. Limitations include the use of one-day dietary intake, thus not reflecting usual intake, along with a low sample of 24-hr recalls collected for Friday and Saturday [53]. This would likely underrepresent days where high intake of discretionary choices might be consumed. Although we adjusted analyses for several characteristics, the possibility of residual confounding impedes definitive conclusions about causality. The survey was conducted in 2011 and dietary intakes, along with changing societal behaviours such as prevalence of obesity and older maternal age, is likely to be different at present compared to 10 years ago.

5. Conclusions

In conclusion we report no differences between younger and older women of reproductive age in meeting dietary recommendations for food groups or macronutrients, and there was no difference in diet quality. Our findings reinforce the continued need for health promotion for women of reproductive age as a key priority to improve their own health but also that of future generations.

Supplementary Materials: The following are available online at https://www.mdpi.com/article/10.3390/nu13113830/s1, Supplementary Table S1: Likelihood for adherence to AGHE and AMDR recommendations among women without compared to with child. Supplementary Table S2: Dietary Guideline Index (DGI) among women without compared to with child

Author Contributions: Conceptualization, J.A.G. and N.H.; Data curation, N.H., K.M.L. and J.A.G.; Formal analysis, N.H. and S.E.; Methodology, N.H., K.M.L. and S.E.; Supervision, J.A.G.; Writing—original draft, J.A.G. and N.H.; Writing—review & editing, N.H., K.M.L., S.E. and J.A.G. All authors have read and agreed to the published version of the manuscript.

Funding: N.H. and J.A.G. have financial support from the National Health and Medical Research Council (NHMRC) Ideas Grant, awarded to J.A.G. [APP2000905]. K.M.L. is supported by a National Health and Medical Research Council Emerging Leadership Fellowship [APP1173803].

Institutional Review Board Statement: As this study is a secondary analysis of the National Nutrition and Physical Activity Survey data that was collected as part of the Australian Health Survey, 2011–2013 no ethics was required.

Informed Consent Statement: The Census and Statistics Act, 1905 provided the Australian Bureau of Statistics with the authority to conduct NNPAS, with all respondents providing written informed consent.

Data Availability Statement: Microdata products are available to approved users. Data are available at https://www.abs.gov.au/websitedbs/D3310114.nsf/home/MicrodataDownload, and upon request to: microdata.access@abs.gov.au.

Acknowledgments: We would like to thank the Australian Bureau of Statistics (ABS) for giving us access to the National Nutrition and Physical Activity Survey data.

Conflicts of Interest: The authors declare no conflict of interest.

References

1. Murray, C.J.; Callender, C.S.; Kulikoff, X.R.; Srinivasan, V.; Abate, D.; Abate, K.H.; Abay, S.M.; Abbasi, N.; Abbastabar, H.; Abdela, J.; et al. Population and fertility by age and sex for 195 countries and territories, 1950–2017: A systematic analysis for the Global Burden of Disease Study 2017. *Lancet* **2018**, *392*, 1995–2051. [CrossRef]
2. Australian Bureau of Statistics. Births Australia. 3301.0 do007. 2009. Available online: https://www.Abs.Gov.Au/ausstats/abs@.Nsf/detailspage/3301.02009 (accessed on 5 June 2021).
3. Australian Institute of Health and Welfare. Australia's Mothers and Babies Data Visualisations. 2018. Available online: https://www.aihw.gov.au/reports/mothers-babies/australias-mothers-babies-data-visualisations/contents/demographics-of-mothers-and-babies/maternal-age (accessed on 1 June 2021).
4. Grieger, J.A. Preconception diet, fertility, and later health in pregnancy. *Curr. Opin. Obstet. Gynecol.* **2020**, *32*, 227–232. [CrossRef]
5. Gaskins, A.J.; Chavarro, J.E. Diet and fertility: A review. *Am. J. Obstet. Gynecol.* **2018**, *218*, 379–389. [CrossRef] [PubMed]
6. Grieger, J.A.; Grzeskowiak, L.; Bianco-Miotto, T.; Jankovic-Karasoulos, T.; Moran, L.J.; Wilson, R.L.; Leemaqz, S.; Poston, L.; McCowan, L.; Kenny, L.C.; et al. Pre-pregnancy fast food and fruit intake is associated with time to pregnancy. *Hum. Reprod.* **2018**, *33*, 1063–1070. [CrossRef]
7. Karayiannis, D.; Kontogianni, M.; Mendorou, C.; Mastrominas, M.; Yiannakouris, N. Adherence to the Mediterranean diet and IVF success rate among non-obese women attempting fertility. *Hum. Reprod.* **2018**, *33*, 494–502. [CrossRef] [PubMed]
8. Raghavan, R.; Dreibelbis, C.; Kingshipp, B.L.; Wong, Y.P.; Abrams, B.; Gernand, A.D.; Rasmussen, K.M.; Siega-Riz, A.M.; Stang, J.; Casavale, K.O.; et al. Dietary patterns before and during pregnancy and maternal outcomes: A systematic review. *Am. J. Clin. Nutr.* **2019**, *109*, 705S–728S. [CrossRef] [PubMed]
9. Schoenaker, D.A.; Mishra, G.D.; Callaway, L.K.; Soedamah-Muthu, S.S. The Role of Energy, Nutrients, Foods, and Dietary Patterns in the Development of Gestational Diabetes Mellitus: A Systematic Review of Observational Studies. *Diabetes Care* **2015**, *39*, 16–23. [CrossRef] [PubMed]
10. Grieger, J.A.; Grzeskowiak, L.; Clifton, V.L. Preconception Dietary Patterns in Human Pregnancies Are Associated with Preterm Delivery. *J. Nutr.* **2014**, *144*, 1075–1080. [CrossRef] [PubMed]
11. Chen, L.-W.; Aubert, A.M.; Shivappa, N.; Bernard, J.Y.; Mensink-Bout, S.M.; Geraghty, A.A.; Mehegan, J.; Suderman, M.; Polanska, K.; Hanke, W.; et al. Associations of maternal dietary inflammatory potential and quality with offspring birth outcomes: An individual participant data pooled analysis of 7 European cohorts in the ALPHABET consortium. *PLoS Med.* **2021**, *18*, e1003491. [CrossRef] [PubMed]
12. Grieger, J.A.; Pelecanos, A.M.; Hurst, C.; Tai, A.; Clifton, V.L. Pre-Conception Maternal Food Intake and the Association with Childhood Allergies. *Nutrients* **2019**, *11*, 1851. [CrossRef] [PubMed]
13. Chen, L.-W.; Aubert, A.M.; Shivappa, N.; Bernard, J.Y.; Mensink-Bout, S.M.; Geraghty, A.A.; Mehegan, J.; Suderman, M.; Polanska, K.; Hanke, W.; et al. Maternal dietary quality, inflammatory potential and childhood adiposity: An individual participant data pooled analysis of seven European cohorts in the ALPHABET consortium. *BMC Med.* **2021**, *19*, 1–14. [CrossRef] [PubMed]
14. Caut, C.; Leach, M.; Steel, A. Dietary guideline adherence during preconception and pregnancy: A systematic review. *Matern. Child. Nutr.* **2019**, *16*, e12916. [CrossRef]
15. Jardí, C.; Aparicio, E.; Bedmar, C.; Aranda, N.; Abajo, S.; March, G.; Basora, J.; Arija, V.; the ECLIPSES Study Group Food Consumption during Pregnancy and Post-Partum. ECLIPSES Study. *Nutrients* **2019**, *11*, 2447. [CrossRef] [PubMed]
16. Malek, L.; Umberger, W.; Makrides, M.; Zhou, S.J. Adherence to the Australian dietary guidelines during pregnancy: Evidence from a national study. *Public Health Nutr.* **2015**, *19*, 1155–1163. [CrossRef]
17. Zhou, S.J.; Flynn, A.C.; Malek, L.; Greco, R.; Moran, L.; Martin, J.C. The Assessment of Diet Quality and Its Effects on Health Outcomes Pre-pregnancy and during Pregnancy. *Semin. Reprod. Med.* **2016**, *34*, 083–092. [CrossRef] [PubMed]
18. Mishra, G.D.; Schoenaker, D.A.; Mihrshahi, S.; Dobson, A.J. How do women's diets compare with the new Australian dietary guidelines? *Public Health Nutr.* **2014**, *18*, 218–225. [CrossRef] [PubMed]
19. Blumfield, M.L.; Hure, A.J.; MacDonald-Wicks, L.K.; Patterson, A.J.; Smith, R.; Collins, C.E. Disparities exist between National food group recommendations and the dietary intakes of women. *BMC Women's Health* **2011**, *11*, 37. [CrossRef]
20. Devarshi, P.P.; Legette, L.L.; Grant, R.W.; Mitmesser, S.H. Total estimated usual nutrient intake and nutrient status biomarkers in women of childbearing age and women of menopausal age. *Am. J. Clin. Nutr.* **2021**, *113*, 1042–1052. [CrossRef]
21. Martin, J.C.; Moran, L.J.; Teede, H.J.; Ranasinha, S.; Lombard, C.B.; Harrison, C.L. Exploring Diet Quality between Urban and Rural Dwelling Women of Reproductive Age. *Nutrients* **2017**, *9*, 586. [CrossRef] [PubMed]
22. Luderer, U.; Li, T.; Fine, J.; Hamman, R.; Stanford, J.; Baker, D. Transitions in pregnancy planning in women recruited for a large prospective cohort study. *Hum. Reprod.* **2017**, *32*, 1325–1333. [CrossRef] [PubMed]
23. Ng, M.; Fleming, T.; Robinson, M.; Thomson, B.; Graetz, N.; Margono, C.; Mullany, E.C.; Biryukov, S.; Abbafati, C.; Abera, S.F.; et al. Global, regional, and national prevalence of overweight and obesity in children and adults during 1980–2013: A systematic analysis for the Global Burden of Disease Study 2013. *Lancet* **2014**, *384*, 766–781. [CrossRef]
24. Centers for Disease Control and Prevention Health. Hyattsville (MD): National Center for Health Statistics. 2008. Available online: https://www.cdc.gov/nchs/index.htm (accessed on 20 August 2021).

25. Australian Bureau of Statistics. ABS. Australian Health Survey: Users' Guide 2011–13 Catalogue No. 4363.0.55.001. 2015. Available online: http://www.abs.gov.au/ausstats/abs@.nsf/Lookup/4363.0.55.001Chapter1002011-13 (accessed on 16 June 2021).
26. Australian Government National Health and Medical Research Council Department of Health and Ageing. Eat for Health. Australian Dietary Guidelines 2013. 21 October 2016. Available online: https://www.eatforhealth.gov.au/sites/default/files/files/the_guidelines/n55_australian_dietary_guidelines.pdf (accessed on 13 February 2021).
27. World Health Organisation. Physical Activity. Adults Aged 18–64 Years. 2020. Available online: https://www.who.int/news-room/fact-sheets/detail/physical-activity (accessed on 13 February 2021).
28. Bliss, R.M. Researchers produce innovation in dietary recall. *Agric. Res.* **2004**, *52*, 10.
29. Willett, W.C. *Nutritional Epidemiology*; Oxford University Press: New York, NY, USA, 1998.
30. National Health and Medical Research Council. NHMRC. *Eat. for Health: Australian Dietary Guidelines*; NHMRC: Canberra, Australia, 2013. Available online: https://www.eatforhealth.gov.au/guidelines (accessed on 12 March 2021).
31. Department of Health and Ageing, National Health and Medical Research Council. Nutrient Reference Values for Australia and New Zealand. 2006. Available online: https://www.nrv.gov.au/ (accessed on 19 June 2011).
32. Thorpe, M.G.; Milte, C.M.; Crawford, D.; McNaughton, S.A. A Revised Australian Dietary Guideline Index and Its Association with Key Sociodemographic Factors, Health Behaviors and Body Mass Index in Peri-Retirement Aged Adults. *Nutrients* **2016**, *8*, 160. [CrossRef]
33. Livingstone, K.M.; McNaughton, S.A. Diet quality is associated with obesity and hypertension in Australian adults: A cross sectional study. *BMC Public Health* **2016**, *16*, 1037. [CrossRef] [PubMed]
34. Data Analysis Australia. Sampling and Weighting—A Better Practice Guide for Practitioners. 2012. Available online: https://www.daa.com.au/articles/analytical-ideas/sampling-and-weighting/ (accessed on 5 June 2021).
35. Bhandari, S.; Thapa, P.; Sayami, M.; Kandel, B.P.; Banjara, M.R. Dietary intake patterns and nutritional status of women of reproductive age in Nepal: Findings from a health survey. *Arch. Public Health* **2016**, *74*, 1–11. [CrossRef]
36. Padmadas, S.; Dias, J.G.; Willekens, F.J. Disentangling women's responses on complex dietary intake patterns from an Indian cross-sectional survey: A latent class analysis. *Public Health Nutr.* **2006**, *9*, 204–211. [CrossRef]
37. Widaman, A.M.; Witbracht, M.G.; Forester, S.M.; Laugero, K.D.; Keim, N.L. Chronic Stress Is Associated with Indicators of Diet Quality in Habitual Breakfast Skippers. *J. Acad. Nutr. Diet.* **2016**, *116*, 1776–1784. [CrossRef]
38. Opie, R.; Ball, K.; Abbott, G.; Crawford, D.; Teychenne, M.; McNaughton, S.A. Adherence to the Australian dietary guidelines and development of depressive symptoms at 5 years follow-up amongst women in the READI cohort study. *Nutr. J.* **2020**, *19*, 30. [CrossRef] [PubMed]
39. Velde, E.R.T. The variability of female reproductive ageing. *Hum. Reprod. Updat.* **2002**, *8*, 141–154. [CrossRef] [PubMed]
40. Grieger, J.A.; Norman, R.J. Menstrual Cycle Length and Patterns in a Global Cohort of Women Using a Mobile Phone App: Retrospective Cohort Study. *J. Med. Internet Res.* **2020**, *22*, e17109. [CrossRef] [PubMed]
41. Department of Economic and Social Affairs, Population Division, United Nations. World Fertility Report 2015—Highlights (ST/ESA/SER.A/415). 2017. Available online: https://www.un.org/en/development/desa/population/publications/pdf/fertility/worldFertilityReport2015_highlights.pdf (accessed on 5 June 2021).
42. American College of Obstetricians and Gynecologists Committee on Gynecologic Practice and Practice Committee. Female age-related fertility decline. *Fertil. Steril.* **2014**, *101*, 633–634. [CrossRef] [PubMed]
43. Chivers, B.R.; Boyle, J.A.; Lang, A.Y.; Teede, H.J.; Moran, L.J.; Harrison, C.L. Preconception Health and Lifestyle Behaviours of Women Planning a Pregnancy: A Cross-Sectional Study. *J. Clin. Med.* **2020**, *9*, 1701. [CrossRef] [PubMed]
44. Stephenson, J.; Patel, D.; Barrett, G.; Howden, B.; Copas, A.; Ojukwu, O.; Pandya, P.; Shawe, J. How Do Women Prepare for Pregnancy? Preconception Experiences of Women Attending Antenatal Services and Views of Health Professionals. *PLoS ONE* **2014**, *9*, e103085. [CrossRef] [PubMed]
45. Pinho, M.G.M.; Mackenbach, J.D.; Charreire, H.; Oppert, J.-M.; Bárdos, H.; Glonti, K.; Rutter, H.; Compernolle, S.; De Bourdeaudhuij, I.; Beulens, J.W.J.; et al. Exploring the relationship between perceived barriers to healthy eating and dietary behaviours in European adults. *Eur. J. Nutr.* **2017**, *57*, 1761–1770. [CrossRef]
46. Bateson, D.J.; Black, K.I. Pre-conception care: An important yet underutilised preventive care strategy. *Med. J. Aust.* **2018**, *209*, 389–391. [CrossRef] [PubMed]
47. Nicklas, T.A.; Baranowski, T.; Baranowski, J.C.; Cullen, K.; Rittenberry, L.; Olvera, N. Family and child-care provider influences on preschool children's fruit, juice, and vegetable consumption. *Nutr. Rev.* **2001**, *59*, 224–235. [CrossRef] [PubMed]
48. Vereecken, C.; Haerens, L.; De Bourdeaudhuij, I.; Maes, L. The relationship between children's home food environment and dietary patterns in childhood and adolescence. *Public Health Nutr.* **2010**, *13*, 1729–1735. [CrossRef] [PubMed]
49. Magarey, A.; Nichols, J.; Boulton, J. Food intake at age 8 2. Frequency, company and place of meals. *J. Paediatr. Child. Health* **1987**, *23*, 179–180. [CrossRef] [PubMed]
50. Bonis-Profumo, G.; Stacey, N.; Brimblecombe, J. Maternal diets matter for children's dietary quality: Seasonal dietary diversity and animal-source foods consumption in rural Timor-Leste. *Matern. Child. Nutr.* **2020**, *17*, e13071. [CrossRef] [PubMed]
51. Bergmeier, H.; Hill, B.; Haycraft, E.; Blewitt, C.; Lim, S.; Meyer, C.; Skouteris, H. Maternal body dissatisfaction in pregnancy, postpartum and early parenting: An overlooked factor implicated in maternal and childhood obesity risk. *Appetite* **2019**, *147*, 104525. [CrossRef]

52. Yager, Z.; Prichard, I.; Hart, L.; Damiano, S.R. Mumbod? A comparison of body image and dietary restraint among women with younger, older, and no children. *J. Health Psychol.* **2020**. [CrossRef] [PubMed]
53. Australian Bureau of Statistics. ABS. *Australian Health Survey: Under-Reporting in Nutrition Surveys*; Australian Bureau of Statistics (ABS): Canberra, Australia, 2015. Available online: http://www.abs.gov.au/ausstats/abs@.nsf/Lookup/4363.0.55.001Chapter651512011-13 (accessed on 28 June 2021).

nutrients MDPI

Article

Factors Related to Diet Quality: A Cross-Sectional Study of 1055 University Students

Enrique Ramón-Arbués [1,2], José-Manuel Granada-López [2,3,4], Blanca Martínez-Abadía [5], Emmanuel Echániz-Serrano [2,3], Isabel Antón-Solanas [3,6,*] and Benjamin Adam Jerue [7]

1 Faculty of Health Sciences, Campus Universitario Villanueva de Gállego, Universidad San Jorge, Villanueva de Gállego, 50830 Zaragoza, Spain; eramon@usj.es
2 Research Group Transfercult (H27_20D), University of Zaragoza, 50009 Zaragoza, Spain; jmgranada@unizar.es (J.-M.G.-L.); eechaniz@unizar.es (E.E.-S.)
3 Department of Physiatrics and Nursing, Faculty of Health Sciences, University of Zaragoza, C/Domingo Miral S/N, 50009 Zaragoza, Spain
4 Research Group Safety and Care (GIISA021), Institute of Research of Aragón, 50009 Zaragoza, Spain
5 Occupational Health and Prevention Service, Zaragoza City Council, P° de La Mina 9, 50001 Zaragoza, Spain; bmartinez@zaragoza.es
6 Research Group Nursing Research in Primary Care in Aragón (GENIAPA) (GIIS094), Institute of Research of Aragón, 50009 Zaragoza, Spain
7 Faculty of Communication and Social Sciences, Campus Universitario Villanueva de Gállego, Universidad San Jorge, Villanueva de Gállego, 50830 Zaragoza, Spain; bajerue@usj.es
* Correspondence: ianton@unizar.es

Citation: Ramón-Arbués, E.; Granada-López, J.-M.; Martínez-Abadía, B.; Echániz-Serrano, E.; Antón-Solanas, I.; Jerue, B.A. Factors Related to Diet Quality: A Cross-Sectional Study of 1055 University Students. *Nutrients* **2021**, *13*, 3512. https://doi.org/10.3390/nu13103512

Academic Editors: Clare Collins and George Moschonis

Received: 30 August 2021
Accepted: 1 October 2021
Published: 5 October 2021

Abstract: Given that there is only a limited body of evidence available concerning the dietary habits of Spanish university students, the present study assesses the quality of this group's diet, their adherence to the National Food-Based Dietary Guidelines, and the predictive factors of their diet quality. To do so, a cross-sectional study was performed on a sample of 1055 students. The quality of the participants' diets was then analysed by using the Spanish Healthy Eating Index, and then their level of compliance was assessed in light of the dietary recommendations put forth by the Spanish Society for Community Nutrition. According to these standards, only 17.4% of the participants had a healthy diet. The level of compliance with the recommendations was poor, highlighting especially the low levels of "fruit" and "vegetables" that they consumed as well as high levels of "cold meats and cuts" and "sweets". The factors that predicted a worse diet are being male, living alone, low levels of physical activity, smoking, high alcohol intake, leading a sedentary lifestyle, psychological distress, and insomnia ($p < 0.005$). Furthermore, participants with low or high body weights showed signs of a higher quality diet ($p < 0.001$). The present findings suggest that a significant proportion of university students ought to change their dietary habits; these also attest to the importance of developing strategies that are directly targeted at university students in order to promote a healthy diet.

Keywords: diet quality; dietary guidelines; university students; cross-sectional study

1. Introduction

Research has repeatedly shown the important role that diet plays in maintaining one's short and long-term health as well as its relation to life expectancy [1,2]. Accordingly, increasing diet quality could be independently associated with a reduced risk of death (by all causes) of up to 28% [3,4]. There is also evidence [5,6] that links the consumption of certain foods with the increased or decreased likelihood of suffering from certain diseases. All of these findings on the importance of diet have been taken into account by various organisations that have published dietary guidelines [7]. The level of compliance with these recommendations has in turn served as the basis for constructing indices that seek to assess the diet quality (DQ) of various groups and populations. Not only have these indices proven to be useful tools for assessing alimentary practices (e.g., diet diversity, moderation, etc.), but their use is also recommended for studies on the DQ of the general population as well as more targeted groups [8]. Internationally, these indices have been used to study the DQ of a range of groups [9–12], including university students [13,14]. Students, in particular, are an important target audience for public health actions, seeing that entering university constitutes a drastic change in lifestyle that can bring about new challenges and meaningfully affect the students' habits and health. Rivalry between classmates, the pressure to succeed academically, changes in workload and support networks, new types of relationships, and, in some instances, moving away from home are all factors that can trigger new, risky behaviours that may compromise the future health of university students [15,16]. These young adults find themselves in a crucial moment in terms of acquiring and reinforcing many habits that impact health. When it comes to dietary habits, university is the time when previously learned patterns can be cemented, or new patterns can be learned and replace old ones [17,18]. Many variables can exert influence on the ways that university students nourish themselves, including individual factors (e.g., the lack of self-discipline or time constraints), support networks (e.g., the influence of peers or the lack of parental monitoring), the local environment (e.g., accessibility or the appeal and price of certain food products) as well as the macro environment (e.g., advertising) [19,20]. Other sociodemographic variables have also been connected to the DQ of university students, including the following: living alone [21], gender [22], satisfaction with one's studies and academic performance [23], lack of information [24] as well as anxiety and depression [25].

In Spain, there have been numerous studies on the DQ of the general population [7,26–28] and even clinical populations [29,30]. That said, more targeted work on the DQ of young people and university students in particular has been scarcer, and the studies that do exist have generally relied on small samples and somewhat indirect approximations of DQ based on the adherence to the Mediterranean diet. Accordingly, there is an important gap in the research that needs to be filled, especially given that universities can easily communicate with large groups of young adults and hence could become excellent agents for promoting healthier dietary practices. With this in mind, this study's objectives were twofold: first, to assess Spanish university students' DQ and adherence to the National Food-Based Dietary Guidelines (NFBDG) [31]; second, to identify possibly linked factors.

2. Materials and Methods

2.1. Design and Study Population

A descriptive cross-sectional study was carried out among a group of undergraduate students from the San Jorge University in Zaragoza (Aragon, Spain). Information about the research objectives was provided and students were recruited in the classroom during the second semester of the 2020–2021 academic year (specifically, in March and April of 2021). A total of 1309 students out of the 2219 enrolled at the university were asked to participate in the study by anonymously filling out a series of questionnaires. There were 151 students who declined to participate, while the responses of an additional 103 students were discarded due to gaps in the provided information (Figure 1).

2.2. Data Collection

Sociodemographic data (age, gender, place of residence, and marital status), anthropometric measurements (height and weight, which were used to calculate BMI), information about mental health history (signs of depression, anxiety, and stress), and lifestyle (current tobacco and alcohol intake, sleep, level of physical activity, time spent sitting, and diet) were collected. The BMI variable was categorised according to the classification of the World Health Organization (WHO) [32], namely as underweight (<18.5 kg/m^2), normal weight (18.5–24.9 kg/m^2), overweight (25–29.9 kg/m^2), and obese ($\geq$30 kg/m^2). However, we combined the participants who were either overweight or obese into one group—overweight/obese ($\geq$25 kg/m^2)—in order to increase the sample-size comparability of the groups. The sociodemographic, anthropometric, and smoking data were all self-reported using a questionnaire made specifically for collecting this information.

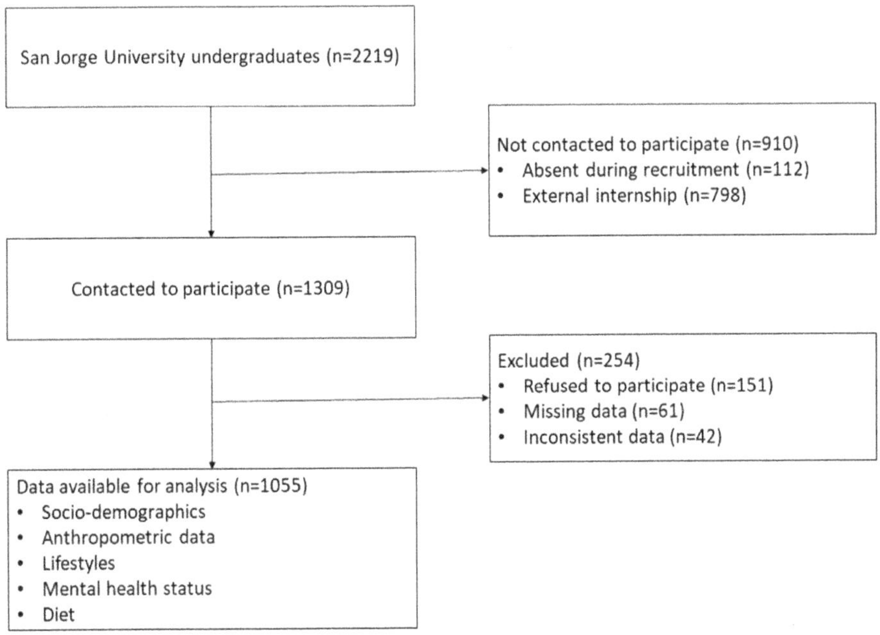

Figure 1. Study flow chart.

Data on the mental health of participating students were gathered through the Depression, Anxiety, Stress Scales-21 (DASS-21) [33]. This scale is an abridged version of the DASS-42 and was validated for the study of Spanish university students in 2010 [34]. DASS-21 consists of three sub-scales (depression, anxiety, and stress) with seven Likert-style questions (with choices between 0 and 3) in each section. The total score of each sub-scale is multiplied by two so that results can be compared with those from the DASS-42. Next, the subjects were classified according to the following criteria:

- Anxiety: Normal (0–7 points), mild (8–9), moderate (10–14), severe (15–19), and extremely severe (>19);
- Depression: Normal (0–9 points), mild (10–13), moderate (14–20), severe (21–27), and extremely severe (>27);
- Stress: Normal (0–14 points), mild (15–18), moderate (19–25), severe (26–33), and extremely severe (>33).

Data on alcohol intake were collected through the CAGE questionnaire, which has been validated for studying Spaniards by Rodríguez Martos et al. [35]. This questionnaire consists of four items with two possible responses (Yes or No). Consumption is deemed problematic when two or more questions are answered affirmatively.

Sleep quality was assessed using the Insomnia Severity Index (ISI) in its Spanish version [36]. This tool has previously been used to measure this construct in similar populations [37,38]. In its Spanish version, the ISI comprises 7 items measuring three different components of insomnia, namely (1) nature of insomnia, (2) severity of insomnia symptoms, and (3) impact of insomnia on daily function. Each item is rated on a 5-point Likert scale ranging from 0 to 4 points. The global score, ranging from 0 to 28, is obtained by adding the scores from each individual item. The results are classified as follows: (1) no insomnia (0–7 points), (2) sub-threshold insomnia (8–14 points), (3) moderate insomnia (15–21 points), severe insomnia (22–28 points).

Physical activity and sedentary time were assessed using the short version of the International Physical Activity Questionnaire (IPAQ-SF). This research tool, which has been validated for the study of Spanish university students [39], measures the intensity, frequency, and duration of physical activity over the last seven days. IPAQ-SF determines a mean of daily sedentary time and allows researchers to obtain two types of data concerning physical activity: first, it offers a calculation of the metabolic equivalent of tasks (METs), taking the type of activity (walking, moderate physical activity, and vigorous physical activity) and the time spent on the activity into account; secondly, the tool allows researchers to classify individuals into three categories of physical activity (low, moderate, high) [40].

DQ was assessed using the Spanish Healthy Eating Index (SHEI) [26]. This tool comprises 10 items measured on a 5-point Likert scale. Points for each answer (0 = no adherence, 2.5, 5, 7.5, or 10 = full adherence) are given based on the participant's degree of adherence to the NFBDG recommendations for the frequency of consumption of specific foods [31]. Specifically, the SHEI measures the frequency of consumption of bread and grains, vegetables, fruit, dairy products, meat (including eggs), legumes, cold meats and cuts, sweets, soft drinks with sugar, and diet variety. The diet variety variable is calculated a posteriori by the researcher based on the participant's report of daily and weekly food consumption (1 point is awarded for each weekly recommendation and 2 points for each daily recommendation that is fully met or adhered to). Supplementary Table S1 details the specific criteria for scoring each of these categories. The final score falls between 0 and 100 points, which is calculated by adding the scores from each category. Based on the results, diet can be classified as follows: healthy (>80), needing change (51–80), and inadequate (<51) [26].

2.3. Data Analysis

The characteristics of the sample were summarised using mean and standard deviation for the continuous variables, and frequency and percentage for the nominal ones. The Kolmogorov–Smirnov test was used to check the normality of DQ (SHEI score). Next, a multiple linear regression analysis was carried out (enter method) to determine which factors were associated with DQ (SHEI score). The covariates included in the multiple linear regression model were age, gender, BMI (WHO categories), life arrangement, marital status, smoking status, alcohol consumption (CAGE categories), physical activity (IPAQ categories), sedentary time, sleep quality (ISI categories), and symptoms of depression, anxiety, and stress (DASS-21 categories).

The model's goodness-of-fit was assessed through R^2. Furthermore, the diagnostic of collinearity of the final regression model showed tolerance levels over 0.6 for all included variables. The statistical analysis of the data was performed with the SPSS statistical package for Windows-Version 21 (IBM Corp, Armonk, NY, USA), accepting a significance level of $p < 0.05$.

3. Results

The size of the study's final sample came to 1055 university students, with an average age of 21.74 ± 5.15. The majority of the participants were women (70.5%), living with family (66.4%), and non-smokers (76.6%). Nearly a third reported high alcohol intake and nearly half reported a low level of physical activity. Furthermore, 33.9% of the students reported some degree of stress, 18.5% reported depression, 23.5% anxiety, and 43.1% insomnia. Other information about the sample is presented in Table 1.

The average SHEI score came up to 68.57 ± 12.17 (100 being the maximum). The vast majority of the participants reported an inadequate diet (6.9%) or a diet needing changes (75.6%), while only 17.4% had a healthy diet (Table 1). The scores obtained by the participants ranged between 4.45 ± 3.28, for the consumption of sweets, and 9.27 ± 2.82, for the consumption of dairy products (Table 2).

Most participants showed a low level of compliance with the NFBDG recommendations concerning the frequency with which certain foods are consumed, especially for "bread and grains", "fruits", "meat", "vegetables"; in contrast, participants surpassed recommendations for the categories "cold meats and cuts" and "sweets" (Figure 2). Men and women reported similar dietary patterns; that said, the women more consistently followed the recommendations for the consumption of fruits and vegetables ($p < 0.05$), whereas the men more rigidly adhered to recommendations concerning meat ($p < 0.05$).

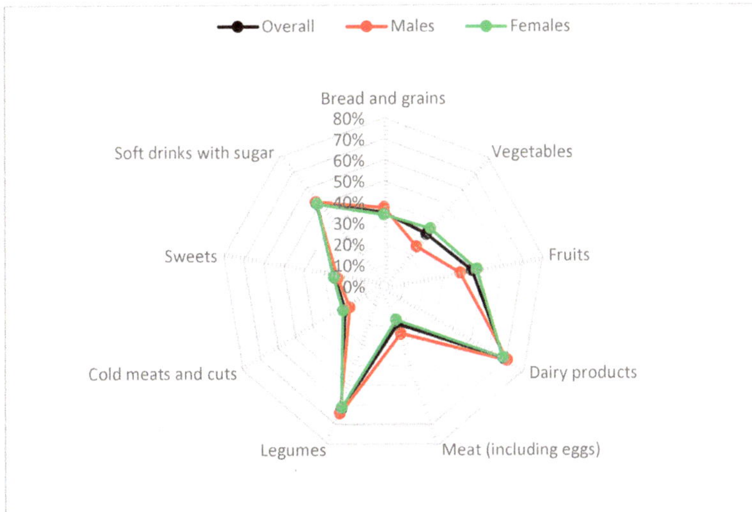

Figure 2. Percentage of students who adhere to the NFBDG-2016 [31] recommendations for the frequency with which certain foods should be consumed every week.

Table 1. Participant characteristics (n = 1055).

Variable		Mean ± SD/*n* (%)
Age		21.74 ± 5.15
Gender	Female	744 (70.5%)
	Male	311 (29.5%)
BMI (kg/m^2)		22.15 ± 3.48
BMI Categories	Underweight (<18.5 kg/m^2)	160 (15.2%)
	Normal weight (18.5–24.9 kg/m^2)	736 (69.8%)
	Overweight/obese (≥25 kg/m^2)	159 (15.1%)
Living arrangement	Living alone	64 (6.1%)
	Living with a partner	291 (27.6%)
	Living with family	700 (66.4%)
Relationship status	Currently in a relationship	494 (46.8%)
	Currently not in a relationship	561 (53.2%)
Smoking status (current)	No	535 (76.6%)
	Yes	163 (23.4%)
CAGE score		0.48 ± 0.78
CAGE categories	Problematic alcohol consumption	343 (32.5%)
	Non-problematic alcohol consumption	712 (67.5%)
SHEI score		68.57 ± 12.17
Diet quality	Inadequate (<51 points)	73 (6.9%)
	Need changes (51–80 points)	798 (75.6%)
	Healthy (>80 points)	184 (17.4%)

Table 1. *Cont.*

Variable		Mean ± SD/*n* (%)
Physical activity (METs/week)		1877.03 ± 1966.54
Physical activity categories	High	236 (22.4%)
	Medium	351 (33.3%)
	Low	468 (44.4%)
Sedentary time (hours/day)		6.76 ± 2.45
Sedentary time categories	<3 h/day	133 (12.6%)
	3–6 h/day	342 (32.4%)
	≥6 h/day	580 (54.9%)
DASS-E score		12.39 ± 8.08
DASS-E categories	No stress	697 (66.1%)
	Mild stress	121 (11.5%)
	Moderate stress	174 (16.5%)
	Severe stress	46 (4.4%)
	Extremely severe stress	17 (1.6%)
DASS-D score		5.45 ± 7.12
DASS-D categories	No depression	859 (81.4%)
	Mild depression	80 (7.6%)
	Moderate depression	48 (4.5%)
	Severe depression	38 (3.6%)
	Extremely severe depression	30 (2.8%)
DASS-A score		4.84 ± 5.75
DASS-A categories	No anxiety	807 (76.5%)
	Mild anxiety	83 (7.9%)
	Moderate anxiety	95 (9.0%)
	Severe anxiety	9 (0.9%)
	Extremely severe anxiety	61 (5.8%)
ISI score		7.91 ± 4.88
Sleep quality	No insomnia	600 (56.9%)
	Sub-threshold insomnia	333 (31.6%)
	Moderate insomnia	114 (10.8%)
	Severe insomnia	8 (0.8%)

Table 2. SHEI scores of the participants (*n* = 1055).

Food Group	Mean ± SD	Min.	Max.	Mode
Bread and grains	7.27 ± 3.25	0	10	10 (Consumed daily)
Vegetables	8.38 ± 2.91	0	10	10 (Consumed daily)
Fruits	8.23 ± 3.54	0	10	10 (Consumed daily)
Dairy products	9.27 ± 2.82	0	10	10 (Consumed daily)
Meat	6.90 ± 2.83	0	10	7.5 (3 or more times a week but not daily)
Legumes	9.17 ± 1.97	0	10	7.5 (3 or more times a week but not daily)
Cold meats and cuts	6.29 ± 3.75	0	10	5 (Once or twice a week)
Sweets	4.45 ± 3.28	0	10	5 (Once or twice a week)
Soft drinks with sugar	8.62 ± 3.36	0	10	7.5 (Less than once a week)
SHEI score	68.57 ± 12.17	25	96.5	70.5 (Need changes)

Through the multiple linear regression analysis, we found that being older, being female, not having a stable partner as well as having a low or high body weight independently correlated with a better DQ ($p < 0.05$). On the other hand, demonstrating signs of depression, anxiety, stress or insomnia, living alone, smoking, having an unactive lifestyle, being sedentary, and a high alcohol intake were all linked independently with lower SHEI scores ($p < 0.05$). This model's predictive power for DQ was determined to be 37.7% ($R^2 = 0.38$) (Table 3).

Table 3. Factors related to diet quality. Multiple linear regression model *.

Independent Variable	B (CI 95%)	Std. Error	β	p
Age. <20 years (Ref.)				
20–24.9	3.54 (2.05, 5.04)	0.76	0.14	0.00
≥25	4.76 (2.68, 6.85)	1.06	0.14	0.00
Gender. Male (Ref.)				
Female	2.47 (0.94, 4.00)	0.781	0.09	0.00
BMI categories. Normal weight (Ref.)				
Underweight (<18.5 kg/m^2)	3.55 (1.63, 5.48)	0.98	0.10	0.00
Overweight/obese (≥25 kg/m^2)	6.42 (4.53, 8.31)	0.96	0.19	0.00
Living arrangement. Living with family (Ref.)				
Living alone	−11.49 (−14.27, −8.71)	1.42	−0.22	0.00
Living with a partner	−0.50 (−2.06, 1.07)	0.80	−0.02	0.53
Relationship status. Currently in a relationship (Ref.)				
Currently not in a relationship	3.63 (2.01, 5.25)	0.83	0.15	0.00
Smoking status. Not a smoker (Ref.)				
Smoker	−2.82 (−4.41, −1.24)	0.81	−0.10	0.00
CAGE Categories. Non-problematic alcohol consumption (Ref.)				
Problematic alcohol consumption	−1.82 (−3.20, −0.45)	0.702	−0.070	0.01
Physical activity. Medium (Ref.)				
High PA	1.74 (−0.05, 3.53)	0.91	0.06	0.06
Low PA	−2.77 (−4.45, −1.09)	0.86	−0.11	0.00
Sedentary time. 3–6 h per day				
<3 h/day	−0.29 (−2.48, 1.90)	1.11	−0.01	0.80
≥6 h/day	−2.40 (−3.86, −0.93)	0.75	−0.10	0.00
DASS-E categories. No stress (Ref.)				
Mild stress	12.10 (9.63, 14.57)	1.26	0.32	0.00
Moderate stress	−1.08 (−3.08, 0.92)	1.02	−0.03	0.29
Severe stress	−0.29 (−3.93, 3.35)	1.85	−0.00	0.88
Extremely severe stress	−5.56 (−11.37, 0.24)	2.96	−0.06	0.06
DASS-D categories. No depression (Ref.)				
Mild depression	2.13 (−1.00, 5.27)	1.60	0.05	0.18
Moderate depression	−3.23 (−6.71, 0.25)	1.77	−0.05	0.07
Severe depression	−18.04 (−22.12, −3.97)	2.07	−0.28	0.00
Extremely severe depression	−7.77 (−12.22, −3.33)	2.26	−0.11	0.00
DASS-A categories. No anxiety (Ref.)				
Mild anxiety	−3.25 (−5.91, −0.60)	1.35	−0.07	0.01
Moderate anxiety	−3.32 (−5.93, −0.70)	1.33	−0.08	0.01
Severe anxiety	−10.96 (−18.25, −3.66)	3.72	−0.08	0.00
Extremely severe anxiety	−1.29 (−5.18, 2.61)	1.98	−0.02	0.52
ISI categories. No insomnia (Ref.)				
Sub-threshold insomnia	−4.93 (−6.50, −3.37)	0.79	−0.19	0.00
Moderate insomnia	−6.62 (−9.11, −4.14)	1.27	−0.17	0.00
Severe insomnia	−13.51 (−21.46, −5.56)	4.05	−0.10	0.00

Ref. = Group of Reference. * Model's Goodness of Fit (R^2) = 0.38. p value (model) = 0.00 (one-way ANOVA).

4. Discussion

Based on the recommendations of the National Food-Based Dietary Guidelines [31], our findings suggest that university students' diet quality is generally poor. Our participants consumed insufficient amounts of "fruit" and "vegetables" and excessive amounts of "cold meats and cuts" and "sweets". Factors that predicted a diet of worse quality were being male, living alone, maintaining low levels of physical activity, smoking, consuming alcohol, leading a sedentary lifestyle, experiencing psychological distress, and insomnia. In contrast, participants with low or high body weights showed signs of a higher quality diet.

Only 17.4% of the participants reported having a healthy diet. The present results are similar to those previously obtained by using SHEI to study Spanish university students [22,41–43]. They are, however, distinctly lower than the results from studies of the general Spanish population, for which between 28% and 35.8% of the participants reported having a healthy diet [26,27,29]. These results could be explained in two ways that are not mutually exclusive. First, the newly found liberty and independence associated with university life could allow students to let themselves go and overindulge in low-quality foods and alcohol. This does not necessarily mean that these individuals will not improve their DQ in the future after finishing their studies; indeed, they very well could do so. In this vein, previous studies carried out in England, Spain, and Lebanon have shown that some students opt for a poorer diet and gain a significant amount of weight in the first year of university, a phenomenon popularly referred to as "the Freshman 15" [44–46]. The second argument is that these trends reflect a more general tendency and could therefore imply that the DQ of Spaniards could decline in the future. The fact that age was positively associated with DQ in our sample lends support to this hypothesis. Indeed, research has shown that there has continually been less adherence to the Mediterranean diet in Spain [47,48], a diet that has been shown to be healthy and traditional in the country. This, however, does not appear to be a trend that is only valid in Spain, since researchers throughout Europe have detected a decrease in DQ over the last decade [49].

Internationally, researchers have found a remarkable range in the percentage of university students who have a healthy diet, ranging between 1.8% and 57% [18,50–53]. These differences, for the most part, can be explained in terms of the different socioeconomic realities and living arrangements of the various countries studied. For example, whereas 57% of Thai students reported following an inadequate diet [50], only 2.03% of Northern European students followed an unhealthy diet [18].

What deserves special attention is how student habits do not conform to the national alimentary guidelines for the majority of food groups. In fact, over 50% of the participants complied with recommendations in only three of the 10 variables included in the SHEI (dairy products, legumes, and soft drinks with sugar). Likewise, the results show a low level of fruit and vegetable consumption (44.3% and 32.5% of recommended frequency, respectively). Prima facie, these results may come as a surprise since Spain has a reputation for the quality of its agricultural products. However, similar trends have already been observed in Spanish university students [54,55] and the general population [7,56] that support the present findings.

In line with previous studies carried out in Tunisia and Canada [52,57], being a woman is associated with a better DQ. The relationship between gender and diet are conditioned by a suite of physiological, psychological, and sociocultural factors. Thus, women generally believe in the importance of a healthy diet, are more likely to monitor their body weight, and frequently express greater concern over their own eating habits [58–60].

The connection between DQ and BMI is controversial. From a biological point of view, it is plausible that a low-quality diet could be associated with deviations (whether higher or lower) from what experts recommend as a healthy body weight. As a corollary, a high-quality diet would be expected to favour healthy body weight. However, various studies have demonstrated how this is not always the case [61,62]. Our analysis found a U-shaped relation between the profiles of BMI and DQ (healthy body weight < low and high weights). These results should be viewed with caution given this study's qualitative means of assessing DQ. However, it is possible that in a developed country such as Spain, young university students who are over or underweight may be more informed and conscious about what constitutes a healthy and balanced diet; perhaps some are influenced by the enduring canon of beauty in the West (based on being thin), while others seek to have a healthier weight.

The participants that lived alone showed a poorer DQ than those who lived with family members or flat mates. This same phenomenon has been repeatedly found in other studies involving samples of European students [21,63]. There are various reasons that explain why students who live alone were less likely to adopt a healthy diet; these include, but are not limited to, the following: changing lifestyle, the comfort and convenience of fast food, taste, students' physical and social environment, and awareness of weight [64].

The fact that being in a stable relationship was associated with a poorer DQ in our sample appears to support the prevalent idea that when we enter a serious relationship, we often do not take as good care of ourselves as before. Available research on the issue has shown that people who are overweight or obese (especially women) have more difficulty finding a partner than those who are not overweight [65]. Developing this idea, van Woerden et al. [66] suggest that there is a selection bias related to weight for beginning (but not ending) romantic relationships. In their study, these authors observed that for students that were single at moment A, the increase of each BMI unit reduced their chances of finding a partner at moment B (four months later) by 9%. Taking these results into account, one could infer that an individual seeking to start a new relationship might be more inclined to regulate his/her diet than someone uninterested in finding a new partner.

Among the study population, a clear association was observed between DQ and both unhealthy lifestyle choices (i.e., low levels of physical activity, a highly sedentary lifestyle, high alcohol intake, or smoking) as well as psychological health (i.e., the presence of stress, anxiety, depression, or insomnia). Previous studies have shown the tendency for unhealthy lifestyle choices (including low-quality diet) to cluster among Spanish university students [67–70]. The same holds for the relation between mental health and DQ [22,23,41]. Unhealthy habits (e.g., high alcohol intake, smoking, or certain dietary behaviours) have often been detected among those suffering from psychological distress and have been identified as passive coping mechanisms based on avoidance and/or escape [71]. However, one should not dismiss a bidirectional relationship between mental health and certain unhealthy lifestyle choices such as poor DQ. In fact, several recent studies have reported a strong correlation between a healthy diet and psychological wellbeing. Therefore, healthy diets such as the Mediterranean, which is rich in fresh fruits and vegetables, could be associated with higher levels of happiness and mental health [72–74], whereas certain gaps in the diet could be associated with a deterioration in mental health [71,75]. A similar connection can be observed when it comes to sleep quality; participants suffering from insomnia also reported a worse DQ. These results are consistent with findings in the broader scholarly literature on the topic. Numerous experimental studies have shown how partial sleep deprivation leads to an increased intake of fats [76,77], snacks [78,79], foods rich in rapidly absorbed carbohydrates [80,81], and inconsistent or shifting mealtimes [76]. Similarly, observational studies have provided further evidence of poorer DQ among people who have a lower quality of sleep in Iran and the USA [82,83]. Different explanations have been proffered to illuminate the phenomenon. More waking hours means more time for eating, changes in the level of hormones that regulate appetite (leptin and ghrelin), increased processing of hedonic stimuli in the brain (providing a greater reward from food), and shifting eating schedules [84]. However, it may not only be lack of sleep that affects diet; certain foods and nutrients can themselves influence sleep quality. For example, high-carb diets and foods that contain tryptophan, melatonin, and phytonutrients (e.g., cherries) seem to be linked with higher sleep quality [85].

As far as the authors are aware, this is the first study that analyses DQ and a large number of sociodemographic and behavioural variables among a large sample of Spanish university students. We believe that the obtained results can be generalised to the larger body of Spanish university students, not only due to the large sample size but also because of the standardised procedures used to collect data as well as the plausibility of the associations detected in the data analysis. Accordingly, this would allow us to trace a reliable picture of university students' DQ as well as its associated factors. Such information is crucial since it can assist in the development and implementation of both diagnostic tools as well as educational activities concerning a healthy diet. That said, the study also has several limitations that need to be underscored. First, the transversal design makes it possible to detect associations, but it does not allow us to determine a cause-and-effect relationship or direction of influence. Second, the type of sampling used, a choice based on convenience and available resources, does impinge on our ability to draw generalisations from these results even though, we should note, the profile of our sample (i.e., predominantly female) does match the broader demographics of university students in Aragon. Third, data was self-reported by the participants, which means that one cannot rule out the possibility of faulty memory or the playing down of certain information such as body weight [86,87]. Fourth, our data was collected when the COVID-19 pandemic and the resulting public health measures were well underway in Spain. This fact provides valuable information about Spanish university students' diet in the current context, and, in all likelihood, our results reflect the pandemic's impact on the lives and dietary habits of university students. However, the data does not allow us to determine the precise ways that the current situation has affected students' diets. Nevertheless, it is worth mentioning that other researchers have observed a decline in DQ since the beginning of the pandemic; lockdown measures have, on the one hand, led to a decline in the consumption of fruits and vegetables [88], and on the other hand, to an increase in the consumption of unhealthy foods (e.g., highly-processed foods, snacks, and frozen foods) [89–91]. Furthermore, the SHEI questionnaire only takes into account the frequency with which foods are consumed and not the quantity that is ingested. For this reason, it cannot offer information concerning the intake of nutrients or calories. Despite these limitations, there were three main reasons that we chose this tool: it is a questionnaire specifically adapted to Spanish alimentary habits; it has repeatedly been shown to be well-equipped to assess the DQ of Spaniards [27,92,93]; finally, the original questionnaire from which it was derived has been validated with plasma biomarkers in previous studies [94,95]. Given the limitations listed above, further research on the present issue is needed, including a longitudinal study as well as a quantitative approach to evaluating the diet of Spanish university students.

5. Conclusions and Recommendations

The present findings reveal that a large portion of university students have a poor DQ and do not closely adhere to alimentary recommendations. Therefore, it is necessary to encourage changes in current dietary patterns. Factors such as living arrangement, certain unhealthy habits (high alcohol intake, a sedentary lifestyle, smoking, and the presence of psychological distress and insomnia) predict DQ and can therefore be used to help tailor and direct action. It is indeed essential that educational institutions and health services undertake future action to promote better DQ among university students. We recommend a global approach to the issue that takes into account the factors related to poor DQ. Any such actions ought to take into consideration the following recommendations:

(1) the early detection of trends of poor DQ among students entering university as part of existing systems that offer students support;
(2) activities that aim to interrupt and prevent unhealthy dietary habits such as providing gender-specific information about immediate health concerns or organising community-wide public health campaigns that ensure that students have access to needed resources and affordable healthy foods;
(3) the empowerment of students by encouraging, for example, the acquisition of skills for making dietary choices and increasing resilience so that they can develop their own adaptive strategies to confront dietary problems and avoid unhealthy dietary habits;

(4) the consideration and handling of any underlying mental health conditions that could be present among university students with poor DQ.

Supplementary Materials: The following are available online at https://www.mdpi.com/article/10.3390/nu13103512/s1, Table S1: Criteria for scoring the Spanish Healthy Eating Index (SHEI).

Author Contributions: Conceptualization, E.R.-A. and B.A.J.; methodology, E.R.-A., I.A.-S., and B.A.J.; formal analysis, E.R.-A., J.-M.G.-L., and E.E.-S.; investigation, E.R.-A., B.A.J., I.A.-S., J.-M.G.-L., E.E.-S., and B.M.-A.; writing—original draft preparation, E.R.-A.; writing—review and editing, B.A.J., I.A.-S., J.-M.G.-L., E.E.-S., and B.M.-A.; supervision, B.A.J. and J.-M.G.-L. All authors have read and agreed to the published version of the manuscript.

Funding: This research received no external funding.

Institutional Review Board Statement: The study was conducted according to the guidelines of the Declaration of Helsinki, and approved by the Research Ethics Committee of the Autonomous Community of Aragón (CEICA) (protocol code C.I. PI09/062X and date of approval 07/08/2017).

Informed Consent Statement: Informed consent was obtained from all subjects involved in the study.

Data Availability Statement: The data presented in this study are available on request from the corresponding author. The data are not publicly available as they contain information that could compromise the privacy of research participants.

Conflicts of Interest: The authors declare no conflict of interest.

References

1. Jankovic, N.; Geelen, A.; Streppel, M.T.; de Groot, L.C.; Kiefte-de Jong, J.C.; Orfanos, P.; Bamia, C.; Trichopoulou, A.; Boffetta, P.; Es Bobak, M.; et al. WHO Guidelines for a Healthy Diet and Mortality from Cardiovascular Disease in European and American Elderly: The CHANCES Project. *Am. J. Clin. Nutr.* **2015**, *102*, 745–756. [CrossRef]
2. Jankovic, N.; Geelen, A.; Streppel, M.T.; de Groot, L.C.P.G.M.; Orfanos, P.; van den Hooven, E.H.; Pikhart, H.; Boffetta, P.; Trichopoulou, A.; Bobak, M.; et al. Adherence to a Healthy Diet According to the World Health Organization Guidelines and All-Cause Mortality in Elderly Adults from Europe and the United States. *Am. J. Epidemiol.* **2014**, *180*, 978–988. [CrossRef] [PubMed]
3. Liese, A.D.; Krebs-Smith, S.M.; Subar, A.F.; George, S.M.; Harmon, B.E.; Neuhouser, M.L.; Boushey, C.J.; Schap, T.E.; Reedy, J. The Dietary Patterns Methods Project: Synthesis of Findings across Cohorts and Relevance to Dietary Guidance. *J. Nutr.* **2015**, *145*, 393–402. [CrossRef] [PubMed]
4. Neelakantan, N.; Koh, W.-P.; Yuan, J.-M.; van Dam, R.M. Diet-Quality Indexes Are Associated with a Lower Risk of Cardiovascular, Respiratory, and All-Cause Mortality among Chinese Adults. *J. Nutr.* **2018**, *148*, 1323–1332. [CrossRef] [PubMed]
5. Micha, R.; Peñalvo, J.L.; Cudhea, F.; Imamura, F.; Rehm, C.D.; Mozaffarian, D. Association Between Dietary Factors and Mortality from Heart Disease, Stroke, and Type 2 Diabetes in the United States. *JAMA* **2017**, *317*, 912–924. [CrossRef]
6. Harrison, S.; Couture, P.; Lamarche, B. Diet Quality, Saturated Fat and Metabolic Syndrome. *Nutrients* **2020**, *12*, 3232. [CrossRef]
7. Martínez Valero, A.P.; Amo-Saus, E.; Pardo-García, I.; Escribano-Sotos, F. Calidad de la dieta en mayores de 65 años y factores socioeconómicos relacionados. *Atención Primaria* **2021**, *53*, 27–35. [CrossRef]
8. Gil, Á. Indicadores de Evaluación de La Calidad de La Dieta. *Nutr. Hosp.* **2015**, 128–144. [CrossRef]
9. Asadi, Z.; Ghaffarian Zirak, R.; Yaghooti Khorasani, M.; Saedi, M.; Parizadeh, S.M.; Jafarzadeh-Esfehani, R.; Khorramruz, F.; Jandari, S.; Mohammadi-Bajgiran, M.; Zare-Feyzabadi, R.; et al. Dietary Inflammatory Index Is Associated with Healthy Eating Index, Alternative Healthy Eating Index, and Dietary Patterns among Iranian Adults. *J. Clin. Lab. Anal.* **2020**, *34*, e23523. [CrossRef]
10. Murakami, K.; Livingstone, M.B.E.; Fujiwara, A.; Sasaki, S. Application of the Healthy Eating Index-2015 and the Nutrient-Rich Food Index 9.3 for Assessing Overall Diet Quality in the Japanese Context: Different Nutritional Concerns from the US. *PLoS ONE* **2020**, *15*, e0228318. [CrossRef]
11. Sedaghat, F.; Heidari, Z.; Jalali, S.; Doustmohammadian, A.; Ehteshami, M.; Rashidkhani, B. Healthy Eating Index 2010 and Breast Cancer Risk. *Nutr. Cancer* **2018**, *70*, 860–866. [CrossRef] [PubMed]
12. Al-Ibrahim, A.A.; Jackson, R.T. Healthy Eating Index versus Alternate Healthy Index in Relation to Diabetes Status and Health Markers in U.S. Adults: NHANES 2007–2010. *Nutr. J.* **2019**, *18*, 26. [CrossRef]
13. Tay, M.E.; Foster, E.; Stevenson, L.; Brownlee, I. The Adherence of Singaporean Students in Different Educational Institutions to National Food-Based Dietary Guidelines. *Nutrients* **2020**, *12*, 2995. [CrossRef]
14. Merhout, F.; Doyle, J. Socioeconomic Status and Diet Quality in College Students. *J. Nutr. Educ. Behav.* **2019**, *51*, 1107–1112. [CrossRef]

15. El Ansari, W.; Stock, C. Is the Health and Wellbeing of University Students Associated with Their Academic Performance? Cross Sectional Findings from the United Kingdom. *Int. J. Environ. Res. Public Health* **2010**, *7*, 509–527. [CrossRef]
16. Deliens, T.; Clarys, P.; De Bourdeaudhuij, I.; Deforche, B. Determinants of Eating Behaviour in University Students: A Qualitative Study Using Focus Group Discussions. *BMC Public Health* **2014**, *14*, 53. [CrossRef] [PubMed]
17. Sogari, G.; Velez-Argumedo, C.; Gómez, M.I.; Mora, C. College Students and Eating Habits: A Study Using an Ecological Model for Healthy Behavior. *Nutrients* **2018**, *10*, 1823. [CrossRef] [PubMed]
18. Suliga, E.; Cieśla, E.; Michel, S.; Kaducakova, H.; Martin, T.; Śliwiński, G.; Braun, A.; Izova, M.; Lehotska, M.; Kozieł, D.; et al. Diet Quality Compared to the Nutritional Knowledge of Polish, German, and Slovakian University Students—Preliminary Research. *Int. J. Environ. Res. Public Health* **2020**, *17*, 9062. [CrossRef]
19. Kabir, A.; Miah, S.; Islam, A. Factors Influencing Eating Behavior and Dietary Intake among Resident Students in a Public University in Bangladesh: A Qualitative Study. *PLoS ONE* **2018**, *13*, e0198801. [CrossRef]
20. Vélez-Toral, M.; Rodríguez-Reinado, C.; Ramallo-Espinosa, A.; Andrés-Villas, M. "It's Important but, on What Level?": Healthy Cooking Meanings and Barriers to Healthy Eating among University Students. *Nutrients* **2020**, *12*, 2309. [CrossRef] [PubMed]
21. Bárbara, R.; Ferreira-Pêgo, C. Changes in Eating Habits among Displaced and Non-Displaced University Students. *Int. J. Environ. Res. Public Health* **2020**, *17*, 5369. [CrossRef]
22. Ramón-Arbués, E.; Martínez Abadía, B.; Granada López, J.M.; Echániz Serrano, E.; Pellicer García, B.; Juárez Vela, R.; Guerrero Portillo, S.; Saéz Guinoa, M. Eating behavior and relationships with stress, anxiety, depression and insomnia in university students. *Nutr. Hosp.* **2019**, *36*, 1339–1345. [CrossRef] [PubMed]
23. Whatnall, M.C.; Patterson, A.J.; Siew, Y.Y.; Kay-Lambkin, F.; Hutchesson, M.J. Are Psychological Distress and Resilience Associated with Dietary Intake Among Australian University Students? *Int. J. Environ. Res. Public Health* **2019**, *16*, 4099. [CrossRef] [PubMed]
24. El Hajj, J.S.; Julien, S.G. Factors Associated with Adherence to the Mediterranean Diet and Dietary Habits among University Students in Lebanon. *J. Nutr. Metab.* **2021**, *2021*, 6688462. [CrossRef] [PubMed]
25. Wattick, R.A.; Hagedorn, R.L.; Olfert, M.D. Relationship between Diet and Mental Health in a Young Adult Appalachian College Population. *Nutrients* **2018**, *10*, 957. [CrossRef] [PubMed]
26. Norte Navarro, A.I.; Ortiz Moncada, R. Spanish diet quality according to the healthy eating index. *Nutr. Hosp.* **2011**, *26*, 330–336. [CrossRef] [PubMed]
27. Hernández Galiot, A.; Goñi Cambrodón, I. Calidad de La Dieta de La Población Española Mayor de 80 Años No Institucionalizada. *Nutr. Hosp.* **2015**, *31*, 2571–2577. [CrossRef]
28. Valdés, J.; Grau, M.; Subirana, I.; Marrugat, J.; Covas, M.-I.; Schröder, H. Secular Trends in Energy Intake and Diet Quality in a Mediterranean Population. *Ann. Nutr. Metab.* **2009**, *54*, 177–183. [CrossRef] [PubMed]
29. Cebrino, J.; Portero de la Cruz, S. Diet Quality According to Mental Status and Associated Factors during Adulthood in Spain. *Nutrients* **2021**, *13*, 1727. [CrossRef]
30. Varoucha-Azcarate, A.C. Analysis of the Diet in a Spanish Prison and the Level of Perception in a Sample of Prisoners. *Rev. Esp. Sanid. Penit.* **2019**, *21*, 18–27. [CrossRef]
31. Bartrina, J.A.; Grupo Colaborativo de la Sociedad Española de Nutrición Comunitaria (SENC); Arija Val, A.; Maíz Aldalur, E.; de la Victoria Muñoz, E.; Ortega Anta, R.M.; Pérez-Rodrigo, C.; Quiles Izquierdo, J.; Rodríguez Martín, A.; Román Viñas, B.; et al. Dietary guidelines for the Spanish population (SENC, December 2016): The new graphic icon of healthy nutrition. *Nutr. Hosp.* **2016**, *33*, 1–48. [CrossRef]
32. World Health Organization. Body Mass Index-BMI. Available online: https://www.euro.who.int/en/health-topics/disease-prevention/nutrition/a-healthy-lifestyle/body-mass-index-bmi (accessed on 11 June 2021).
33. Lovibond, P.F.; Lovibond, S.H. The Structure of Negative Emotional States: Comparison of the Depression Anxiety Stress Scales (DASS) with the Beck Depression and Anxiety Inventories. *Behav. Res. Ther.* **1995**, *33*, 335–343. [CrossRef]
34. Pedrero, E.F.; Piñeiro, M.; de las, M.P.; Giráldez, S.L.; Fernández, J.M. Propiedades psicométricas de la Depresión Anxiety and Stress Scales-21 (DASS-21) en universitarios españoles. *Ansiedad Estrés* **2010**, *16*, 215–226.
35. Rodríguez Martos, A.; Navarro, R.; Vecino, C.; Pérez, R. Validación de Los Cuestionarios KFA (CBA) y CAGE Para El Diagnóstico Del Alcoholismo. *Droga-Alcohol* **1986**, *11*, 132–139.
36. Sierra-Guerra, K.L.; Viveros-Contreras, C.; Martínez-Carrillo, G.; Hernández-León, O.; Caballero-Ambriz, G. Calidad de Vida En Pacientes Con Cáncer de Próstata, Operados de Prostatectomía Radical Laparoscópica. *Rev. Mex. Urol.* **2014**, *74*, 133–140. [CrossRef]
37. Dietch, J.R.; Taylor, D.J.; Sethi, K.; Kelly, K.; Bramoweth, A.D.; Roane, B.M. Psychometric Evaluation of the PSQI in U.S. College Students. *J. Clin. Sleep Med.* **2016**, *12*, 1121–1129. [CrossRef]
38. Veqar, Z.; Hussain, M.E. Validity and Reliability of Insomnia Severity Index and Its Correlation with Pittsburgh Sleep Quality Index in Poor Sleepers among Indian University Students. *Int. J. Adolesc. Med. Health* **2017**, *32*, 20160090. [CrossRef]
39. Rodríguez-Muñoz, S.; Corella, C.; Abarca-Sos, A.; Zaragoza, J. Validation of Three Short Physical Activity Questionnaires with Accelerometers among University Students in Spain. *J. Sports Med. Phys. Fit.* **2017**, *57*, 1660–1668. [CrossRef]
40. IPAQ. Scoring, Protocol-International Physical Activity Questionnaire. Available online: https://sites.google.com/site/theipaq/scoring-protocol (accessed on 24 July 2021).

41. Ramón-Arbués, E.; Gea-Caballero, V.; Granada-López, J.M.; Juárez-Vela, R.; Pellicer-García, B.; Antón-Solanas, I. The Prevalence of Depression, Anxiety and Stress and Their Associated Factors in College Students. *Int. J. Environ. Res. Public Health* **2020**, *17*, 7001. [CrossRef]
42. Amaral Alves, D.; Hernández Regidor, N.; Basabe Baraño, N.; Rocandio Pablo, A.M.; Arroyo Izaga, M. Body satisfaction and diet quality in female university students from the Basque Country. *Endocrinol. Nutr.* **2012**, *59*, 239–245. [CrossRef]
43. Telleria-Aramburu, N.; Bermúdez-Marín, N.; Rocandio, A.M.; Telletxea, S.; Basabe, N.; Rebato, E.; Arroyo-Izaga, M. Nutritional Quality and Carbon Footprint of University Students' Diets: Results from the EHU12/24 Study. *Public Health Nutr.* **2021**, 1–13. [CrossRef] [PubMed]
44. Vadeboncoeur, C.; Foster, C.; Townsend, N. Freshman 15 in England: A Longitudinal Evaluation of First Year University Student's Weight Change. *BMC Obes.* **2016**, *3*, 45. [CrossRef]
45. Haidar, S.A.; de Vries, N.K.; Papandreou, D.; Rizk, R.; Karavetian, M. The Freshman Weight Gain Phenomenon: Does It Apply To. *Open Access Maced. J. Med. Sci.* **2018**, *6*, 2214–2220. [CrossRef]
46. Mihalopoulos, N.L.; Auinger, P.; Klein, J.D. The Freshman 15: Is It Real? *J. Am. Coll. Health* **2008**, *56*, 531–533. [CrossRef] [PubMed]
47. Bach-Faig, A.; Fuentes-Bol, C.; Ramos, D.; Carrasco, J.L.; Roman, B.; Bertomeu, I.F.; Cristià, E.; Geleva, D.; Serra-Majem, L. The Mediterranean Diet in Spain: Adherence Trends during the Past Two Decades Using the Mediterranean Adequacy Index. *Public Health Nutr.* **2011**, *14*, 622–628. [CrossRef] [PubMed]
48. García Cabrera, S.; Herrera Fernández, N.; Rodríguez Hernández, C.; Nissensohn, M.; Román-Viñas, B.; Serra-Majem, L. KIDMED Test; Prevalence of Low Adherence to the Mediterranean Diet in Children and Young: A Systematic Review. *Nutr. Hosp.* **2015**, *32*, 2390–2399. [CrossRef]
49. Riccardi, G.; Vitale, M.; Vaccaro, O. Are Europeans Moving towards Dietary Habits More Suitable for Reducing Cardiovascular Disease Risk? *Nutr. Metab. Cardiovasc. Dis.* **2020**, *30*, 1857–1860. [CrossRef] [PubMed]
50. Calderon, R.; Pupanead, S.; Prachakul, W.; Kim, G. Happiness, Perceived Stress, Psychological Well-Being, and Health Behaviors of Thai University Students: Preliminary Results from a Multinational Study on Well-Being. *J. Am. Coll. Health* **2021**, *69*, 176–184. [CrossRef] [PubMed]
51. Quehl, R.; Haines, J.; Lewis, S.P.; Buchholz, A.C. Food and Mood: Diet Quality Is Inversely Associated with Depressive Symptoms in Female University Students. *Can. J. Diet. Pract. Res.* **2017**, *78*, 124–128. [CrossRef]
52. Delicado-Soria, A.; Serrano-Urrea, R.; Cervera-Burriel, F.; Daouas, T.; García-Meseguer, M.-J. Food Consumption in Tunisian University Students and Its Association with Sociodemographic Characteristics and Lifestyle Behaviours. *Public Health Nutr.* **2020**, *24*, 4949–4964. [CrossRef]
53. Cervera Burriel, F.; Serrano Urrea, R.; Daouas, T.; Delicado Soria, A.; García Meseguer, M.J. Food habits and nutritional assessment in a tunisian university population. *Nutr. Hosp.* **2014**, *30*, 1350–1358. [CrossRef] [PubMed]
54. García-Meseguer, M.J.; Burriel, F.C.; García, C.V.; Serrano-Urrea, R. Adherence to Mediterranean Diet in a Spanish University Population. *Appetite* **2014**, *78*, 156–164. [CrossRef]
55. Ejeda-Manzanera, J.M.; Rodrigo-Vega, M. Hábitos de alimentación y calidad de dieta en estudiantes universitarias de magisterio en relación a su adherencia a la dieta mediterránea. *Rev. Española Salud Pública* **2021**, *95*, e1–e14.
56. Salas, R.; del Mar Bibiloni, M.; Zapata, M.E.; Coll, J.L.; Pons, A.; Tur, J.A. Balearic Adults Have Low Intakes of Fruits and Vegetables Compared with the Dietary Guidelines for Adults in Spain. *Nutr. Res.* **2013**, *33*, 204–210. [CrossRef]
57. Beaudry, K.M.; Ludwa, I.A.; Thomas, A.M.; Ward, W.E.; Falk, B.; Josse, A.R. First-Year University Is Associated with Greater Body Weight, Body Composition and Adverse Dietary Changes in Males than Females. *PLoS ONE* **2019**, *14*, e0218554. [CrossRef] [PubMed]
58. Leblanc, V.; Bégin, C.; Corneau, L.; Dodin, S.; Lemieux, S. Gender Differences in Dietary Intakes: What Is the Contribution of Motivational Variables? *J. Hum. Nutr. Diet.* **2015**, *28*, 37–46. [CrossRef] [PubMed]
59. Menozzi, D.; Sogari, G.; Mora, C. Explaining Vegetable Consumption among Young Adults: An Application of the Theory of Planned Behaviour. *Nutrients* **2015**, *7*, 7633–7650. [CrossRef] [PubMed]
60. Grzymisławska, M.; Puch, E.A.; Zawada, A.; Grzymisławski, M. Do Nutritional Behaviors Depend on Biological Sex and Cultural Gender? *Adv. Clin. Exp. Med.* **2020**, *29*, 165–172. [CrossRef]
61. Aljadani, H.M.; Patterson, A.J.; Sibbritt, D.; Collins, C.E. Diet Quality and Six-Year Risk of Overweight and Obesity among Mid-Age Australian Women Who Were Initially in the Healthy Weight Range. *Health Promot. J. Austr.* **2016**, *27*, 29–35. [CrossRef] [PubMed]
62. Aljadani, H.M.A.; Sibbritt, D.; Patterson, A.; Collins, C. The Australian Recommended Food Score Did Not Predict Weight Gain in Middle-Aged Australian Women during Six Years of Follow-Up. *Aust. N. Z. J. Public Health* **2013**, *37*, 322–328. [CrossRef]
63. El Ansari, W.; Stock, C.; Mikolajczyk, R.T. Relationships between Food Consumption and Living Arrangements among University Students in Four European Countries—A Cross-Sectional Study. *Nutr. J.* **2012**, *11*, 28. [CrossRef] [PubMed]
64. Lupi, S.; Bagordo, F.; Stefanati, A.; Grassi, T.; Piccinni, L.; Bergamini, M.; Donno, A.D. Assessment of Lifestyle and Eating Habits among Undergraduate Students in Northern Italy. *Ann. Ist. Super. Sanità* **2015**, *51*, 154–161. [CrossRef]
65. Côté, M.; Bégin, C. Review of the Experience of Weight-Based Stigmatization in Romantic Relationships. *Curr. Obes. Rep.* **2020**, *9*, 280–287. [CrossRef]
66. van Woerden, I.; Brewis, A.; Hruschka, D.; Dunton, G.; Adams, M.A.; Bruening, M. Young Adults' BMI and Changes in Romantic Relationship Status during the First Semester of College. *PLoS ONE* **2020**, *15*, e0230806. [CrossRef]

67. Moreno-Gómez, C.; Romaguera-Bosch, D.; Tauler-Riera, P.; Bennasar-Veny, M.; Pericas-Beltran, J.; Martinez-Andreu, S.; Aguilo-Pons, A. Clustering of Lifestyle Factors in Spanish University Students: The Relationship between Smoking, Alcohol Consumption, Physical Activity and Diet Quality. *Public Health Nutr.* **2012**, *15*, 2131–2139. [CrossRef]
68. Romaguera, D.; Tauler, P.; Bennasar, M.; Pericas, J.; Moreno, C.; Martinez, S.; Aguilo, A. Determinants and Patterns of Physical Activity Practice among Spanish University Students. *J. Sports Sci.* **2011**, *29*, 989–997. [CrossRef] [PubMed]
69. Sánchez-Ojeda, M.A.; De Luna-Bertos, E. Healthy lifestyles of the university population. *Nutr. Hosp.* **2015**, *31*, 1910–1919. [CrossRef] [PubMed]
70. Bennasar-Veny, M.; Yañez, A.M.; Pericas, J.; Ballester, L.; Fernandez-Dominguez, J.C.; Tauler, P.; Aguilo, A. Cluster Analysis of Health-Related Lifestyles in University Students. *Int. J. Environ. Res. Public Health* **2020**, *17*, 1776. [CrossRef]
71. Adan, R.A.H.; van der Beek, E.M.; Buitelaar, J.K.; Cryan, J.F.; Hebebrand, J.; Higgs, S.; Schellekens, H.; Dickson, S.L. Nutritional Psychiatry: Towards Improving Mental Health by What You Eat. *Eur. Neuropsychopharmacol.* **2019**, *29*, 1321–1332. [CrossRef]
72. Moreno-Agostino, D.; Caballero, F.F.; Martín-María, N.; Tyrovolas, S.; López-García, P.; Rodríguez-Artalejo, F.; Haro, J.M.; Ayuso-Mateos, J.L.; Miret, M. Mediterranean Diet and Wellbeing: Evidence from a Nationwide Survey. *Psychol. Health* **2019**, *34*, 321–335. [CrossRef]
73. Emerson, S.D.; Carbert, N.S. An Apple a Day: Protective Associations between Nutrition and the Mental Health of Immigrants in Canada. *Soc. Psychiatry Psychiatr. Epidemiol.* **2019**, *54*, 567–578. [CrossRef]
74. Fresán, U.; Bes-Rastrollo, M.; Segovia-Siapco, G.; Sanchez-Villegas, A.; Lahortiga, F.; de la Rosa, P.-A.; Martínez-Gonzalez, M.-A. Does the MIND Diet Decrease Depression Risk? A Comparison with Mediterranean Diet in the SUN Cohort. *Eur. J. Nutr.* **2019**, *58*, 1271–1282. [CrossRef]
75. Smith, A.D.; Warren, M.J.; Refsum, H. Chapter Six-Vitamin B12. In *Advances in Food and Nutrition Research*; New Research and Developments of Water-Soluble Vitamins; Eskin, N.A.M., Ed.; Academic Press: Cambridge, MA, USA, 2018; Volume 83, pp. 215–279.
76. Spaeth, A.M.; Dinges, D.F.; Goel, N. Sex and Race Differences in Caloric Intake during Sleep Restriction in Healthy Adults. *Am. J. Clin. Nutr* **2014**, *100*, 559–566. [CrossRef]
77. Fang, Z.; Spaeth, A.M.; Ma, N.; Zhu, S.; Hu, S.; Goel, N.; Detre, J.A.; Dinges, D.F.; Rao, H. Altered Salience Network Connectivity Predicts Macronutrient Intake after Sleep Deprivation. *Sci. Rep.* **2015**, *5*, 8215. [CrossRef] [PubMed]
78. Heath, G.; Roach, G.D.; Dorrian, J.; Ferguson, S.A.; Darwent, D.; Sargent, C. The Effect of Sleep Restriction on Snacking Behaviour during a Week of Simulated Shiftwork. *Accid. Anal. Prev.* **2012**, *45*, 62–67. [CrossRef]
79. Mozaffarian, N.; Heshmat, R.; Ataie-Jafari, A.; Motlagh, M.E.; Ziaodini, H.; Shafiee, G.; Taheri, M.; Mansourian, M.; Qorbani, M.; Kelishadi, R. Association of Sleep Duration and Snack Consumption in Children and Adolescents: The CASPIAN-V Study. *Food Sci. Nutr.* **2020**, *8*, 1888–1897. [CrossRef] [PubMed]
80. Martinez, S.M.; Tschann, J.M.; Butte, N.F.; Gregorich, S.E.; Penilla, C.; Flores, E.; Greenspan, L.C.; Pasch, L.A.; Deardorff, J. Short Sleep Duration Is Associated with Eating More Carbohydrates and Less Dietary Fat in Mexican American Children. *Sleep* **2017**, *40*, zsw057. [CrossRef] [PubMed]
81. Nedeltcheva, A.V.; Kilkus, J.M.; Imperial, J.; Kasza, K.; Schoeller, D.A.; Penev, P.D. Sleep Curtailment Is Accompanied by Increased Intake of Calories from Snacks. *Am. J. Clin. Nutr.* **2009**, *89*, 126–133. [CrossRef]
82. Stern, J.H.; Grant, A.S.; Thomson, C.A.; Tinker, L.; Hale, L.; Brennan, K.M.; Woods, N.F.; Chen, Z. Short Sleep Duration Is Associated with Decreased Serum Leptin, Increased Energy Intake and Decreased Diet Quality in Postmenopausal Women. *Obesity* **2014**, *22*, E55–E61. [CrossRef]
83. Haghighatdoost, F.; Karimi, G.; Esmaillzadeh, A.; Azadbakht, L. Sleep Deprivation Is Associated with Lower Diet Quality Indices and Higher Rate of General and Central Obesity among Young Female Students in Iran. *Nutrition* **2012**, *28*, 1146–1150. [CrossRef]
84. Dashti, H.S.; Scheer, F.A.; Jacques, P.F.; Lamon-Fava, S.; Ordovás, J.M. Short Sleep Duration and Dietary Intake: Epidemiologic Evidence, Mechanisms, and Health Implications. *Adv. Nutr.* **2015**, *6*, 648–659. [CrossRef]
85. Binks, H.E.; Vincent, G.; Gupta, C.; Irwin, C.; Khalesi, S. Effects of Diet on Sleep: A Narrative Review. *Nutrients* **2020**, *12*, 936. [CrossRef]
86. King, B.M.; Cespedes, V.M.; Burden, G.K.; Brady, S.K.; Clement, L.R.; Abbott, E.M.; Baughman, K.S.; Joyner, S.E.; Clark, M.M.; Pury, C.L.S. Extreme Under-Reporting of Body Weight by Young Adults with Obesity: Relation to Social Desirability. *Obes. Sci. Pract.* **2018**, *4*, 129–133. [CrossRef]
87. Burke, M.A.; Carman, K.G. You Can Be Too Thin (but Not Too Tall): Social Desirability Bias in Self-Reports of Weight and Height. *Econ. Hum. Biol.* **2017**, *27*, 198–222. [CrossRef]
88. Mattioli, A.V.; Sciomer, S.; Cocchi, C.; Maffei, S.; Gallina, S. Quarantine during COVID-19 Outbreak: Changes in Diet and Physical Activity Increase the Risk of Cardiovascular Disease. *Nutr. Metab. Cardiovasc. Dis.* **2020**, *30*, 1409–1417. [CrossRef]
89. Izzo, L.; Santonastaso, A.; Cotticelli, G.; Federico, A.; Pacifico, S.; Castaldo, L.; Colao, A.; Ritieni, A. An Italian Survey on Dietary Habits and Changes during the COVID-19 Lockdown. *Nutrients* **2021**, *13*, 1197. [CrossRef] [PubMed]
90. Ferrante, G.; Camussi, E.; Piccinelli, C.; Senore, C.; Armaroli, P.; Ortale, A.; Garena, F.; Giordano, L. Did Social Isolation during the SARS-CoV-2 Epidemic Have an Impact on the Lifestyles of Citizens? *Epidemiol. Prev.* **2020**, *44*, 353–362. [CrossRef]
91. Sidor, A.; Rzymski, P. Dietary Choices and Habits during COVID-19 Lockdown: Experience from Poland. *Nutrients* **2020**, *12*, 1657. [CrossRef] [PubMed]

92. Alegria-Lertxundi, I.; Rocandio, A.M.; Telletxea, S.; Rincón, E.; Arroyo-Izaga, M. Relación Entre El Índice de Consumo de Pescado y Carne y La Adecuación y Calidad de La Dieta En Mujeres Jóvenes Universitarias. *Nutr. Hosp.* **2014**, *30*, 1135–1143. [CrossRef] [PubMed]
93. Rodríguez-Rodríguez, E.; López-Sobaler, A.M.; Ortega, R.M.; Delgado-Losada, M.L.; López-Parra, A.M.; Aparicio, A. Association between Neutrophil-to-Lymphocyte Ratio with Abdominal Obesity and Healthy Eating Index in a Representative Older Spanish Population. *Nutrients* **2020**, *12*, 855. [CrossRef] [PubMed]
94. Weinstein, S.J.; Vogt, T.M.; Gerrior, S.A. Healthy Eating Index Scores Are Associated with Blood Nutrient Concentrations in the Third National Health and Nutrition Examination Survey. *J. Am. Diet. Assoc.* **2004**, *104*, 576–584. [CrossRef] [PubMed]
95. Fallaize, R.; Livingstone, K.M.; Celis-Morales, C.; Macready, A.L.; San-Cristobal, R.; Navas-Carretero, S.; Marsaux, C.F.M.; O'Donovan, C.B.; Kolossa, S.; Moschonis, G.; et al. Association between Diet-Quality Scores, Adiposity, Total Cholesterol and Markers of Nutritional Status in European Adults: Findings from the Food4Me Study. *Nutrients* **2018**, *10*, 49. [CrossRef] [PubMed]

nutrients

MDPI

Article

Food-Based Dietary Guidelines around the World: A Comparative Analysis to Update AESAN Scientific Committee Dietary Recommendations

Montaña Cámara [1,*], Rosa María Giner [2], Elena González-Fandos [3], Esther López-García [4], Jordi Mañes [5], María P. Portillo [6], Magdalena Rafecas [7], Laura Domínguez [1] and José Alfredo Martínez [8]

1 Nutrition and Food Science Department, Pharmacy Faculty, Complutense University of Madrid (UCM), Plaza Ramón y Cajal, s/n, 28040 Madrid, Spain; ladoming@ucm.es
2 Department of Pharmacology, Faculty of Pharmacy, University of Valencia, 46100 Burjassot, Spain; Rosa.M.Giner@uv.es
3 Department of Food Technology, CIVA Research Center, University of La Rioja, Madre de Dios, 26006 Logroño, Spain; elena.gonzalez@unirioja.es
4 Department of Preventive Medicine and Public Health, School of Medicine, Universidad Autónoma de Madrid, Instituto de Investigación Sanitaria Hospital Universitario La Paz (IdiPAZ), CIBER of Epidemiology and Public Health (CIBERESP), 28029 Madrid, Spain; esther.lopez@uam.es
5 Department of Preventive Medicine and Public Health, Food Sciences, Toxicology and Forensic Medicine, Faculty of Pharmacy, University of Valencia, 46100 Burjassot, Spain; jordi.manes@uv.es
6 Nutrition and Obesity Group, Department of Pharmacy and Food Sciences, University of the Basque Country (UPV/EHU) and CIBERobn Physiopathology of Obesity and Nutrition, Institute of Health Carlos III, and BIOARABA Health Research Institute, 01006 Vitoria-Gasteiz, Spain; mariapuy.portillo@ehu.eus
7 Departament de Nutrition, Food Science and Gastonomy, Faculty of Farmacy and Food Science, University of Barcelona, 08028 Barcelona, Spain; magdarafecas@ub.edu
8 IMDEA + CSIC/UAM y CIBEROBN, 28049 Madrid, Spain; jalfredo.martinez@imdea.org
* Correspondence: mcamara@ucm.es; Tel.: +34-91-394-1802; Fax: +34-91-394-1799

Citation: Cámara, M.; Giner, R.M.; González-Fandos, E.; López-García, E.; Mañes, J.; Portillo, M.P.; Rafecas, M.; Domínguez, L.; Martínez, J.A. Food-Based Dietary Guidelines around the World: A Comparative Analysis to Update AESAN Scientific Committee Dietary Recommendations. *Nutrients* **2021**, *13*, 3131. https://doi.org/10.3390/nu13093131

Academic Editors: Clare Collins and George Moschonis

Received: 18 July 2021
Accepted: 5 September 2021
Published: 8 September 2021

Abstract: Food-Based Dietary Guidelines (FBDG) include dietary recommendations based on food groups according to the general and accepted nutrition principles and current scientific evidence. Adoption of FBDG contributes to the prevention of malnutrition in all its forms, promotes human health, and reduces environmental impact. The present review aims to perform an international comparative analysis of the FBDG adopted in different countries from three different continents (America, Asia, and Europe), with particular reference to the Spanish Food Safety and Nutrition Agency (AESAN, Agencia Española de Seguridad Alimentaria y Nutrición) Scientific Committee dietary recommendations. A total of twelve countries with the most updated FBDG and/or closest to the traditional and cultural preferences of Spain were finally selected. All the reviewed FBDG provided recommendations for fruits, vegetables, cereals, legumes, nuts, milk and dairy products, meat and derivatives, fish, eggs, water, and oil; however, remarkable differences regarding recommended amounts were found among countries.

Keywords: food-based dietary guidelines; national dietary recommendations; healthy eating; health promotion; public health

1. Introduction

Foods are sources of macronutrients (carbohydrates, proteins, fats) and micronutrients (vitamins and minerals) necessary to cover human metabolism requirements for life and survival, concerning energy demands for sustainability, growth, development, and reproduction [1]. In addition, foods contain biologically active components called "bioactive compounds" or "phytochemicals", which are able to contribute to achieving an adequate health status [2].

The knowledge of food composition (nutrients and bioactive compounds) as well as defining the different food groups, where they are categorized, is fundamental for food intake decision-making and promoting human health [1,3]. The consumption of foodstuffs from different food groups in balanced proportions ensures the adequate intake of nutrients and bioactive compounds with potential benefits for human health [4]. Scientific evidence has demonstrated that a varied and balanced diet with a predominant consumption of plant-based food groups (fruits, vegetables, legumes, cereals, nuts, etc.) over food groups of animal origin promotes health and reduces environmental impact [5]. According to EAT-Lancet Commission, the adoption of healthy and sustainable diets could reduce 19.0–23.6% of global deaths (10.8–11.6 million) every year [6]. Thus, focusing exclusively on human health is not sufficient as inadequate eating patterns adversely affect the environment and jeopardize well-being, quality of life, and survival of present and future generations [7,8].

In general, dietary recommendations are based on Dietary Reference Values (DRV) (also named Recommended Nutrient Intake, RNI; or Recommended Dietary Allowances, RDAs), which refer to specific nutrients and their recommended intake for each particular group of the population in order to avoid nutritional deficiencies that can compromise health. One example is Spain, where the Scientific Committee of the Spanish Agency for Food Safety and Nutrition (AESAN) in 2019 approved a scientific report to update DRVs of 15 minerals and 13 vitamins for the Spanish population [9].

The European Food Safety Authority (EFSA) has encouraged Member States of the European Union (EU) to establish dietary recommendations focused on food groups based on DRVs [10]. In this context, The World Health Organization (WHO) and the Food and Agriculture Organization of the United Nations (FAO) have promoted the development of national food-based dietary recommendations in line with the Sustainable Healthy Diets; that is, considering the economic, cultural, social, and environmental conditions of each country [11].

In this context, Food-Based Dietary Guidelines (FBDG) are considered short messages expressed as dietary recommendations based on food groups, in accordance with the general and accepted nutrition principles and current scientific evidence [7]. FBDG are focused on preventing malnutrition in all its forms, promoting human health, as well as reducing environmental impact through the incorporation of the concept of sustainability within the healthy diet definition [7,12,13].

The objective of the present review is to perform an international comparative analysis of the FBDG adopted in different countries from three different continents (America, Asia, and Europe), with particular reference to the AESAN (Agencia Española de Seguridad Alimentaria y Nutrición) Scientific Committee dietary recommendations.

2. Materials and Methods

Different countries have established FBDG. On its website (http://www.fao.org/nutrition/education/food-dietary-guidelines/en/, accessed on 6 September 2021), FAO [14] offers a general description of food guides that include recommendations for approved food groups in diverse countries. Inclusion criteria established to select FBDG subjected to this review include the most updated dietary guidelines as well as those that are closest to the traditional and cultural preferences of Spain.

Twelve countries were selected considering the inclusion criteria. As shown in Table 1, the present work critically reviews the international food guides of the United States, China, the Nordic countries (Finland, Norway, and Sweden), the United Kingdom, Germany, the Netherlands, France, Portugal, Italy, and Spain.

Table 1. International overview of Food-Based Dietary Guidelines established in North America (United States), Asia (China), and Europe (Finland, Norway, Sweden, United Kingdom, Germany, The Netherlands, France, Portugal, Italy, and Spain). Adapted from [5,14].

Region/Country	Food-Based Dietary Guidelines	Reference
North America		
United States	Dietary guidelines for Americans 2015–2020	[15]
Asia		
China	Chinese Dietary Guidelines	[16]
Europe		
Finland	Finnish nutrition recommendations 2014	[17]
Norway	Norwegian guidelines on diet, nutrition, and physical activity	[18]
Sweden	Find your way to eat greener, not too much, and to be active!	[19]
United Kingdom	The Balance of Good Health	[20]
Germany	Ten guidelines for wholesome eating and drinking from the German Nutrition Society	[21]
The Netherlands	Dutch dietary guidelines 2015	[22]
France	The French National Nutrition and Health Program's dietary guidelines	[23]
Portugal	Food wheel guide	[24]
Italy	Dietary Guidelines for Healthy Eating	[25]
Spain	NAOS Strategy.	[26,27]
	GENCAT Strategy (Generalitat de Catalunya)	[28]

3. Results and Discussion

In general, all the national and international dietary guidelines selected and reviewed in the present work were in accordance with the Sustainable Healthy Diets (healthy eating models with a low environmental impact) [29], as they provided the following recommendations:

- A varied, balanced diet: eat a wide range of food products from different food groups and maintain an adequate balance between the energy ingested and the expenditure of the individuals.
- A diet based mainly on plant-based food; that is, fruits, vegetables, minimally processed tubers, cereals (preferably whole grains), unsalted seeds and nuts, as well as oils and fats with a beneficial omega 3:6 ratio.
- Moderate consumption of meat and its derivatives and dairy products. The diet should incorporate small amounts of fish and aquatic products from certified fisheries.
- Very limited consumption of food rich in fats, simple sugars, or salt, as well as low in micronutrients (e.g., fried potatoes, confectionery products, sugary drinks, etc.).
- Intake of water as the main drink, limiting the consumption of other drinks, particularly sugary soft drinks.

3.1. Illustrations Included in the Selected Food Guides

The most commonly used graphic representation in the reviewed dietary guidelines was an illustration with comprehensible and clear key messages and traffic light colors: green, amber/yellow, and red. The first one (green color) recommends an increase of the consumption of certain food groups, above all plant-based food (fruits, vegetables, legumes, etc.). The amber color promotes a replacement of one specific food group by a better option (e.g., refined cereals by whole grains). Finally, the red color recommends a reduction in the consumption of particular food groups, generally red and processed meat, salt, sugar, and alcohol. The dietary guidelines of Sweden, The Netherlands, France, and Spain (GENCAT, Generalitat de Catalunya) used this graphic representation [19,22,23,28].

The nutritional circle, oval, or wheel as well as the plate were the next illustrations most often used in the selected dietary guidelines. Germany, the United Kingdom, and Portugal used the nutritional circle, oval, and wheel, respectively [20,21,24], whereas the United States, China, and Finland included the plate model in their food guides [15–17]. Except for the Finnish model, both types of graphic representations are divided into segments with a different size, which reflects how different food groups should contribute towards the total diet. Although both illustrations depict the relative weight of each food group, the nutritional circle, oval, and wheel refer to the whole diet, while the plate represents a single meal.

The pyramid model was used in the dietary guidelines of Finland and Spain (AESAN) and it is divided in segments or steps according to the contribution of each food group to the whole diet, so that the lower the level (close to the bottom level), the higher the importance in the diet [17,26,27].

The Chinese and Swedish food guides included other illustrations not used in other countries, such as the pagoda and the abacus as well as the keyhole symbol, respectively [16,19]. The pagoda model is similar to the pyramid as the most important food groups are located in the lower levels. The abacus is directed to children (8–11 years old) and it contains 6 rows with colored beads. Each food group is represented by a specific color, and the number of beads in each row indicates the portions recommended [16]. The Italian food guides do not include graphic representations [25].

Table 2 provides a summary of the illustrations used in the selected food guides.

Table 2. International overview of Food-Based Dietary Guidelines established in North America (United States), Asia (China), and Europe (Finland, Norway, Sweden, United Kingdom, Germany, The Netherlands, France, Portugal, Italy, and Spain). Adapted from [5,14].

Graphic Representations	Country/Region												
	United States	China	Finland	Norway	Sweden	United Kingdom	Germany	The Netherlands	France	Portugal	Italy *	Spain	
												AESAN	GENCAT
Abacus		X											
Key messages (e.g., traffic light)					X			X	X				X
Keyhole symbol					X								
Nutritional circle, oval, or wheel						X	X			X			
Pagoda		X											
Plate	X	X	X										
Pyramid			X									X	

* The Italian guidelines do not include graphical representations. X: information included in the National Dietary Guidelines.

Herforth et al. carried out an interesting review of the current FBDG whose information was available in the repository of the FAO in order to evaluate the similarities and differences in the key nutrition messages among countries, although they do not include information about FBDG that use key messages as graphic representations of the food groups [30]. In the present manuscript, a total number of 90 FBDG from different regions of the world were finally selected and reviewed: Europe (33 FBDG), Latin America and the Caribbean (27), Asia and the Pacific (17), Africa (7), Near East (4), and North America (2). The results revealed that the illustrations most commonly used in the above-mentioned FBDG were the pyramid and the circle or plate (39.7% and 26.9%, respectively). In addition, this review was mainly focused on the Spanish dietary recommendations.

Soy milk in the food group "dairy products" (milk, yogurt, cheese, etc.) as an alternative of the above-mentioned products was only considered in the United States and the United Kingdom. In addition, Norway was the only country that specifically recommended the consumption of lean dairy products.

3.2. Comparative Analysis of the Food Groups

The results from the comparative analysis of the selected national and international food guides carried out by the authors of the present work are summarized in Table 3.

Table 3. Food groups and other important categories for which the international food guides have established dietary recommendations.

Food Group	Country/region												
	United States	China	Finland	Norway	Sweden	United Kingdom	Germany	The Netherlands	France	Portugal	Italy	Spain	
												AESAN	GENCAT
Fruits	X	X	X	X	X	X	X	X	X	X	X	X	X
Vegetables	X	X	X	X	X	X	X	X	X	X	X	X	X
Starchy foods	X	X	X	X	X	X	X	X	X	X	X	X	X
Legumes	X	X	X	X	X	X	X	X	X	X	X	X	X
Nuts	X	X	X	X	X	X	X	X	X	X	X	X	X
Soy products	X	X	n.a.	n.a.	-	-	-	-	-	-	-	-	-
Dairy products	X	X	X	X	X	X	X	X	X	X	X	X	X
Meat and its products	X	X	X	X	X	X	X	X	X	X	X	X	X
Fish	X	X	X	X	X	X	X	X	X	X	X	X	X
Seafood	X	-	-	-	X	-	-	-	-	-	X	-	X
Eggs	X	X	X	X	X	X	X	X	X	X	X	X	X
Water and other liquids (tea, etc.)	X	X	X	X	X	X	X	X	X	X	X	X	X
Oil	X	X	X	X	X	X	X	X	X	X	X	X	X
Salt	X	X	X	n.a.	X	X	-	X	-	X	X	X	X
Sugar	X	X	n.a.	n.a.	X	-	-	-	-	-	X	-	X
Alcohol	X	X	n.a.	n.a.	X	-	-	X	X	-	X	-	-
Physical activity	X	X	X	X	X	X	X	X	X	X	X	X	X

X: information included in the National Dietary Guidelines; n.a.: Information not available in the official English version of the National Dietary Guidelines; -: food or food group not mentioned in the National Dietary Guidelines.

Focusing on plant-based food groups, it is important to highlight that the dietary guidelines from Finland, Norway, Italy, and Spain (GENCAT) specifically recommended the consumption of whole grains. In the rest of the countries (United States, China, Sweden, United Kingdom, Germany, The Netherlands, France, Portugal, and Spain (AESAN)), it was indicated that the consumption of whole products should be promoted versus the consumption of refined ones. With respect to the soy products, advised consumption was only recommended in the food guides of the United States and China.

Regarding the food groups of animal origin, all the selected dietary guidelines generally recommended reducing the consumption of meat, mainly red and/or processed meat. The inclusion of seafood within the food group "fish" was only considered in the food guides of the United States, Sweden, Italy, and Spain (GENCAT).

The consumption of virgin olive oil was particularly promoted in some of the countries, except for the United States, China, The Netherlands, France, and Portugal. All the reviewed dietary guidelines generally recommended reducing the intake of salt, simple sugars, and alcohol, but only few countries suggested a maximum daily intake. Finally, the performance of daily physical activity was promoted in all countries.

These results are in accordance with the studies by Montagnese et al. and Herforth et al. [30,31]. Montagnese et al. performed a comprehensive comparative analysis of the FBDG of 34 European countries. Although important differences among these dietary guidelines were found due to geographical, social, and cultural factors, the great majority of the key nutritional points were similar among countries (e.g., promotion of the consumption of plant-based food such as fruits, vegetables, and cereals, and reduction of the consumption of animal products, fats, sugars, and salt). Likewise, Herforth et al. reported that most of the reviewed food guides recommended following a varied diet, with a clear predominance of plant-based food groups (fruits, vegetables, legumes) and a limited consumption of fat, salt, and sugar. The recommendations related to nuts, dairy products, red meat, and oil were more variable among countries. In addition, the consumption of nuts, whole grains, and healthy fats was not promoted in all the countries despite the WHO recommendations.

3.3. Recommendations for Specific Food Groups: Established Daily Intakes

A more comprehensive comparative analysis of the selected food guides regarding the specific recommendations established for each food group was carried out. Tables 4–6 summarize the most important findings of all the reviewed dietary guidelines (see Table 1 for references). It is important to highlight that the Italian dietary guidelines establish various daily and weekly intakes for each food group according to three different caloric intakes (1500, 2000, and 2500 kcal/day). In the present work, Italian recommendations will be provided as a range of the three caloric intakes.

Fruits and vegetables are low-energy density foods whose regular consumption contributes to a diversified and nutritious diet by providing a wide range of micronutrients, such as minerals (mainly magnesium and potassium) and water-soluble vitamins (C and B_9 or folic acid), and bioactive compounds, when consumed fresh and uncooked. Dietary fiber is another important bioactive compound in these food groups, with a general predominance of the soluble fraction (pectins, gums, mucilages) in fruits. Carotenoids without provitamin-A activity are present in some fruits and vegetables; for instance, lycopene (above all in watermelon and tomato) and zeaxanthin (especially in corn), among others [1].

Cereals, particularly whole grains, contain high quantities of insoluble dietary fiber (cellulose, hemicellulose, lignin), whereas the soluble fraction of fiber is present in significant amounts in oat. An adequate daily intake of cereals also provides soluble and insoluble carbohydrates, B-group vitamins such as B_1, B_3, B_6, and B_9, and minerals such as magnesium, zinc, calcium, and iron (especially in whole grains) [1].

Legumes are foods high in carbohydrates, fiber, and protein, with an important nutritional value. Starch, stachyose, and raffinose represent the main carbohydrates in these plant-based foods. Except for methionine (present in grains), legumes contain all amino acids, including lysine, which is limited in cereals. For this reason, it is recommended to combine the consumption of legumes and cereals in the same meal to increase its nutritional value. Other important compounds present in legumes are vitamins (B_1, B_2, B_3, B_9, C, carotenes) and minerals (calcium, magnesium, zinc, potassium, iron). Fruits, vegetables, and cereals' fat content is low. Legumes have a proper lipid profile as monounsaturated and polyunsaturated fatty acids are the predominant ones [1,32,33].

Nuts (walnuts, almonds, hazelnuts, peanuts) are high-energy foods due to their important quantity of fat (nearly 50%); however, the lipid profile is adequate as nuts contain mostly monounsaturated and polyunsaturated fatty acids, such as linoleic acid. The consumption of nuts also provides some vitamins (B_6, E) and minerals (magnesium, potassium) [1,3,34].

Focusing on the plant-based food groups (Table 4), all the reviewed dietary guidelines, with the exception of the Swedish one, suggested specific recommendations for fruits and vegetables. Norway, the United Kingdom, Germany, France, Italy, and Spain (AESAN and GENCAT) recommended eating at least 5 servings/day. The Portuguese food guide proposed a higher number of servings, as it recommended 3–5 servings/day for fruits and 3–5 servings/day for vegetables; that is, a total of 6–10 servings/day counting both food groups. China, Finland, and The Netherlands directly suggested specific amounts (at least 200 g/day), instead of servings. In summary, all the selected dietary guidelines promote the consumption of a great variety of fruits and vegetables, which contribute to the maintenance of an appropriate health status. According to López-González et al., the higher the quantity and variety in fruit and vegetables' consumption, the better nutrient adequacy and diet quality [35].

Table 4. Dietary recommendations for food groups of plant origin established by the international food guides selected in the present work.

Country/Region	Food Groups of Plant Origin					
	Fruits	Vegetables	Starchy Foods	Legumes	Nuts	Soy Products
United States	2 cups-eq/day	$2\frac{1}{2}$ cups-eq/day	6 oz-eq/day	$1\frac{1}{2}$ cups-eq/week	5 oz-eq/week	
China	200–350 g/day	300–500 g/day (150–250 g of dark green vegetables)	250–400 g/day (50–150 g of whole grains and legumes, 50–100 g of tubers)		-	At least 25 g/day
Finland	>500 g/day (potatoes not included)		-	-	-	-
Norway	At least 5 servings/day		-	-	-	n.a.
Sweden	-	-	-	-	-	-
United Kingdom	At least 5 servings/day		-	-	-	-
Germany	At least 5 servings/day		-	-	-	-
The Netherlands	At least 200 g/day	At least 200 g/day	At least 90 g/day of whole grain bread or other whole grain products	-	At least 15 g/day of unsalted nuts	-
France	At least 5 servings/day (80–100 g/day)		1 portion/meal	-	A handful/day	-
Portugal	3–5 servings/day (1 piece of fruit; medium size = 160 g)	3–5 servings/day (2 cups of raw vegetables = 180 g/day; 1 cup of cooked vegetables = 140 g/day)	4–11 servings/day (1 loaf of bread = 50 g; 1 thin slice of corn bread = 70 g; 1 and 1/2 potato (medium size = 125 g); 5 tablespoons of breakfast cereal = 35 g; 6 biscuits = 35 g; 2 tablespoons of uncooked rice/pasta = 35 g; 4 tablespoons of cooked rice/pasta = 110 g)	1–2 servings/day (1 tablespoon of dried raw legumes (chickpeas, beans, lentils) = 25 g; 3 tablespoons of fresh raw legumes (peas, beans) = 80 g; 3 tablespoons of cooked/ fresh legumes = 80 g)	-	-
Italy	2–3 servings/day (1 serving = 150 g)	$2\frac{1}{2}$–3 servings/day (1 serving = 200 g)	$2\frac{1}{2}$–$4\frac{1}{2}$ servings bread/day (1 serving = 50 g)1–$1\frac{1}{2}$ servings rice and/or pasta/ day (1 serving = 80 g)$1\frac{1}{2}$–3 servings breakfast cereals/week (1 serving = 30 g)1–2 servings potatoes/week (1 serving = 200 g)	3 servings/week (1 serving = 150 g)	1–$1\frac{1}{2}$ servings/week (1 serving = 30 g)	-
Spain: AESAN	3 servings/day (120 g or a medium piece/a slice of pineapple/two slices melon/watermelon; 150 mL of fresh fruit juice)	2 servings/day (150 g raw in the form of a salad (tomato, lettuce, etc.); 1 serving of sautéed/cooked vegetables as a main course or as garnish of meat, fish or eggs (zucchini, green beans, etc.)	-	At least 2–3 times/week	-	-
Spain: GENCAT	3 servings/day = 1 piece of fruit (1 orange, apple; 2–3 apricots, tangerines, plums, etc.); or 1 bowl cherries, strawberries, grapes; or 1–2 slices of melon, watermelon, pineapple)	2 servings/day (1 dish of cooked vegetables (green beans, puree, stew); 1–2 tomatoes, carrots, cucumbers; 1 pepper, 1 zucchini, 1 eggplant)	-	At least 3–4 times/week	A handful/day; 3–7 handfuls/week	-

n.a.: Information not available in the official English version of the National Dietary Guidelines; -: food or food group not mentioned in the National Dietary Guidelines; c-eq: cup-equivalents; oz-eq = ounce-equivalents.

Table 5. Dietary recommendations for food groups of animal origin established by the international food guides selected in the present work.

Country/Region	Food Group of Animal Origin				
	Dairy Products	Meat and Its Products	Fish	Seafood	Eggs
United States	3 cups-eq/day	26 oz-eq/week (meats, poultry, eggs)	-	8 oz-eq/week	26 oz-eq/week (meats, poultry, eggs)
China	300 g of milk/day	280–525 g of poultry or lean meat/week	280–525 g/week	-	280–350 g/week
Finland	5–6 dL of milk/day; 2–3 slices of low-fat cheese	<500 g/week	-	-	-
Norway	-	-	-	-	-
Sweden	-	<500 g/week	-	-	-
United Kingdom	-	-	2 servings/week (at least one of them must be oily fish)	-	-
Germany	-	-	-	-	-
The Netherlands	-	-	1 serving/week (preferably oily fish)	-	-
France	2 servings/day (one serving = 150 mL of milk or 125 g of yogurt or 30 g of cheese)	<500 g/week	-	-	-
Portugal	2–3 servings/day (1 cup of milk = 250 mL; 1 liquid yogurt or 1 and 1/2 solid yogurt = 200 g; 2 thin slices of cheese = 40 g; 1/4 of fresh cheese (medium size) = 50 g; 1/2 curd (medium size) = 100 g)	1.5–4.5 servings/day (raw meat/fish = 30 g; cooked meat/fish = 25 g)		-	1 egg (medium size) = 55 g
Italy	3 servings milk and fermented products/day (1 serving = 125 mL milk, 125 g yogurt)3 servings cheese/week (1 serving = 100 g)	1–3 servings lean meat/week (1 serving = 100 g)1 serving red meat/week (1 serving = 100 g)	2–3 servings/week (1 serving = 150 g of fish including seafood)		2–4 times/week; 1 egg (medium size) = 50 g
Spain – AESAN	-	-	2–4 servings of fish/week (1 serving ≈ 100–125 g of filleted fish or 200–250 g of whole fish (not filleted)	-	-
Spain – GENCAT	1–3 times/day	3–4 times/week (in case of red meat, maximum twice/week)	3–4 servings of fish/week (alternate oily fish with lean fish)	-	3–4 times/week

n.a.: Information not available in the official English version of the National Dietary Guidelines; -: food or food group not mentioned in the National Dietary Guidelines.

Table 6. Dietary recommendations for water and other liquids, oil, salt, sugar, and alcohol established by the international food guides selected in the present work.

Country/Region	Water and Other Liquids	Oil	Salt	Sugar	Alcohol
United States	-	27 g/day	5.75 g/day	<10% of the daily energy intake from added sugars	No more than 2 alcoholic drinks/day (men) and 1 alcoholic drink/day (women)
China	7–8 cups of water (1500–1700 mL/day)	<25–30 g/day	<6 g/day	<50 g/day; <10% of the daily energy intake	<25 g/day (men); <15 g/day (women)
Finland	-	-	<5 g/day	n.a.	n.a.
Norway	-	-	n.a.	n.a.	n.a.
Sweden	-	-	<6 g/day	<10% of the daily energy intake	<20 g/day (men); <10 g/day (women)
United Kingdom	6–8 glasses or cups of water/day	-	<6 g/day	-	-
Germany	At least 1.5 L/day	-	-	-	-
The Netherlands	3 cups of tea/day	-	<6 g/day	-	Do not consume alcohol or no more than 1 glass/day (1 glass ≈ 10 g of alcohol; 250 mL of beer ≈ 5% alcohol, 100 mL of wine ≈ 12% alcohol; 35 mL of alcohol ≈ 35% alcohol)
France	-	-	-	-	No more than 2 glasses/day and not everyday
Portugal	-	1–3 servings/day (1 tablespoon of olive oil/oil = 10 g; 1 teaspoon of lard = 10 g; 4 tablespoons of cream = 30 mL; 1 tablespoon of butter/margarine = 15 g)	<5 g/day	-	-
Italy	1.2–2 L/day (at least 6–10 glasses of water)	2–4 servings/day (1 serving = 10 mL olive and/or vegetable oil)	<5 g/day	5–10 g/day	No more than 2 alcoholic drinks/day (men) and 1 alcoholic drink/day (women)
Spain AESAN	At least 1.5 L/day (5–8 glasses of water or other liquids/day)	-	<5 g/day	-	-
GENCAT	-	-	<5 g/day	<10% of the daily energy intake	-

n.a.: Information not available in the official English version of the National Dietary Guidelines; -: food or food group not mentioned in the National Dietary Guidelines.

Regarding the starchy foods (cereals, preferably whole grains, bread, pasta, rice, and potatoes), Portugal proposed the highest amounts (4–11 servings/day) as well as the best-described recommendations for this group by indicating household measurement for each food product and its equivalent in grams. Italy established different servings for each food item (daily amounts for bread and pasta/rice, and weekly intakes for breakfast cereals and potatoes), France 1 portion/meal, and the Chinese, Dutch, and the Italian guidelines provided a specific daily amount for starchy foods.

The food group with the lowest number of specific recommendations was soy products (only two food guides: the United States and China), followed by nuts (five countries: the United States, The Netherlands, France, Italy, and Spain (GENCAT)) and legumes (six food guides: the United States, China, Portugal, Italy, and Spain (AESAN and GENCAT)). Spain only established the frequency for legumes' consumption (2–3 times/week in AESAN food guide and 3–4 times/week in GENCAT food guide) but not a specific weekly amount.

Finally, it is important to underline that the only country that provided specific recommendations for all the plant-based food groups was the United States, where they are expressed as cup-equivalents (c-eq) and/or ounce-equivalents (oz-eq), where 1 ounce = 0.25 cup = 29.6 mL.

Regarding recommendations for foods of animal origin, most of the dietary guidelines include milk, dairy products, fish, eggs, meat, and derivatives.

Milk is considered the most complete food item in terms of nutritional composition as it contains all essential nutrients for humans except for dietary fiber, vitamin C, and iron. Dairy products (yogurt, cheese, etc.) are an excellent option to achieve an adequate intake of certain nutrients such as calcium, phosphorus, retinol, vitamin D, and vitamin B_{12} [1].

Fish are high-protein foods with important quantities of fat (polyunsaturated fatty acids) in oily fish such as salmon, tuna, mackerel, sardines, and herring, among others. Liver fish or blue fish are good sources of vitamin D for humans. Eicosapentaenoic and docosahexaenoic acids (EPA and DHA), other vitamins (retinol, B_{12}), and minerals (calcium, potassium, zinc, iron, phosphorus, iodine, selenium) are present in fish as well [1,32,33].

Eggs contain important quantities of proteins of high biological value (albumin, ovovitellin, etc.), vitamins D, E, B_2, and B_{12}, retinol, iron, and iodine. Water and proteins are mainly contained in the egg white, whereas the yolk is high-fat (cholesterol) and has significant amounts of vitamin D [1,3,34].

Meat and its derivatives are high-protein and high-fat foods with important quantities of iron, zinc, retinol, and vitamins B_1, B_2, B_3, B_6, and B_{12}; however, the lipid profile (in terms of fatty acids) is not entirely adequate and lean meat is preferred. In addition, the content of vitamins E and K is very low, and they do not contain dietary fiber, carbohydrates (except for glycogen and lactose in processed meat), or vitamin C [1].

With regard to the recommended intake of foods of animal origin (Table 5), the United States, France, and Portugal provided similar recommendations for dairy products (3 cup-equivalents/day, 2 servings/day, and 2–3 servings/day, respectively). The Chinese, Finnish, and Italian dietary guidelines recommended specific amounts for milk (300 g/day, 5–6 dL/day, and 125–375 mL/day, respectively) and for cheese, in the case of Finland (2–3 slices of low-fat cheese/day) and Italy (300 g cheese/week). Norway, Sweden, the United Kingdom, Germany, The Netherlands, and Spain have no specific recommendations about daily intakes for dairy products. Spain (GENCAT) only established the frequency for dairy products' consumption (1–3 times/day) but not a specific daily amount. The weekly recommendations for meat and its products, as well as for fish, were quite equal in China, Finland, Sweden, and France (<500–525 g meat/week). China was the only country that directly recommended the consumption of poultry or lean meat, and Italy provided different weekly servings for lean and red meat. Norway, the United Kingdom, Germany, and The Netherlands did not include specific amounts for fish, meat, and its products in their national dietary guidelines. Food groups with the least number of recommendations were seafood and eggs. Out of the thirteen selected dietary guidelines, only one (United States food guide) included one specific recommendation for seafood (8 oz-eq/week) and four for eggs (United States, China, Portugal, and Italy). Spain (GENCAT) only established the frequency for eggs' consumption (3–4 times/week). Last but not least, the dietary guidelines of the United States, Portugal, and Italy established one specific recommendation that covers several food groups; that is, 26 oz-eq/week for meats, poultry, and eggs (United States), 1.5–4.5 servings/day for meat and fish (raw meat/fish = 30 g; cooked meat/fish = 25 g) (Portugal), and 2–3 servings/week for fish and seafood (1 serving = 150 g) (Italy).

Water is fundamental for organism survival as it regulates temperature, protects tissues and organs, allows nutrient absorption and transportation to cells, and other vital bodily functions. For that reason, all national dietary guidelines selected in the present study established recommendations related to water consumption, at least 1.2 L/day. The recommendations of water and other liquids' consumption were similar among countries. China, the United Kingdom, Germany, Italy, and Spain (GENCAT) suggested a daily consumption of at least 1.2 L/day; that is, between 5 and 8 cups/glasses of water. However, it is important to highlight that in The Netherlands, the recommended daily intake was established in just 3 cups of tea/day. This fact demonstrates once again the strong influence of the cultural, social, and geographical factors.

Olive oil is one of the pillars of the Mediterranean Diet. It consists primarily of oleic acid (C18:1, ω-9, cis) (80–90%), fatty acids such as linoleic acid (C18:2, ω-6, cis) and palmitic acid (C16:0), and other bioactive compounds such as vitamin E (α-tocopherol), phytosterols (especially β-sitosterol), and polyphenols (e.g., oleuropein, tyrosol) [32,33,36]. The dietary guidelines of the United States, China, Portugal, and Italy were the only ones that recommend a specific daily intake of oil (27 g/day, <25–30 g/day, 10–30 g/day, and 20–40 mL/day, respectively).

Regarding salt consumption, most selected countries were in line with the WHO recommendations about the maximum daily intake (<5 g/day). The United States suggested a slightly higher amount (<5.75 g/day), whereas China, Sweden, the United Kingdom, and The Netherlands proposed the highest daily intake (<6 g/day). The United States, China, Sweden, France, Italy, and Spain (GENCAT) proposed a maximum daily intake of sugar. Another recommendation provided by some countries (United States, China, Sweden, France, and Spain (GENCAT)) was related to the caloric intake from the consumption of sugar, which should not exceed 10% of the total daily energy intake.

Finally, the consumption of alcohol was particularly limited in the food guides of the United States, China, Sweden, The Netherlands, France, and Italy. Dutch guidelines had the most restrictive limit, with the recommendation of no consumption (or not more than 1 glass/day, equivalent to 10 g of alcohol per day). This is followed by France (not everyone should consume alcohol; <2 glasses/day ≈ 20 g alcohol/day), the United States, Sweden, and Italy (<2 glasses/day in men ≈ 20 g alcohol/day; <1 glass/day in women ≈ 10 g alcohol/day), and finally China with the highest limit (<25 g alcohol/day in men and <15 g alcohol/day in women).

The dietary recommendations for water and other liquids, oil, salt, sugar, and alcohol established by the selected international food guides are included in Table 6.

Based on previous considerations explained throughout the main text, the Scientific Committee of AESAN has updated the dietary recommendations regarding each food group for the Spanish population (Table 7), with the incorporation of portion sizes. According to Almiron-Roig et al., the establishment of adequate food portion sizes is essential to avoid misunderstandings amongst consumers about the amounts of food that should be consumed as well as to decrease their likelihood of overeating [37].

Table 7. Dietary recommendations for each food group and other important categories proposed by the Scientific Committee of AESAN. Adapted from [5].

Food Group	Frequency of Consumption	Weight of Each Serving
Fruits	3–5 servings/day Sporadically substitute for juice	120–200 g of fresh fruit 150 mL of juice
Vegetables	2–4 servings/day Combine different products (raw and cooked)	150–200 g
Starchy foods (preferably whole grains)	Daily consumption 4–6 servings/day	40–60 g of bread
		60–80 g of pasta, rice
Legumes	2–4 servings/week	50–60 g
Nuts	Weekly, several times	20–30 g No salt added
Dairy products	Daily consumption 2–4 servings/day	200–250 mL of milk
		80–125 g of fresh cheese 40–60 g of mature cheese
		125 g of yogurt, and other fermented milks, with no added sugar
Meat and its products	2–4 servings/week Preferably chicken or rabbit meat No more than 2 servings of red meat/week	100–125 g
Fish/seafood	At least 2 servings/week 1–2 servings of oily fish/week	125–150 g
Eggs	2–4 eggs/week	Medium size (53–63 g)
Water	1.5–2.5 L/day	200–250 mL
Virgin olive oil	Daily consumption Preferably raw	10 mL
Salt	<5 g salt/day = 2 g sodium/day Do not add during cooking Avoid food with added salt	-
Sugar	<30 g/day Avoid foods with added sugar	5–10 g

4. Conclusions

All the reviewed dietary guidelines provided recommendations for the following food groups: fruits, vegetables, starchy foods (cereals, preferably whole grains, bread, pasta, rice, potatoes), legumes, nuts, milk and dairy products (yogurt, cheese), meat and derivatives, fish, eggs, water, and oil (vegetable oils, most importantly virgin olive oil).

Spanish dietary recommendations proposed by the Scientific Committee of AESAN include a varied and balanced diet characterized by a predominance of plant-based foods and moderate consumption of foods from animal origin. That is, 3–5 servings of fruits/day (it could occasionally be replaced by juice), 2–4 servings of vegetables (raw and cooked)/day, 4–6 servings of cereals/day (preferably whole grains), 2–4 servings of legumes/week, 2–4 servings of milk and dairy products/day, $\geq$2 servings of fish/week (if possible, 1–2 servings oily fish/week), 2–4 eggs/week, and 2–4 servings of meat/week, preferably chicken or rabbit, and consumption of red meat must not exceed 2 servings/week. Consumption of nuts without added salt as well as virgin olive oil (preferably raw) is recommended as well. Finally, 1.5–2.5 L of water/day should be consumed, and daily intakes of salt and sugar must not exceed 5 and 30 g, respectively.

The present work provided a valuable international overview of twelve food-based dietary guidelines from three different continents (Asia, North America, and Europe). This selection includes dietary guidelines from diverse cultures and traditions directly linked to their eating habits and patterns; however, a more comprehensive comparative analysis including more Food-Based Dietary Guidelines approved in other countries and geographic regions around the world could be addressed in future works based on the results of the present study.

Author Contributions: Conceptualization, M.C. and L.D.; methodology, M.C., L.D., R.M.G., E.G.-F., E.L.-G., J.M., M.P.P., M.R. and J.A.M.; investigation, M.C., L.D. and J.A.M.; writing—original draft preparation, M.C. and L.D.; writing—review and editing, M.C., L.D., R.M.G., E.G.-F., E.L.-G., J.M., M.P.P., M.R. and J.A.M.; funding acquisition, M.C. All authors have read and agreed to the published version of the manuscript.

Funding: This research was funded by UCM ALIMNOVA Research Group, Ref: 951505, and Project OTRI Art. 83, Ref: 252-2017, UCM-Fundación Sabor y Salud. Laura Domínguez is grateful for her PhD grant (UCM-Santander; Ref: CT42/18-CT43/18).

Institutional Review Board Statement: Not applicable.

Informed Consent Statement: Not applicable.

Data Availability Statement: Not applicable.

Acknowledgments: This paper is related to the Report of the Scientific Committee of the Spanish Agency for Food Safety and Nutrition (AESAN) on the review and update of Dietary Recommendations for the Spanish population. The authors are grateful to all the members of the Scientific Committee of AESAN (2019–2021) and AESAN staff from NAOS Strategy and Sub-directorate-General for Food Safety Promotion.

Conflicts of Interest: The authors declare no conflict of interest.

References

1. Moreiras, O.; Carbajal, A.; Cabrera, L.; Cuadrado, C. *Tablas de Composición de Alimentos. Guía de Prácticas*, 9th ed.; Ediciones Pirámide: Madrid, Spain, 2018.
2. Domínguez Díaz, L.; Fernández-Ruiz, V.; Cámara, M. Phytochemicals and Nutraceuticals with Particular Health-Promoting Effects. *Pharmatech* **2020**, *48*, 74–78.
3. Ortega Anta, R.M.; López Sobaler, A.M.; Requejo Marcos, A.M.; Andrés Carvajales, P. *La composición de los Alimentos. Herramienta Básica para la Valoración Nutricional*, 1st ed.; Editorial Complutense: Madrid, Spain, 2004.
4. OMS—Alimentación Sana. Available online: https://www.who.int/es/news-room/fact-sheets/detail/healthy-diet (accessed on 26 May 2021).
5. AESAN (Working Group); Martínez, J.A.; Cámara, M.; Giner, R.; González, E.; López, E.; Mañes, J.; Portillo, M.P.; Rafecas, M.; Gutiérrez, E.; et al. Report of the Scientific Committee of the Spanish Agency for Food Safety and Nutrition (AESAN) on the Review and Update of Dietary Recommendations for the Spanish Population. Available online: https://www.aesan.gob.es/AECOSAN/docs/documentos/seguridad_alimentaria/evaluacion_riesgos/informes_cc_ingles/DIETARY_RECOMMENDATIONS.pdf (accessed on 30 August 2021).
6. Willett, W.; Rockström, J.; Loken, B.; Springmann, M.; Lang, T.; Vermeulen, S.; Garnett, T.; Tilman, D.; DeClerck, F.; Wood, A.; et al. Food in the Anthropocene: The EAT-Lancet Commission on healthy diets from sustainable food systems. *Lancet Commissions* **2019**, *393*, 447–492. [CrossRef]
7. Bechthold, A.; Boeing, H.; Tetens, I.; Schwingshackl, L.; Nöthlings, U. Perspective: Food-based dietary guidelines in Europe-scientific concepts, current status, and perspectives. *Adv. Nutr.* **2018**, *9*, 544–560. [CrossRef] [PubMed]
8. Tuomisto, H.L. Importance of considering environmental sustainability in dietary guidelines. *Lancet Planet Health* **2018**, *2*, e331–e332. [CrossRef]
9. AESAN. Report of the Scientific Committee of the Spanish Agency for Food Safety and Nutrition (AESAN) on the Nutritional Reference Intakes for the Spanish Population. Available online: https://www.aesan.gob.es/AECOSAN/docs/documentos/seguridad_alimentaria/evaluacion_riesgos/informes_cc_ingles/NUTRITIONAL_REFERENCE_INTAKES.pdf (accessed on 30 August 2021).
10. EFSA. Scientific Opinion on establishing Food-Based Dietary Guidelines. *EFSA J.* **2010**, *8*, 1460.
11. FAO/WHO. *Sustainable Healthy Diets—Guiding Principles*; FAO: Rome, Italy, 2019; ISBN 978-92-5-131875-1.
12. Blackstone, N.T.; El-Abbadi, N.H.; McCabe, M.S.; Griffin, T.S.; Nelson, M.E. Linking sustainability to the healthy eating patterns of the Dietary Guidelines for Americans: A modelling study. *Lancet Planet Health* **2018**, *2*, 344–352. [CrossRef]
13. Buttriss, J.L.; Briend, A.; Darmon, N.; Ferguson, E.L.; Maillot, M.; Lluch, A. Diet modelling: How it can inform the development of dietary recommendations and public health policy. *Nutr. Bull.* **2014**, *39*, 115–125. [CrossRef]

14. FAO—Food-Based Dietary Guidelines. Available online: http://www.fao.org/nutrition/education/food-dietary-guidelines/en/ (accessed on 6 September 2021).
15. USDHHS/USDA—Dietary Guidelines for Americans 2015–2020. Available online: http://health.gov/dietaryguidelines/2015/guidelines/ (accessed on 29 May 2021).
16. Chinese Nutrition Society—Dietary Guidelines for Chinese Residents. Available online: http://www.fao.org/nutrition/education/food-dietary-guidelines/regions/countries/China/en (accessed on 30 May 2021).
17. National Nutrition Council—Finnish Nutrition Recommendations. Available online: http://www.fao.org/nutrition/education/food-dietary-guidelines/regions/countries/finland/en/ (accessed on 29 May 2021).
18. Norwegian Directorate of Health—Norwegian Guidelines on Diet, Nutrition and Physical Activity. Available online: http://www.fao.org/nutrition/education/food-dietary-guidelines/regions/countries/norway/en/ (accessed on 27 May 2021).
19. Swedish National Food Agency—Sweden's Dietary Guidelines: "Find Your Way to Eat Greener, Not Too Much and to Be Active!". Available online: http://www.fao.org/nutrition/education/food-dietary-guidelines/regions/countries/sweden/en/ (accessed on 26 May 2021).
20. Public Health England—Eatwell Guide. Available online: http://www.fao.org/nutrition/education/food-dietary-guidelines/regions/countries/united-kingdom/en/ (accessed on 27 May 2021).
21. German Nutrition Society—Ten Guidelines for Wholesome Eating and Drinking. Available online: http://www.fao.org/nutrition/education/food-dietary-guidelines/regions/countries/germany/en/ (accessed on 26 May 2021).
22. Health Council of The Netherlands—Dutch Dietary Guidelines 2015. Available online: https://www.healthcouncil.nl/documents/advisory-reports/2015/11/04/dutch-dietary-guidelines-2015 (accessed on 26 May 2021).
23. Santé Publique France—Recommandations Relatives à L'alimentation, à L'activité physique et à la Sédentarité Pour les Adultes. Available online: https://static.cnsf.asso.fr/wp-content/uploads/2019/01/2019_SPF_reco-alimentation-activite-physique-sedentarite-adultes.pdf (accessed on 28 May 2021).
24. FCNAUP—Guia Alimentar Mediterrânico. Relatório Justificativo Do Seu Desenvolvimento. Available online: https://nutrimento.pt/noticias/guia-alimentar-mediterranico-relatorio-justificativo-do-seu-desenvolvimento/ (accessed on 29 May 2021).
25. CREA (Centro di Ricerca Alimenti e Nutrizione)—Linee Guida per una Sana Alimentazione. Available online: https://www.crea.gov.it/web/alimenti-e-nutrizione/-/linee-guida-per-una-sana-alimentazione-2018 (accessed on 25 August 2021).
26. AESAN—Estrategia Para la Nutrición, Actividad Física y Prevención de la Obesidad" (Estrategia NAOS). Available online: http://www.aecosan.msssi.gob.es/AECOSAN/web/nutricion/seccion/estrategia_naos.htm (accessed on 29 May 2021).
27. AESAN—Decálogo "Come Sano y Muévete: 12 Decisiones Saludables"—Estrategia NAOS. Available online: http://www.aecosan.msssi.gob.es/AECOSAN/docs/documentos/nutricion/educanaos/come_sano_muevete.pdf (accessed on 27 May 2021).
28. GENCAT—Pequeños Cambios Para Comer Mejor. Generalitat de Catalunya. Available online: http://salutpublica.gencat.cat/web/.content/minisite/aspcat/promocio_salut/alimentacio_saludable/02Publicacions/pub_alim_salu_tothom/Petits-canvis/La-guia-peq-cambios-castella.pdf (accessed on 28 May 2021).
29. FAO/FCRN. *Plates, Pyramids, Planet. Developments in National Healthy and Sustainable Dietary Guidelines: A State of Play Assessment*; FAO: Rome, Italy, 2016; ISBN 978-92-5-109222-4.
30. Herforth, A.; Arimond, M.; Álvarez-Sánchez, C.; Coates, J.; Christianson, K.; Muehlhoff, E. A Global Review of Food-Based Dietary Guidelines. *Adv. Nutr.* **2019**, *10*, 590–605. [CrossRef] [PubMed]
31. Montagnese, C.; Santarpia, L.; Buonifacio, M.; Nardelli, A.; Caldara, A.R.; Silvestri, E.; Contaldo, F.; Pasanisi, F. European food-based dietary guidelines: A comparison and update. *Nutrition* **2015**, *31*, 908–915. [CrossRef] [PubMed]
32. Souci, S.; Fachmann, W.; Kraut, H.; Kirchho, E. *Food Composition and Nutrition Tables*, 17th ed.; MedPharm Scientific Publishers: Stuttgart, Germany, 2008.
33. USDA—Food Composition Databases. Available online: https://ndb.nal.usda.gov/ndb/foods (accessed on 27 May 2021).
34. Mataix, J.; Mañas, M.; Llopis, J.; Martínez, E. *Tabla de Composición de Alimentos*, 5th ed.; Biblioteca de Ciencias de la Salud, Servicio de Publicaciones de la Universidad de Granada: Granada, Spain, 2009.
35. López-González, L.; Becerra-Tomás, N.; Babio, N.; Martínez-González, M.Á.; Díaz-López, A.; Corella, D.; Goday, A.; Romaguera, D.; Vioque, J.; Alonso-Gómez, Á.M.; et al. Variety in fruits and vegetables, diet quality and lifestyle in an older adult mediterranean population. *Clin. Nutr.* **2021**, *40*, 1510–1518. [CrossRef] [PubMed]
36. Rothwell, J.; Pérez-Jiménez, J.; Neveu, V.; Medina-Remón, A.; M'Hiri, N.; García-Lobato, P.; Manach, C.; Knox, C.; Eisner, R.; Wishart, D.S.; et al. Phenol-Explorer 3.0: A major update of the Phenol-Explorer database to incorporate data on the effects of food processing on polyphenol content. *Database* **2013**, *2013*, bat070. [CrossRef] [PubMed]
37. Almiron-Roig, E.; Navas-Carretero, S.; Emery, P.; Martínez, J.A. Research into food portion size: Methodological aspects and applications. *Food Funct.* **2017**, *9*, 715–739. [CrossRef] [PubMed]

nutrients

Article

Cost and Affordability of Healthy, Equitable and Sustainable Diets in Low Socioeconomic Groups in Australia

Meron Lewis [1,2,*], Sarah A. McNaughton [3], Lucie Rychetnik [2,4] and Amanda J. Lee [1]

1 School of Public Health, Faculty of Medicine, The University of Queensland, Herston, QLD 4006, Australia; amanda.lee@uq.edu.au
2 The Australian Prevention Partnership Centre, The Sax Institute, Glebe, NSW 2037, Australia; lucie.rychetnik@saxinstitute.org.au
3 Institute for Physical Activity and Nutrition, School of Exercise and Nutrition Sciences, Deakin University, Geelong, VIC 3217, Australia; sarah.mcnaughton@deakin.edu.au
4 School of Public Health, University of Sydney, Camperdown, NSW 2006, Australia
* Correspondence: meron.lewis@uq.net.au

Abstract: Few Australians consume a healthy, equitable and more sustainable diet consistent with the Australian Dietary Guidelines (ADGs). Low socioeconomic groups (SEGs) suffer particularly poor diet-related health problems. However, granular information on dietary intakes and affordability of recommended diets was lacking for low SEGs. The Healthy Diets Australian Standardised Affordability and Pricing protocol was modified for low SEGs to align with relevant dietary intakes reported in the National Nutrition Survey 2011–2012(which included less healthy and more discretionary options than the broader population), household structures, food purchasing habits, and incomes. Cost and affordability of habitual and recommended diets of low SEGs were calculated using prices of 'standard brands' and 'cheapest options'. With 'standard brands', recommended diets cost less than habitual diets, but were unaffordable for low SEGs. With 'cheapest options', both diets were more affordable, but recommended diets cost more than habitual diets for some low SEGs, potentially contributing to perceptions that healthy food is unaffordable. The study confirms the need for an equity lens to better target dietary guidelines for low SEGs. It also highlights urgent policy action is needed to help improve affordability of recommended diets.

Keywords: diet cost; diet affordability; low socioeconomic; low income; healthy eating; dietary guidelines; Australia

Citation: Lewis, M.; McNaughton, S.A.; Rychetnik, L.; Lee, A.J. Cost and Affordability of Healthy, Equitable and Sustainable Diets in Low Socioeconomic Groups in Australia. *Nutrients* **2021**, *13*, 2900. https://doi.org/10.3390/nu13082900

Academic Editors: Clare Collins and George Moschonis

Received: 21 July 2021
Accepted: 19 August 2021
Published: 23 August 2021

1. Introduction

There is an urgent need for food system transformation to produce healthy, equitable and more environmentally sustainable diets for all people [1,2]. Poor diet is a leading contributor to the burden of disease in Australia [3,4]. Fewer than 4% of Australians consume a healthy, equitable and more sustainable diet consistent with the Australian Dietary Guidelines (ADGs) [5,6]. More than one-third of adults' and more than 40% of children's energy intake comes from "discretionary" food and drinks. These discretionary food and drinks are not needed for health and are high in saturated fat, added sugar, salt and/or alcohol [6]. Low socioeconomic groups (SEGs) suffer poorer diet-related health problems than the broader population, including higher rates of chronic disease such as diabetes, heart disease, and some cancers [7–9].

1.1. *Key Considerations in Understanding Determinants of Inequitable Dietary Patterns*

A recent systematic review of habitual dietary intake of low SEGs in Australia found that while total diet quality is generally lower in low SEGs compared to higher SEGs, findings were inconsistent across studies for all reported food groups and SEG measures due to variation between study metrics, definitions, dietary assessment methods, and granularity of analysis [10]. Most often, intakes of fruits and vegetables were used as markers of a healthy diet [10]. Quantitative intakes of ADG food groups by SEGs were reported rarely, and were not available readily from national survey data [5].

The inequities of healthy eating are complex, and strongly influenced by environmental, economic and social determinants [11]. The affordability of healthy food has been identified as a key leverage point in models of inequitable healthy eating, and is influenced by both household income and the cost of healthy food and drinks [12]. However, the relative cost of healthy and unhealthy food and drinks must be considered within the context of dietary patterns, rather than as individual components [13].

1.2. Food Habits and Incomes of Low SEGs

Low SEGs implement various food purchasing strategies to stretch the food budget. Low income households purchase a higher proportion of 'own brand' (also called generic brand, private label or home brand) products compared to higher income households [14]. The number of 'own brand' products in major Australian supermarket chains has been increasing [15] and purchasing those alternatives can deliver large cost savings [16]. The number of 'budget' supermarkets in Australia has also been increasing, providing a popular source of low cost groceries [15]. Additionally, household expenditure surveys have shown that low income households spend less on eating out and takeaway foods than higher income households: purchase of convenience foods from supermarkets by low SEGs approximates that of foods consumed away from home by high SEGs [17].

Two-thirds (65%) of households in the lowest household income quintile in Australia report government pensions and allowances as their main source of income [18]. Assessment of healthy food affordability for households receiving a low income or reliant on payments such as unemployment benefits or aged pension will highlight the inequities faced by these vulnerable groups.

1.3. The Healthy Diets ASAP Protocol

In Australia, there was an urgent need for comparable food cost and affordability data to inform fiscal policy from a health perspective. A previous review identified 11 different methods that had been used in Australia and there was a lack of comparability across all metrics, with approaches rarely fully aligned with recommendations of the ADGs, and only one attempted comparison with the cost of a typical diet. [19]. The Healthy Diets Australian Standardised Affordability and Pricing (ASAP) method protocol was developed to compare the cost, cost differential and affordability of habitual (current, typically unhealthy) and recommended (healthy, equitable and more sustainable) omnivorous diets for the mean population in Australia [20].

This standardised approach includes a five-part protocol:

1. Habitual (current, unhealthy) and recommended (healthy, equitable, more sustainable) diet pricing tools, including foods commonly consumed by the Australian population, for reference households
2. Store location and sampling
3. Food and drink price data collection
4. Calculation of median household income, and low-income household income (minimum wage plus welfare payments) for the reference households
5. Analysis and reporting

The types and amounts of the food and drinks in the habitual diet pricing tool were sourced from mean dietary intakes reported by reference household members in the most recent national survey [21]. The recommended diet pricing tool includes those healthy food and drinks in the habitual diet pricing tool, in higher quantities reflecting ADG recommendations. Recommended diets in Australia promote health and wellbeing, are equitable [6] and are more environmentally sustainable with modelling reporting generation of 25% less greenhouse gas emissions, than habitual diets [22].

Implementation of the protocol has shown that, under present fiscal policy settings in Australia where basic healthy food and drinks do not incur the 10% Goods and Service Tax (GST), healthy diets are between 16–24% less expensive than habitual diets but are still unaffordable for many Australians. [23–25]

Consultations with academic, government and non-government organisations to inform development of the Healthy Diets ASAP protocol for the mean population noted requests to also develop methods specific to low socioeconomic and other groups [20]. The protocol was modified subsequently to reflect dietary intakes and circumstances of Aboriginal and Torres Strait Islander peoples, which resulted in a more sensitive tool to describe the cost and affordability of habitual and recommended diets in these population groups [23].

Modification of the Healthy Diets ASAP protocol for low SEGs would provide more granular evidence to better target dietary guidelines for low SEGs and inform policies and practices to help low SEGs purchase and consume healthy diets and improve diet-related health. Improved health outcomes for low SEGs may result in reduced health costs, improved workforce and social participation, improved education outcomes for children, and reduced social inequality [9].

The aim of this study was twofold: (i) to modify the relevant components of the original Healthy Diets ASAP protocol to accommodate habitual dietary intakes, household structures, food purchasing habits, and income sources and amounts, of low SEGs in Australia; and (ii) to test the low SEG Healthy Diets ASAP protocol to assess the cost, cost differential and affordability of habitual and recommended diets for low SEG households in Australia.

2. Materials and Methods

2.1. Development of the Healthy Diets ASAP Protocol for Low SEGs in Australia

As relevant quantitative habitual dietary intake data were not available (as noted above) reported dietary intakes of individuals in low SEGs from the most recent Australian Health Survey National Nutrition and Physical Activity Survey (AHS NNPAS) in 2011–2012 were used to modify the habitual diet pricing tool [26]. The recommended diet pricing tool did not require modification, as healthy, equitable and more sustainable dietary recommendations are similar for all Australians [6]. The modified pricing tools were tested iteratively and results informed development of the low SEG protocols. The methods and results for the tools and testing are reported separately.

2.1.1. Selection of SEG Measure

Household income was used as the indicator of SEG in this study, as this metric reflects household resources to purchase food, and is available for all persons surveyed in the AHS NNPAS. When examining categories of income, low sample numbers within subcategories in the AHS NNPAS (see Table S1) dictated use of income quintiles, rather than the deciles reported publicly [21]. Low SEGs were defined as those in the lowest income quintile.

2.1.2. Selection of Low SEG Reference Households

Three common household compositions among low SEGs in Australia comparable with households in the Healthy Diets ASAP protocol [18] were included. Additionally, to account for low sample numbers within age subcategories in the AHS NNPAS (Table S1), the original included age range for the children was expanded. The low SEG reference households were:

- Household A: Two adults (female 31–50 years, male 31–50 years) and two children (boy 14–18 years, child 4–8 years)
- Household B: One adult (female 31–50 years) and two children (boy 14–18 years, child 4–8 years)
- Household C: Older, retired couple (female 70+ years, male 70+ years)

2.1.3. Modification of the Habitual Diet Pricing Tool for Low SEGs

Dietary intake was collected in the AHS NNPAS [21] using 24-h dietary recall. The Confidential Unit Record Files of the AHS NNPAS were assessed and analysed to determine mean intake of food and drinks of members of the reference households, by age, gender, and household income quintile. The mean intakes of all food and drinks for the lowest income quintile for each reference household (sum of mean intakes of household members) were then mapped to the 75 representative food and drinks of the habitual diet pricing tool (Table S2). The low SEG habitual diet pricing tool was analysed for energy content using the FoodWorks 9th Edition computer program [27].

2.1.4. Modification of the Store Location and Sampling Methods for Low SEGs

For the store location and sampling methods, 'budget' supermarkets (e.g., ALDI® stores), were included, in addition to the major supermarkets and other food outlets of the original Healthy Diets ASAP protocol.

2.1.5. Modification of the Price Collection Methods for Low SEGs

In the low SEG price collection methods, prices were collected for the most commonly purchased brands in Australia as a whole ('standard brands'), as per the original Healthy Diets ASAP protocol, and prices were also collected for the 'cheapest option' available, usually an 'own brand' product. As non-packaged produce such as fruit, vegetables, and meats are not branded, these items were selected by type alone and the same prices were included in both 'standard brands' and 'cheapest option' price collections.

2.1.6. Household Income Calculations for Low SEGs

The low-minimum disposable household income of the original Healthy Diets ASAP protocol was calculated including minimum wage rates [28], tax payable [29] and any applicable welfare payments [30], and this was retained for the low SEG protocol. A welfare dependent household income, calculated to include only welfare payments such as unemployment benefits, was added to the low SEG protocol.

2.1.7. Modification of the Analysis and Reporting Methods for Low SEGs

The analysis and reporting component of the low SEG Healthy Diets ASAP protocol was modified to include additional calculation of costs and affordability using the 'cheapest option' price collection. Costs for habitual and recommended diets were reported as total cost and cost of each ADG food group or food group component, for the 'standard brands' and 'cheapest option' price collections.

The cost of 'healthy' food in the habitual diet was the sum of costs of those foods and drinks listed in the recommended diet together with artificially sweetened drinks. The cost of 'discretionary' food and drinks in the habitual diet was the sum of costs of those food and drinks not included in the recommended diet.

Diet costs were deemed unaffordable if they were more than 30% of household income [31]. If diet costs were more than 25% of disposable household income, the household was considered to be in food stress [32,33].

2.2. Testing the Healthy Diets ASAP Protocol for Low SEGs in Australia

2.2.1. Food and Drink Price Collection

To test the low SEG protocol, food and drink prices were collected in June 2020 from one conveniently sampled Statistical Area 2 (SA2) in Brisbane, Queensland, Australia, using the Healthy Diets ASAP web-based data collection portal [34]. Due to restrictions related to the SARS-CoV-2 pandemic at the time, the majority of food and drink prices were collected online from two major supermarket and liquor store chains. Food and drink prices at a budget supermarket (ALDI®) and prices from other stores included in the original protocol (independent bakery, fish and chip store, burger restaurant chain store, and pizza chain store) were collected in-store as these were unavailable online. Prices collected included both 'standard brands' and 'cheapest option' packaged products.

2.2.2. Data Analysis

Data analysis was conducted using algorithms with the following steps: item prices and sizes were entered into the Healthy Diets ASAP web-based data collection portal; prices were converted to price per gram or millilitre, adjusted by an edible portion factor (to account for cooking or inedible parts), and then multiplied by the amount consumed by the reference household per fortnight as per the diet pricing tools. Individual food and drink prices were then summed to provide a total cost for each ADG food group or food group component, and the total diet cost per household per fortnight. Diet costs were calculated based on the 'standard brands' price collection (from major supermarkets) and the 'cheapest option' price collection (from major supermarkets and the budget supermarket) for each of the three low SEG households.

Household income was calculated in two different ways where relevant for each of the three low SEG households: (i) for those on a welfare only income, and (ii) for those working age adults on a minimum wage-based income. Detailed calculations of the household incomes are included in Table S3. Affordability of both habitual and recommended diets was calculated for each household and relevant income levels.

3. Results

3.1. The Low SEG Healthy Diets ASAP Protocol

The components of the original Healthy Diets ASAP protocol and the low SEG Healthy Diets ASAP protocol are shown in Table 1, with further details below.

Table 1. Components of the original Healthy Diets ASAP protocol and the Low SEG Healthy Diets ASAP protocol.

Protocol Component	Original Healthy Diets ASAP Protocol	Low SEG Healthy Diets ASAP Protocol **
Reference households	Household A: Adult male (31–50 years), Adult female (31–50 years), Boy (14 years), Girl (8 years) Household B: Adult female (31–50 years), Boy (14 years), Girl (8 years) Household C: Senior male (71+ years), Senior female (71+ years)	Household A: Adult male (31–50 years), Adult female (31–50 years), Boy (***14–18 years***), Child (***4–8 years***) Household B: Adult female (31–50 years), Boy (***14–18 years***), Child (***4–8 years***) Household C: Senior male (71+ years), Senior female (71+ years)
Habitual (current, unhealthy) diet pricing tool	Mean dietary intakes reported by specific age and gender individuals in AHS NNPAS, abridged and combined to provide household diet per fortnight	Mean dietary intakes reported by specific age and gender individuals ***of lowest household income quintile*** in AHS NNPAS, abridged and combined to provide household diet per fortnight
Recommended (healthy, equitable, sustainable) diet pricing tool	Healthy food and drinks included in Habitual diet pricing tool in amounts reflecting ADG.	Healthy food and drinks included in Habitual diet pricing tool in amounts reflecting ADG.
Store location and sampling methods	Major supermarkets and other food outlets	Major supermarkets, ***budget supermarkets*** and other food outlets
Food and drink price data collection methods	Prices collected of non-packaged items and packaged products of major Australian brands	Standard brand price collection: prices collected of non-packaged items and packaged products of major Australian brands ***'Cheapest options' price collection: prices collected of non-packaged items and packaged products of cheapest equivalent of standard brand product (including 'own brands')***
Household income calculation methods	Median gross household income of area sampled Low-minimum disposable household income	Low-minimum disposable household income ***Welfare dependent household income***
Analysis and reporting methods	Cost and affordability of habitual and recommended diets reported	Cost and affordability of habitual and recommended diets reported for both 'standard brand' price collection ***and 'cheapest option' price collection.***

** Key changes from the Original Healthy Diets ASAP Protocol are highlighted in ***bold italics***.

3.1.1. The Low SEG Habitual Diet Pricing Tools

Details of the low SEG habitual diet pricing tool for Household A (two adults, two children) are shown in Table 2, together with the composition of the original Healthy Diets ASAP habitual diet pricing tool. Equivalent data for Households B (one adult, two children) and C (older, retired couple) are presented in Table S4A,B.

Table 2. Composition of original Healthy Diets ASAP habitual diet pricing tool for mean Australian population and Low SEG Healthy Diets ASAP habitual diet pricing tool, and recommended diet pricing tool, for Household A (two adult, two children).

Food Item	Habitual Diet (g/Fortnight)		Recommended Diet (g/Fortnight)
	Original Healthy Diets ASAP	**Low SEG Healthy Diets ASAP**	**Original Healthy Diets ASAP**
Energy (kJ/day)	33,602 kJ	32,517 kJ	32,996 kJ
	Water		
Water, bottled (mL)	5296	3485 (34% < Original)	5296
	Fruit		
Apples (g)	3497	3638	5460
Bananas (g)	899	795	5460
Oranges (g)	1664	971	5460
Fruit salad, canned in juice (g)	2046	1544	0
Total Fruit (g)	11,133	9614 (14% < Original)	16,380
	Vegetables and Legumes		
Potato, loose (g)	1460	1844	2320
Broccoli, loose (g)	422	389	1470
White cabbage, loose (g)	235	175	1470
Iceberg lettuce, whole (g)	795	704	1470
Carrot, loose (g)	753	618	2205
Pumpkin (g)	240	330	2205
Onion, loose (g)	84	106	1638
Tomatoes, loose (g)	488	654	1638
Sweetcorn, canned (g)	206	216	1160
Four bean mix, canned (g)	74	61	1005
Diced tomatoes, canned (g)	235	175	1638
Baked Beans, canned (g)	369	237	1005
Frozen mixed vegetables (g)	1184	746	1638
Frozen peas (g)	273	334	1638
Total Vegetables and Legumes (g)	7584	7136 (6% < Original)	22,500
	Grain (Cereal) Foods—Wholegrain and Refined		
Wholemeal bread, pre-packaged (g)	1054	870	4272
White bread, pre-packaged (g)	3033	3001	893
Rolled oats (g)	870	578	6648
Breakfast cereal, corn flakes (g)	680	509	670
Breakfast cereal, wheat biscuits (g)	430	243	2216
White pasta (g)	1326	988	2042
White rice (g)	1622	1904	2042
Dry wheat crackers, water crackers (g)	258	89	781
Total Grain (Cereal) Foods (g)	9393	8336 (11% < Original)	19,564

Table 2. *Cont.*

Food Item	Habitual Diet (g/Fortnight)		Recommended Diet (g/Fortnight)
	Original Healthy Diets ASAP	Low SEG Healthy Diets ASAP	Original Healthy Diets ASAP
Lean Meats and Poultry, Fish, Eggs, Nuts and Seeds			
Tuna, canned in oil (g)	1052	760	1841
Beef mince, lean (g)	267	163	1168
Lamb loin chops (g)	257	333	1169
Beef rump steak (g)	1056	1042	1172
Eggs (g)	872	884	2208
Chicken, cooked whole (g)	1661	1093	1471
Peanuts, roasted, unsalted (g)	0	0	780
Total Lean Meats and Poultry, Fish, Eggs, Nuts and Seeds (g)	5931	4822 (19% < Original)	9809
Milk, Yoghurt, Cheese and Alternatives			
Cheddar cheese, full fat (g)	624	682	704
Cheddar cheese, reduced fat (g)	44	49	516
Milk, full fat (mL)	5961	7301	6438
Milk, reduced fat (mL)	2929	1839	12,000
Flavoured milk (mL)	2416	2187	0
Yoghurt, full fat, plain (g)	204	101	2576
Yoghurt, flavoured reduced fat (g)	676	722	5100
Total Milk, Yoghurt, Cheese and Alternatives (g)	12,854	12,881 (0.2% > Original)	27,334
Unsaturated Oils and Spreads (or foods from which these are derived)			
Sunflower oil (mL)	7	15	291
Olive oil (mL)	7	15	291
Canola margarine (g)	170	197	412
Total Unsaturated Oils and Spreads (g)	184	227 (23% > Original)	994
Discretionary Choices—other			
Chicken soup, canned (g)	1340	2219	0
Muffin, commercial (g)	1455	922	0
Instant noodles, wheat based (g)	381	227	0
White sugar (g)	566	714	0
Cream-filled sweet biscuit, pre-packaged (g)	496	628	0
Muesli bar, pre-packaged (g)	373	339	0
Savoury flavoured biscuits (g)	222	207	0
Nuts, mixed, salted (g)	255	262	0
Confectionary (g)	418	396	0
Chocolate (g)	441	359	0
Potato crisps, pre-packaged (g)	518	650	0
Salad dressing (g)	277	211	0
Tomato sauce (g)	569	511	0
Beef sausages (g)	1047	1036	0
Butter (g)	280	195	0
Ham (g)	189	143	0
Frozen lasagne, pre-packaged (g)	4322	3684	0
Fish fillet crumbed, pre-packaged (g)	302	433	0
Ice cream (g)	1830	1307	0
Total Discretionary Choices—other (g)	18,308	17109 (7% < Original)	0
Alcoholic Drinks			
Beer, full strength (mL)	4661	5060	0
White wine, sparkling (mL)	863	546	0
Whisky (mL)	266	453	0
Red wine (mL)	1078	519	0
Total Alcoholic Drinks (mL)	6868	6578 (4% < Original)	0

Table 2. *Cont.*

Food Item	Habitual Diet (g/Fortnight)		Recommended Diet (g/Fortnight)
	Original Healthy Diets ASAP	Low SEG Healthy Diets ASAP	Original Healthy Diets ASAP
	Takeaway foods		
Pizza, commercial (g)	1182	1800	0
Meat pie, commercial (g)	1638	1554	0
Hamburger, commercial (g)	2413	2710	0
Potato chips, commercial (g)	670	833	0
Total Takeaway Foods (g)	5903	6897 (17% > Original)	0
	Sugar sweetened beverages		
Sugar-sweetened soft drink (mL)	12,012	16,288 (36% > Original)	0
	Artificially sweetened drinks		
Artificially sweetened soft drink (mL)	2390	1406 (41% < Original)	0
	Items allocated to more than one food group		
Sandwich, pre-made, white bread, chicken, and salad * (g)	361	462	360
Canned meat and vegetable casserole ** (g)	1291	786	0
Orange fruit juice *** (mL)	6053	5331	0

* Divided equally between Grains etc, Lean meats etc, and Vegetables; ** Divided equally between Lean meats etc and Vegetables; *** Divided equally between Fruit and Discretionary choices—other.

The habitual diets of low SEG Households A, B and C provided 97%, 98% and 99% respectively of the energy content of habitual diets for the mean Australian population (that is, as described in the original Healthy Diets ASAP protocol) (Table 2 and Table S4A,B), and 99%, 99% and 98%, respectively, of the total energy intake reported by members of these households in the AHS NNPAS [21]. The energy content of the habitual diets of low SEG Households A, B and C provided 99%, 99% and 95% respectively of the energy content of the recommended diets for the same households (Table 2 and Table S4A,B).

Overall, energy derived from healthy food and drinks in the habitual diets of low SEGs was 10%, 11% and 3% lower, respectively, for Households A, B, and C than habitual diets of the mean population (Table 2). Energy derived from discretionary food and drinks in the habitual diets of low SEGs was 2% higher, 6% higher and no different, respectively for Households A, B, and C, than habitual diets of the mean population.

Compared to habitual diets of the mean population, habitual diets of low SEGs included, by weight, for Households A, B and C respectively: 14%, 14% and 8% less fruit; 6%, 13% and 4% less vegetables and legumes; 11% less, 14% less and 10% more grain (cereal) foods, and 19%, 17% and 6% less lean meats, poultry, fish, eggs, nuts, and seeds ("lean meats etc."). However, habitual diets of low SEGs included, by weight, for Households A, B and C respectively: 17%, 21% and 5% more takeaway foods; 36% more, 58% more and 2% less sugar sweetened beverages (SSBs); and 41%, 60% and 27% less artificially sweetened soft drinks than habitual diets of the mean population (Table 2 and Table S4A,B).

3.1.2. Price Collection

When the food price collection methods were modified to accommodate 'cheapest option' items in the low SEG protocol, the revised wording for data collection was: "When collecting the 'cheapest option' prices, the price of the cheapest equivalent product (selected from all brands including 'own brands') in the specified size is collected. For the items pie, pizza, and chips, usually sourced from other stores, the price of a frozen equivalent item from the supermarket is collected, selecting the cheapest option from all brands, including 'own brands', in the specified size. The takeaway burger item should be priced from the burger restaurant as per the original protocol. If the specified size is not available, choose the nearest larger size. If a larger size is not available, choose the nearest smaller size." Testing the low SEG protocol showed that including 'cheapest option' products resulted in marked cost reductions compared to the 'standard brands' products. Of the 60 packaged foods priced in supermarkets and discount supermarkets, 52 (87%) were an 'own brand' equivalent, five (8%) were a 'cheapest brand' equivalent, and three (5%) were 'standard brands'.

3.1.3. Modifications of Sources and Amounts of Household Income

The welfare dependent household income and low-minimum disposable household income amounts for each reference household, and the assumptions made in their calculation for the low SEG protocol, are shown in Table S5.

3.2. Testing of the Low SEG Healthy Diets ASAP Protocol

The costs of habitual and recommended diets for the three reference households, calculated by application of the low SEG protocol for both 'standard brands' and 'cheapest options', and the costs calculated by application of the original Healthy Diets ASAP protocol (mean population intakes), are shown in Figure 1, and detailed below.

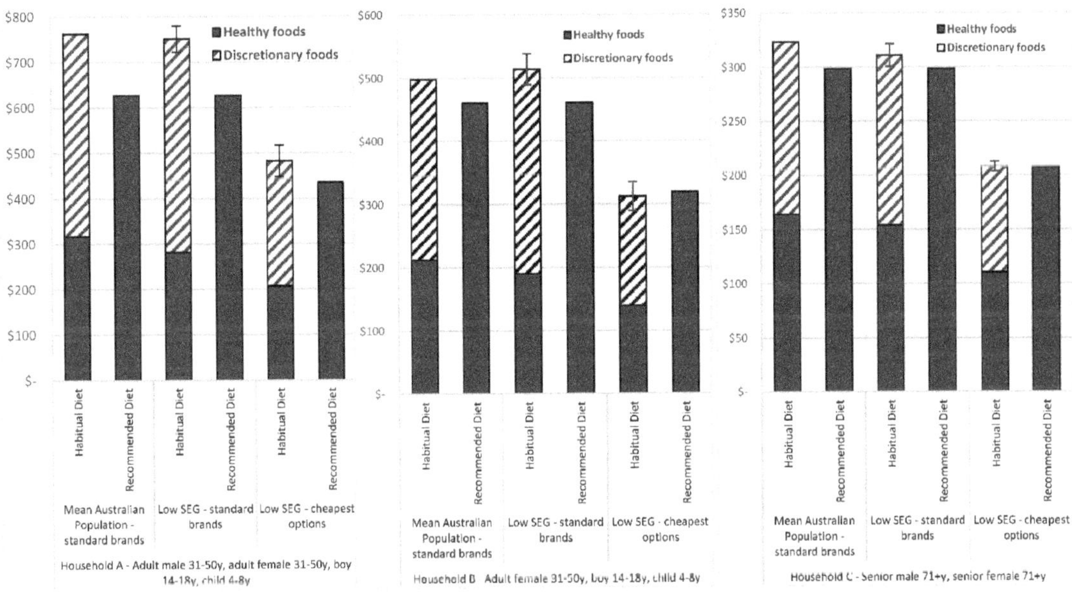

Figure 1. Costs of habitual and recommended diets for mean population and low SEG reference households (using 'standard brands' and 'cheapest options') per fortnight. Error bars reflect standard errors. y = years.

Detailed costs of the component food groups of habitual and recommended diets, for the mean population and low SEG reference households per fortnight, are shown in Table S6A–C.

3.2.1. Comparison of Habitual and Recommended Diet Costs Determined by the Low SEG Protocol and the Original Healthy Diets ASAP Protocol Using 'Standard Brands'

Comparison of Total Costs of Diets Calculated by the Low SEG Protocol and the Original Healthy Diets ASAP Protocol

When 'standard brands' were priced, the total costs of the habitual diets of low SEGs were 1% lower ($11 per fortnight) for Household A, 3% higher ($16 per fortnight) for

Household B, and 4% lower ($13 per fortnight) for Household C, than habitual diet costs for the mean population (Figure 1). As the recommended diet pricing tool was the same, the cost of the recommended diet for low SEGs and the mean population was also the same.

Comparison of Diet Costs of Food Groups and Food Group Components Calculated by the Low SEG Protocol and the Original Healthy Diets ASAP Protocol

When 'standard brands' were priced, the healthy food and drink costs of the habitual diets of low SEG were 11% ($36 per fortnight) lower for Household A, 10% ($22 per fortnight) lower for Household B and 6% ($10 per fortnight) lower for Household C, than healthy food and drink costs for the mean population. The discretionary food and drink costs of the habitual diets of low SEG were 6% higher ($25 per fortnight) for Household A, 13% higher ($38 per fortnight) for Household B, and 1% lower ($2 per fortnight) for Household C than the discretionary food and drink costs of the mean population (Figure 1). Costs in habitual diets of low SEGs for fruit, vegetables and legumes; grain (cereal) foods; lean meats and poultry, fish, eggs, nuts and seeds; and artificially sweetened soft drinks, were lower, and costs for: takeaway foods and SSBs were higher than costs for the mean population, in all low SEG households. (Table S6A–C).

Comparison of Habitual Diet and Recommended Diet Costs

When 'standard brands' were priced, the cost of the recommended diet was less expensive than the habitual diets of low SEGs, by 17% ($124 per fortnight) for Household A, 10% ($53 per fortnight) for Household B, and 4% ($13 per fortnight) for Household C (Figure 1).

Proportion of Total Habitual Diet Costs Spent on Discretionary Food and Drinks

When 'standard brands' were priced, the proportion of the food budget of low SEGs spent on discretionary items was 63% ($470 per fortnight) for Household A, 63% ($324 per fortnight) for Household B, and 50% ($157 per fortnight) Household C (Figure 1).

3.2.2. Habitual Diet Cost Differences between 'Standard Brands' and 'Cheapest Options'

When 'cheapest options' were priced instead of 'standard brands', the cost of habitual diets of low SEGs reduced by around 36%, and the cost of the recommended diets reduced by around 31%. (Figure 1). When 'cheapest options' were priced instead of 'standard brands', the cost of the recommended diet was 10% less ($48 per fortnight) for Household A, 2% more ($7 per fortnight) for Household B, and equal cost to the habitual diet for Household C.

3.2.3. Affordability of Habitual and Recommended Diets Using 'Standard Brands' and 'Cheapest Options'

The affordability of habitual and recommended diets for mean population and low SEG reference households (using 'standard brands' and 'cheapest options' prices) are shown in Figure 2. Affordability of the diets are shown for Households A and B at two calculated household incomes: a low-minimum disposable and a welfare only income, and for Household C, at a calculated welfare only income (as both members of this household are retired and not receiving employment income).

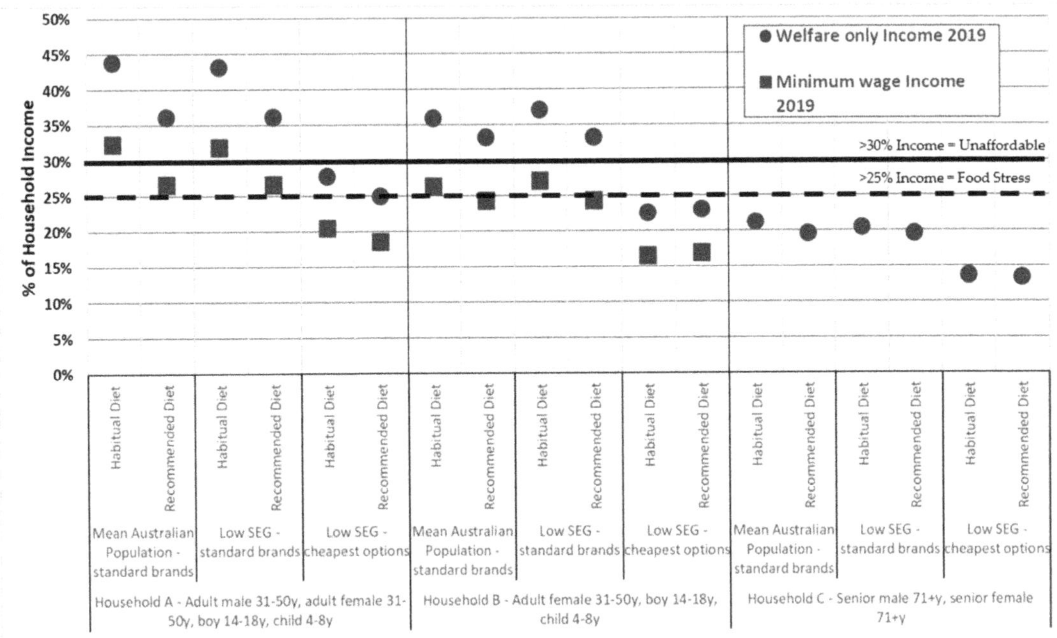

Figure 2. Affordability of habitual and recommended diets for mean population and low SEG reference households receiving welfare only and minimum wage incomes (using 'standard brands' and 'cheapest options'). y = years.

Affordability of Habitual and Recommended Diets for Household A (Two Adults, Two Children)

For Household A receiving the low-minimum disposable income, when 'standard brands' were priced, habitual diets of low SEGs cost 32% of household income. Recommended diets cost 27% of household income. When purchasing 'cheapest options' habitual diets of low SEGs and recommended diets required 20% and 18%, respectively of the low-minimum household income (Figure 2).

For Household A receiving a welfare only income, when 'standard brands' were priced, habitual diets of low SEGs cost 43% of household income (Figure 2). Recommended diets required 36% of the welfare household income. If the household purchased 'cheapest options', habitual and recommended diets required 28% and 25%, respectively of the welfare household income (Figure 2).

Affordability of Habitual and Recommended Diets for Household B (One Adult, Two Children)

For Household B receiving the low-minimum disposable income, when 'standard brands' were priced, habitual diets of low SEGs cost 27% of household income. Recommended diets cost 24% of household income. When purchasing 'cheapest options', habitual and recommended diets required 16% and 17%, respectively, of the low-minimum disposable income (Figure 2).

For Household B receiving a welfare only income, when 'standard brands' were priced, habitual diets of low SEGs cost 37% of the welfare household income. Recommended diets required 33% of the welfare household income. When 'cheapest options' were purchased, both the habitual diet and the recommended diet required 23% of the welfare household income (Figure 2).

Affordability of Habitual and Recommended Diets for Household C (Older, Retired Couple)

For Household C on a welfare only income, when 'standard brands' were priced, habitual diets of low SEGs cost 20% of the welfare household income. Recommended diets also required 20% of the welfare household income. When 'cheapest options' were purchased, habitual and recommended diets required 14% and 13%, respectively, of the welfare household income (Figure 2).

4. Discussion

4.1. Summary of Findings

Development and testing of the low SEG Healthy Diets ASAP protocol showed that overall energy content and cost of habitual diets for each reference low SEG household was similar to that of the corresponding mean population reference households (assessed by the original Healthy Diets ASAP protocol). However, in the habitual diets of low SEGs a higher proportion of energy, and cost, was derived from discretionary food and drinks, particularly SSBs and takeaway foods, with a corresponding decrease in energy and cost derived from healthy food and drinks and artificially sweetened beverages.

The habitual diet was more expensive than the recommended diet for all three low SEG reference households when 'standard brands' were purchased. However, when the 'cheapest options' were purchased instead of 'standard brands', habitual diets of low SEGs cost the same as recommended diets for Household C (older, retired couple), became less expensive than recommended diets for Household B (one adult, two children), but remained more expensive than recommended diets for Household A (two adults, two children).

For recommended diets to be affordable (<30% of disposable income) for Households A and B receiving a minimum wage income, it was necessary to employ strategies such as purchasing 'cheapest option' products. When Households A and B were reliant upon welfare benefits, affording recommended diets would be even more challenging. Recommended diets for Household C receiving a welfare only income would be more affordable than the other households on a welfare only income.

4.2. Differences between Habitual Diet of Low SEGs and the Mean Population

When 'standard brands' were priced, the habitual diet of low SEGs was more expensive than recommended diets, consistent with the findings of previous applications of the original Healthy Diets ASAP protocol [23,25,35]. This is partially due to exemption of basic, healthy food and drinks from GST in Australia [36].

Total diet costs and affordability of habitual diets priced using 'standard brands' were similar for low SEGs and the mean Australian population. However, analysis of each food group showed lower cost contributions from healthy food and drinks, and higher cost contributions from discretionary food and drinks in the habitual diets of low SEGs compared to those of the mean population. These cost differences reflect dietary intake differences between low SEGs and the mean Australian population, as captured in the respective diet pricing tools. Such variation may relate to differing perceptions that healthy foods are too expensive, lack of food preparation time and resources among different SEGs, and higher promotion of unhealthy foods in the food environment in low SEG areas [2,11,37,38]. Additionally, many complex social barriers affect access to resources, which in turn influence food choice in low SEGs [10,39].

The costs of habitual diets in all low SEG reference households (exemplified here by data for Household A) included a higher proportion spent on SSBs (5.5% of total habitual diets in low SEG), and lower proportion spent on artificially sweetened beverages (0.5% of total habitual diets in low SEG), in comparison to the mean population (4.0% and 0.8%, respectively, of total habitual diets in the mean population). These differences may be one reason that, although potentially regressive (i.e., having greater impact on low SEGs), other studies have postulated greater health benefits of a tax on SSBs to low SEGs than the rest of the population [40].

Similarly, costs of habitual diets of all low SEG reference households included a higher proportion from takeaway foods compared to the mean population. In contrast, household expenditure surveys show that low SEGs spend less on 'meals out and fast foods' than higher SEGs [17]. However, expenditure surveys solely reflect the purchase location, rather than the nutritional quality of food being purchased. Our results correlate with other studies that suggest that when low SEGs consume food prepared outside the home, they tend to purchase 'fast food' rather than healthier meals, such as in restaurants [41,42].

4.3. *Choice of 'Cheapest Options' as a Coping Strategy to Stretch the Budget*

Purchase of 'cheapest options' instead of 'standard brands' resulted in cost savings of 31% for recommended diets, and 36% for habitual diets. These differences arose as more packaged products are included in the latter than the former. The cost differential between habitual and recommended diets reduced to zero for Household C, and habitual diets became less expensive than recommended diets for Household B. For Household A, habitual diets were still more expensive than recommended diets when 'cheapest options' were purchased instead of 'standard brands', but the cost differential was smaller. This reduction and reversal in the cost differential may help explain the common perception that healthy food is more expensive than unhealthy food [11], and may be a driver for the consumption of unhealthy packaged foods over fresh healthy foods in low SEGs.

Other coping strategies that may be used by low SEG households to stretch their food budget include taking advantage of price promotions. However, a previous study found price promotions may save only a small (3%) proportion of cost for both habitual and recommended diets [14]. Discounted food and drinks tend to be less healthy than other products, and thus this can reduce the quality of habitual diets [43]. Therefore, households that adjust their shopping habits by stockpiling price promoted products to consume later may be able to save in the medium term, but this practice can also lead to increased consumption [44].

4.4. *Affordability of Diets*

Recommended diets were unaffordable for Households A and B, when receiving welfare benefits, but were affordable for Household C receiving the aged pension. The aged pension is indexed to average wages in Australia, whereas unemployment benefits are indexed to inflation. The aged pension has increased at a greater rate than unemployment benefits, which did not increase in real terms from 2009 to 2020 [45].

4.5. *Strengths of the Low SEG Healthy Diets ASAP Protocol*

Face validity of the low SEG habitual diet pricing tool was supported, as the energy content of the low SEG habitual diet for each reference household was within 2% of the energy content of corresponding reported energy intakes in the AHS NNPAS [21].

4.5.1. Selection of SEG Measure

For the purposes of this study, household income was selected as the measure of low SEGs as it reflected household resources for food purchases, even if a recent lifestyle change had occurred, such as job loss or family separation. Many households comprised of older people may report a low income, despite having access to retirement savings and superannuation for daily expenditure. However, household income was preferred over household asset levels to indicate the SEG of older households, as such assets are not usually available to spend on daily expenses. Other SEG measures used in dietary intake studies in Australia included education, occupation, disadvantage level of the residential area, and/or combinations thereof, although household income was most commonly used [10]. Some previous studies found differences in SEG gradients of dietary intake using different measures of SEG [46–48], however measures such as education and occupation are not available in the AHS NNPAS for all reference household members [26].

4.5.2. Selection of Low SEG Households

By including three types of low SEG households instead of just one, we have increased the range of relevant tools available to future users of the low SEG Healthy Diets ASAP. This study was also able to demonstrate how the cost, cost differential, and affordability of diets varied for different, common, low SEG household composition types.

4.6. Limitations

There are inherent limitations of the original Healthy Diets ASAP protocol that also apply to the low SEG protocol [20]. These include underlying assumptions: that food is equitably shared with all household members; that there is minimal food wastage; and that food is not acquired through home production. Measurement of dietary intake by 24-h recall (as in the AHS NNPAS) is known to be biased due to social desirability, particularly among low SEGs [26,49]. As with the original protocol, no adjustments have been made to account for the likely under-reporting of overall food intake and over-reporting of healthier foods. Hence, the findings of this study present a 'best-case' scenario.

As with the original Healthy Diets ASAP protocol, due to the sampling methods of the AHS NNPAS, it was not possible to analyse dietary intakes of actual family groups, as only one adult, or one adult and one child, were selected from households included in the national dietary survey [26]. This may have impacted particularly the low SEG habitual diet pricing tools as, for example, dietary intakes of children in single parent households may differ from those of children in two parent households. Further, low sample size numbers within subcategories of some age/gender/income groups in the AHS NNPAS 2011–2012 [21] affected the reliability of mean dietary intakes calculated for teenage boys (included in Households A and B), and older adults (included in Household C). However, despite these limitations, the AHS NNPAS 2011–2012 was the most detailed, recent, national source of population dietary intake data for this study [10].

For monitoring and surveillance purposes, it is essential that a standardised tool is used to collect current food and drink prices. The AHS NNPAS (2011–2013) data used in the development of the standardised habitual diet pricing tool are the most recent available in Australia, but are now 10 years old, and dietary intake patterns may have altered over those years. While few changes were noted between the 1995 National Nutrition Survey and the AHS NNPAS 16 years later [50], recent food environment changes (such as the rise in online food delivery options) may have influenced current dietary intakes. Additionally, the effects of the SARS-CoV-2 pandemic on employment (affecting income) and movement restrictions (affecting locations available for food shopping) may have been particularly challenging for low SEGs.

Testing the low SEG protocol used prices from a major city location. Regional and/or remote areas are likely to experience higher food prices [51] and a relative lack of 'own brand' products and budget supermarkets [52]. Therefore, diet cost and affordability results in this study reflect a 'best case scenario' for low SEGs.

Incomes were calculated at 2019 rates to avoid enumerating complex economic support supplements instituted by the Australian Government in response to the SARS-CoV-2 pandemic. The consumer price index for food in Queensland increased by 3.5% between June 2019 and June 2020, and thus diet affordability may be slightly underestimated [53].

The low SEG Healthy Diets ASAP protocol targets those in the lowest quintile of household income. However, some of these low SEG households experience particular challenges, such as very low incomes (due to ineligibility for welfare benefits), homelessness or unstable housing, limited access to food stores, and/or particular cultural food requirements. The low SEG Healthy Diets ASAP protocol does not specifically capture dietary intakes or incomes of these extremely vulnerable groups.

Additional coping strategies that may be used by low SEGs to stretch the food budget, such as shopping at market stalls or culturally specific stores, bulk purchasing, and/or accessing food banks, charitable donations, subsidised meals or food provided by family or friends, have not been included in this study [54–56].

4.7. Policy Implications

Our findings reflect reported dietary intake differences between low SEGs and the broader population, which have not been quantified previously across all ADG food groups [10]. This study confirms the need for an equity lens to better target the ADGs to low SEGs in Australia [6].

One measure to improve affordability of healthy, equitable and more sustainable diets is to increase household income. In the early months of the SARS-CoV-2 pandemic in 2020 the Australian Government implemented a number of economic stimulus measures to combat the sudden increase in unemployment [57]. This resulted in an increased income for many welfare dependent households and thus improved affordability of recommended diets [58]. A national survey found 83% of welfare dependent families reported eating healthier and more regularly compared to pre-pandemic times [59]. While these economic measures were only of short duration, this tangible example demonstrated the beneficial impact of increasing welfare support to adequate levels.

The results of the study also suggest that there is an opportunity to encourage purchase and consumption of recommended diets by making unhealthy foods relatively more expensive than healthy foods. Provision of vouchers for healthy food, such as the Special Supplemental Nutrition Program for Women, Infants and Children (WIC) in the USA, have been shown to increase consumption of healthy foods [60]. Promotion and discounting of healthy, rather than unhealthy, foods and beverages may also encourage their purchase [43]. In Australia, in remote Aboriginal and Torres Strait Islander communities, a study restricting promotion of unhealthy foods decreased their consumption [61]. Further research testing the impact of providing discounts for healthy foods for families with young children is currently underway (Ferguson et al., unpublished results), contributing to important evidence of potential policy changes to address inequities in dietary patterns.

Increasing taxation of unhealthy foods has also been suggested [25,62]. Increasing the GST rate on unhealthy foods and retaining the current exemption of GST on basic, healthy foods, increases the relative cost of unhealthy foods. Modelling has shown that increasing the rate of GST to 20% on unhealthy foods would make recommended diets 9% more affordable than habitual diets and raise revenue that could be used for health promotion programs [24].

By creating more supportive fiscal environments, such regulatory policy measures would help address the dietary inequities faced by low SEGs [39,63]. Reduction of economic barriers to healthy eating would also provide greater opportunity for low SEG households to benefit from nutrition education and food literacy programs [39,63].

5. Conclusions

Development of the low SEG Healthy Diets ASAP protocol enables calculation of habitual and recommended diet costs and affordability that assimilate the habitual dietary intakes, household structures, food purchasing habits, and income sources and amounts of low SEGs in Australia. The low SEG habitual diet pricing tool incorporates differences in dietary intake between low SEGs and the mean Australian population including lower quantities of healthy food and drinks and higher quantities of key discretionary food and drinks, particularly takeaway foods and SSBs.

Testing the low SEG protocol showed affordability of both diets improved when 'cheapest options' were purchased, but that the cost differential between habitual and recommended diets decreased. The finding that for some low SEG households recommended diets became more expensive than habitual low SEG diets could partly explain commonly-held perceptions that healthy food is unaffordable [11].

Policy action is necessary to increase affordability of recommended diets for low SEGs by reducing healthy food and drink costs and ensuring all household incomes are sufficient. This should include measures aimed at increasing the differential between costs of habitual and recommended diets, and at supporting and encouraging low SEGs to purchase and consume healthy diets.

Further application of the low SEG Healthy Diets ASAP protocol will provide additional data to inform policy and practice change. Improving diet-related health will lead to reduced health costs, improved workforce and social participation, improved education outcomes for children, and reduced social inequality, thus benefiting all Australians.

Supplementary Materials: The following are available online at https://www.mdpi.com/article/10.3390/nu13082900/s1, Table S1: Participant numbers in subcategories in the ABS National Nutrition and Physical Activity Survey; Table S2: Concordance between ABS NNPAS food codes and food and drink items of the Healthy Diets ASAP habitual diet pricing tool; Table S3: Calculations for minimum wage and welfare only household incomes for 2019; Table S4A: Composition of original Healthy Diets ASAP habitual diet pricing tool for mean Australian population and, Low SEG Healthy Diets ASAP habitual diet pricing tool, and recommended diet pricing tool, for Household B (one adult, two children); Table S4B: Composition of original Healthy Diets ASAP habitual diet pricing tool for mean Australian population and Low SEG Healthy Diets ASAP habitual diet pricing tool, and recommended diet pricing tool for Household C (older retired couple); Table S5: Assumptions and resultant incomes for minimum wage and welfare only incomes for reference Households A, B and C in 2019; Table S6A: Dietary costs and affordability by food group and food group components of low SEG habitual and recommended diets, using 'standard brand' and 'cheapest option' prices, and comparison to the mean Australian population, for reference Household A: Two adults, two children; Table S6B: Dietary costs and affordability by food group and food group components of low SEG habitual and recommended diets, using 'standard brand' and 'cheapest option' prices, and comparison to the mean Australian population, for reference Household B: One adult, two children; Table S6C: Dietary costs and affordability by food group and food group components of low SEG habitual and recommended diets, using 'standard brand' and 'cheapest option' prices, and comparison to the mean Australian population, for reference Household C: Older retired couple.

Author Contributions: Conceptualization, M.L. and A.J.L.; methodology, M.L.; validation, M.L.; formal analysis, M.L.; writing—original draft preparation, M.L.; writing—review and editing, A.J.L., S.A.M., L.R.; supervision, A.J.L., S.A.M., L.R.; funding acquisition, M.L. and A.J.L. All authors have read and agreed to the published version of the manuscript.

Funding: M.L. was supported by a Research Training Program Scholarship provided by The University of Queensland, and a Top Up Scholarship provided by The Australian Prevention Partnership Centre, The Sax Institute.

Institutional Review Board Statement: The University of Queensland Research Ethics Committee assessed this study as meeting the conditions for exemption from Human Research Ethics Committee review and approval in accordance with Section 5.1.22 of the National Statement on Ethical Conduct in Human Research (2007). The Ethics Clearance number is 2019000561. All data were obtained from publicly available sources and did not involve human participants.

Informed Consent Statement: Not applicable.

Data Availability Statement: The data presented in this study are available in this article and its Supplementary Materials.

Conflicts of Interest: The authors declare no conflict of interest. The funders had no role in the design of the study; in the collection, analyses, or interpretation of data; in the writing of the manuscript, or in the decision to publish the results.

References

1. Lee, A.J.; Cullerton, K.; Herron, L.-M. Achieving food system transformation: Insights from a retrospective review of nutrition policy (in)action in high-income countries. *Int. J. Health Policy Manag.* **2020**. [CrossRef] [PubMed]
2. Burns, C. The Vulnerable and the Disadvantaged. *Aust. Econ. Rev.* **2008**, *41*, 90–96. [CrossRef]

3. Australian Institute of Health and Welfare. Australian Burden of Disease Study: Impact and Causes of Illness and Death in Australia 2011. Available online: https://www.aihw.gov.au/reports/burden-of-disease/abds-impact-and-causes-of-illness-death-2011/contents/table-of-contents (accessed on 19 June 2019).
4. GBD 2019 Risk Factors Collaborators. Global burden of 87 risk factors in 204 countries and territories, 1990–2019: A systematic analysis for the Global Burden of Disease Study 2019. *Lancet* **2020**, *396*, 1223–1249. [CrossRef]
5. Australian Bureau of Statistics. 4364.0.55.007 Australian Health Survey: Nutrition First Results—Foods and Nutrients, 2011–2012. Available online: http://www.abs.gov.au/AUSSTATS/abs@.nsf/DetailsPage/4364.0.55.0072011-12?OpenDocument (accessed on 12 November 2017).
6. National Health and Medical Research Council. *Australian Dietary Guidelines—Providing the Scientific Evidence for Healthier Australian Diets*; National Health and Medical Research Council: Canberra, Australia, 2013. Available online: https://www.eatforhealth.gov.au/sites/default/files/content/n55_australian_dietary_guidelines.pdf (accessed on 9 February 2016).
7. Australian Institute of Health and Welfare. Australia's Health 2016—Health of Population Groups: Health across SOCIOECONOMIC Groups. Available online: https://www.aihw.gov.au/reports/australias-health/australias-health-2016/contents/chapter-5-health-of-population-groups (accessed on 27 May 2019).
8. Stringhini, S.; Carmeli, C.; Jokela, M.; Avendaño, M.; Muennig, P.; Guida, F.; Ricceri, F.; d'Errico, A.; Barros, H.; Bochud, M.; et al. Socioeconomic status and the 25 × 25 risk factors as determinants of premature mortality: A multicohort study and meta-analysis of 1.7 million men and women. *Lancet* **2017**, *389*, 1229–1237. [CrossRef]
9. Harris, B.; Fetherston, H.; Calder, R. *Australia's Health Tracker by Socio-Economic Status 2017*; Australian Health Policy Collaboration Victoria University: Melbourne, VIC, Australia, 2017.
10. Lewis, M.; Lee, A.J. Dietary inequity? A systematic scoping review of dietary intake in low socio-economic groups compared with high socio-economic groups in Australia. *Public Health Nutr.* **2021**, *24*, 393–411. [CrossRef]
11. Zorbas, C.; Palermo, C.; Chung, A.; Iguacel, I.; Peeters, A.; Bennett, R.; Backholer, K. Factors perceived to influence healthy eating: A systematic review and meta-ethnographic synthesis of the literature. *Nutr. Rev.* **2018**, *76*, 861–874. [CrossRef]
12. Friel, S.; Pescud, M.; Malbon, E.; Lee, A.; Carter, R.; Greenfield, J.; Cobcroft, M.; Potter, J.; Rychetnik, L.; Meertens, B. Using systems science to understand the determinants of inequities in healthy eating. *PLoS ONE* **2017**, *12*, e0188872. [CrossRef]
13. Lee, A.; Ni Mhurchu, C.; Sacks, G.; Swinburn, B.; Snowdon, W.; Vandevijvere, S.; Hawkes, C.M.; Labbe, M.R.; Rayner, M.; Sanders, D.A.R.; et al. Monitoring the price and affordability of foods and diets globally. *Obes. Rev.* **2013**, *14*, 82–95. [CrossRef]
14. Zorbas, C.; Lee, A.; Peeters, A.; Lewis, M.; Landrigan, T.; Backholer, K. Streamlined data-gathering techniques to estimate the price and affordability of healthy and unhealthy diets under different pricing scenarios. *Public Health Nutr.* **2021**, *24*, 1–11. [CrossRef]
15. Youl, T.; Supermarkets and Grocery Stores in Australia. AU Industry (ANZSIC) Report G4111. Available online: https://my.ibisworld.com/download/au/en/industry/1834/1/0/pdf (accessed on 10 September 2020).
16. Chapman, K.; Innes-Hughes, C.; Goldsbury, D.; Kelly, B.; Bauman, A.; Allman-Farinelli, M. A comparison of the cost of generic and branded food products in Australian supermarkets. *Public Health Nutr.* **2012**, *16*, 894–900. [CrossRef]
17. Australian Bureau of Statistics. 6530.0—Household Expenditure Survey, Australia: Summary of Results, 2015–2016. Available online: https://www.abs.gov.au/AUSSTATS/abs@.nsf/Lookup/6530.0Main+Features12015-16?OpenDocument (accessed on 22 May 2019).
18. Australian Bureau of Statistics. 6523.0—Household Income and Wealth, Australia, 2015–2016. Available online: http://abs.gov.au/household-income (accessed on 12 November 2017).
19. Lewis, M.; Lee, A. Costing 'healthy' food baskets in Australia—A systematic review of food price and affordability monitoring tools, protocols and methods. *Public Health Nutr.* **2016**, *19*, 2872–2886. [CrossRef]
20. Lee, A.J.; Kane, S.; Lewis, M.; Good, E.; Pollard, C.M.; Landrigan, T.J.; Dick, M. Healthy diets ASAP—Australian Standardised Affordability and Pricing methods protocol. *Nutr. J.* **2018**, *17*, 1–14. [CrossRef]
21. Australian Bureau of Statistics. 4324.0.55.002 Microdata: Australian Health Survey: Nutrition and Physical Activity, 2011–2012. Available online: http://www.abs.gov.au/ausstats/abs@.nsf/PrimaryMainFeatures/4324.0.55.002?OpenDocument (accessed on 12 November 2017).
22. Hendrie, G.A.; Ridoutt, B.G.; Wiedmann, T.O.; Noakes, M. Greenhouse Gas Emissions and the Australian Diet—Comparing Dietary Recommendations with Average Intakes. *Nutrients* **2014**, *6*, 289–303. [CrossRef]
23. Lee, A.; Lewis, M. Testing the Price of Healthy and Current Diets in Remote Aboriginal Communities to Improve Food Security: Development of the Aboriginal and Torres Strait Islander Healthy Diets ASAP (Australian Standardised Affordability and Pricing) Methods. *Int. J. Environ. Res. Public Health* **2018**, *15*, 2912. [CrossRef] [PubMed]
24. Lee, A.J.; Kane, S.; Ramsey, R.; Good, E.; Dick, M. Testing the price and affordability of healthy and current (unhealthy) diets and the potential impacts of policy change in Australia. *BMC Public Health* **2016**, *16*, 315. [CrossRef] [PubMed]
25. Love, P.; Whelan, J.; Bell, C.; Grainger, F.; Russell, C.; Lewis, M.; Lee, A. Healthy Diets in Rural Victoria—Cheaper than Unhealthy Alternatives, Yet Unaffordable. *Int. J. Environ. Res. Public Health* **2018**, *15*, 2469. [CrossRef] [PubMed]
26. Australian Bureau of Statistics. 4364.0.55.001—Australian Health Survey: Users' Guide, 2011–2013. Available online: https://www.abs.gov.au/ausstats/abs@.nsf/Lookup/5209F2553DE3B084CA257BBB0014D160?opendocument (accessed on 31 May 2017).
27. Xyris Software (Australia) Pty Ltd. *FoodWorks Professional*, 9th ed.; Xyris Software (Australia) Pty Ltd.: Brisbane, Australia, 2019.

28. Fair Work Ombudsman. Minimum Wages. Available online: https://www.fairwork.gov.au/how-we-will-help/templates-and-guides/fact-sheets/minimum-workplace-entitlements/minimum-wages (accessed on 22 October 2015).
29. Australian Taxation Office. Simple Tax Calculator. Available online: www.ato.gov.au/calculators-and-tools/simple-tax-calculator/ (accessed on 12 November 2017).
30. Services Australia. Payment and Service Finder. Available online: https://www.servicesaustralia.gov.au/ (accessed on 22 October 2015).
31. Burns, C.; Friel, S. It's time to determine the cost of a healthy diet in Australia. *Aust. N. Z. J. Public Health* **2007**, *31*, 363–365. [CrossRef] [PubMed]
32. Landrigan, T.J.; Kerr, D.A.; Dhaliwal, S.S.; Pollard, C.M. Protocol for the Development of a Food Stress Index to Identify Households Most at Risk of Food Insecurity in Western Australia. *Int. J. Environ. Res. Public Health* **2018**, *16*, 79. [CrossRef]
33. Ward, P.R.; Verity, F.; Carter, P.; Tsourtos, G.; Coveney, J.; Wong, K.C. Food Stress in Adelaide: The Relationship between Low Income and the Affordability of Healthy Food. *J. Environ. Public Health* **2013**, *2013*, 1–10. [CrossRef] [PubMed]
34. Lee, A.J.; Lewis, M. Healthy Diets ASAP Portal. Available online: https://healthydiets.azurewebsites.net/ (accessed on 10 August 2020).
35. Lee, A.J.; Kane, S.; Herron, L.-M.; Matsuyama, M.; Lewis, M. A tale of two cities: The cost, price-differential and affordability of current and healthy diets in Sydney and Canberra, Australia. *Int. J. Behav. Nutr. Phys. Act.* **2020**, *17*, 1–13. [CrossRef]
36. Australian Taxation Office. GST-free Sales. Available online: https://www.ato.gov.au/business/gst/when-to-charge-gst-(and-when-not-to)/gst-free-sales/ (accessed on 23 March 2021).
37. Ball, K.; Crawford, D.; Mishra, G. Socio-economic inequalities in women's fruit and vegetable intakes: A multilevel study of individual, social and environmental mediators. *Public Health Nutr.* **2007**, *9*, 623–630. [CrossRef] [PubMed]
38. Thornton, L.E.; Lamb, K.E.; Ball, K. Fast food restaurant locations according to socioeconomic disadvantage, urban–regional locality, and schools within Victoria, Australia. *SSM Popul. Health* **2016**, *2*, 1–9. [CrossRef] [PubMed]
39. Marmot, M.; Allen, J.; Bell, R.; Bloomer, E.; Goldblatt, P. WHO European review of social determinants of health and the health divide. *Lancet* **2012**, *380*, 1011–1029. [CrossRef]
40. Backholer, K.; Sarink, D.; Beauchamp, A.; Keating, C.; Loh, V.H.Y.; Ball, K.; Martin, J.; Peeters, A. The impact of a tax on sugar-sweetened beverages according to socio-economic position: A systematic review of the evidence. *Public Health Nutr.* **2016**, *19*, 3070–3084. [CrossRef]
41. Thornton, L.E.; Bentley, R.; Kavanagh, A. Individual and area-level socioeconomic associations with fast food purchasing. *J. Epidemiol. Community Health* **2010**, *65*, 873–880. [CrossRef]
42. Miura, K.; Giskes, K.M.; Turrell, G. Socio-economic differences in takeaway food consumption among adults. *Public Health Nutr.* **2011**, *15*, 218–226. [CrossRef] [PubMed]
43. Sacks, G.; Schultz, S.; Grigsby-Duffy, L.; Robinson, E.; Orellana, L.; Marshall, J.; Cameron, A.J. *Inside our Supermarkets: Assessment of the Healthiness of Australian Supermarkets*; Deakin University: Melbourne, Australia, 2020.
44. Backholer, K.; Sacks, G.; Cameron, A.J. Food and Beverage Price Promotions: An Untapped Policy Target for Improving Population Diets and Health. *Curr. Nutr. Rep.* **2019**, *8*, 250–255. [CrossRef] [PubMed]
45. Phillips, B.; Gray, M.; Joesph, C.; Webster, R. *Research Note: Newstart and other Government Allowances: Incomes, Financial Stress and Poverty*; ANU Centre for Social Research & Methods; Australian National University: Canberra, Australia, 2019.
46. Livingstone, K.M.; Olstad, D.L.; Leech, R.M.; Ball, K.; Meertens, B.; Potter, J.; Cleanthous, X.; Reynolds, R.; McNaughton, S.A. Socioeconomic Inequities in Diet Quality and Nutrient Intakes among Australian Adults: Findings from a Nationally Representative Cross-Sectional Study. *Nutrients* **2017**, *9*, 1092. [CrossRef] [PubMed]
47. Turrell, G.; Hewitt, B.; Patterson, C.; Oldenburg, B. Measuring socio-economic position in dietary research: Is choice of socio-economic indicator important? *Public Health Nutr.* **2003**, *6*, 191–200. [CrossRef] [PubMed]
48. Zarnowiecki, D.; Ball, K.; Parletta, N.; Dollman, J. Describing socioeconomic gradients in children's diets—does the socioeconomic indicator used matter? *Int. J. Behav. Nutr. Phys. Act.* **2014**, *11*, 44. [CrossRef]
49. Giskes, K.; Turrell, G.; Patterson, C.; Newman, B. Socio-economic differences in fruit and vegetable consumption among Australian adolescents and adults. *Public Health Nutr.* **2002**, *5*, 663–669. [CrossRef]
50. Olstad, D.L.; Leech, R.M.; Livingstone, K.M.; Ball, K.; Thomas, B.; Potter, J.; Cleanthous, X.; Reynolds, R.; McNaughton, S.A. Are dietary inequalities among Australian adults changing? A nationally representative analysis of dietary change according to socioeconomic position between 1995 and 2011–2013. *Int. J. Behav. Nutr. Phys. Act.* **2018**, *15*, 1–19. [CrossRef]
51. Lee, A.; Patay, D.; Herron, L.-M.; Harrison, E.P.; Lewis, M. Affordability of current, and healthy, more equitable, sustainable diets by area of socioeconomic disadvantage and remoteness in Queensland: Insights into food choice. *Int. J. Equity Health* **2021**, *20*, 1–17. [CrossRef]
52. Whelan, J.; Millar, L.; Bell, C.; Russell, C.; Grainger, F.; Allender, S.; Love, P. You Can't Find Healthy Food in the Bush: Poor Accessibility, Availability and Adequacy of Food in Rural Australia. *Int. J. Environ. Res. Public Health* **2018**, *15*, 2316. [CrossRef]
53. Australian Bureau of Statistics. 6401.0—Consumer Price Index, Australia, Dec 2020. Available online: https://www.abs.gov.au/statistics/economy/price-indexes-and-inflation/consumer-price-index-australia/latest-release (accessed on 25 February 2021).
54. Burns, C.; Cook, K.; Mavoa, H. Role of expendable income and price in food choice by low income families. *Appetite* **2013**, *71*, 209–217. [CrossRef]

55. Jovanovski, N.; Cook, K. How Australian welfare reforms shape low-income single mothers' food provisioning practices and their children's nutritional health. *Crit. Public Health* **2019**, *30*, 340–351. [CrossRef]
56. McKenzie, H.J. Food as a discretionary item: The impact of welfare payment changes on low-income single mother's food choices and strategies. *J. Poverty Soc. Justice* **2017**, *25*, 35–48. [CrossRef]
57. The Treasury of the Australian Government. Economic Response to the Coronavirus. Available online: https://treasury.gov.au/coronavirus (accessed on 12 February 2021).
58. Lewis, M.; Lee, A.J. Affording health during the COVID-19 pandemic and associated economic downturn. *Aust. N. Z. J. Public Health* **2020**, *44*, 519–520. [CrossRef] [PubMed]
59. Australian Council of Social Service. Survey of 955 people receiving the new rate of jobseeker and other allowances. Available online: https://www.acoss.org.au/wp-content/uploads/2020/06/200624-I-Can-Finally-Eat-Fresh-Fruit-And-Vegetables-Results-Of-The-Coronaviru_pdf (accessed on 29 July 2020).
60. Whaley, S.E.; Ritchie, L.D.; Spector, P.; Gomez, J. Revised WIC Food Package Improves Diets of WIC Families. *J. Nutr. Educ. Behav.* **2012**, *44*, 204–209. [CrossRef]
61. Bryce, S.; Scales, I.; Herron, L.-M.; Wigginton, B.; Lewis, M.; Lee, A.; Ngaanyatjarra Pitjantjatjara Yankunytjatjara (NPY) Women's Council. Maitjara Wangkanyi: Insights from an ethnographic study of food practices of households in remote australian aboriginal communities. *Int. J. Environ. Res. Public Health* **2020**, *17*, 8109. [CrossRef] [PubMed]
62. Sacks, G.; Veerman, J.L.; Moodie, M.; Swinburn, B. 'Traffic-light' nutrition labelling and 'junk-food' tax: A modelled comparison of cost-effectiveness for obesity prevention. *Int. J. Obs.* **2011**, 1001–1009. [CrossRef] [PubMed]
63. World Health Organization. *Ottawa Charter for Health Promotion*; WHO: Ottowa, ON, Canada, 1986.

nutrients

MDPI

Article

Increasing Fruit and Vegetable Variety over Time Is Associated with Lower 15-Year Healthcare Costs: Results from the Australian Longitudinal Study on Women's Health

Jennifer N. Baldwin [1,2], Lee M. Ashton [1,2], Peta M. Forder [3], Rebecca L. Haslam [1,2], Alexis J. Hure [3,4,5], Deborah J. Loxton [3], Amanda J. Patterson [1,2] and Clare E. Collins [1,2,*]

1 Priority Research Centre for Physical Activity and Nutrition, University of Newcastle, Callaghan, NSW 2308, Australia; jennifer.baldwin@newcastle.edu.au (J.N.B.); lee.ashton@newcastle.edu.au (L.M.A.); rebecca.williams@newcastle.edu.au (R.L.H.); amanda.patterson@newcastle.edu.au (A.J.P.)
2 School of Health Sciences, College of Health, Medicine and Wellbeing, University of Newcastle, Callaghan, NSW 2308, Australia
3 Priority Research Centre for Generational Health and Ageing, University of Newcastle, Callaghan, NSW 2308, Australia; peta.forder@newcastle.edu.au (P.M.F.); alexis.hure@newcastle.edu.au (A.J.H.); deborah.loxton@newcastle.edu.au (D.J.L.)
4 School of Medicine and Public Health, College of Health, Medicine and Wellbeing, University of Newcastle, Callaghan, NSW 2308, Australia
5 Hunter Medical Research Institute, New Lambton Heights, NSW 2305, Australia
* Correspondence: clare.collins@newcastle.edu.au; Tel.: +61-2-4921-5000

Citation: Baldwin, J.N.; Ashton, L.M.; Forder, P.M.; Haslam, R.L.; Hure, A.J.; Loxton, D.J.; Patterson, A.J.; Collins, C.E. Increasing Fruit and Vegetable Variety over Time Is Associated with Lower 15-Year Healthcare Costs: Results from the Australian Longitudinal Study on Women's Health. *Nutrients* **2021**, *13*, 2829. https://doi.org/10.3390/nu13082829

Academic Editor: Francesca Giampieri

Received: 30 June 2021
Accepted: 14 August 2021
Published: 18 August 2021

Abstract: Healthcare costs are lower for adults who consume more vegetables; however, the association between healthcare costs and fruit and vegetable varieties is unclear. Our aim was to investigate the association between (i) baseline fruit and vegetable (F&V) varieties, and (ii) changes in F&V varieties over time with 15-year healthcare costs in an Australian Longitudinal Study on Women's Health. The data for Survey 3 (n = 8833 women, aged 50–55 years) and Survey 7 (n = 6955, aged 62–67 years) of the 1946–1951 cohort were used. The F&V variety was assessed using the Fruit and Vegetable Variety (FAVVA) index calculated from the Cancer Council of Victoria's Dietary Questionnaire for Epidemiological Studies food frequency questionnaire. The baseline FAVVA and change in FAVVA were analysed as continuous predictors of Medicare claims/costs by using multiple regression analyses. Healthy weight women made, on average, 4.3 (95% confidence interval (CI) 1.7–6.8) fewer claims for every 10-point-higher FAVVA. Healthy weight women with higher fruit varieties incurred fewer charges; however, this was reversed for women overweight/obese. Across the sample, for every 10-point increase in FAVVA over time, women made 4.3 (95% CI 1.9–6.8) fewer claims and incurred $309.1 (95% CI $129.3–488.8) less in charges over 15 years. A higher F&V variety is associated with a small reduction in healthcare claims for healthy weight women only. An increasing F&V variety over time is associated with lower healthcare costs.

Keywords: fruit; vegetables; diet quality; health care costs; Medicare; women's health

1. Introduction

An adequate intake of fruit and vegetables (F&V) is associated with a lower risk of cardiovascular disease, cancer and all-cause mortality [1,2]. However, globally, 78% of adults consume less than five daily portions of F&V [3]. Low F&V consumption is among the leading dietary risk factors for mortality, each accounting for more than 2% of global deaths [4].

Poor diets are costly for governments. In Canada, inadequate F&V intake generates an economic burden of approximately $CAN 3.3 billion per year, including $CAN 1 billion in healthcare costs [5]. The results from two previous cohort studies have shown that the cumulative healthcare costs were lower for men [6] and women [7] who consumed more vegetables. However, the evidence for the association with fruit intake is mixed. The Chicago Western Electric Study reported lower healthcare costs for men in the highest tertile of fruit intake [6], while our analysis of Australian women found that healthcare costs increased as fruit consumption increased [7].

The variety of F&V intake, in addition to frequency, is important for health benefits. The dietary guidelines in the US, UK and Australia all recommend increasing the F&V variety to increase both the quantity and diversity of the nutrients consumed [8–10]. The frequency and variety of the F&V intake were each inversely associated with the risk of type 2 diabetes [11]. Green leafy vegetables were associated with a reduced risk of coronary heart disease (relative risk (RR) 0.83 (95% CI 0.75–0.91)), while cruciferous vegetables were associated with a reduced risk of cancer (RR 0.84 (95% CI 0.72–0.97)) [1].

Knowledge of the association between the F&V variety with healthcare costs is lacking and could potentially inform future approaches to population dietary interventions and health policies. The aim of the current study of mid-aged women in the Australian Longitudinal Study on Women's Health (ALSWH) was to investigate the association between (i) Part I: the F&V variety at the baseline and (ii) Part II: changes in the F&V variety over time with cumulative 15-year healthcare costs.

2. Materials and Methods

2.1. *Australian Longitudinal Study on Women's Health (ALSWH)*

This study uses data from the ALSWH [12]. Women in three cohorts (born 1973–1978, 1946–1951 and 1921–1926) were randomly selected from the Medicare database (Australia's government funds universal health coverage, which includes all permanent residents) to take part in Survey 1 in 1996 [12]. The surveys were initially mailed; however, participants have had the option of online surveys since 2011. Participants living in rural/remote areas were intentionally oversampled [13]. The original sample was a representative sample of over 40,000 Australian women, although women from non-English speaking backgrounds were under-represented [14]. Ethical approvals were granted by the University of Newcastle (h-076-0795) and the University of Queensland (200400224). Medicare data consent was provided for the overall ALSWH study, and the use of the linked Medicare Benefits Schedule data was granted by the ALSWH Data Access Committee.

2.2. *Participants: The 1946–1951 Cohort*

For this analysis, the data for Survey 3 (2001) (n = 11,228 women, aged 50–55 years) and Survey 7 (2013) (n = 9151, then aged 62–67 years) of the 1946–1951 cohort were used. The response rates for Surveys 3 and 7 were 85% and 81%, respectively, excluding women who had died or withdrawn since Survey 1 [15].

One thousand and seven (n = 1007, 7.3%) women opted out of the Medicare Benefits Schedule (MBS) data linkage. Women with the highest 1% (n = 128, total charges > $79,525) and lowest 1% ($n$ = 445, total charges = $0) of cumulative MBS charges over the 15-year period were excluded from the analyses to avoid anomalies associated with extreme values. The Fruit and Vegetable Variety Index (FAVVA) data were available for n = 9526 during Survey 3 and n = 7648 during both Survey 3 and Survey 7. Women with missing/incomplete dietary data were more likely to find it difficult/impossible to manage on their current income, live in outer regional Australia, be a smoker and be sedentary and were less likely to have a healthy body mass index (BMI) compared with women who had data at both time points. Baseline BMI data were missing for n = 569 women, residential area data for n = 37 women and socioeconomic data for n = 87 women, who were excluded from analyses. A total sample size of n = 8833 was used for the baseline FAVVA with healthcare costs (Part I) and n = 6955 for changes in the FAVVA with healthcare costs (Part II) (Figure 1).

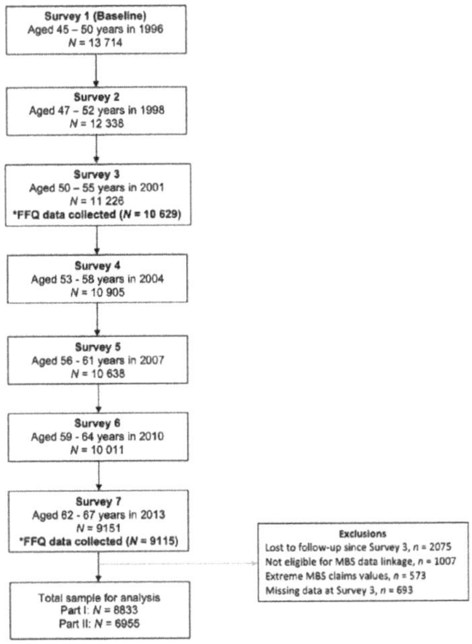

Figure 1. Flow chart of the participant selection using the 1946–1951 ALSWH cohort. Note: *FFQ, food frequency questionnaire; MBS, Medicare Benefits Schedule.

2.3. *Sociodemographic Characteristics and Anthropometry*

The Accessibility Remoteness Index of Australia (ARIA) provided a measure of residential area, categorised as 'major cities', 'inner regional', 'outer regional', 'remote' or 'very remote' [16]. Financial stress was assessed by a self-reported ability to manage on their current income, collected by a single-item question and categorised as 'easy', 'not too bad', 'difficult some of the time', 'difficult all of the time' or 'impossible'. The BMI was calculated using self-reported height and weight data and categorised as underweight (<18.5 kg/m^2), healthy weight (18.5–24.99 kg/m^2) or overweight/obese (≥25 kg/m^2) [17].

2.4. *Assessment of Dietary Intake*

The Cancer Council of Victoria's Dietary Questionnaire for Epidemiological Studies (DQES) Version 2 food frequency questionnaire (FFQ) was used to assess the dietary intake [18,19]. The DQES asks participants to report their usual consumption of 74 foods and beverages over the past 12 months on a 10-point frequency option ('never' up to '3 to 4 times/day'). Portion size photographs were used to calculate a single portion size factor (PSF) to indicate whether, on average, a person eats median-size servings (PSF = 1), more than the median (PSF > 1) or less than the median (PSF < 1) and was used to scale the reported serving sizes for vegetables, meat and casseroles.

The mean total daily F&V intake was derived from responses to individual items for fruits (11 items) and vegetables (24 items) and summed to generate a total intake of fruits, vegetables and F&V (g/day). The nutrient intakes were computed from NUTTAB 1995 by the Cancer Council of Victoria [20]. The development of DQES [21] and validation using plasma biomarkers to estimate polyunsaturated and monounsaturated fats and F&V intakes has been reported [22,23].

2.5. *Fruit and Vegetable Variety Index (FAVVA)*

The FAVVA [24] scores were derived using DQES data [18]. FAVVA captures both the frequency and variety of the F&V intake and has demonstrated moderate-to-strong positive correlations with dietary intakes of key nutrients (vitamin C, vitamin A, fibre, potassium and magnesium) and plasma concentrations of carotenoids rich in fruits and vegetables [24]. As the original FAVVA was developed using the Australian Eating Survey FFQ, the FAVVA was modified slightly in the current study to align with the data collected by the DQES FFQ. Supplemental Table S1 details the scoring method for items in the modified FAVVA used in the current study, while Supplemental Table S2 outlines the differences in the scoring methods for the modified and original FAVVA. For the modified FAVVA used in the current study, points were awarded incrementally based on the frequency of different types of F&V, as assessed by the DQES, such that zero points were awarded for 'Never', 1 point for 'Less than 1 per month', 2 points for '1–3 per month', 3 points for 'once per week', 4 points for '2–4 per week' and 5 points for '5 or more per week'. The F&V typically consumed frequently (e.g., bananas and carrots) had additional response options of 5 points for 5 to 6 times per week, 6 points for 'Once per day' and 7 points for '2 or more times per day'. Additional points were awarded for the total number of different F&V servings consumed per day. The items were summed to calculate the total FAVVA scores, ranging from 0 to 185 points (a maximum of 66 points for the Fruit subscale and 119 points for the Vegetable subscale). Changes in the FAVVA were calculated by subtracting the baseline FAVVA (2001) from Survey 7 FAVVA (2013), where negative scores indicated that the FAVVA score worsened, and positive scores indicated that the FAVVA improved over time.

2.6. Medicare Benefit Schedule Data

Medicare is Australia's universal healthcare coverage provided by the Australian government. Healthcare coverage under Medicare includes services that are eligible for rebate according to the Medicare Benefits Schedule (MBS). The MBS provides benefits for doctor consultations, scheduled fees for out-of-hospital services for doctors (including examinations and tests ordered by doctors), specialist consultations and service fees, many surgical and other therapeutic procedures performed by doctors, some surgical procedures performed by dentists, eye tests performed by optometrists and other allied health consultations, as well as specified items under nominated care schemes (e.g., Cleft Lip and Palate Scheme and Better Access Scheme).

The MBS variables included the number of claims made, the 'charge' (the total cost of the service, as charged by the provider), the 'benefit' (the amount paid by Medicare back to the patient) and the 'gap' (the difference between the charge and the benefit, i.e., the patient's out-of-pocket or direct costs). The MBS data were provided by Medicare in 2016 for the years 2001–2015. The cumulative number of claims, charges, benefits and gap costs were calculated across the 15-year period for each woman. Zero values were assumed for women who had no records of MBS claims during 2001–2015 (n = 445), as data were only provided for women who had made claims. Women with the highest 1% (n = 128, total charges > $79,525) and lowest 1% ($n$ = 445, total charges = $0) of cumulative MBS charges over the 15-year period were excluded from the analyses to avoid anomalies associated with extreme values.

2.7. Statistical Methods

The statistical analyses were conducted using STATA IC, Version 13 (StataCorp LP, College Station, TX, USA). FAVVA quintiles were generated using the xtile function in STATA. Descriptive statistics were calculated for sociodemographic, anthropometric and fruit and vegetable intakes for the included women at Survey 3 by FAVVA quintiles. Differences between the FAVVA quintiles were explored using chi-square analyses (categorical data) and one-way ANOVA (continuous data). The FAVVA scores were normally distributed; however, as the MBS data were highly skewed to the right, nonparametric statistics were used. Multiple linear regression modelling was performed, adjusting for the area of residence, self-reported financial stress and total energy intake at Survey 3. For the 'Underweight' category, regression modelling was not performed on account of the small sample size.

The Part I Baseline F&V frequency and variety with the 15-year Medicare claims/costs: Median 15-year cumulative Medicare claims, charges, benefits and gap costs were reported by the quintiles of FAVVA at Survey 3. The FAVVA quintiles were treated as a categorical predictor of each MBS variable presented by the BMI category, with FAVVA quintile 1 (lowest F&V intake) set as the reference group. In addition, the FAVVA total and Fruit and Vegetable subscales were treated as continuous predictors of the MBS variables. The Part II Change in F&V frequency and variety with the 15-year Medicare claims/costs: For each BMI category, changes in the FAVVA total and subscale scores were treated as continuous predictors of the MBS variables.

3. Results

Among the women with baseline dietary and MBS data ($n = 8833$), 34.6% ($n = 2924$) lived in major cities, and 62.6% ($n = 5290$) found it easy/not too bad to manage on their current income, while over half (56.2%, $n = 4750$) had a high BMI (overweight/obesity). The mean baseline FAVVA was 87.7 ± 21.2 points (maximum 185 points), the fruit intake was 216.5 ± 139.8 g/day (recommended target 300 g/day) and the vegetable intake was 176.5 ± 80.4 g/day (recommended target 375 g/day) [8].

There were no differences in the age, weight or area of residence across the FAVVA quintiles at the baseline (Table 1). The women in FAVVA quintile 1 (lowest) were more likely to find it difficult to manage on their current income and be overweight/obese compared with those in FAVVA quintile 5 ($p < 0.05$).

Table 1. Characteristics of the women in the 1946–1951 ALSWH cohort according to the Fruit and Vegetable Variety (FAVVA) scores for Survey 3 (2001, $n = 8833$).

	FAVVA Quintile					
	Q1	Q2	Q3	Q4	Q5	All
n	1796	1840	1699	1761	1737	8833
FAVVA score [a]	58.1 ± 10.7	77.4 ± 3.7	88.6 ± 2.9	99.1 ± 3.5	117.0 ± 10.5	87.7 ± 21.2
FAVVA range	≤70	71–83	84–93	94–105	≥106	
FAVVA Fruit [b]	15.8 ± 6.5	22.6 ± 6.4	27.0 ± 6.0	31.3 ± 6.0	39.2 ± 7.1	27.1 ± 10.2
FAVVA Vegetable [c]	42.3 ± 9.6	54.8 ± 6.6	61.5 ± 6.2	67.7 ± 6.2	77.9 ± 8.2	60.7 ± 14.1
Age (y)	52.5 ± 1.4	52.5 ± 1.5	52.5 ± 1.5	52.5 ± 1.5	52.5 ± 1.5	52.5 ± 1.5
Area of residence						
Major cities	35.0 (629)	33.8 (621)	36.8 (625)	33.3 (587)	33.8 (587)	34.5 (3049)
Inner regional	41.2 (740)	42.3 (779)	40.4 (687)	41.3 (728)	43.8 (761)	41.8 (3695)
Outer regional	20.7 (371)	20.2 (372)	19.5 (332)	21.8 (384)	18.7 (325)	20.2 (1784)
Remote	2.3 (41)	3.2 (59)	2.8 (48)	3.0 (52)	3.1 (53)	2.9 (253)
Very remote	0.8 (15)	0.5 (9)	0.4 (7)	0.6 (10)	0.6 (11)	0.6 (52)
Self-reported ability to manage on their current income						
Easy	14.4 (259)	19.3 (355)	18.9 (321)	19.2 (338)	21.0 (365)	18.5 (1638)
Not too bad	39.4 (708)	43.0 (791)	46.5 (790)	44.6 (786)	44.6 (775)	43.6 (3850)
Difficult some of the time	30.6 (550)	25.9 (476)	24.5 (416)	27.1 (477)	26.4 (458)	26.9 (2377)
Difficult all of the time	13.3 (239)	10.5 (194)	9.3 (158)	7.4 (131)	7.1 (123)	9.6 (845)
Impossible	2.2 (40)	1.3 (24)	0.8 (14)	1.6 (29)	0.9 (16)	1.4 (139)
Weight (kg)	71.4 ± 16.1	71.6 ± 14.9	71.0 ± 14.5	71.6 ± 14.7	71.0 ± 14.7	71.4 ± 15.0
BMI (kg/m^2)	27.1 ± 5.9	27.0 ± 5.6	26.7 ± 5.3	26.9 ± 5.3	26.6 ± 5.2	26.9 ± 5.5
BMI category						
Underweight	1.9 (35)	1.6 (30)	1.2 (20)	0.9 (16)	1.0 (18)	1.3 (119)
Healthy weight	41.1 (738)	40.9 (753)	43.6 (740)	41.6 (732)	44.9 (780)	42.4 (3743)
Overweight/obese	57.0 (1023)	57.4 (1057)	55.3 (939)	57.5 (1013)	54.1 (939)	56.3 (4971)
Energy intake (kJ/day)	5972.7 ± 2323.3	6487.2 ± 2287.5	6625.3 ± 2237.0	6872.1 ± 2392.7	7457.2 ± 2938.7	6676.6 ± 2494.6
Fruit and vegetable intake (g/day) [d]	268.2 ± 136.4	345.5 ± 147.5	385.7 ± 152.0	443.1 ± 163.5	528.4 ± 185.7	393.0 ± 180.6
Fruit intake (g/day) [d]	124.9 ± 100.4	176.2 ± 119.9	211.8 ± 122.8	255.0 ± 130.3	319.4 ± 138.8	216.5 ± 139.8
Vegetable intake (g/day) [d]	143.3 ± 81.2	169.4 ± 75.2	174.0 ± 74.5	188.1 ± 75.7	209.0 ± 80.4	176.5 ± 80.4

[a] FAVVA maximum score = 185. [b] FAVVA Fruit maximum score = 66. [c] FAVVA Vegetable maximum score = 119. [d] Recommended intakes for Australians: 300 g fruit per day, 375 g vegetables per day and 675 g fruit/vegetables per day, according to the Australian Dietary Guidelines.

3.1. Part I: Baseline F&V Variety with 15-Year Healthcare Claims/Costs

Healthy weight women (BMI = 18.5–24.99 kg/m^2) in the highest FAVVA quintile made six fewer claims over 15 years compared with those in quintile 1 (220 claims (95% CI 144–318) compared with 226 claims (145–358), Table 2). For all women, those in FAVVA quintiles 2–5 incurred higher gap (out-of-pocket) costs compared with those in FAVVA quintile 1.

Table 2. Median 15-year (2001–2015) cumulative Medicare claims and costs ($AU) for Australian women born in 1946–1951 by the quintile of the baseline FAVVA score (1 = lowest and 5 = highest FAVVA quintiles) and baseline BMI category (n = 8833) [a].

		Under Weight [b] n = 119		Healthy Weight n = 3743		Overweight/Obese n = 4971		ALL n = 8833	
BMI, Mean ± SD		17.6 ± 0.9		22.6 ± 1.6		30.4 ± 4.8		26.9 ± 5.5	
2001 FAVVA Quintile	Medicare Variable	Median	Q1, Q3	Median	Q1, Q3	Median	Q1, Q3	Median	Q1, Q3
1 (lowest)	n	37		748		1041		1826	
	FAVVA	62	45, 68	62	53, 70	63	53, 70	62	53, 70
	Claims (n) [c]	228	147, 441	226	145, 358	266	170, 401	250	157, 387
	Charge ($) [d]	12,580	7504, 27,566	13,262	7782, 23,063	15,169	8787, 24,673	14,261	8195, 24,246
	Benefit ($) [e]	11,393	6798, 20,669	10,055	6066, 17,603	12,230	7223, 19,636	11,265	6620, 18,910
	Gap ($) [f]	2190	705, 3988	2583	923, 5458	2168	759, 5631	2345	802, 5540
2	n	32		835		1119		1986	
	FAVVA	79	72, 85	79	73, 86	79	72, 86	79	73, 86
	Claims (n)	192	109, 321	219	147, 315	260	163, 381	240	156, 353
	Charge ($)	10,845	6253, 17,903	13,404	8099, 22,050	15,839	8811, 24,764	14,614	8450, 23,615
	Benefit ($)	8158	4764, 15,694	10,044	6242, 15,647	12,021	7016, 19,020	10,984	6512, 17,497
	Gap ($)	2019	878, 3858	3028 *	1320, 6087	2821	949, 6345	2886 *	1081, 6206
3	n	22		699		919		1640	
	FAVVA	89	85, 96	89	83, 95	89	83, 95	89	83, 95
	Claims (n)	226	128, 283	224 *	156, 320	269	182, 392	246	170, 363
	Charge ($)	15,045	8061, 20,111	13,553	8435, 22,154	16,770	9852, 27,132	15,290	9336, 25,061
	Benefit ($)	11,122	6818, 14,200	10,085	6605, 15,905	12,881	7772, 19,952	11,470	7132, 18,301
	Gap ($)	2850	1620, 6143	3131 *	1268, 5983	3308 *	1399, 7317	3230 *	1330, 6702
4	n	15		703		910		1628	
	FAVVA	100	98, 106	99	92, 106	98	91, 104	98	92, 105
	Claims (n)	431	202, 532	223 *	150, 326	252	167, 379	239	161, 358
	Charge ($)	22,803	15,527, 33,031	13,728	8293, 22,532	15,331	9060, 25,531	14,788	8844, 24,292
	Benefit ($)	18,016	8683, 29,663	10,327	6336, 16,445	11,754	7155, 18,994	10,859	6800, 18,019
	Gap ($)	3729	1548, 6974	3070 *	1440, 6128	3434 *	1351, 6895	3251 *	1387, 6586
5 (highest)	n	13		758		982		1753	
	FAVVA	114	109, 123	112	105, 120	111	104, 121	112	104, 121
	Claims (n)	208	176, 277	220 *	144, 318	260	167, 393	237	154, 357
	Charge ($)	13,988	11,982, 16,097	14,010	8008, 21,279	16,813	9206, 26,808	15,251	8695, 24,394
	Benefit ($)	11,357	8319, 13,101	9878	6091, 15,673	12,262	7058, 20,286	11,250	6618, 18,151
	Gap ($)	2666	686, 4740	3552	1375, 6399	3250 *	1249, 7242	3448 *	1321, 6761

Abbreviations: BMI, body mass index; FAVVA, Fruit and Vegetable Variety index; SD, standard deviation; * $p < 0.05$: linear regression modelling by BMI category with adjustment for area of residence, ability to manage on current income and total energy intake, with FAVVA Quintile 1 set as reference group. [a] Data presented are unadjusted medians and IQRs. [b] Women with 'Underweight' BMI were excluded from the analysis due to the small sample size. [c] Number of healthcare services received under the Medicare Benefits Schedule. [d] Total cost of services (as charged by the healthcare provider). [e] Amount paid back to the patient by Medicare. [f] Out-of-pocket costs paid by the patient.

Among healthy weight women, higher FAVVA and FAVVA Vegetable scores were associated with fewer claims and benefits (Table 3). For every 10-point-higher FAVVA, healthy weight women made, on average, 4.3 (95% confidence interval (CI) 1.7–6.8) fewer claims over 15 years. For every 10-point-higher FAVVA Vegetable score, healthy weight women made 7.1 (95% CI 3.3–10.9) fewer claims and incurred $AUD 293.0 (95% CI $8.6–57.4) less in charges. Among the women overweight/obese, a higher FAVVA was associated with higher charges and out-of-pocket (gap) costs, while a higher FAVVA Fruit score was associated with higher claims and all costs. For every 10-point-higher FAVVA, women overweight/obese incurred $187.8 (95% CI S2.4–373.2) more in charges over 15 years. For all women, higher FAVVA, Vegetable and Fruit subscales were associated with higher out-of-pocket costs.

Table 3. Coefficients and 95% confidence intervals per 10-unit-higher baseline FAVVA as predictors of the 15-year (2001–2015) cumulative Medicare claims and costs for Australian women born in 1946–1951 (n = 8833) and within the baseline BMI category [a].

2001 Fruit and Vegetable Intake	Medicare Variable	Healthy Weight n = 3743	Overweight/Obese n = 4971	All n = 8833
FAVVA Total	Claims (n) [b]	−4.3 (−6.8, −1.7) *	0.3 (−2.3, 2.9)	−1.6 (−3.4, 0.2)
	Charge ($AUD) [c]	−132.6 (−321.6, 56.5)	187.8 (2.4, 373.2) *	47.1 (−85.7, 179.9)
	Benefit ($AUD) [d]	−188.0 (−325.8, −50.1) *	66.9 (−69.2, 203.0)	−45.0 (−142.6, 52.5)
	Gap ($AUD) [e]	55.4 (−10.4, 121.2)	120.9 (56.3, 185.5) *	92.2 (46.2, 138.1) *
FAVVA Fruit	Claims (n)	−4.9 (−10.2, 0.3)	5.6 (0.2, 10.9) *	1.4 (−2.5, 5.2)
	Charge ($AUD)	−13.9 (−409.9, 382.1)	567.4 (184.0, 950.7) *	324.8 (48.2, 601.4) *
	Benefit ($AUD)	−182.7 (−471.6, 106.2)	336.7 (55.2, 618.1) *	119.5 (−83.8, 322.8)
	Gap ($AUD)	168.8 (31.1, 306.5) *	230.7 (97.0, 364.4) *	205.3 (109.6, 301.0) *
FAVVA Vegetable	Claims (n)	−7.1 (−10.9, −3.3) *	−2.2 (−6.1, 1.7)	−4.4 (−7.1, −1.6) *
	Charge ($AUD)	−293.0 (−577.4, −8.6) *	122.3 (−153.6, 398.1)	−61.9 (−260.4, 136.5)
	Benefit ($AUD)	−331.4 (−538.7, −124.0) *	−26.0 (−228.4, 176.5)	−162.0 (−307.8, −16.3) *
	Gap ($AUD)	38.3 (−60.7, 137.3)	148.3 (52.1, 244.4) *	100.1 (31.4, 168.8) *

Abbreviations: BMI, body mass index; FAVVA, Fruit and Vegetable Variety index. * $p < 0.05$; linear regression modelling with adjustment for the area of residence, ability to manage on their current income and total energy intake. [a] Women with 'Underweight' BMI were excluded from the analysis due to the small sample size (n = 113). [b] The number of healthcare services received under the Medicare Benefits Schedule. [c] Total cost of the services (as charged by the healthcare provider). [d] Amount paid back to the patient by Medicare. [e] Out-of-pocket costs paid by the patient.

A higher total fruit and vegetable intake (g/day) and total fruit intake were each associated with higher claims, charges and benefits for women overweight/obese only. For every 100-g-higher intake of fruit consumed per day, women overweight/obese made, on average, 3.7 (95% CI 0.9–6.4) more claims and incurred $253.6 (95% CI $52.9–454.4) more in charges (Supplemental Table S3).

3.2. *Part II: Change in F&V Variety over Time with 15-Year Healthcare Claims/Costs*

Across the sample, the mean changes in the FAVVA, FAVVA Vegetable and FAVVA Fruit scores (2001–2013) were 0.94 ± 17.1 points, 1.0 ± 11.9 points and −0.1 ± 9.0 points, respectively (n = 6955). The mean change in the total FAVVA was 1.7 ± 17.5 points for women with underweight BMI (n = 96), 1.4 ± 17.2 points for women with healthy BMI (n = 3007) and 0.6 ± 17.1 points for women overweight/obese (n = 3854).

The changes in the total FAVVA, FAVVA Vegetable and FAVVA Fruit scores were inversely associated with the cumulative total claims and charges over 15 years (Table 4). For every 10-point increase in the FAVVA over time, on average, women made 4.3 (95% CI 1.9–6.8) fewer claims and incurred $309.1 (95% CI $129.3–488.8) less in charges.

The change in the total daily grams of F&V consumed was also inversely associated with the cumulative total charges incurred over 15 years. For every 100-g-increase in the daily F&V intake over time, on average, women made 6.5 (95% CI 3.6–9.4) fewer claims and incurred $480.0 (95% CI $265.2–694.7) less in charges (Supplemental Table S4).

Table 4. Coefficients and 95% confidence intervals (CI) per 10-unit changes in the FAVVA (2001–2013) as a predictor of the 15-year (2001–2015) cumulative Medicare claims and costs for Australian women born in 1946–1951 (n = 6955) and within the baseline BMI category.

Change in Intake 2001–2013	Medicare Variable	Healthy Weight n = 3007	Overweight/Obese n = 3857	All n = 6955
FAVVA Total	Claims (n)	−2.1 (−5.3, 1.2)	−4.9 (−8.3, −1.5) *	−4.3 (−6.8, −1.9) *
	Charge ($AUD)	−152.9 (−402.8, 97.1)	−368.1 (−623.0, −113.1) *	−309.1 (−488.8, −129.3) *
	Benefit ($AUD)	−141.3 (−322.6, 40.0)	−280.6 (−466.0, −95.3) *	−252.0 (−383.0, −121.0) *
	Gap ($AUD)	−11.6 (−99.5, 76.4)	−87.4 (−177.5, 2.6)	−57.0 (−120.0, 5.9)
FAVVA Fruit	Claims (n)	−1.9 (−8.2, 4.4)	−4.9 (−11.4, 1.6)	−4.7 (−9.3, −0.03) *
	Charge ($AUD)	−175.5 (−657.4, 306.4)	−452.8 (−933.6, 28.0)	−392.6 (−735.4, −49.7) *
	Benefit ($AUD)	−159.3 (−508.8, 190.3)	−315.3 (−664.9, 34.2)	−297.6 (−547.6, −47.7) *
	Gap ($AUD)	−16.2 (−185.8, 153.3)	−137.5 (−307.2, 32.2)	−94.9 (−215.0, 25.1)
FAVVA Vegetables	Claims (n)	−3.3 (−8.1, 1.5)	−7.3 (−12.1, −2.3) *	−6.4 (−9.9, −2.9) *
	Charge ($AUD)	−227.0 (−593.4, 139.3)	−494.9 (−860.6, −129.3) *	−421.1 (−681.3, −161.0) *
	Benefit ($AUD)	−211.6 (−477.3, 54.1)	−394.7 (−660.5, −128.8) *	−356.4 (−546.0, −166.8) *
	Gap ($AUD)	−15.5 (−144.4, 113.4)	−100.3 (−229.4, 28.9)	−64.8 (−156.0, 26.4)

Abbreviations: BMI, body mass index; FAVVA, Fruit and Vegetable Variety index. * $p < 0.05$; linear regression modelling with adjustment for the area of residence, ability to manage on their current income, total energy intake and baseline FAVVA. Note: Women with 'Underweight' BMI were excluded from the analysis due to the small sample size.

4. Discussion

In this analysis, from the 1946–1951 cohort of the Australian Longitudinal Study on Women's Health, we found that a higher baseline F&V frequency and variety was associated with fewer cumulative 15-year healthcare claims among healthy weight women but not women overweight/obese. A higher baseline vegetable intake was associated with fewer healthcare claims for healthy weight women and increasing the F&V intake over time was associated with fewer healthcare claims and charges among all the women. These findings were largely in keeping with our expectations, given the known benefits of F&V consumption [6,7,25]. However, the positive association between fruit intake and healthcare claims and costs among women overweight or obese was unexpected and requires further investigation.

Our results indicate that increasing the variety and frequency of F&V regularly consumed over time, regardless of the baseline intake or weight status, is associated with lower healthcare costs. Improving the diet quality over time conveys a reduced risk of cardiovascular disease and all-cause mortality [26–28]. Despite the national dietary guidelines advocating regular F&V consumption, the current intakes remain low [3]. The Australian Dietary Guidelines recommend consuming 300 g of fruit (two servings at 150 g/serving) and 375 g of vegetables (five servings at 75 g per serving) per day [8]. The national data from 2017 to 2018 showed that fewer than one in ten Australian adults met the vegetable consumption target [29]. Given our findings, one potential strategy to address long-term healthcare costs could be the development of population health interventions that focus on increasing F&V consumption by consuming one new variety of fruit or vegetable per week. A cost-effectiveness modelling study showed that a subsidy on F&V, when combined with taxes on saturated fat, sugar, salt and sugar-sweetened beverages, could save the Australian health sector $AU 3.4 billion annually [30]. The economic modelling in Canada demonstrates that increasing the F&V consumption by one serving per day would avoid approximately $CAN 9 billion in total costs [5]. In the US, a 30% subsidy on F&V would prevent approximately 1.9 million deaths and save $US 40 billion in healthcare costs [31]. However, while public health interventions are important, multisectoral action across nutrition, agriculture and technology to increase the global supply of F&V and reduce food waste is also needed [32].

The association between lower healthcare costs and a higher vegetable variety observed among healthy weight women is consistent with the literature. We showed that a higher vegetable intake was associated with fewer healthcare services and costs over

10 years in both women of a healthy weight and women overweight [7]. The previous study assessed the vegetable intake using the vegetable subscale of the Australian Recommended Food Score (ARFS), which allocates one point for each additional type of vegetable usually consumed at least weekly. While the ARFS vegetable subscale does take into account variety, it considers frequency based only on weekly consumption and not more frequently. By comparison, the FAVVA considers the variety in addition to frequency across the full spectrum of intake, as responses from 'never' up to '3 to 4 times/day' are used to calculate the score. Thus, a higher FAVVA score indicates both a greater frequency and variety and, hence, a greater volume (grams per day).

A higher F&V intake has been associated with a lower risk of all causes and cardiovascular mortality [1,33]. A large, 11-year cohort study (n = 3704) nested in the European Prospective Investigation into Cancer and Nutrition-Norfolk study found that a greater quantity of vegetables consumed was associated with a 24% reduction in the risk of developing type 2 diabetes, while a greater variety of vegetables consumed was associated with a 23% risk reduction [11]. We have previously found that higher fruit and vegetable consumptions (measured using the Fruit and Vegetable Index (FAVI)) were associated with less weight gain among young women [34]. Our study adds to this body of knowledge by demonstrating the importance of both the frequency and variety of vegetable intakes in terms of their association with future healthcare costs.

Our findings regarding the association between fruit consumption and healthcare costs are slightly at odds. While women reporting higher fruit intakes incurred fewer healthcare charges, when the data were analysed by the BMI category, this association was reversed for women overweight/obese. For those women overweight, a higher variety and frequency of fruit consumed, consistent with a higher score, could reflect either an excess overall intake or potentially be due to over-reporting of their intake or could be associated with other characteristics, such as lower physical activity levels. One cohort study reported lower healthcare charges for men with the highest fruit intake [6], although this study was not nationally representative and examined the quantity of the fruits consumed, not variety [6]. A systematic review found no association between whole, fresh fruit consumption and excess energy intake or adiposity [35]. There are likely further confounding factors, such as food insecurity which has a complex relationship with being bodyweight and healthcare expenditures in older adults [36], as well as other sociodemographic and lifestyle factors influencing the changes in diet quality over time [37].

Not all healthcare services appear in the national MBS data. The MBS scheme in Australia includes medical information relating to claims for healthcare services that are eligible for rebate under the Medicare funding scheme. Public hospital and outpatient services are not captured, as these services are funded entirely by Medicare (and are therefore not applicable for rebate). Women who do not have private health insurance are more likely to use public hospital and public outpatient services; hence, information relating to their usage of public services will not appear in the MBS data, as these public services are funded entirely by Medicare and do not appear in the MBS. Hence, our results could be affected by residual confounding due to factors and/or variables not captured, including private health insurance status and health outcomes. Our analyses only included women who had both dietary and Medicare data, possibly influencing the findings, as these women had higher health statuses and lower financial stress. We recognise that the use of self-reported methods to collect dietary data potentially overestimates the F&V intake [38]. Dietary data were only collected at the two time points in 2001 and 2013; thus, it was not possible to ascertain at what point in time between 2001 and 2013 any changes in F&V consumption may have occurred, although the dietary patterns in this cohort remained relatively stable over time [39]. Although the data were from a large cohort of mid-aged Australian women, the results may not be generalisable among the broader population. The cohort study design precluded drawing inferences regarding cause and effect. There was also likely a residual confounding due to the variables that may not have been accounted for (e.g., health status, physical activity level and smoking and alcohol intake); the current analysis adds to the current literature regarding the association between F&V intake and long-term healthcare costs.

5. Conclusions

A higher F&V frequency and variety is associated with a small reduction in healthcare claims for healthy weight women, although a higher fruit intake among women overweight/obese is associated with higher costs. Increasing their F&V frequency and variety over time is associated with lower healthcare costs.

Supplementary Materials: The following are available online at https://www.mdpi.com/article/10.3390/nu13082829/s1: Table S1: Modified FAVVA index. Table S2: Differences in the methods used to calculate the FAVVA index derived from the AES FFQ and the DQESv2 FFQ. Table S3: Coefficients and 95% confidence intervals for the baseline fruit and vegetable intakes (g/day) as a predictor of the 15-year (2001–2015) cumulative Medicare claims and costs for Australian women born in 1946–1951 by the baseline BMI category (n = 8833). Table S4: Coefficients and 95% confidence intervals (CI) for the changes in the daily fruit and vegetable intakes (2001–2013) as a predictor of the 15-year (2001–2015) cumulative Medicare claims and costs for Australian women born in 1946–1951 by the BMI category (n = 6955).

Author Contributions: Conceptualization, J.N.B., L.M.A. and C.E.C.; methodology, J.N.B., L.M.A. and P.M.F.; formal analysis, J.N.B. and P.M.F.; data curation, D.J.L. and P.M.F.; writing—original draft preparation, J.N.B., L.M.A. and C.E.C.; writing—review and editing, J.N.B., L.M.A., P.M.F., R.L.H., A.J.H., D.J.L., A.J.P. and C.E.C. and funding acquisition, C.E.C. All authors have read and agreed to the published version of the manuscript.

Funding: This research was supported by a National Health and Medical Research Council of Australia Senior Research Fellowship and a Gladys M Brawn Senior Research Fellowship from the Faculty of Health and Medicine, the University of Newcastle, Australia (C.E.C.).

Institutional Review Board Statement: This study was conducted according to the guidelines of the Declaration of Helsinki and approved by the University of Newcastle (h-076-0795) and the University of Queensland (200400224). Medicare data consent was provided for the overall ALSWH study, and use of the linked Medicare Benefits Schedule data was granted by the ALSWH Data Access Committee.

Informed Consent Statement: Informed consent was obtained from all subjects involved in the study. Medicare data consent was provided for the overall ALSWH study, and use of the linked Medicare Benefits Schedule data was granted by the ALSWH Data Access Committee.

Data Availability Statement: Restrictions apply to the availability of these data.

Acknowledgments: The research on which this paper is based was conducted as part of the Australian Longitudinal Study on Women's Health by the University of Queensland and the University of Newcastle. The authors are grateful to the Australian Department of Health for funding the ALSWH and to the women who provided the survey data. The authors acknowledge the Department of Health and Medicare Australia for providing Medicare Benefits Schedule data and the Australian Institute of Health and Welfare (AIHW) as the integrating authority. The authors thank Graham Giles of the Cancer Epidemiology Centre of Cancer Council Victoria for permission to use the Dietary Questionnaire for Epidemiological Studies (Version 2), Melbourne: Cancer Council Victoria, 1996.

Conflicts of Interest: The authors declare no conflict of interest. The funders had no role in the design of the study; in the collection, analyses or interpretation of the data; in the writing of the manuscript or in the decision to publish the results.

References

1. Aune, D.; Giovanucci, E.; Boffetta, P.; Fadnes, L.T.; Keum, N.; Norat, T.; Greenwood, D.; Riboli, E.; Vatten, L.J.; Tonstad, S. Fruit and vegetable intake and the risk of cardiovascular disease, total cancer and all-cause mortality: A systematic review and dose-response meta-analysis of prospective studies. *Int. J. Epidemiol.* **2017**, *46*, 1029–1056. [CrossRef]
2. World Health Organization. *Joint WHO/FAO Expert Consultation on Diet, Nutrition and the Prevention of Chronic Diseases*; World Health Organization: Geneva, Switzerland, 2002.

3. Hall, J.N.; Moore, S.; Harper, S.B.; Lynch, J.W. Global variability in fruit and vegetable consumption. *Am. J. Prev. Med.* **2009**, *36*, 402–409.e5. [CrossRef]
4. Afshin, A.; Sur, P.J.; Fay, K.A.; Cornaby, L.; Ferrara, G.; Salama, J.S.; Mullany, E.C.; Abate, K.H.; Abbafati, C.; Abebe, Z.; et al. Health effects of dietary risks in 195 countries, 1990–2017: A systematic analysis for the Global Burden of Disease Study 2017. *Lancet* **2019**, *393*, 1958–1972. [CrossRef]
5. Ekwaru, J.P.; Ohinmaa, A.; Loehr, S.; Setayeshgar, S.; Thanh, N.X.; Veugelers, P.J. The economic burden of inadequate consumption of vegetables and fruit in Canada. *Public Health Nutr.* **2017**, *20*, 515–523. [CrossRef]
6. Daviglus, M.L.; Liu, K.; Pirzada, A.; Yan, L.L.; Garside, D.B.; Wang, R.; Van Horn, L.; Manning, W.G.; Manheim, L.M.; Dyer, A.R. Relationship of fruit and vegetable consumption in middle-aged men to medicare expenditures in older age: The Chicago Western Electric Study. *J. Am. Diet Assoc.* **2005**, *105*, 1735–1744. [CrossRef] [PubMed]
7. Patterson, A.; Hure, A.; Burrows, T.; Jackson, J.; Collins, C. Diet quality and 10-year healthcare costs by BMI categories in the mid-age cohort of the Australian Longitudinal Study on Women's Health. *J. Hum. Nutr. Diet* **2018**, *31*, 463–472. [CrossRef] [PubMed]
8. National Health and Medical Research Council. *Australian Dietary Guidelines*; National Health and Medical Research Council: Canberra, Australia, 2013.
9. Public Health England. *Government Dietary Recommendations: Government. Recommendations for Energy and Nutrients for Males and Females Aged 1–18 Years and 19+ Years*; Department of Health: London, UK, 2016. Available online: https://assets.publishing.service.gov.uk/government/uploads/system/uploads/attachment_data/file/618167/government_dietary_recommendations.pdf (accessed on 17 September 2019).
10. US Department of Health and Human Services; US Department of Agriculture. *2015–2020 Dietary Guidelines for Americans*, 8th ed.; USDA: Washington, DC, USA, 2015. Available online: http://health.gov/dietaryguidelines/2015/guidelines/ (accessed on 17 September 2019).
11. Cooper, A.J.; Sharp, S.J.; Lentjes, M.A.; Luben, R.N.; Khaw, K.-T.; Wareham, N.J.; Forouhi, N.G. A prospective study of the association between quantity and variety of fruit and vegetable intake and incident type 2 diabetes. *Diabetes Care* **2012**, *35*, 1293–1300. [CrossRef]
12. Brown, W.J.; Bryson, L.; Byles, J.E.; Dobson, A.J.; Lee, C.; Mishra, G.; Schofield, M. Women's Health Australia: Recruitment for a national longitudinal cohort study. *Women Health* **1999**, *28*, 23–40. [CrossRef] [PubMed]
13. Brown, W.J.; Young, A.F.; Byles, J.E. Tyranny of distance? The health of mid–age women living in five geographical areas of Australia. *Aust. J. Rural Health* **1999**, *7*, 148–154. [CrossRef]
14. Lee, C.; Dobson, A.J.; Brown, W.J.; Bryson, L.; Byles, J.; Warner-Smith, P.; Young, A.F. Cohort profile: The Australian Longitudinal Study on Women's Health. *Int. J. Epidemiol.* **2005**, *34*, 987–991. [CrossRef]
15. Women's Health Australia. Australian Longitudinal Study on Women's Health: Sample. 2019. Available online: https://www.alswh.org.au/about/sample (accessed on 17 September 2019).
16. Department of Health and Aged Care (GISCA). *Measuring Remoteness: Accessibility/Remoteness Index of Australia (ARIA)*; Commonwealth of Australia: Canberra, Australia, 2001.
17. World Health Organization. *Obesity: Preventing and Managing the Global Epidemic*; World Health Organization: Geneva, Switzerland, 2000.
18. Giles, G.; Ireland, P. *Dietary Questionnaire for Epidemiological Studies (Version 2)*; The Cancer Council Victoria: Melbourne, Australia, 1996.
19. Hodge, A.; Patterson, A.J.; Brown, W.J.; Ireland, P.; Giles, G. The Anti Cancer Council of Victoria FFQ: Relative validity of nutrient intakes compared with weighed food records in young to middle-aged women in a study of iron supplementation. *Aust. N. Z. J. Public Health* **2000**, *24*, 576–583. [CrossRef] [PubMed]
20. Lewis, J.; Milligan, G.C.; Hunt, A. *NUTTAB96: Nutrient Data Table for Use in Australia*; Australian Government Publishing Service: Canberra, Australia, 1995.
21. Ireland, P.; Jolley, D.; Giles, G.; O'Dea, K.; Powles, J.; Rutishauser, I.; Wahlqvist, M.L.; Williams, J. Development of the Melbourne FFQ: A food frequency questionnaire for use in an Australian prospective study involving an ethnically diverse cohort. *Asia Pac. J. Clin. Nutr.* **1994**, *3*, 19–31. [PubMed]
22. Hodge, A.M.; Simpson, J.A.; Fridman, M.; Rowley, K.; English, D.R.; Giles, G.G.; Su, Q.; O'Dea, K. Evaluation of an FFQ for assessment of antioxidant intake using plasma biomarkers in an ethnically diverse population. *Public Health Nutr.* **2009**, *12*, 2438–2447. [CrossRef] [PubMed]
23. Hodge, A.M.; Simpson, J.A.; Gibson, R.A.; Sinclair, A.J.; Makrides, M.; O'Dea, K.; English, D.R.; Giles, G.G. Plasma phospholipid fatty acid composition as a biomarker of habitual dietary fat intake in an ethnically diverse cohort. *Nutr. Metab. Cardiovasc Dis.* **2007**, *17*, 415–426. [CrossRef]
24. Ashton, L.; Williams, R.; Wood, L.; Schumacher, T.; Burrows, T.; Rollo, M.; Pezdirc, K.; Callister, R.; Collins, C.E. The comparative validity of a brief diet screening tool for adults: The Fruit and Vegetable VAriety index (FAVVA). *Clin. Nutr. ESPEN* **2019**, *29*, 189–197. [CrossRef]
25. Del Pozo Rubio, R.; Moya-Martinez, P.; Escribano-Sotos, F.; Amo Saus, M.E. Costs of health services associated with fruit and vegetable consumption habits. *Nutr. Hosp.* **2018**, *35*, 920–927. [CrossRef]

26. Sotos-Prieto, M.; Bhupathiraju, S.N.; Mattei, J.; Fung, T.T.; Li, Y.; Pan, A.; Willett, W.C.; Rimm, E.B.; Hu, F.B. Changes in diet quality scores and risk of cardiovascular disease among US men and women. *Circulation* **2015**, *132*, 2212–2219. [CrossRef]
27. Baden, M.Y.; Liu, G.; Satija, A.; Li, Y.; Sun, Q.; Fung, T.T.; Rimm, E.B.; Willett, W.C.; Hu, F.B.; Bhupathiraju, S.N. Changes in plant-based diet quality and total and cause-specific mortality. *Circulation* **2019**, *140*, 979–991. [CrossRef]
28. Sotos-Prieto, M.; Bhupathiraju, S.N.; Mattei, J.; Fung, T.T.; Li, Y.; Pan, A.; Willett, W.C.; Rimm, E.B.; Hu, F.B. Association of changes in diet quality with total and cause-specific mortality. *N. Engl. J. Med.* **2017**, *377*, 143–153. [CrossRef]
29. Australian Bureau of Statistics. *National Health Survey: First Results*; Australian Government: Canberra, Australia, 2017. Available online: https://www.abs.gov.au/statistics/health/health-conditions-and-risks/national-health-survey-first-results/latest-release (accessed on 17 September 2019).
30. Cobiac, L.J.; Tam, K.; Veerman, L.; Blakely, T. Taxes and Subsidies for Improving Diet and Population Health in Australia: A Cost-Effectiveness Modelling Study. *PLoS Med.* **2017**, *14*, e1002232. [CrossRef]
31. Lee, Y.; Mozaffarian, D.; Sy, S.; Huang, Y.; Liu, J.; Wilde, P.E.; Abrahams-Gessel, S.; Jardim, T.d.S.V.; Gaziano, T.A.; Micha, R. Cost-effectiveness of financial incentives for improving diet and health through Medicare and Medicaid: A microsimulation study. *PLoS Med.* **2019**, *16*, e1002761. [CrossRef]
32. Siegel, K.R. Insufficient consumption of fruits and vegetables among individuals 15 years and older in 28 low- and middle-income countries: What can be done? *J. Nutr.* **2019**, *149*, 1105–1106. [CrossRef] [PubMed]
33. Wang, X.; Ouyang, Y.; Liu, J.; Zhu, M.; Zhao, G.; Bao, W.; Hu, F.B. Fruit and vegetable consumption and mortality from all causes, cardiovascular disease, and cancer: Systematic review and dose-response meta-analysis of prospective cohort studies. *BMJ* **2014**, *349*, g4490. [CrossRef]
34. Aljadani, H.M.; Patterson, A.; Sibbritt, D.; Hutchesson, M.J.; Jensen, M.E.; Collins, C.E. Diet quality, measured by fruit and vegetable intake, predicts weight change in young women. *J. Obes.* **2013**, *2013*, 525161. [CrossRef]
35. Guyenet, S.J. Impact of whole, fresh fruit consumption on energy intake and adiposity: A systematic review. *Front. Nutr.* **2019**, *6*, 66–84. [CrossRef] [PubMed]
36. Bhargava, V.; Lee, J.S.; Jain, R.; Johnson, M.A.; Brown, A. Food insecurity is negatively associated with home health and out-of-pocket expenditures in older adults. *J. Nutr.* **2012**, *142*, 1888–1895. [CrossRef]
37. Park, S.-Y.; Shvetsov, Y.B.; Kang, M.; Setiawan, V.W.; Wilkens, L.R.; Le Marchand, L.; Boushey, C.J. Changes in diet quality over 10 years are associated with baseline sociodemographic and lifestyle factors in the multiethnic cohort study. *J. Nutr* **2020**, *150*, 1880–1888. [CrossRef]
38. Subar, A.F.; Freedman, L.S.; Tooze, J.A.; Kirkpatrick, S.I.; Boushey, C.; Neuhouser, M.L.; Thompson, F.E.; Potischman, N.; Guenther, P.M.; Tarasuk, V.; et al. Addressing current criticism regarding the value of self-seport dietary data. *J. Nutr.* **2015**, *145*, 2639–2645. [CrossRef] [PubMed]
39. Baldwin, J.N.; Forder, P.M.; Haslam, R.L.; Hure, A.J.; Loxton, D.J.; Patterson, A.J.; Collins, C.E. Change in diet quality over 12 years in the 1946–1951 cohort of the Australian Longitudinal Study on Women's Health. *Nutrients* **2020**, *12*, 147. [CrossRef] [PubMed]

nutrients

MDPI

Article

The Adherence of Singaporean Students in Different Educational Institutions to National Food-Based Dietary Guidelines

Mia Eng Tay [1,2], Emma Foster [3], Leo Stevenson [1,4] and Iain Brownlee [1,5,*]

1 Newcastle Research and Innovation Institute, Devan Nair Building, Singapore 600201, Singapore; tay_mia_eng@nyp.edu.sg (M.E.T.); stevenl2@hope.ac.uk (L.S.)
2 School of Chemical & Life Sciences, Nanyang Polytechnic, Singapore 569830, Singapore
3 Human Nutrition Research Centre, Population Health Sciences Institute, Newcastle University, Newcastle upon Tyne NE2 4HH, UK; dremmafoster@outlook.com
4 School of Health Sciences, Liverpool Hope University, Hope Park, Liverpool L16 9JD, UK
5 Faculty of Health and Life Sciences, Northumbria University, Newcastle-upon-Tyne NE1 8ST, UK
* Correspondence: iain.brownlee@northumbria.ac.uk; Tel.: +44-(0)191-227-4187

Received: 24 August 2020; Accepted: 27 September 2020; Published: 30 September 2020

Abstract: There are currently limited data on the dietary habits of young Singaporeans. This study aimed to evaluate the adherence of 17–21 year olds attending different educational institutions using a novel diet-quality scoring method. Dietary data were collected using a single weekday 24 h dietary recall in a cross section of 536 Singaporeans aged 17–21 years. An 11 category scoring system (0.0–100.0) was used to define adherence to food based dietary guidelines. Demographic and self-reported data were also collected via a questionnaire, BMI status, and using Mann-Whitney and Kruskal-Wallis (non-parametric) tests, with post-hoc Bonferroni-corrected tests. The median diet quality score was 48.5 (IQR 40.5, 56.4) for this cohort, with component scores for "Total fruit", "Whole fruit", "Total vegetables", "Dark green leafy & orange vegetables", "Whole grains", "Dairy products", and "Sodium" frequently scoring the minimum value. Median diet quality scores were statistically different for groups by ethnic origin ($p < 0.001$) and by educational institution ($p < 0.001$). Intake of fruit, vegetables, and whole grains is minimal, while sodium intake is frequently too high in young Singaporeans. Differences across ethnic groups and types of educational institutions suggest the need for targeted interventions to improve dietary habits in this population.

Keywords: food-based dietary guidelines; diet quality; salt intake; fruit and vegetable consumption

1. Introduction

Adolescence is the transitional stage that lies between childhood and adulthood and has previously been defined as the time between 10–19 years old [1]. The transition from adolescence to adulthood is a period of the life course where there is a rapid change in nutritional requirements [2]; social, physical, and environmental influences [3,4]; and often increased independence in decision-making, including decisions that relate to dietary habits and lifestyle [5,6]. This period of transition has been suggested to be important in developing dietary habits that may track into later life [7], thereby affecting lifelong disease trajectory [8–10]. Previous reports suggest that dietary habits in adolescent populations are frequently sub-optimal with a high intake of saturated and total fat, but a low intake of fruit, vegetables, fibre, and calcium-rich foods [11–13].

Singapore is an island nation that has rapidly developed a world-class reputation in education [14]. The majority of Singaporeans are from three major ethnic groups (Chinese, Malay, and Indian) which form the core of multicultural culinary offerings in Singapore [15]. Existing data from adult cross-sectional studies suggest that ethnicity is linked to divergent dietary habits [16] and health outcomes [17,18]. Nationally-representative dietary data have been collected in Singaporean adults (aged 18 to 69 years) within the National Nutrition Study (NNS) since 1993 [19] using food frequency questionnaire methods. However, dietary habits specific to students have only been collected previously as part of the Students' Health Survey, using a short-form dietary questionnaire [20]. As such, information on current dietary habits in Singaporean adolescents is limited, particularly in relation to the educational institution that they are attending.

Within the Singaporean education system, almost all adolescents (at the age of approximately 17 years) enter post-secondary education into one of three types of institutes: an Institute of Technical Education (ITE—23.7% of all individuals after secondary school completion), a polytechnic (47.8%), or a junior college (28%) [21]. Each type of educational institution has specific core pedagogic missions. It is also important to note that only junior colleges are monitored by the Ministry of Health for the standards of food made available on-campus [22,23].

Approaches to estimate the adherence of individuals to notional ideals of dietary habits have been utilized more frequently in nutrition research since the 1990s, with earlier iterations in existence since the 1940s [24,25]. Such methodologies frequently compare estimates of dietary intake against food or nutrient based dietary guidelines [26,27], providing a single numeric indicator from complex dietary data [28,29]. Such approaches have been used to provide feedback to individuals on overall dietary habits [30,31] and could help focus future public health efforts for specific populations [32]. Such approaches may also be less prone to confounding factors than an evaluation of intake of single or multiple nutrients and food groups [33]. While approaches to estimate overall dietary quality have been published for Singaporean infants and children [34,35], the authors believe that no such method has currently been defined for late adolescents and young adults.

This study therefore aimed to fill current gaps in knowledge by assessing dietary habits (on school days) in a cross-section of Singaporean late adolescents/early adults attending the three main types of post-secondary educational institution. In order to do this, a novel diet quality scoring approach was developed to assess the adherence of individuals in this cohort to Singaporean food-based dietary guidelines, as estimated through a single weekday 24 h dietary recall.

2. Materials and Methods

The study method was approved by the Ethics Committee (Faculty of Science, Agriculture, and Engineering), Newcastle University on the 24 October 2014 and Institutional Review Board and Nanyang Polytechnic (NYP IRB Ref: SCL-2014-001) on the 18 September 2014. As the participants included students from a junior college, additional approval from the Ministry of Education, Singapore was obtained on the 23 February 2015. Email approval was obtained from the principal of ITE College Central on 19 March 2015.

The eligible target population was Singaporean nationals, aged 17–21 years (the standard age range in which individuals attend post-secondary education). Participants of Chinese, Malay, and Indian ethnic origin were subsequently recruited via school portals and posters. Posters were displayed on students' notice boards for the attention of students and to encourage word of mouth recruitment through friends. On-site recruitment was also performed where responses from school portal or posters was low. Interested participants contacted the research lead (M.E.T.) and received additional information on the project prior to collection of informed consent. For participants aged 17 years, parental consent was also obtained. Following this, a separate participant data form was developed to collect details of their name, contact details, address, ethnicity, sex, date of birth, education institute, self-reported weight, and height. Two separate recruitment drives were undertaken. The first recruited students were from the polytechnic site only, using a purposeful sampling approach to ensure inclusion of adequate numbers of individuals by ethnic origin and sex. This approach ensured an adequate representation of participants of Malay and Indian ethnic origin and increased the number of male participants. The second recruited an additional 100 individuals from the Institute of Technical Education and the Junior College by convenience sampling (i.e., all individuals who agreed to take part were recruited) to allow comparisons between institutions. Data were from a total of 536 participants (collected/recruited between November 2014 and August 2015). The most conservative estimate of a representative sample from a population of approximately 100,000 individuals [21] with 95% chance of estimating the true population mean and desired accuracy within 5% would require a total of 383 participants [36]. Additional individuals were recruited to help ensure additional statistical power for sub-analyses within the time constraints of the proposed study.

The 24 h recall form was adapted for use from The UK Low Income Diet and Nutrition Survey [37]. A multiple-pass approach was taken to collecting dietary data from participants. This approach was adapted from the USDA 5-step multiple-pass method [38,39] to help improve the accuracy of the dietary recall [40]. Data were collected by a trained researcher at the student's particular educational institute. Model plates, bowls, and cutlery alongside a compendium of local food pictures [41] were developed to improve the quality of the portion size estimation by the participants. Food composition data were collated from local tables as well as international tables (Malaysia, Australia, and UK) as previously described [34].

The scoring system for the Healthy Eating Index for Singaporean adolescents (HEI-SGA) was based on similar approaches used to design the Healthy Eating Index 2010 [42,43] and the Healthy Eating Index for pregnant women in Singapore, HEI-SGP [44], but modified according to Singaporean food-based dietary guidelines for individuals of this age range [45]. The Singaporean Health Promotion Board launched My Healthy Plate in 2014 in order to better communicate the stipulated dietary guidelines [45]. The current approach to assess adherence to these guidelines included 11 components (presented in Table 1 below).

Table 1. Scoring elements used to calculate the Healthy Eating Index for Singaporean Adolescents (HEI-SGA).

No.	Component	Standards for Minimum Score of Zero	Standards for Maximum Score	Maximum Score
1	Total fruit	No fruit	≥0.87 serves/1000 kcal	5
2	Whole fruit	No whole fruit	≥0.43 serves/1000 kcal	5
3	Total vegetables	No vegetables	≥0.87 serves/1000 kcal	5
4	Dark green leafy & orange vegetables	No dark green leafy and orange vegetables	≥0.43 serves/1000 kcal	5
5	Whole grains	No whole grains	≥1.30 serves/1000 kcal	10
6	Dairy and alternatives	No dairy and alternatives	≥0.43 serves/1000 kcal	10
7	Total protein foods	No protein food	≥1.08 serves/1000 kcal	10
8	Total rice & alternatives	No rice and alternatives	≥3.04 serves/1000 kcal	10
9	Total fat	≥40% of energy	≤30% of energy	10
10	Saturated fat	≥20% of energy	≤10% of energy	10
11	Sodium	≥870 mg/1000 kcal	≤435 mg/1000 kcal	10
-	TOTAL	-	-	90

A score for each component was calculated based on Singapore's My Healthy Plate and dietary guidelines and adjusted based on recommended energy intake for individuals of that particular sex and age [45,46]. For example, if an individual was recommended to consume 2 servings of fruit with a total dietary energy intake of 2300 kcal diet/day, the maximum standard for the "Total fruit" (i.e., all forms including juice) component was calculated as ≥0.87 servings/1000 kcal diet. Zero points were allocated if no fruit in any form was consumed, while a maximum of 5 points were allocated if more than 0.87 servings of fruit per 1000 kcal were consumed. The sum of all component scores was then divided by 90 and multiplied by 100 to give a total score that could hypothetically range from 0–100.

All statistical analyses were performed using the Statistical Package for Social Sciences, SPSS, version 26.0 for Windows (IBM Corp., Armonk, NY, USA) and statistical significance for all the tests was defined at p-value < 0.05. Total HEI-SGA scores for the cohort were parametrically distributed, but sub-groups were not. As all component scores were non-parametric, it was decided to carry out comparisons between groups using Mann-Whitney and Kruskal-Wallis (non-parametric) tests, with post-hoc Bonferroni-corrected tests.

3. Results

Complete 24 h food recall and questionnaire data were collected for all participants. Overall, the median HEI-SGA score was low at 48.5 (IQR 40.5, 56.4) out of 100. Component scores for "Total fruit", "Whole fruit", "Total vegetables", "Dark green leafy & orange vegetables", "Whole grains", "Dairy products", and "Sodium" were frequently zero or close to zero within this cohort, while component scores for "Total rice and alternatives", "Total protein foods", "Total fat", and "Saturated fat" were towards maximal for the majority of the population (see Table 2 for additional detail). Male (median 48.2, IQR 40.1–56.4) and female (48.8, 42.1–56.4) participants had similar total HEI-SGA scores ($p = 0.883$), with female participants scoring statistically higher component scores for "Whole fruit", "Total vegetables", "Dark green leafy & orange vegetables", and "Total rice and alternatives" when compared by independent sample Mann Whitney U test ($p < 0.05$, see Table 2) despite similar median values. A higher proportion of males appeared to score a maximum score for the "Total protein foods" category ($p < 0.001$), although again, median scores were similar (males median = 10, IQR 9.2–10.0 vs. females 10.0, 5.7–10.0), see Table 2).

Table 2. Median component and total HEI-SGA values across all participants and by sex.

	All (n = 536)	Female (n = 304)	Male (n = 232)	
Components	**Median (IQR)**	**Median (IQR)**	**Median (IQR)**	* p-**Value**
Total fruit	0.0 (0.0, 4.1)	0.0 (0.0, 4.8)	0.0 (0.0, 3.2)	0.001
Whole fruit	0.0 (0.0, 5.0)	0.0 (0.0, 5.0)	0.0 (0.0, 0.0)	<0.001
Total vegetables	0.6 (0.0, 2.4)	0.9 (0.0, 2.7)	0.3 (0.0, 1.7)	0.014
DGLOV	0.0 (0.0, 0.0)	0.0 (0.0, 0.0)	0.0 (0.0, 0.0)	0.009
Total rice & alternatives	10.0 (7.9, 10.0)	10.0 (7.4, 10.0)	10.0 (8.5, 10.0)	0.013
Whole grains	0.0 (0.0, 0.0)	0.0 (0.0, 0.0)	0.0 (0.0, 0.0)	0.956
Dairy and alternatives	1.9 (0.0, 7.0)	1.9 (0.0, 7.5)	2.1 (0.0, 6.4)	0.811
Total protein foods	10 (6.9, 10.0)	10.0 (5.7, 10.0)	10.0 (9.2, 10.0)	<0.001
Total Fat	10 (8.4, 10.0)	10.0 (8.0, 10.0)	10.0 (8.8, 10.0)	0.621
Saturated fat	10.0 (7.1, 10.0)	9.8 (6.9, 10.0)	10.0 (7.4, 10.0)	0.097
Sodium	0.0 (0.0, 0.0)	0.0 (0.0, 0.0)	0.0 (0.0, 0.0)	0.722
Total HEI-SGA score	48.5 (40.5, 56.4)	48.2 (40.1, 56.4)	48.8 (42.1, 56.4)	0.883

* Based on independent sample Mann-Whitney U Tests between males and females. DGLOV—dark green leafy and orange vegetables, HEI-SGA—Healthy Eating Index for Singaporean adolescents, IQR—diet quality score.

There was no significant difference among the median total HEI-SGA and component scores for different categories of BMI (see Table 3), but the highest BMI category group appeared to consume fewer energy-adjusted portions of "Rice and alternatives" and "Dairy and alternatives" compared to other groups ($p = 0.007$ and 0.008, respectively).

Table 3. Median component and total HEI-SGA values across all participants and by BMI category.

	Median (IQR) Component or Total Score				
	At Risk of Nutrient Deficiency (n = 106)	Healthy (n = 281)	Moderate Risk (n = 95)	High Risk (n = 54)	* p-Value
Total fruit	0.0 (0.0, 3.5)	0.0 (0.0, 4.2)	0.0 (0.0, 4.8)	0.0 (0.0, 4.1)	0.757
Whole fruit	0.0 (0.0, 3.9)	0.0 (0.0, 5.0)	0.0 (0.0, 3.8)	0.0 (0.0, 5.0)	0.349
Total vegetables	0.0 (0.0, 1.5)	0.5 (0.0, 2.5)	0.6 (0.0, 2.6)	1.3 (0.0, 2.4)	0.328
DGLOV	0.0 (0.0, 0.0)	0.0 (0.0, 0.0)	0.0 (0.0, 0.0)	0.0 (0.0, 0.0)	0.402
Total rice & alternatives	10.0 (7.7, 10.0) ^{b}	10.0 (8.3, 10.0) ^{b}	10.0 (8.0, 10.0) ^{b}	8.5 (7.2, 10.0) ^{a}	0.007
Whole grains	0.0 (0.0, 0.0)	0.0 (0.0, 0.0)	0.0 (0.0, 0.0)	0.0 (0.0, 0.0)	0.581
Dairy	2.6 (0.0, 5.4) ^{b}	2.1 (0.0, 7.0) ^{b}	2.9 (0.0, 9.4) ^{b}	0.0 (0.0, 2.9) ^{a}	0.008
Total protein foods	10.0 (7.8, 10.0)	10.0 (6.9, 10.0)	10.0 (5.8, 10.0)	10.0 (6.2, 10.0)	0.766
Total Fat	10.0 (8.6, 10.0)	10.0 (7.2, 10.0)	10.0 (9.8, 10.0)	10.0 (8.4, 10.0)	0.372
Saturated fat	9.7 (7.3, 10.0)	9.7 (7.0, 10.0)	10.0 (7.7, 10.0)	10.0 (7.0, 10.0)	0.476
Sodium	0.0 (0.0, 0.0)	0.0 (0.0, 0.0)	0.0 (0.0, 0.0)	0.0 (0.0, 0.0)	0.462
Total HEI-SGA score	47.5 (41.7, 55.2)	48.8 (40.1, 56.1)	49.1 (41.9, 59.7)	47.0 (40.1, 52.6)	0.470

* Based on independent samples, Kruskal-Wallis. Groups that do not share a superscript are significantly different from each other by post-hoc Bonferroni tests. DGLOV—dark green leafy and orange vegetables. BMI categories used in Singapore for this age group: "At risk of nutrient deficiency" < 18.5; "Heathy range" 18.5–22.9; "Moderate risk (of developing cardiovascular diseases) 23.0–27.0; "High risk" > 27.0 [17].

Tables 4 and 5 highlight that the majority of component scores differed across ethnic groups and educational institutions. Participants of Chinese ethnic origin had the statistically highest ($p < 0.001$) Total HEI-SGA score (median 52.4, IQR 44.4–60.4) followed by those of Indian (47.6 38.5–54.9) and Malay (44.4, 37.2–50.2) ethnic origin (see Table 4). Students from the Junior College had a statistically higher ($p < 0.001$) Total HEI-SGA score (56.6, 48.1–64.4) than those attending the polytechnic (47.4, 38.2–54.7) or ITE (47.4, 40.2–52.6). Junior College students appeared to have markedly higher median scores for "Total fruit", "Whole Fruit", and "Total vegetables" than students from other educational institutions (see Table 5 for further detail).

Table 4. Median component and total HEI-SGA values across all participants by ethnicity.

	Median (IQR) Component and Total Scores			
	Chinese (n = 257)	Indian (n = 134)	Malay (n = 145)	p-Value *
Total fruit	0.0 (0.0, 5.0) ^{a}	0.0 (0.0, 3.5) ^{b}	0.0 (0.0, 1.0) ^{b}	<0.001
Whole fruit	0.0 (0.0, 5.0) ^{a}	0.0 (0.0, 3.2) ^{b}	0.0 (0.0, 0.0) ^{b}	<0.001
Total vegetables	1.4 (0.0, 3.6) ^{a}	0.3 (0.0, 1.5) ^{b}	0.0 (0.0, 0.9) ^{b}	<0.001
DGLOV	0.0 (0.0, 3.7) ^{a}	0.0 (0.0, 0.0) ^{b}	0.0 (0.0, 0.0) ^{b}	<0.001
Total rice & alternatives	10.0 (8.0, 10.0)	10.0 (7.9, 10.0)	10.0 (7.4, 10.0)	0.458
Whole grains	0.0 (0.0, 0.0) ^{a}	0.0 (0.0, 0.0) ^{a,b}	0.0 (0.0, 0.0) ^{b}	0.001
Dairy	2.2 (0.0, 7.0) ^{a,b}	2.8 (0.0, 7.8) ^{a}	0.0 (0.0, 5.3) ^{b}	0.013
Total protein foods	10.0 (6.9, 10.0)	10.0 (6.6, 10.0)	10.0 (7.1, 10.0)	0.705
Total Fat	10.0 (9.7, 10.0) ^{a}	10.0 (6.7, 10.0) ^{b}	10.0 (6.0, 10.0) ^{b}	0.001
Saturated fat	10.0 (8.1, 10.0) ^{a}	9.5 (5.8, 10.0) ^{b}	9.1 (6.4, 10.0) ^{b}	<0.001
Sodium	0.0 (0.0, 0.0) ^{b}	0.0 (0.0, 0.0) ^{a}	0.0 (0.0, 0.0) ^{a}	0.009
Total HEI-SGA score	52.4 (44.4, 60.4) ^{a}	47.6 (38.5, 54.9) ^{b}	44.4 (37.2, 50.2) ^{c}	<0.001

* Based on independent samples, Kruskal-Wallis. Groups that do not share a superscript are significantly different from each other by post-hoc Bonferroni tests. DGLOV—dark green leafy and orange vegetables.

Table 5. Median component and total HEI-SGA values in Singaporean students attending different educational institutions.

	Median (IQR) Component and Total Scores			
Components	**ITE ($n = 100$)**	**JC ($n = 100$)**	**POLY ($n = 334$)**	**p-Values ***
Total fruit	0.0 (0.0, 3.2) [b]	4.6 (0.0, 5.0) [a]	0.0 (0.0, 3.2) [b]	<0.001
Whole fruit	0.0 (0.0, 0.4) [b]	4.2 (0.0, 5.0) [a]	0.0 (0.0, 4.0) [b]	<0.001
Total vegetables	0.7 (0.0, 2.6) [b]	2.7 (0.0, 5.0) [a]	0.0 (0.0, 1.5) [b]	<0.001
DGLOV	0.0 (0.0, 0.0) [b]	0.0 (0.0, 3.7) [a]	0.0 (0.0, 0.0) [b]	<0.001
Total rice & alternatives	10.0 (6.3, 10.0) [b]	10.0 (8.8, 10.0) [a]	10.0 (7.9, 10.0) [a,b]	0.015
Whole grains	0.0 (0.0, 0.0) [a]	0.0 (0.0, 0.0) [b]	0.0 (0.0, 0.0) [b]	0.004
Dairy	0.0 (0.0, 4.0) [b]	3.4 (0.0, 8.4) [a]	2.1 (0.0, 7.3) [a,b]	0.002
Total protein foods	10.0 (6.7, 10.0)	10.0 (7.6, 10.0)	10.0 (6.4, 10.0)	0.433
Total Fat	10.0 (9.8, 10.0)	10.0 (9.4, 10.0)	10.0 (7.0, 10.0)	0.034
Saturated fat	10.0 (8.6, 10.0) [b]	10.0 (7.7, 10.0) [a,b]	9.7 (6.5, 10.0) [a]	0.008
Sodium	0.0 (0.0, 0.0)	0.0 (0.0, 0.0)	0.0 (0.0, 0.0)	0.788
Total HEI-SGA score	47.4 (40.2, 52.6) [b]	56.6 (48.1, 64.4) [a]	47.4 (38.2, 54.7) [b]	<0.001

* Based on independent samples, Kruskal-Wallis. Groups that do not share a superscript are significantly different from each other by post-hoc Bonferroni-corrected tests. ITE—Institute of Technical Education, JC—Junior College, POLY—polytechnic, DGLOV–dark green leafy and orange vegetable.

4. Discussion

With accelerated economic development and urbanization over the past decades, Singapore faces current and future public health challenges with non-communicable diseases [47], despite having one of the highest estimates of healthy life expectancy of any country or territory globally [48]. The use of diet quality indices has allowed researchers to consider overall dietary habits in relation to measures of a population's health using a single useful indicator with varying degrees of complexity [42]. The authors believe that the approach described in this paper provides a rational means to look at overall dietary habits in this population group. As information of dietary intake within Singaporean late adolescents/early adults is extremely limited, the current dataset should also provide support to future national public health efforts. The approaches taken to consider how educational institution and other factors are associated with diet quality in a diverse cross-section may have wider applications for similar future studies globally.

The HEI-SGA scores across the cohort suggested that dietary intake was frequently divergent from dietary guidelines in this cohort, with the median score of the current sample (48.5 out of 100) appearing lower than similar estimates of diet quality in Singaporean pre-teen (median 65.4 out of 100) and infants (mean 44.2 out of 65) noted in recent studies [34,35].

While wider data on dietary habits in late adolescents/young adults remain limited, previous studies have suggested similar findings within individuals of this age range elsewhere in the world. Cross-sectional data from the UK National Diet and Nutrition Survey highlight that diet quality is far from ideal within this age range [49,50], with US cross-sectional data also highlighting that individuals aged 14–18 years tended to have lower diet quality estimates than younger children [51,52]. Analysis of the Norwegian Longitudinal Health Behaviour Study dataset (which includes dietary data collection from a Norwegian longitudinal cohort at eight time-points between 14 and 30 years) highlighted a dip in fruit and vegetable consumption in early adulthood (until age 21 years and 23 years, respectively), alongside an increased intake of sugar-sweetened beverages and confectionary items between the ages of 14 years and 18 years [53]. A similar study in the US suggested that the diet quality of individuals may improve modestly between the ages of 16 years and 20 years [54].

The component scores that most frequently scored highly (i.e., individuals met or exceeded dietary guidelines) were for "Total rice and alternatives" and "Total protein foods". These findings were similar to previous studies, where intake of carbohydrates and proteins in late adolescents and early adults in developed countries was rarely below the recommendation [55,56]. Although almost all participants met or exceeded "Total rice & alternatives" recommendations, the component score for "Whole grains" was negligible across the cohort. This somewhat aligns with data on adult intake (aged 18 to 69 years) from the Singapore National Nutrition Survey (NNS) conducted in 2010, where it was noted that only 27% of Singaporeans consumed one serving or more of wholegrain products per day [19], up from 8.4% in 2004. O'Neil et al. (2011) reviewed the consumption of whole grains in USA children and adolescents using the National Health and Nutrition Examination Survey (NHANES) 1999–2004 [57]. It was concluded that the consumption of whole grains was low, with a mean serving of 0.63 servings of whole grains/d for adolescents, aged 13–18 years. Factors that have been suggested to drive low intake of whole grains within this age group include poor expected palatability, limited availability outside of the home, and consumers' inability to identify wholegrain products [58,59]. There has been increased public health promotion of wholegrain consumption in Singapore, including increasing the availability of whole grains by working with the food manufacturers to produce more whole grain products and actively broadcasting the benefits of whole grains through initiatives such as supermarket tours and school talks (Health Hub, 2017). In 2016 (after the end of data collection for the current study), a major shift was made in the Heathy Meals in Schools Programme to stipulate that at least 20% of the rice or alternative cereal-based foods should be whole grains and only wholemeal bread can be used to prepare the sandwiches [22]. However, this programme is not mandatory for all post-secondary education establishments. Currently, only food provision at Junior Colleges falls under the purview of the Ministry of Education guidelines. Evaluation of whether this update in recommended food provision has increased wholegrain food intake in Junior College students would be interesting and should be possible through collection of further dietary data in this population.

The median component scores for the "Total fruit", "Whole fruit", "Total vegetables", and "Dark green leafy & orange vegetables" components were also low across the cohort. Data from the Singaporean National Nutrition Survey suggests that intake of fruit and vegetables may have gone down in adults over time, with a lower percentage of individuals meeting fruit and vegetable recommendations in 2010 versus 2004. The intake of fruit is lowest in 18–29 year-olds, but vegetable intake tends to be higher both for males and females in this age range than for older groups [19]. Low intake of fruit and vegetables appears relatively common in late adolescents/early adults in many parts of the world [13]. For example, a recent study conducted in India found that adolescent girls' consumption of vegetables and fruit was also considerably below the national Recommended Dietary Intake [60].

The approach taken here was based on the wording of the food-based dietary guidelines in Singapore. Weighting was used within scoring categories to ensure that intake of specific items (e.g., whole fruits and green leafy and orange vegetables) was included in the criteria for maximal scoring. Individuals who scored high for "Whole fruit" and "Dark green leafy & orange vegetables" would also score highly for "Total fruit" and "Total vegetables". While the current approach aligns well with food-based dietary guidelines, an alternative scoring approach could have been to limit the number of servings (of, for example, fruit juices or smoothies) that could be credited with a score. Due to the low intake of fruits and vegetables in the current cross-section (>60% of all participants scored zero for all fruit and vegetable component scores), this appears unlikely to have affected the overall findings of the current study.

The lowest-scoring nutrient-based category in the HEI-SGA was sodium, for which the majority of individuals scored less than 1.5 out of 10. The high sodium intake could possibly be attributed to the frequent consumption of out-of-home food consumption previously noted in Singapore [61], where many popular dishes (both of Asian and Western origin) tend to have high sodium content [62]. While attempts were made to estimate total salt (including elective salt) consumption accurately during collection of 24 h recall information, previous studies would suggest that total salt intake may be under-reported using such methods [63].

It appears that the dietary habits among the students attending Junior College were closer to the ideal. Students attending this institution tend to start and end the school day earlier compared to the Polytechnic and ITE students. This could be driven by confounding factors like socio-economic status linked to educational attainment [64,65] that have not been collected within the current study. It is also unclear whether on-campus food provision was a major driver for more or less positive dietary habits. Our current analysis has not separated site of food consumption beyond whether items were consumed within the home and out-of-home, but this would form a rational focus for future research.

The HEI-SGA provides an approach to systematically evaluate the diet quality of Singaporean late adolescents/early adults against the Health Promotion Board's recommendations. The method used to estimate HEI-SGA scores was largely based on the previous HEI-2010 method but was adapted to Singaporean dietary guidelines. This previous method included energy adjustments for each component score. Due to the potential for the methods for dietary intake estimation (24 h food recall) to under-report intake, the authors felt that energy adjustment would help mitigate these potential limitations [41,43]. It would have been more ideal to estimate physical activity levels in this cohort to better define target energy intake [34]. However, the design of the current study did not allow this. Estimation of physical activity energy expenditure is particularly relevant for similar future studies where guidelines for total dietary energy intake differ based on physical activity levels.

Weight and height of the respondents were obtained based on self-declaration. This approach is not as accurate as direct measurement methods [66] and may skew the HEI-SGA scoring for under- and over-reporters. The proportion of individuals in this cohort who were self-reported as high risk/obese (10.4%) was similar to the proportion recently estimated to exist in the adult population (8.7%) in Singapore [17]. A novel food atlas was developed for culturally-relevant food items in Singapore and used to support the collection of dietary recall data [41]. While similar tools have been used in other populations effectively [67,68], it must be noted that the current tool has not been validated. Nonetheless, the authors believe that this approach helped to ensure better estimation of food portion sizes by respondents, thereby benefitting the overarching study outcomes. Ideally, dietary data collection would also have involved replicate collection across 3–4 days [69]. However, neither direct measurement of height and weight or additional dietary data collection were possible within the time scale and were not available resources of the current study. Due to the scarcity of data of dietary habits in Singaporeans of this age, it was decided to recruit a larger and more representative cohort for this cross-sectional study. The design of this study aimed to evaluate the dietary habits of this population in relation to the educational institution setting and so only dietary recall data from weekdays was collected. While the current study had a sample size that would be likely to adequately represent the overall population of post-secondary Singaporean students, the sub-analyses carried out here on sex, ethnicity, BMI status, and institution of study may not have been adequately powered. The current comparison only included data from three specific institutions that may not have represented the wider range of educational institutions in Singapore. Future studies should consider more extensive sampling across a wider range of institutions and advertising for participants through more inclusive and widely-accessed methods (like institutional emails or social media platforms). Repeated and/or more objective approaches for dietary data collection like weighed food diaries and height and weight measurements should be measured directly by future study teams to improve confidence in dietary and body weight status data. Additional record-keeping of individuals who declined participation or withdrew would help align with consensus guidelines on best practice (see Appendix A) for the running of observational studies [70].

Many savoury food items consumed by participants (e.g., fried rice, stir-fried noodles, and curry chicken) contained proportions of food items from multiple food groups. Estimation of the contribution of these items to the intake of each food group required utilization of available recipes and thus, may not accurately depict the actual food consumed.

There appears to be a future research need to develop interventions (for instance, to encourage fruit and vegetables consumption) for this targeted group of post secondary school students over a period of time and then to review the impact of the intervention by calculating and comparing the HEI-SG before and after the interventions. The multi-vendor nature of each cafeteria/eatery in Singaporean educational institutions reduces potential issues of access to positive choices [22]. Our findings suggest that such interventions may need to focus on improving personal choice of food items towards better meeting food-based dietary guidelines. The existing standards for more prudent food provision (currently recommended/enforced at Junior Colleges) could be considered at both polytechnics and ITEs.

5. Conclusions

This work proposes a means of assessing diet quality in Singaporean late adolescents/young adults and also highlights some of the major areas for improvement in the diet for this population. Public health strategies should be customized to address the low intake of fruit and vegetables, whole grains, and dairy products and the high intake of sodium for this group of adolescents, with particular consideration for approaches that effectively engage students at different types of educational institutions and from different ethnic groups.

Author Contributions: Conceptualization, L.S., I.B., E.F., and M.E.T.; methodology, L.S., I.B., E.F., and M.E.T.; data collection, M.E.T., formal analysis, M.E.T.; investigation, data curation, M.E.T.; writing—original draft preparation I.B.; writing—review and editing, M.E.T., L.S., and E.F.; supervision, L.S., E.F., and I.B.; project administration, L.S. and I.B. All authors have read and agreed to the published version of the manuscript.

Funding: This research received no external funding and was fully funded by Nanyang Polytechnic and Newcastle University.

Acknowledgments: The authors would like to acknowledge Kwan Su Yan for supporting data collection and thank all participants for their time and effort put into this study.

Conflicts of Interest: The authors declare no conflict of interest.

Appendix A

Table A1. Strengthening the reporting of observation studies in epidemiology (STROBE) checklist of recommended items that should be included in reports of cross-sectional studies.

Section	Item	Recommendation	Reported in
Title and abstract	1	(a) Indicate the study's design with a commonly used term in the title or the abstract	Title and Abstract (p. 1 lines 19–20)
		(b) Provide in the abstract an informative and balanced summary of what was done and what was found	Abstract (p. 1)
		Introduction	
Background/rationale	2	Explain the scientific background and rationale for the investigation being reported	Introduction (p. 1–2)
Objectives	3	State specific objectives, including any prespecified hypotheses	Objectives p. 1, lines 71–73. No prespecified hypotheses included.
		Methods	
Study design	4	Present key elements of the study design early in the paper	Abstract, Introduction, and Methods
Setting	5	Describe the setting, locations, and relevant dates, including periods of recruitment, exposure, follow-up, and data collection	Exposure and follow-up not relevant to study design. Recruitment data collection dates included (Methods, p. 3, line 97).
Participants	6	(a) Give the eligibility criteria and the sources and methods of selection of participants	Methods, p. 3, lines 81–83)
Variables	7	Clearly define all outcomes, exposures, predictors, potential confounders, and effect modifiers. Give diagnostic criteria, if applicable	Outcomes defined throughout Methods section. Unmeasured potential confounders discussed (Discussion, line 256–262 and lines 269–272). Exposures and diagnostic criteria not applicable to current study.
Data sources/measurement	8	For each variable of interest, give sources of data and details of methods of assessment (measurement). Describe comparability of assessment methods if there is more than one group	Presented throughout the Methods section
Bias	9	Describe any efforts to address potential sources of bias	Methods, particularly lines 85–96

Table A1. *Cont.*

Section	Item	Recommendation	Reported in
Study size	10	Explain how the study size was arrived at	Only an estimate of the adequacy of total population was considered, with broader convenience sampling based on available study timeline (Methods, lines 97–101)
Quantitative variables	11	Explain how quantitative variables were handled in the analyses. If applicable, describe which groupings were chosen and why	Data handling described in Methods (lines 86–128)
Statistical methods	12	(a) Describe all statistical methods, including those used to control for confounding variables	Methods (lines 129–134)
		(b) Describe any methods used to examine subgroups and interactions	Methods and Results
		(c) Explain how missing data were addressed	Not applicable (see Results line 136)
		(d) If applicable, describe analytical methods taking account of sampling strategy	Not carried out
		(e) Describe any sensitivity analyses	Not carried out. Potential unmeasured confounders discussed
		Results	
Participants	13	(a) Report numbers of individuals at each stage of study—e.g., numbers potentially eligible, examined for eligibility, confirmed eligible, included in the study, completing follow-up, and analysed	No data collected on potential eligibility or number of individuals who declined to take part.
		(b) Give reasons for non-participation at each stage	Not applicable (see 13 (a)).
		(c) Consider use of a flow diagram	Not applicable (see 13 (a))
Descriptive data	14	(a) Give characteristics of the study participants (e.g., demographic, clinical, social) and information on exposures and potential confounders	Results Tables 1–5
		(b) Indicate the number of participants with missing data for each variable of interest	Not applicable (see 13 (a))
Outcome data	15	Report numbers of outcome events or summary measures	Results Tables 1–5

Table A1. *Cont.*

Section	Item	Recommendation	Reported in
Main results	16	(a) Give unadjusted estimates and if applicable, confounder-adjusted estimates and their precision (e.g., 95% confidence interval). Make clear which confounders were adjusted for and why they were included	Confounder-adjusted estimates not applicable to the current study design
		(b) Report category boundaries when continuous variables were categorized	BMI categories used noted in Results (Table 3, lines 159–161).
		(c) If relevant, consider translating estimates of relative risk into absolute risk for a meaningful time period	Not applicable
Other analyses	17	Report other analyses done—e.g., analyses of subgroups and interactions and sensitivity analyses	Analyses of sub-groups described throughout Results. Interaction and sensitivity analyses not carried out.
		Discussion	
Key results	18	Summarise key results with reference to study objectives	Discussion (lines 191–257)
Limitations	19	Discuss limitations of the study, taking into account sources of potential bias or imprecision. Discuss both the direction and magnitude of any potential bias	Discussion (lines 241–250, lines 258–264, lines 269–274, lines 275–301)
Interpretation	20	Give a cautious overall interpretation of results considering objectives, limitations, multiplicity of analyses, results from similar studies, and other relevant evidence	Major interpretations of results presented in lines 317–318 of Conclusions.
Generalisability	21	Discuss the generalisability (external validity) of the study results	Considered in relation to broader limitations of the study design (lines 275–301). Conclusions related to this are presented on lines 318–322
		Other information	
Funding	22	Give the source of funding and the role of the funders for the present study and if applicable, for the original study on which the present article is based	Presented post-Conclusions (lines 329–330)

References

1. World Health Organisation. WHO|Adolescent Health. 2016. Available online: /topics/adolescent_health/en/index.html (accessed on 5 August 2020).
2. Thana'Y, A.; Takruri, H.R.; Tayyem, R.F. Dietary Practices and Nutrient Intake among Adolescents: A General Review. *Obes. Med.* **2019**, *16*, 100145.
3. Neumark-Sztainer, D.; Story, M.; Perry, C.; Casey, M.A. Factors Influencing Food Choices of Adolescents: Findings from Focus-Group Discussions with Adolescents. *J. Am. Diet. Assoc.* **1999**, *99*, 929–937. [CrossRef]
4. Story, M.; Neumark-Sztainer, D.; French, S. Individual and environmental influences on adolescent eating behaviors. *J. Am. Diet. Assoc.* **2002**, *102*, S40–S51. [CrossRef]
5. Christoph, M.J.; Larson, N.I.; Winkler, M.R.; Wall, M.M.; Neumark-Sztainer, D. Longitudinal trajectories and prevalence of meeting dietary guidelines during the transition from adolescence to young adulthood. *Am. J. Clin. Nutr.* **2019**, *109*, 656–664. [CrossRef]
6. Lowe, C.J.; Morton, J.B.; Reichelt, A.C. Adolescent obesity and dietary decision making—A brain-health perspective. *Lancet Child Adolesc. Health* **2020**, *4*, 388–396. [CrossRef]
7. Hovdenak, I.M.; Stea, T.H.; Twisk, J.; te Velde, S.J.; Klepp, K.-I.; Bere, E. Tracking of fruit, vegetables and unhealthy snacks consumption from childhood to adulthood (15 year period): Does exposure to a free school fruit programme modify the observed tracking? *Int. J. Behav. Nutr. Phys. Act.* **2019**, *16*, 22. [CrossRef]
8. Birch, L.L. Development of food preferences. *Annu. Rev. Nutr.* **1999**, *19*, 41–62. [CrossRef]
9. Craigie, A.M.; Lake, A.A.; Kelly, S.A.; Adamson, A.J.; Mathers, J.C. Tracking of obesity-related behaviours from childhood to adulthood: A systematic review. *Maturitas* **2011**, *70*, 266–284. [CrossRef]
10. Ormel, J.; Oldehinkel, A.J.; Sijtsema, J.; van Oort, F.; Raven, D.; Veenstra, R.; Vollebergh, W.A.; Verhulst, F.C. The TRacking Adolescents' Individual Lives Survey (TRAILS): Design, current status, and selected findings. *J. Am. Acad. Child Adolesc. Psychiatry* **2012**, *51*, 1020–1036. [CrossRef]
11. Eicher-Miller, H.A.; Boushey, C.J.; Bailey, R.L.; Yang, Y.J. Frequently consumed foods and energy contributions among food secure and insecure U.S. children and adolescents. *Nutrients* **2020**, *12*, 304. [CrossRef]
12. French, S.A.; Story, M.; Neumark-Sztainer, D.; Fulkerson, J.A.; Hannan, P. Fast food restaurant use among adolescents: Associations with nutrient intake, food choices and behavioral and psychosocial variables. *Int. J. Obes.* **2001**, *25*, 1823. [CrossRef] [PubMed]
13. World Health Organization. Guideline: Implementing Effective Actions for Improving Adolescent Nutrition. 2018. Available online: https://apps.who.int/iris/bitstream/handle/10665/260297/9789241513708-eng.pdf;jsessionid=6C93746038CAB361A625201EB52A221E?sequence=1 (accessed on 10 August 2020).
14. Organisation for Economic Co-Operation and Development. Singapore: Rapid Improvement Followed by Strong Performance. In *Lessons from PISA for the United States*; OECD Publishing: Paris, France, 2010.
15. Leong-Salobir, C. Singapore: Tasting the City. In *Urban Food Culture*; Springer: Berlin/Heidelberg, Germany, 2019; pp. 83–111.
16. Health Promotion Board Singapore. *National Nutrition Survey 2010, Singapore—BookSG—National Library Board*; Health Promotion Board Singapore: Singapore, 2017.
17. Ministry of Health. Executive Summary on National Population Health Survey 2016/17. Available online: https://www.moh.gov.sg/docs/librariesprovider5/resources-statistics/reports/executive-summary-nphs-2016_17.pdf (accessed on 29 September 2020).
18. Ministry of Health. Obesity Rate in Singapore. 2015. Available online: https://www.google.com.sg/?gfe_rd=cr&ei=bcmGWKavBZeDoAPv-LnICw&gws_rd=ssl#q=obesity+rate+in+singapore+2015 (accessed on 24 January 2020).
19. Health Promotion Board Singapore. National Nutrition Survey. 2010. Available online: https://www.hpb.gov.sg/docs/default-source/pdf/nns-2010-report.pdf?sfvrsn=18e3f172_2 (accessed on 11 August 2020).
20. Health Promotion Board. Students' Health Survey. Available online: https://data.gov.sg/dataset/students-health-survey?resource_id=93a05d55-a41b-44f8-9052-94aa7d563d7f (accessed on 24 August 2020).
21. Ministry of Education Singapore. *Education Statistics Digest 2019*; Ministry of Education: Singapore, 2019.
22. Health Promotion Board Singapore. Healthy Meals in Schools Programme. Available online: https://www.hpb.gov.sg/docs/default-source/default-document-library/healthy-meals-in-schools-programme-criteria28038bf6468366dea7adff00000d8c5a.pdf?sfvrsn=0 (accessed on 13 November 2019).

23. Health Promotion Board Singapore. Eating Healthily at the School Canteen. Available online: https://www.hpb.gov.sg/HOPPortal/health-article/2818 (accessed on 31 January 2020).
24. Kant, A.K. Indexes of overall diet quality: A review. *J. Am. Diet. Assoc.* **1996**, *96*, 785–791. [CrossRef]
25. Coulston, A.M. The Search Continues for A Tool to Evaluate Dietary Quality. *Am. J. Clin. Nutr.* **2001**, *74*, 417. [CrossRef] [PubMed]
26. Kant, A.K. Dietary patterns and health outcomes. *J. Am. Diet. Assoc.* **2004**, *104*, 615–635. [CrossRef] [PubMed]
27. Krebs-Smith, S.M.; Pannucci, T.E.; Subar, A.F.; Kirkpatrick, S.I.; Lerman, J.L.; Tooze, J.A.; Wilson, M.M.; Reedy, J. Update of the Healthy Eating Index: HEI-2015. *J. Acad. Nutr. Diet.* **2018**, *118*, 1591–1602. [CrossRef]
28. Jacobs, S.; Harmon, B.E.; Boushey, C.J.; Morimoto, Y.; Wilkens, L.R.; Le Marchand, L.; Kröger, J.; Schulze, M.B.; Kolonel, L.N.; Maskarinec, G. A priori-defined diet quality indexes and risk of type 2 diabetes: The Multiethnic Cohort. *Diabetologia* **2015**, *58*, 98–112. [CrossRef]
29. Schwingshackl, L.; Bogensberger, B.; Hoffmann, G. Diet quality as assessed by the healthy eating index, alternate healthy eating index, dietary approaches to stop hypertension score, and health outcomes: An updated systematic review and meta-analysis of cohort studies. *J. Acad. Nutr. Diet.* **2018**, *118*, 74–100.e111. [CrossRef]
30. Brauer, P.; Royall, D.; Li, A.; Rodrigues, A.; Green, J.; Macklin, S.; Craig, A.; Pasanen, J.; Brunelle, L.; Maitland, S.; et al. Nutrient intake and dietary quality changes within a personalized lifestyle intervention program for metabolic syndrome in primary care. *Appl. Physiol. Nutr. Metab.* **2019**, *44*, 1297–1304. [CrossRef]
31. Hendrie, G.A.; Baird, D.; Golley, R.K.; Noakes, M. The CSIRO healthy diet score: An online survey to estimate compliance with the Australian dietary guidelines. *Nutrients* **2017**, *9*, 47. [CrossRef]
32. Waijers, P.M.; Feskens, E.J.; Ocké, M.C. A critical review of predefined diet quality scores. *Br. J. Nutr.* **2007**, *97*, 219–231. [CrossRef]
33. Kirkpatrick, S.I.; Reedy, J.; Krebs-Smith, S.M.; Pannucci, T.E.; Subar, A.F.; Wilson, M.M.; Lerman, J.L.; Tooze, J.A. Applications of the Healthy Eating Index for surveillance, epidemiology, and intervention research: Considerations and caveats. *J. Acad. Nutr. Diet.* **2018**, *118*, 1603–1621. [CrossRef] [PubMed]
34. Brownlee, I.A.; Low, J.; Duriraju, N.; Chun, M.; Ong, J.X.Y.; Tay, M.E.; Hendrie, G.A.; Santos-Merx, L. Evaluation of the Proximity of Singaporean Children's Dietary Habits to Food-Based Dietary Guidelines. *Nutrients* **2019**, *11*, 2615. [CrossRef] [PubMed]
35. Chen, L.W.; Fung, S.M.; Fok, D.; Leong, L.P.; Toh, J.Y.; Lim, H.X.; Pang, W.W.; Tan, K.H.; Chong, Y.S.; Yap, F.; et al. The development and evaluation of a diet quality index for Asian toddlers and its perinatal correlates: The GUSTO cohort study. *Nutrients* **2019**, *11*, 535. [CrossRef] [PubMed]
36. Australian Bureau of Statistics Sample Size Calculator. Available online: https://www.abs.gov.au/websitedbs/D3310114.nsf/home/Sample+Size+Calculator (accessed on 8 September 2020).
37. Hamer, M.; Mishra, G. Dietary patterns and cardiovascular risk markers in the UK Low Income Diet and Nutrition Survey. *Nutr. Metab. Cardiovasc. Dis.* **2010**, *20*, 491–497. [CrossRef] [PubMed]
38. Moshfegh, A.J.; Borrud, L.; Perloff, B.; LaComb, R. Improved method for the 24-hour dietary recall for use in national surveys. *FASEB J.* **1999**, *13*, A603.
39. Moshfegh, A.; Raper, N.; Ingwersen, L.; Cleveland, L.; Anand, J.; Goldman, J.; LaComb, R. An improved approach to 24-hour dietary recall methodology. *Ann. Nutr. Metab.* **2001**, *45*, 156.
40. Conway, J.M.; Ingwersen, L.A.; Vinyard, B.T.; Moshfegh, A.J. Effectiveness of the US Department of Agriculture 5-step multiple-pass method in assessing food intake in obese and nonobese women. *Am. J. Clin. Nutr.* **2003**, *77*, 1171–1178. [CrossRef] [PubMed]
41. Health Promotion Board & Nanyang Polytechnic. *A Compendium of Food Pictures: For Dietitians and Nutritionists*; Health Promotion Board & Nanyang Polytechnic: Singapore, 2018.
42. Guenther, P.M.; Reedy, J.; Krebs-Smith, S.M. Development of the healthy eating index-2005. *J. Am. Diet. Assoc.* **2008**, *108*, 1896–1901. [CrossRef]
43. Guenther, P.M.; Casavale, K.O.; Reedy, J.; Kirkpatrick, S.I.; Hiza, H.A.; Kuczynski, K.J.; Kahle, L.L.; Krebs-Smith, S.M. Update of the healthy eating index: HEI-2010. *J. Acad. Nutr. Diet.* **2013**, *113*, 569–580. [CrossRef]
44. Han, C.Y.; Colega, M.; Quah, E.P.L.; Chan, Y.H.; Godfrey, K.M.; Kwek, K.; Saw, S.-M.; Gluckman, P.D.; Chong, Y.-S.; Chong, M.F.-F. A healthy eating index to measure diet quality in pregnant women in Singapore: A cross-sectional study. *BMC Nutr.* **2015**, *1*, 39. [CrossRef]

45. Health Promotion Board. Food-Based Dietary Guidelines for Adults. 2017. Available online: https://www.healthhub.sg/live-healthy/15/dietary_guidelines_adults (accessed on 8 September 2020).
46. Health Hub Ministry of Health Singapore. Build a Healthy Food Foundation. Available online: https://www.healthhub.sg/live-healthy/10/build_healthy_food_foundation (accessed on 10 August 2020).
47. Martinez, R.; Lloyd-Sherlock, P.; Soliz, P.; Ebrahim, S.; Vega, E.; Ordunez, P.; McKee, M. Trends in premature avertable mortality from non-communicable diseases for 195 countries and territories, 1990–2017: A population-based study. *Lancet Glob. Health* **2020**, *8*, e511–e523. [CrossRef]
48. Hay, S.I.; Abajobir, A.A.; Abate, K.H.; Abbafati, C.; Abbas, K.M.; Abd-Allah, F.; Abdulle, A.M.; Abebo, T.A.; Abera, S.F.; Aboyans, V.; et al. Global, regional, and national disability-adjusted life-years (DALYs) for 333 diseases and injuries and healthy life expectancy (HALE) for 195 countries and territories, 1990-2016: A systematic analysis for the Global Burden of Disease Study 2016. *Lancet* **2017**, *390*, 1260–1344. [CrossRef]
49. Llauradó, E.; Albar, S.; Giralt, M.; Solà, R.; Evans, C. The effect of snacking and eating frequency on dietary quality in British adolescents. *Eur. J. Nutr.* **2016**, *55*, 1789–1797. [CrossRef]
50. Winpenny, E.M.; Greenslade, S.; Corder, K.; Van Sluijs, E.M. Diet Quality through Adolescence and Early Adulthood: Cross-Sectional Associations of the Dietary Approaches to Stop Hypertension Diet Index and Component Food Groups with Age. *Nutrients* **2018**, *10*, 1585. [CrossRef]
51. Banfield, E.C.; Liu, Y.; Davis, J.S.; Chang, S.; Frazier-Wood, A.C. Poor adherence to US dietary guidelines for children and adolescents in the national health and nutrition examination survey population. *J. Acad. Nutr. Diet.* **2016**, *116*, 21–27. [CrossRef] [PubMed]
52. Hiza, H.A.; Casavale, K.O.; Guenther, P.M.; Davis, C.A. Diet quality of Americans differs by age, sex, race/ethnicity, income, and education level. *J. Acad. Nutr. Diet.* **2013**, *113*, 297–306. [CrossRef] [PubMed]
53. Winpenny, E.M.; van Sluijs, E.M.; White, M.; Klepp, K.-I.; Wold, B.; Lien, N. Changes in diet through adolescence and early adulthood: Longitudinal trajectories and association with key life transitions. *Int. J. Behav. Nutr. Phys. Act.* **2018**, *15*, 86. [CrossRef]
54. Lipsky, L.M.; Nansel, T.R.; Haynie, D.L.; Liu, D.; Li, K.; Pratt, C.A.; Iannotti, R.J.; Dempster, K.W.; Simons-Morton, B. Diet quality of US adolescents during the transition to adulthood: Changes and predictors. *Am. J. Clin. Nutr.* **2017**, *105*, 1424–1432. [CrossRef]
55. Fulgoni, V.L. Current protein intake in America: Analysis of the National Health and Nutrition Examination Survey, 2003–2004. *Am. J. Clin. Nutr.* **2008**, *87*, 1554S–1557S. [CrossRef] [PubMed]
56. Rolland-Cachera, M.F.; Bellisle, F.; Deheeger, M. Nutritional status and food intake in adolescents living in Western Europe. *Eur. J. Clin. Nutr.* **2000**, *54*, S41. [CrossRef] [PubMed]
57. O'Neil, C.F.; Nicklas, T.A.; Zanovec, M.; Cho, S.S.; Kleinman, R. Consumption of whole grains is associated with improved diet quality and nutrient intake in children and adolescents: The National Health and Nutrition Examination Survey 1999–2004. *Public Health Nutr.* **2011**, *14*, 347–355. [CrossRef] [PubMed]
58. Kamar, M.; Evans, C.; Hugh-Jones, S. Factors influencing adolescent whole grain intake: A theory-based qualitative study. *Appetite* **2016**, *101*, 125–133. [CrossRef] [PubMed]
59. Neo, J.E.; Brownlee, I.A. Wholegrain food acceptance in young Singaporean adults. *Nutrients* **2017**, *9*, 371. [CrossRef] [PubMed]
60. Sharma, V.; Singh, V. Impact Assessment of Nutrition Education Programme on Nutritional Status of Adolescent Girls. *J. Nutr. Food Sci.* **2017**, *7*, 1–5. [CrossRef]
61. Naidoo, N.; van Dam, R.M.; Ng, S.; Tan, C.S.; Chen, S.; Lim, J.Y.; Chan, M.F.; Chew, L.; Rebello, S.A. Determinants of eating at local and western fast-food venues in an urban Asian population: A mixed methods approach. *Int. J. Behav. Nutr. Phys. Act.* **2017**, *14*, 69. [CrossRef]
62. Rebello, S.A.; Koh, H.; Chen, C.; Naidoo, N.; Odegaard, A.O.; Koh, W.P.; Butler, L.M.; Yuan, J.M.; Van Dam, R.M. Amount, type, and sources of carbohydrates in relation to ischemic heart disease mortality in a Chinese population: A prospective cohort study. *Am. J. Clin. Nutr.* **2014**, *100*, 53–64. [CrossRef]
63. McLean, R.; Cameron, C.; Butcher, E.; Cook, N.R.; Woodward, M.; Campbell, N.R.C. Comparison of 24-hour urine and 24-hour diet recall for estimating dietary sodium intake in populations: A systematic review and meta-analysis. *J. Clin. Hypertens.* **2019**, *21*, 1753–1762. [CrossRef]
64. Chiong, C.; Dimmock, C. Building trust: How low-income parents navigate neoliberalism in Singapore's education system. *Comp. Educ.* **2020**, *56*, 1–15. [CrossRef]
65. Chua, V.; Swee, E.L.; Wellman, B. Getting ahead in Singapore: How neighborhoods, gender, and ethnicity affect enrollment into elite schools. *Sociol. Educ.* **2019**, *92*, 176–198. [CrossRef]

66. Tsigilis, N. Can secondary school students' self-reported measures of height and weight be trusted? An effect size approach. *Eur. J. Public Health* **2006**, *16*, 532–535. [CrossRef] [PubMed]
67. Frobisher, C.; Maxwell, S. The estimation of food portion sizes: A comparison between using descriptions of portion sizes and a photographic food atlas by children and adults. *J. Hum. Nutr. Diet.* **2003**, *16*, 181–188. [CrossRef] [PubMed]
68. Harris-Fry, H.; Paudel, P.; Karn, M.; Mishra, N.; Thakur, J.; Paudel, V.; Harrisson, T.; Shrestha, B.; Manandhar, D.; Costello, A. Development and validation of a photographic food atlas for portion size assessment in the southern plains of Nepal. *Public Health Nutr.* **2016**, *19*, 2495–2507. [CrossRef]
69. Cade, J.E.; Warthon-Medina, M.; Albar, S.; Alwan, N.A.; Ness, A.; Roe, M.; Wark, P.A.; Greathead, K.; Burley, V.J.; Finglas, P. DIET@ NET: Best Practice Guidelines for dietary assessment in health research. *BMC Med.* **2017**, *15*, 202. [CrossRef] [PubMed]
70. Von Elm, E.; Altman, D.G.; Egger, M.; Pocock, S.J.; Gøtzsche, P.C.; Vandenbroucke, J.P. Strobe Initiative. The Strengthening the Reporting of Observational Studies in Epidemiology (STROBE) Statement: Guidelines for reporting observational studies. *Int. J. Surg.* **2014**, *12*, 1495–1499. [CrossRef] [PubMed]

nutrients

MDPI

Review

Adherence to Food-Based Dietary Guidelines: A Systemic Review of High-Income and Low- and Middle-Income Countries

Ana Carolina B. Leme [1,2,*], Sophia Hou [1], Regina Mara Fisberg [3], Mauro Fisberg [2] and Jess Haines [1]

1 Department of Family Relations and Applied Nutrition, University of Guelph, Guelph, ON N1G 2W1, Canada; shou01@uoguelph.ca (S.H.); jhaines@uoguelph.ca (J.H.)
2 Center of Excellence in Nutrition and Feeding Difficulties, PENSI Institute, Sabará Children's Hospital, José Luis Egydio Setúbal Foundation, São Paulo 01228-200, Brazil; mauro.fisberg@pensi.org.br
3 Department of Nutrition, School of Public University of São Paulo, São Paulo 01246-904, Brazil; regina.fisberg@gmail.com
* Correspondence: acarol.leme@gmail.com

Abstract: Research comparing the adherence to food-based dietary guidelines (FBDGs) across countries with different socio-economic status is lacking, which may be a concern for developing nutrition policies. The aim was to report on the adherence to FBDGs in high-income (HIC) and low-and-middle-income countries (LMIC). A systematic review with searches in six databases was performed up to June 2020. English language articles were included if they investigated a population of healthy children and adults (7–65 years), using an observational or experimental design evaluating adherence to national FBDGs. Findings indicate that almost 40% of populations in both HIC and LMIC do not adhere to their national FBDGs. Fruit and vegetables (FV) were most adhered to and the prevalence of adhering FV guidelines was between 7% to 67.3%. HIC have higher consumption of discretionary foods, while results were mixed for LMIC. Grains and dairy were consumed below recommendations in both HIC and LMIC. Consumption of animal proteins (>30%), particularly red meat, exceeded the recommendations. Individuals from HIC and LMIC may be falling short of at least one dietary recommendation from their country's guidelines. Future health policies, behavioral-change strategies, and dietary guidelines may consider these results in their development.

Keywords: dietary guidelines; adherence; diet intake; high-income countries; low- and middle-income countries

Citation: Leme, A.C.B.; Hou, S.; Fisberg, R.M.; Fisberg, M.; Haines, J. Adherence to Food-Based Dietary Guidelines: A Systemic Review of High-Income and Low- and Middle-Income Countries. *Nutrients* **2021**, *13*, 1038. https://doi.org/10.3390/nu13031038

Academic Editors: Clare Collins and George Moschon

Received: 18 February 2021
Accepted: 16 March 2021
Published: 23 March 2021

1. Introduction

The obesity epidemic is becoming the greatest public health concern worldwide. Globally, current data suggest that 1307 million adults are overweight and 671 million are obese, and the number of cases in low- and middle-income countries (LMIC) are rapidly reaching those observed in high-income countries (HIC) [1]. Morbidity and mortality related to obesity have been shown to follow a socio-economic gradient, with higher rates of chronic non-communicable diseases (NCD) among those from lower socio-economic positions [2]. Diet, along with other lifestyle behaviors, is an important risk factor for many NCD, and a large number of dietary components have been shown to be socio-economically patterned [3–5]. The sharing of cultural ideas is enhanced with the rapid development of the flow of goods, services, and capital, and the broadening of social networks via advanced communication technologies and enhanced transportation systems. Thus, globalization has accelerated diet and lifestyle changes—as seen with the westernization of diet quality [6].

Although first demonstrated in HIC, changes in diet quality have also been found in LMIC [7,8]. For instance, results from multi-center cross-sectional study, assessing the diet quality of individuals (n = 9218) for eight Latin American countries, showed that better scores for healthy eating were found in higher socio-economic populations, while scores for unhealthy diet were observed in lower socio-economic populations [9]. Similar results were found in an Australian population-based study (*n* = 11,247) [10]. Promoting the consumption of a different food sources and high-quality diet among populations across countries with different socio-economic status is an essential challenge to overcome [9,10].

A high diet quality consists of a variety of fruit and vegetables, lean meat and alternatives, low-fat dairy, whole grains, and an adequate ratio of fatty acids (i.e., omega 6 and 3 fatty acids), while minimizing the consumption of discretionary foods, such as those rich in added sugars, saturated fat, alcohol, and sodium [11–13]. Country-specific food-based dietary guidelines (FBDGs) are crucial for policy reference standards in food and nutrition, health, and agriculture [11,14]. FBDGs provide individuals dietary advice to promote health, prevent diet-related diseases.

More than 100 countries have developed or are currently developing their FBDG [11,15]. To date, reviews on FBDGs have focused on providing a descriptive summary of current global FBDG, evaluating differences and similarities of key elements of a healthy diet [16]. However, there is gap in reviews that evaluate adherence to FBDGs. Given that adherence to FBDG has important implications for the diet and health of individuals and populations, exploring levels of adherence to FBDG is important to inform public health policies, and behavior-change strategies. Furthermore, understanding how adherence may differ among HIC and LMIC is important given the disparities in diet quality across different parts of the world [17].

Identification of trends and dietary inadequacies and inequalities can help inform more targeted policies and behavior-change strategies to improve population health across different socio-economic countries [18]. However, research comparing adherence to FBDGs are lacking, which may be a concern for the development of nutrition policies. The aim of this study was to review the content of all available FBDGs and report on the adherence to the national FBDGs available in both HIC and LMIC, identified according to the Food and Agriculture Organization/World Health Organization (FAO/WHO) list of guidelines [13]. The comparison between HIC and LMIC adherence to national FBDGs will inform potential areas for improvements in future dietary guidelines.

2. Materials and Methods

The protocol for this systematic review was registered with PROSPERO (CRD 42020191131) [19] accessible at https://www.crd.york.ac.uk/prospero/, (17 March 2021) and has been reported according to Preferred Reporting Items for Systematic Reviews and Meta-Analysis (PRISMA) guidelines [20].

2.1. Identification of the Studies

A systematic search of six electronic databases (i.e., CINAHL, Lilacs/SciElo, ProQuest, PubMed, Scopus, Web of Science) was performed up to June 2020. Search results indexed within each database from the date of inception to the search date were screened by two authors (AL and SH). The following structured search strings were used: Adult OR Young Adult OR Male OR Female AND Dietary Guidelines OR Food Guidelines OR Dietary Recommendations OR Recommended Diet AND Socio-Economic OR Parental Education OR Paternal Education OR Maternal Education OR Income AND Dietary Intake OR Food Consumption OR Feeding Behavior OR Fruit OR Vegetable OR Fat OR Sodium OR Sugar. Relevant truncations and adjacencies were used to enhance results by allowing variations of the search terms. Manual review of the reference lists was conducted to identify studies that may have been missed. Records were downloaded to EndNote X9.2 and duplicates removed. Records were first assessed by title and abstract and then full text. All records were assessed for inclusion based on the defined criteria. Any uncertainties regarding the inclusion of a study were resolved through discussion among A.L. and S.H. or J.H.

2.2. Eligibility Criteria

This review was limited to studies published in English. All studies were assessed according to the following inclusion and exclusion criteria summarized according to the PICO (Participants, Intervention, Comparison, and Outcome) framework:

Participants: Studies were eligible if they included free-living children, adolescents, and adults until 60–65 years. The cut-off of 60 y was used in studies in LMIC and 65 y was used for studies in HIC, which was based on the countries' definition for older adults. National FBDGs generally focus on these populations [11] as individuals outside of this age range typically have special energy and nutrient needs [21,22] Studies that included participants with a pre-existing disease, an organic cause for obesity and other chronic NCD, or who were taking medication that could affect diet were excluded.

Intervention/Exposure: Studies were included if they used FBDGs to evaluate dietary intake in their own country. Guidelines developed by non-government institutions were excluded. Studies were included if they assess FBDGs through dietary assessment methods, such as food records, 24 h recalls (24hDR) and food frequency questionnaires (FFQ). Studies assessing diet quality and/or adherence to guideline using indexes (e.g., adherence to Dietary Guidelines for Americans using Healthy Eating Index, Alternate Healthy Eating Index, and Dietary Diversity Score) were excluded because they may have assessed additional items outside the FBDGs. Adherence to recommendations in national FBDGS was assessed based on individual level meeting or not meeting the national FBDGs food groups recommendations.

Comparison: Different study designs, i.e., cross-sectional, cohort, and interventions (randomized and non-randomized trials) were included in this review. If intervention design was used, no exclusion criteria were placed on duration, length of follow-up or date.

Outcome: The key outcome of this review was to assess the adherence of participants' dietary intake to their respective national FBDGs. Studies were excluded if they focused on an outcome other than adherence to a national FBDG, i.e., obesity or other chronic NCD.

A secondary outcome of this review was to assess the difference in adherence to each national FDBG according to their socio-economic classification for each country. Countries were dichotomized into two types of economy: HIC and LMIC; upper-middle, lower-middle, and low-income countries were identified as LMIC [23,24].

2.3. Data Extraction

Data were independently extracted from eligible studies by two reviewers (A.L. and S.H.) and cross-checked for accuracy by a third reviewer (J.H.). The extracted data included sample characteristics (age, sex, race/ethnicity, educational level), country, guideline used (name) and adherence to the guideline (reported as mean (± standard deviation/error, SD/SE) or frequency (%)).

2.4. Data Synthesis

Due to the heterogeneity of the study population and FBDG features (i.e., focused components, e.g., energy and nutrients vs. other degree of food processing), it was not possible to perform a meta-analysis. A narrative summary of the findings was conducted.

2.5. Quality Assessment and Risk of Bias

Study quality was assessed using a designed appraised tool developed by Effective Public Health Practice Project (EPHPP) [25,26] for observational, cross-sectional, before and after studies, and randomized controlled trials. Individual component and overall quality ratings were scores as 1 for strong, 2 for moderate, and 3 for weak.

3. Results

3.1. Literature Search and Screening

Studies included in this review are summarized in Figure 1. A total of 12,557 eligible papers were identified: 2851 from CIANHL/EBSCO, 411 from Lilacs/SciElo, 1307 from ProQuest, 2413 from PubMed, 4508 from Scopus, and 1052 from Web of Science. After excluding duplicates and reading titles, 2802 studies were assessed for eligibility. Finally, 616 full-text articles met the inclusion criteria and 49 were considered for the qualitative synthesis.

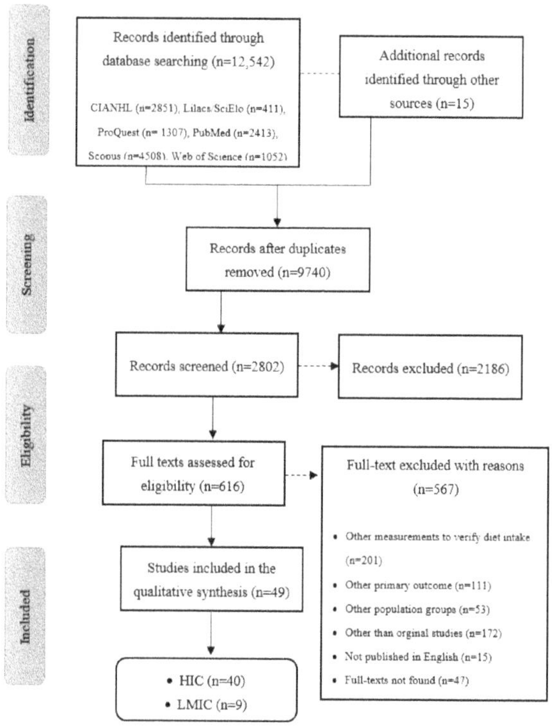

Figure 1. Flowchart of the included studies in the systematic review.

3.2. *Study Design Characteristics of the High-Income (HIC) and Low- and Middle-Income Countries (LMIC)*

From the 49 articles included, only 1 article (2.0%) was case-control [27] while 83.7% of the studies (*n* = 41) were cross-sectional, 4 (8.2%) longitudinal [28–31], and 3 (6.1%) randomized controlled trial [32–34]. From the 41 cross-sectional studies, 21 (42.9%) were performed in representative samples of individuals [35–51]. Table 1 shows details of the studies, which included the FBDG from each country. Thirty-nine studies were conducted in HIC, while the other 10 studies were from LMIC [41,42,51–58].

The average sample size for the HIC studies were 12,355 ranging from 32 [34] to 25,2425 [30], while average sample size for the LMIC were 745,050 ranging from 490 [57] to 32,898 [51]. The studies were conducted in the following countries: United States of America (USA) (*n* = 17) [27,32,34,35,46,48–50,59–66], Canada (*n* = 6) [31,36,44,67–69], Brazil (*n* = 4) [42,51,53,54], Switzerland (*n* = 4) [29,37,40,43], Australia (*n* = 3) [70–72], China (*n* = 2) [55,58], Belgium (*n* = 2) [38,73], Spain (*n* = 2) [30,47], Denmark (*n* = 1) [28], Egypt (*n* = 1) [52], Germany (*n* = 1) [74], Greenland (*n* = 1) [75], Iceland (*n* = 1) [33], Malaysia (*n* = 1) [56], Mexico (*n* = 1) [41], Qatar (*n* = 1) [39], South Korea (*n* = 1) [45], and Sri Lanka (*n* = 1) [57]. Most of the studies (*n* = 32, 65.3%) were conducted in adults ranging from 18 to 65 years old [27–29,32,34–37,39,40,42,43,48,50–55,57,59–61,64,65,67,70,71], five (10.2%) [30,38,44,62,73] include all age groups, but stratifying them (i.e., children, adolescents and/or adults), six (12.2%) [31,45,58,69,72,75] included only adolescents (10–19 years old), and four (8.2%) [33,49,56,63] included children and/or adolescents (2–19 years).

Table 1. Study characteristics and adherence to dietary guidelines.

Reference	Study Design	Country	N and Sex (% Female)	Age	Race/Ethnicity	Dietary Measurement	Dietary Guideline
High-Income countries							
Ewers et al., 2020 [28]	Longitudinal (2003–2015)	Denmark	100,191 45.2% female	20–30 y–40–100 y 58.0 ± 13.1	NR	FFQ	Danish Food Based Dietary Guidelines
Schwartz and Vernarelli 2019 [35]	Cross-sectional	USA	3194	≥18 yo	NR	1× 24hR	Dietary Guidelines for Americans/MyPlate or MyPyramid
Schuh et al., 2019 [29]	Longitudinal (1993–2016)	Switzerland	M = 689 50.5% female	35–74: 51.9 yo ± 11 yo	Non-Swiss: 31.4%	FFQ	Swiss Dietary Guidelines
Schroeter et al., 2019 [27]	Case-study	USA	57	19.94 ± 1.20	NR	1× 24hR	Dietary Guidelines for Americans/MyPlate
Irwin et al., 2019 [70]	Cross-sectional	Australia	115 67.8% female	M = 22 ± 5 y	NR	Records	Australian Dietary Guidelines
Harrison et al., 2019 [36]	Cross-sectional	Canada	50.2% female	M = 45.0 ± 0.3 y	NR	1× 24hR	2019 Canada Food Guide
Dıaz-Méndez and Garcıa-Espejo 2019 [30]	Longitudinal (2006–2011–12)	Spain	M = 25,2425	≥16 yo	NR	FFQ	Guide to Healthy Eating/Spanish Society for Community Nutrition
Mestral et al. 2019 [37]	Cross-Sectional	Switzerland	15450 53.0% female	48.8 ± 17.4 y	NR	FFQ	Swiss Dietary Guidelines
Bel et al. 2019 [38]	Cross-Sectional	Belgium	3146	3–64 y: stratified by age	NR	1× 24hR + FFQ	Flemish Active Food Triangle
Schwartz and Vernarelli et al. 2018 [35]	Cross-sectional	USA	3194	18–50+ y	NR	1× 24hR	Dietary Guidelines for Americans/MyPlate or MyPyramid
Jun et al., 2018 [59]	Cross-sectional	USA	3142 100% female	19–70 y	Non-Hispanic, White: 51.8% Non-Hispanic, Black: 19.3% Hispanic: 22.2%	1× 24hR	Dietary Guidelines for Americans/MyPlate
Jones et al. 2018	Cross-sectional	UK	2045 56.5% female	≥18 y	NR	3d food record	UK Government Scientific Advisory Committee on Nutrition

Table 1. *Cont.*

Reference	Study Design	Country	N and Sex (% Female)	Age	Race/Ethnicity	Dietary Measurement	Dietary Guideline
Brassard et al. 2018 [67]	Cross-sectional	Canada	1147 50.2% female	18–65 y	Caucasian: 94.3% African-American: 2.4% Hispanic: 1.7% Other: 1.6%	3× 24hR	2007 Canada Food Guide
Al Thani et al., 2018 [39]	Cross-sectional	Qatar	1109 48.6% female	18–64 y	NR	FFQ	Qatar Dietary Guidelines
Stroebele-Benschop et al. 2018 [74]	Cross-sectional	German	103 75.7% female	18–30: 24.3 ± 3.1 y	NR	FFQ	German Nutrition Society
Chatelan et al., 2017 [40]	Cross-sectional	Switzerland	2086 54.7% female	18–75: 46.8 ± 15.8 y	NR	2× 24hR	Swiss Dietary Guidelines
Mishra et al., 2015 [71]	Cross-sectional	Australia	16227 100% female	18–75: 43.5 ± 1.5 y	NR	FFQ	Australian Guide to Healthy Eating
Schumacher et al., 2014 [72]	Cross-sectional	Australia	332 100% female	13.7: 13.4–13.9 y	Australian: 86% (Aboriginal and Torres Strait Islander: 11%) European: 10% Asian: 1% Other: 3%	FFQ	Australian Guide to Healthy Eating
Yen and Lewis 2013 [32]	Randomized controlled trial	USA	85:41 intervention vs. 44 control 100% female	53.8 ± 6.6 y	Control vs. Intervention White: 95.5 vs. 100% African-American: 2.3% Hispanic: 2.3%	FFQ	Dietary Guidelines for Americans/MyPlate
Abreu et al., 2013 [43]	Cross-sectional	Switzerland	4371 53.8% female	35–75: 57.6 ± 10.5 y	Switzerland: 65.1%	FFQ	Swiss Dietary Guidelines
Black and Billette 2013 [44]	Cross-sectional	Canada	33,850 43.2% female	2–51+ y	French-British Canadian: 57% Other: 43.1%	2× 24hR	2007 Canada Food Guide

Table 1. *Cont.*

Reference	Study Design	Country	N and Sex (% Female)	Age	Race/Ethnicity	Dietary Measurement	Dietary Guideline
Rossiter et al., 2012 [31]	Longitudinal (2002 and 2005)	Canada	247 46.4% female	14–16 y	NR	FFQ	2007 Canada Food Guide
Park et al., 2012 [45]	Cross-sectional	South Korea	394 53.8% female	13.96 ± 0.44 y	NR	1× 24hR	Korean National Dietary Guidelines
McDaniel and Belury, 2012 [60]	Cross-sectional	USA	60 50.0% female	25.5 ± 6.3 y	Non-Hispanic, White: 78.3% Non-Hispanic, Black: 5.0% Asian: 11.7% Indian: 5.0%	FFQ	Dietary Guidelines for Americans, MyPyramid
Kirkpatrick et al., 2012 [46]	Cross-sectional	USA	16,338 adults and children		Non-Hispanic, White: 41.1% Non-Hispanic, Black: 25.8% Mexican-American: 25.3%	1× 24hR	Dietary Guidelines for Americans, MyPyramid
Allen et al., 2011 [68]	Cross-sectional	Canada	291 71.7% female	20–35+ y	NR	Food record	2007 Canada Dietary Guide
Winham and Florian 2010 [61]	Cross-sectional	USA	171 100% female	18–60: 34.4 ± 9.1 y	Hispanic: 76.7% Bicultural or English dominant: 23.4%	FFQ	Dietary Guidelines for Americans, MyPyramid
Niclasen and Schnor 2010 [75]	Cross-sectional	Greenland	2462	11–17 y	NR	FFQ	Greenlandic Board of Nutrition
Kristjansdottir et al., 2010 [33]	Randomized controlled trial	Iceland	106: 58 intervention and 48 control	3–9 y	NR	3d food records	Food-based Dietary Guidelines set for Icelandic population
Kreb-smith et al., 2010 [62]	Cross-sectional	USA	16338	2–71+ y (stratified by age group and sex)	NR	2× 24hR	Dietary Guidelines for Americans, MyPyramid
Vandevijvere et al., 2009 [73]	Cross-sectional	Belgium	3168 43.4% female	≥15 y (stratified by age)	NR	2× 24hR + FFQ	Flemish Active Food Triangle

Table 1. *Cont.*

Reference	Study Design	Country	N and Sex (% Female)	Age	Race/Ethnicity	Dietary Measurement	Dietary Guideline
Kranz et al., 2009 [63]	Cross-sectional	USA	214 45.8% female	2–12 y (stratified age)	Non-Hispanic, White: 47.7% Non-Hispanic, Black: 43.5% Non-Hispanic, Asian: 18.7% Other: 10.3% Hispanic: 14.0%	3× 24hR	Dietary Guidelines for Americans, MyPyramid
John et al., 2008 [69]	Cross-sectional	Canada	1410	Grade 7 and 11 students	NR	1× 24hR + FFQ	2007 Canada Food Guide
Serra-Majem et al., 2007 [47]	Cross-sectional	Spain	2160 53.9% female	NR	NR	2× 24hR + FFQ	Guide to Healthy Eating/Spanish Society for Community Nutrition
Tande et al., 2004 [48]	Cross-sectional	USA	9111 51.4% female	20–59: 37.4 ± 0.2 y	Non-Hispanic, White: 75% Non-Hispanic, Black: 10.4% Mexican-American: 5.9% Others: 8.5%	1× 24hR	Dietary Guidelines for Americans, Food Pyramid
Pullen and Walker, 2002 [64]	Cross-sectional	USA	371 100% female	34–86: 62 y	White: 92.6% Black: 0.5% Hispanic: 2.2% Asian: 3.3% Native American: 0.8% Other: 0.5%	FFQ	Dietary Guidelines for Americans, Food Pyramid
Anding et al., 2001 [65]	Cross-sectional	USA	103 100% female	17–42: 21.6 ± 4.6 y	Black: 23% White: 32% Asian: 20% Hispanic: 23%	3d food records	Dietary Guidelines for Americans, Food Pyramid
Brady et al., 2000 [66]	Cross-sectional	USA	109 56.9% female	7–14:10.2 ± 1.7 y	NR	1× 24hR	Dietary Guidelines for Americans, Food Pyramid

Table 1. *Cont.*

Reference	Study Design	Country	N and Sex (% Female)	Age	Race/Ethnicity	Dietary Measurement	Dietary Guideline
Munõz et al., 1997 [49]	Cross-sectional	USA	3307 50.2% female	2–19: stratified by age	White, Non-Hispanic: 67.9% Black, Non-Hispanic: 16.6% Hispanic: 11.9%	2× 24hR	Dietary Guidelines for Americans, Food Pyramid
Cleveland et al., 1997 [50]	Cross-sectional	USA	8181 58.7% female	20–60+: stratified by age	White, Non-Hispanic:77.1% Black, Non-Hispanic: 11.8% Hispanic: 8.3% Others: 2.8%	1× 24hR + 2 food records	Dietary Guidelines for Americans, Food Pyramid
Gambera et al., 1995 [34]	Randomized-trial	USA	32 37.5% female	33.3 ± 6 y	NR	3d food records	Dietary Guidelines for Americans, Food Pyramid
Low- and middle-income countries							
Steele et al., 2020 [54]	Cross-sectional	Brazil	10,116 78.0% female	18–60+ y: stratified by age	NR	FFQ	Dietary Guideline for the Brazilian Population 2014
Ansari and Samara 2018 [52]	Cross-sectional	Egypt	2422 53.8% female	18.9 ± 1.4 y	NR	FFQ	WHO dietary guidelines for Eastern Mediterranean region
Sousa and Costa 2018 [53]	Cross-sectional	Brazil	506 57.0% female	20–50+ y: stratified by age	NR	2× 24hR	Brazilian Dietary Guideline 2006/Food Pyramid
Louzada et al., 2018 [51]	Cross-sectional	Brazil	32,898	≥19 y	NR	2× 24hR	Dietary Guideline for the Brazilian Population 2014
Tian et al., 2017 [55]	Cross-sectional	China	14,452 51.9% female	20–59: 42.8 ± 10.3 y	NR	3× 24hR	Chinese Food Pagoda
Batis et al.., 2016 [41]	Cross-sectional	Mexico	7983 50.6% female	5–20+ y: stratified by age	NR	1× 24hR	Mexican Dietary Guidelines
Chin Koo et al., 2016 [56]	Cross-sectional	Malaysia	1773 48.6% female	7–12: stratified by age	Malay: 59.2% Chinese: 19.5% Indian: 6.7% Others: 14.7%	FFQ	Malaysian Dietary Guidelines
Verly-Jr et al. 2013 [42]	Cross-sectional	Brazil	1661 56.5% female	37.7 ± 29.9 y	NR	2× 24hR	Dietary Guidelines for Brazilian population/Pyramid

Table 1. *Cont.*

Reference	Study Design	Country	N and Sex (% Female)	Age	Race/Ethnicity	Dietary Measurement	Dietary Guideline
Jayawardena et al., 2013 [57]	Cross-sectional	Sri Lanka	490 65.5% female	48.3 ± 15.6 y	Sinhalese: 75.6% Muslim: 5.9% Sri Lankan Tamil: 9.5% Indian Tamil: 9%	2× 24hR	Food-based Dietary Guidelines for Sri Lanka and Dietary Guidelines for Brazilian population/Pyramid
Zhang et al., 2012 [58]	Cross-sectional	China	2204 53.8% female	12–17: 15.1 ± 1.9 y	NR	FFQ	Chinese Food Pagoda

24hR: 24 h recall; M = mean; FFQ: Food Frequency Questionnaire, NR: Not Reported; Y = years. Note: Countries were identified as high and low- to middle-income countries based on the World Bank criteria.

3.3. *Adherence to the National Food-Based Dietary Guidelines (FBDGs)*

The adherence to the dietary guidelines is reported on Table 2. The majority of the studies reported adherence to the national FBDGs as percentage of meeting the recommendations [28–30,35–41,43,44,46–48,51–53,56,58,59,61,64,65,68,72,74,75], while only four [35,45,48,70] reported as mean (±SD/SE) servings/day of a certain food group. Almost 40% of the population from both HIC and LMIC do not adhere their national FBDGs [28,29,37,43,44,51,52,56,61–63,65,75].

Adherence to National FBDGs in HIC and LMIC by Food Groups

The percentages of meeting the guidelines in the HIC ranged from 14.0% [75] in Greenland to 43.0% [65] in the USA, and in the LMIC from 40.0% [56] with Malaysians and 45.0% [52] with Egyptians meeting at least one recommendation from their country-specific FBDG. The food groups that were most frequently reported as having been met for the dietary guidelines were fruits and vegetables (n = 19, 38.8%) [27,30,35,37,38,40,41, 43,44,48,52,53,56,64,70,72,74,75]. The adherence to fruit group recommendations in HIC varies from 14% in a population of school-age children from Greenland [75] to 67.3% in the overall Spanish population [30], and in LMIC from 13.4% in Malaysian children and adolescents [56] to 49.4% in the overall Brazilian population [53]. The adherence to vegetable group guidelines in HIC varies from 11.4% in the US population [59] to 43.7% in the Spanish population [30], and in LMIC varies from 9.5% in Malaysian adolescents [56] to 74.1% in the Brazilian population [53]. Some HIC and LMIC reported the combined fruit and vegetable guideline adherence: 18% in Swiss population [40], 7–16% in Mexican population [41] and 33.4% in Egyptian adolescents [52]. The adherence reported in HIC was less than 1.5 and 3 servings/day for fruit and vegetables (FV), respectively [48,70]. More specifically, a Canadian study with 33,850 individuals over 2 years reported the adherence to recommendations for dark green vegetables and orange fruits of 12% and 8%, respectively [44].

Dietary intake of discretionary foods, i.e., foods high in fat and oils, sugars and sweets, and sodium, were reported by 11 studies (22.4%) [30,35,36,38,41,51–53,70,74,75]. In HIC, studies were mixed in regards to reporting food groups, i.e., one study reported that 36.5% were exceeding the recommendations for sweets [30], 90.1% for oils [74], and 14.7% and 18.6% for cookies and soft-drinks, respectively [75]. The average servings/day for discretionary foods and fats/oils were 1.5 [70]. Studies in LMIC, also varied when reporting the groups of discretionary foods: 99.6% and 58.3% of adults from Brazil exceeded recommendations for fats/oils and sugars [53]; 56.4% and 58.9% of adolescents from Egypt for sweets, fast-food and canned foods [52]; and 84% and 72% of children and adolescents in Mexico for sugar-sweetened beverages and high-saturated fat and added sugars [41]. Louzada et al. [51] showed that only 20.4% of the Brazilian population were eating ultra-processed foods.

Other food groups from national FBDGs reported in the studies included: grains (whole vs. refined), proteins (eggs, meats, and fish), and dairy and alternatives. Reported adherence to guidelines for grains and cereals were 3.8% for women in the USA [64], 79.2% for Greenlandic adolescents consuming potatoes [75] and 50.5% of Germans consuming whole grains [74]. Schwartz and Vernarelli [35] found that individuals that used the MyPlate® guideline to inform eating patterns had higher intakes of whole grains (1.1 to 0.8 servings/day) and refined grains (6.0 to 6.6 servings/day) as compared to those who did not use the guideline. In LMIC, less than 40% population of the met recommendations for adequate grain intake in their national FBDGs, [53,56,58], especially among younger participants. In HIC, adherence to milk and alternatives guidelines ranged from 8.4% in Switzerland [43] to 51.9% in US women [64]; and in LMIC from 5.5% with Malaysian youth [56] to 12.5% in an overall sample of Brazilian adolescents and adults [53]. One Australian [70] and one USA [48] study reported an average of 1.0 serving/day of dairy group. Finally, HIC studies that evaluated the adherence to guidelines for meat and alternatives showed an average intake 30.0% higher than the recommendations [30,37,43,64,74,75], with one study showing 95% of the population meeting the recommendations [74]. Alternatively, the adherence to guidelines for meat and alternatives in LMIC showed mixed results. In Brazil [53] and in China [58] adherence was greater than 65.0%, but in Egypt [52], Malaysia [56], and Mexico [41] it was less than 23.0%. Koo et al. [56] only reported the intake for fish and seafood, and the majority of the studies both from HIC and LMIC reported a high prevalence for (red) meat consumption.

3.4. Risk of Bias of the Included Studies

From all the included studies, selection bias (2.2 ± SD 0.5) was the most reported bias, while study design (0.1 ± SD 1.2) the less reported bias. Figure 2 shows the risk of bias of each component rating for the included studies.

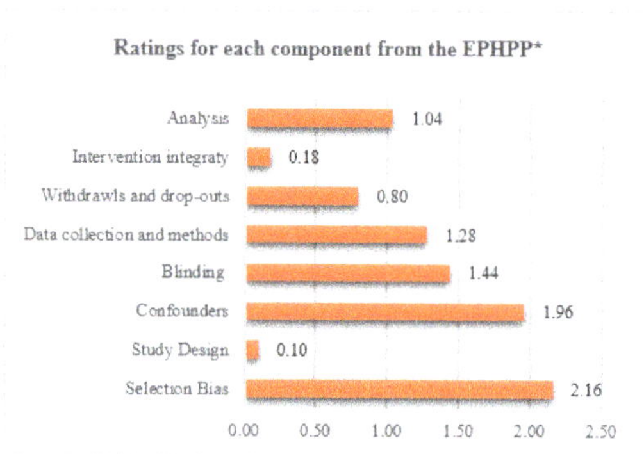

*EPHPP: Effective Public Health Practice Project

Figure 2. Risk of bias of the included studies based on the Effective Public Health Practice Project: ratings for each component.

Table 2. Population adherence to the dietary guidelines across different high- and low- to middle-income countries.

Reference	Dietary Guidelines	Pictorial Image	Food Groups	Include Physical Activity Messages	Summary Results
			High-income countries		
Ewers et al., 2020 [28]	Danish Food Based Dietary Guidelines	No image Key messages	Fruits and vegetables Fish Whole Grains Lean meats and lean cold meats Low-fat dairy products Saturated fat sources Sodium sources Sugar Water	Yes	Only 10% of the participants were identified as very high adherence; 17.3% high adherence; 54.4% intermediate adherence; 8.3% low adherence; and 9.9% very low-adherence. Based on table categorization of meeting the guideline proposed by the authors.
Schwartz and Vernarelli 2019 [35]	Dietary Guidelines for Americans	Plate and Pyramid	Fruits Vegetables Grains Dairy Protein Foods	No	Following MyPlate and MyPyramid showed better adherence to the recommendations than those who did not follow. More whole grains (1.1 vs. 0.8 servings), and vegetables (1.5 vs. 1.4 servings) Less refined grains (6 vs. 6.6 servings) and added sugar (18.6 vs. 20.5 tbs) sources
Schroeter et al., 2019 [27]	Dietary Guidelines for Americans	Plate and Pyramid	Fruits Vegetables Grains Dairy Protein Foods	No	Increased consumption of food groups after participating in education groups Fruit and vegetables and whole grains
Schuh et al., 2019 [29]	Swiss Dietary Guidelines	Pyramid	Beverages Vegetables and Fruits Grains, potatoes and pulses Dairy products, meat, eggs, fish and tofu Oils, fats, and nuts Sweets, salty snacks, alcohol	Yes	Participants are not meeting the guidelines five year after issuing the guideline, regardless of socio-demographic characteristics. Meeting at least three recommendations 1993: 26.1% 2006: 24.9%

Table 2. *Cont.*

Reference	Dietary Guidelines	Pictorial Image	Food Groups	Include Physical Activity Messages	Summary Results
Irwin et al., 2019 [70]	Australian Dietary Guidelines	Plate	Grains (mostly whole grains) Vegetables and legumes/beans Lean meats, and poultry, fish, eggs, tofu, nuts and seeds, and legumes/beans Milk, yogurt, cheese and/or alternatives mostly reduced fat Fruit Use small amounts of oils and fats Only sometimes and small amounts: sugar sweetened beverages, salty snacks and sweets.	No	Participants are not meeting the guidelines for the majority of the food groups Lean meats, and alternatives were the only group that students were meeting the recommendations Meeting the recommendations (female vs. male): Fruit: 0.7 vs. 1.3 servings/day Vegetables: 2.7 vs. 3.2 Meat and Alternatives: 3.0 vs. 2.2 Dairy and Alternatives: 1.3 Bread, cereals, grains: 4.3 vs. 3.3 Discretionary: 1.3 vs. 2.0 Fats and oils: 1.7 vs. 1.0
Harrison et al., 2019 [36]	2019 Canada Food Guide	Plate	Vegetables and Fruits Protein foods Whole grains Water	No	Greater consumption of saturated fats from all the food groups of the Canada Food Guide Protein Foods (milk and alternatives; and meats and alternatives) contributed 47.8% in total for saturated fats. "All other foods" were main contributors: fruit juices, refined grains, and salty snacks.
Diaz-Mendez and García-Espejo 2019 [30]	Guide to Healthy Eating–Spanish Society for Community Nutrition	Pyramid	Whole grains Fruits Vegetables and legumes Oils (especially olive oils) Lean meats, poultry, fish, eggs Beans and nuts Milk and dairy Water	Yes	Percent of participants meeting the guidelines: Fruits: 67.3% Vegetables: 43.7% Meat: 52.3% Breads: 86.6% Percent of participants not meeting the guidelines: Eggs: 59.3% Fish: 46.4% Pasta-rice-potatoes: 47.3% Sweets: 36.5%

Table 2. *Cont.*

Reference	Dietary Guidelines	Pictorial Image	Food Groups	Include Physical Activity Messages	Summary Results
Mestral et al., 2019 [37]	Swiss Dietary Guidelines	Pyramid	Beverages Vegetables and Fruits Grains, potatoes and pulses Dairy products, meat, eggs, fish and tofu Oils, fats, and nuts Sweets, salty snacks, alcohol	Yes	Less than 40% of the participants adhere to all of the guidelines Percent of participants meeting the guidelines: Fruits: 38.8% Vegetables: 20.5% Dairy: 19.4% Fish: 22.5% Meat: 9.1% Liquids (beverages): 39.4%
Bel et al., 2019 [38]	Flemish Active Food Triangle	Triangle	Cereals and Potatoes Vegetables Fruits Meat, fish, eggs, and meat alternatives Dairy and calcium-enriched products Oils and fatty products Sugary products Unsweetened beverages (water and tea)	Yes	Between years the participants adherence to guidelines deteriorated over the time for most groups Change in percent of participants meeting the guidelines: Water and sugar-free drinks: △+7% Bread and cereals: △−15% Potato, rice, and pasta: △+2% Vegetable: △−1% Fruit (including juices): △−3% Fruit (excluding juices): △−1% Dairy products and calcium-enriched products: △−1% Cheese: △+4% Meat, eggs, fish, and substitutes: △−2% Spreadable and cooking fat: △−4%
Schwartz and Vernarelli, 2018 [35]	Dietary Guidelines for Americans	MyPlate	Fruits Vegetables Grains Dairy Protein Foods	No	Participants who follow a MyPlate plan were able to meet the food groups requirements for the following groups: Dark green and orange vegetables Refined grains Whole grains Total meat Milk and dairy Sodium sources

Table 2. *Cont.*

Reference	Dietary Guidelines	Pictorial Image	Food Groups	Include Physical Activity Messages	Summary Results
Jun et al., 2018 [59]	Dietary Guidelines for Americans	MyPlate	Fruits Vegetables Grains Dairy Protein Foods	No	A small percentage of participants met the dietary guidelines: Fruits: 21.3% Vegetables: 11.4% Whole grains: 4.3%
Brassard et al., 2018 [67]	2007 Canada's Food Guide	Rainbow	Vegetables and fruits Grain products Milk and alternatives Meat and alternatives	No	Participants were consuming less than the recommendations for fruits and vegetables, and grain-products. Milk and alternatives; and Meat and alternatives are in line with the recommendations.
Stroebele-Benschop et al., 2018 [74]	German Dietary Guidelines	Circle	Cereals and potatoes Vegetables Fruits Milk and dairy products Meat, sausages, fish, and eggs Fats and oils	No	Participants were not meeting the recommendations for most of the food groups. Percentage of participants that met the recommendations: Vegetables: 12.9% Fruit: 37.6% Whole grain: 50.5% Milk and milk products: 45.5% Meat and meat products: 95.0% Fish: 15.8% Eggs: 80.2% Oil: 90.1% Fat: 89.1% Water and unsweetened beverages: 76.2%
Chatelan et al., 2017 [40]	Swiss Dietary Guidelines	Pyramid	Beverages Vegetables and Fruits Grains, potatoes and pulses Dairy products, meat, eggs, fish and tofu Oils, fats, and nuts Sweets, salty snacks, alcohol	Yes	Less than 1% follow all the food groups. Percentage of participants that met the recommendations: Fruit and vegetables: 18.0% Non-caloric beverages: 75.0%

Table 2. *Cont.*

Reference	Dietary Guidelines	Pictorial Image	Food Groups	Include Physical Activity Messages	Summary Results
Mishra et al., 2015 [71]	Australian Dietary Guidelines	Plate	Grains (mostly whole grains) Vegetables and legumes/beans Lean meats, and poultry, fish, eggs, tofu, nuts and seeds, and legumes/beans Milk, yogurt, cheese and/or alternatives mostly reduced fat Fruit Use small amounts of oils and fats Only sometimes and small amounts: sugar sweetened beverages, salty snacks and sweets.	No	Younger age participants were not meeting the recommendations for all the food groups. Middle-age participants were not meeting the recommendations for cereals, vegetables, and meat and alternatives.
Schumacher et al., 2014 [72]	Australian Dietary Guidelines	Plate	Grains (mostly whole grains) Vegetables and legumes/beans Lean meats, and poultry, fish, eggs, tofu, nuts and seeds, and legumes/beans Milk, yogurt, cheese and/or alternatives mostly reduced fat Fruit Use small amounts of oils and fats Only sometimes and small amounts: sugar sweetened beverages, salty snacks and sweets.	No	Participants were meeting the recommendations for the guideline for the majority of the groups. Fruit: 23.8% Vegetables: 28.6% Dairy: 15.7% Breads and Cereals: 5.7% The only exception was for the meat and substitutes group, where 69.3% were meeting them.
Yen and Lewis 2013 [32]	Dietary Guidelines for Americans	MyPlate	Fruits Vegetables Grains Dairy Protein Foods	No	After participating in an educational program, participants did not improve their intake for the groups: grains, vegetables, and meat and alternatives. They improved their intake for fruit, dairy, and oil.

Table 2. *Cont.*

Reference	Dietary Guidelines	Pictorial Image	Food Groups	Include Physical Activity Messages	Summary Results
De Abreu et al. 2013 [43]	Swiss Dietary Guidelines	Pyramid	Beverages Vegetables and Fruits Grains, potatoes and pulses Dairy products, meat, eggs, fish and tofu Oils, fats, and nuts Sweets, salty snacks, alcohol	Yes	Only 23% of the sample were meeting at least 3 recommendations. Fruits: 39.4% Vegetables: 7.1% Dairy: 8.4% Majority were meeting the recommendations for meat and fish. Meat: 61.3% Fish: 66.4%
Black and Billette, 2013 [44]	2007 Canada's Food Guide	Rainbow	Vegetables and fruits Grain products Milk and alternatives Meat and alternatives	No	Only 26.3% of participants met all of the recommendations. Dark green: 12% Orange fruit: 8% Potatoes: 10% Other: 43%
Rossiter et al., 2012 [31]	2007 Canada's Food Guide	Rainbow	Vegetables and fruits Grain products Milk and alternatives Meat and alternatives	No	Participants were consuming below the recommendations for fruits and vegetables, and grains. Milk and dairy were consumed in the recommendation range. Meat and alternatives were consumed above the recommendations.
Park et al., 2012 [45]	Korean National Dietary Guidelines	Wheels	Fruits Vegetables Meat, fish, eggs, and beans Milk Grains	Yes	Overall adherence was 3.23 (1–5 Likert scale) for meeting the recommendations.
Kirpatrick et al., 2012 [46]	Dietary Guidelines for Americans	MyPlate	Fruits Vegetables Grains Dairy Protein Foods	No	Over 50% of adults met the recommendations for total grains, meats, and beans; less then 20% of adults met the recommendations for other groups

Table 2. *Cont.*

Reference	Dietary Guidelines	Pictorial Image	Food Groups	Include Physical Activity Messages	Summary Results
Mc Daniel and Belury 2012 [60]	Dietary Guidelines for Americans	MyPlate	Fruits Vegetables Grains Dairy Protein Foods	No	Participants' intakes of fruit and vegetables were below the recommendations. Meat and beans; and Milk and dairy were within the recommendations. Grains were above the recommendations Oils were below the recommendations.
Allen et al., 2011 [68]	2007 Canada's Food Guide	Rainbow	Vegetables and fruits Grain products Milk and alternatives Meat and alternatives	No	Less than 48% of the sample were meeting the recommendations for all groups (with females having a better adherence then males) Male vs. Female Vegetables and fruits: 9.5% vs. 17.9% Milk and alternatives: 16.2% vs. 22.2% Grain products: 16.2% vs. 38.2%
Winham and Florian, 2011 [61]	Dietary Guidelines for Americans	Pyramid	Fruits Vegetables Grains Milk Meat	Yes	Less than 30% of Hispanics adhere to the guidelines 7% of bi-racial group adhere to the guidelines.
Niclasen and Schnor, 2011 [75]	Greenlandic (similar to the Danish guidelines)	No image	Fruits Vegetables Traditional foods Whole grains Fat Sugar Water	Yes	Students meeting the guidelines varied from 14% to 87% depending on the groups. Diet variety: 87.0% Marine animals: 31.6% Local terrestrial animals and birds: 37.1% Fish: 31.8% Fruit: 14.8% Vegetables: 38.9% Potatoes: 79.7% Candies: 14.7% Soft-drinks: 18.6% Pre-cooked dinner: 83.4%

Table 2. *Cont.*

Reference	Dietary Guidelines	Pictorial Image	Food Groups	Include Physical Activity Messages	Summary Results
Kristjansdottir et al., 2010 [33]	Food-based dietary Guidelines set for Icelandic Population	Circle/Plate	Fruits and vegetables Cereals and cereal products Dairy products Animal source foods and nuts Oils and visible fats Water	Yes	After the intervention there was an improvement on the food groups intake, however, the participants from both intervention and control groups were still not meeting the recommendations.
Krebs-Smith et al., 2010 [62]	Dietary Guidelines for Americans	Pyramid	Fruits Vegetables Grains Milk Meat	Yes	Majority of the population did not meet the recommendations for all the food groups, with exception for total grains, and meat and beans.
Vandevijvere et al., 2009 [73]	Flemish Active Food Triangle	Triangle	Cereals and Potatoes Vegetables Fruits Meat, fish, eggs, and meat alternatives Dairy and calcium-enriched products Oils and fatty products Sugary products Unsweetened beverages (water and tea)	Yes	Population was consuming below the recommendations for liquids, grains, vegetables, fruits, and milk and soya products. Population was consuming above the recommendations for meats/fish/eggs/legumes/nuts/substitutes
Kranz et al., 2009 [63]	Dietary Guidelines for Americans	Pyramid	Fruits Vegetables Grains Milk Meat	Yes	Younger children presented a higher adherence to the guidelines than older children. Older children have less than 40% adherence for fruit and vegetables.
St. John et al., 2009 [69]	2007 Canada's Food Guide	Rainbow	Vegetables and fruits Grain products Milk and alternatives Meat and alternatives	No	Fruit and vegetables are the groups for which the children have the lowest adherence. Milk and dairy; and meat and alternatives have been less adherent to some specific subgroups: normal weight and overweight.

Table 2. *Cont.*

Reference	Dietary Guidelines	Pictorial Image	Food Groups	Include Physical Activity Messages	Summary Results
Serra-Majem et al., 2008 [47]	Guide to Healthy Eating–Spanish Society for Community Nutrition	Pyramid	Whole grains Fruits Vegetables and legumes Oils (especially olive oils) Lean meats, poultry, fish, eggs Beans and nuts Milk and dairy Water	Yes	Majority of the population were not meeting the recommendations for fruits (72.7%), vegetables (57.6%), and beans (58.1%). Majority of the population exceeded recommendation for intake of fatty meats and sausages (56.1%). Intake for bake goods was 20.2%, soft-drinks 21.8%, and fats 23.6%, and sugars 33.5%.
Tande et al., 2004 [48]	1992 Dietary Guidelines for Americans	Pyramid	Bread, Cereal, Rice, Pasta Fruit Vegetable Meat, Poultry, Fish. Dry Beans, Eggs, and Nuts Milk, Yogurt, Cheese Fats and oils Sweets	No	Participants were not meeting the recommendations for all the groups, consuming fewer than the recommended. Serving/1000 kcal Dairy: 0.95 Fruit: 0.70 Vegetables: 1.55 Grain: 3.19 Meat: 1.06
Pullen and Walker, 2002 [64]	1992 Dietary Guidelines for Americans	Pyramid	Bread, Cereal, Rice, Pasta Fruit Vegetable Meat, Poultry, Fish, Dry Beans, Eggs, and Nuts Milk, Yogurt, Cheese Fats and oils Sweets	No	Women are not adhering the recommendations for the pyramid groups, with exception for fruits that have adherence of 65.4%. Meat: 38.6% Dairy: 48.1% Vegetables: 22.3% Grain products: 3.8%
Anding et al., 2001 [65]	1992 Dietary Guidelines for Americans	Pyramid	Bread, Cereal, Rice, Pasta Fruit Vegetable Meat, Poultry, Fish, Dry Beans, Eggs, and Nuts Milk, Yogurt, Cheese Fats and oils Sweets	No	Less than 43% of the participants followed at least one recommendation from the guideline. Fruits, vegetables, and milk were consumed less than the recommendations. More than 60% of the participants exceeded the recommendations for fats, sugar and sodium.

Table 2. *Cont.*

Reference	Dietary Guidelines	Pictorial Image	Food Groups	Include Physical Activity Messages	Summary Results
Brady et al., 2000 [66]	1992 Dietary Guidelines for Americans	Pyramid	Bread, Cereal, Rice, Pasta Fruit Vegetable Meat, Poultry, Fish, Dry Beans, Eggs, and Nuts Milk, Yogurt, Cheese Fats and oils Sweets	No	Participants from both sexes and ethnicities were consuming less than the recommendations for fruits and dairy. Participants also exceeded the recommendations for sugar and discretionary foods.
Muñoz et al., 1997 [49]	1992 Dietary Guidelines for Americans	Pyramid	Bread, Cereal, Rice, Pasta Fruit Vegetable Meat, Poultry, Fish, Dry Beans, Eggs, and Nuts Milk, Yogurt, Cheese Fats and oils Sweets	No	Participants were not meeting (consuming less) the recommendations for fruit, vegetables, and grains. Dairy and meat intake met the recommendations.
Cleveland et al., 1997 [50]	1992 Dietary Guidelines for Americans	Pyramid	Bread, Cereal, Rice, Pasta Fruit Vegetable Meat, Poultry, Fish, Dry Beans, Eggs, and Nuts Milk, Yogurt, Cheese Fats and oils Sweets	No	Participants were not meeting the recommendations (consuming less) for grains, dairy and fruits. Vegetables and meats were within the recommendations.
Gambera et al., 1995 [34]	1992 Dietary Guidelines for Americans	Pyramid	Bread, Cereal, Rice, Pasta Fruit Vegetable Meat, Poultry, Fish, Dry Beans, Eggs, and Nuts Milk, Yogurt, Cheese Fats and oils Sweets	No	After intervention participants increased their intake for milk, vegetables, fruits, and grains, and decrease intake of meats.

Table 2. *Cont.*

Reference	Dietary Guidelines	Pictorial Image	Food Groups	Include Physical Activity Messages	Summary Results
			Low- and middle-income countries		
Steele et al., 2020 [54]	Dietary Guidelines for the Brazilian population 2014	No	Unprocessed or minimally processed foods Processed culinary ingredients Processed foods Ultra-processed foods	No	Slight increase in consumption of unprocessed/minimally processed foods after coronavirus disease 2019 (COVID-19) pandemic. Consumption of ultra-processed foods remains the same after COVID-19.
Sousa and Costa, 2018 [53]	Dietary Guidelines for the Brazilian population 2006	Pyramid	Rice, bread, pasta, potato, cassava Fruits Vegetables Beans and nuts Milk, cheese, and yogurt Sugar and sweets Oils and fats	No	Participants were not meeting the guidelines for most of the food groups: Grains: 95.8% Vegetables: 74.1% Fruits: 49.4% Meat: 97.2% Beans: 93.5% Dairy products: 87.5% Fats and oils: 99.6% Sugars: 58.3%
Ansari and Samara 2018 [52]	WHO Dietary Guidelines for the Eastern Mediterranean region	Plate	Bread, cereals, potatoes, and rice Milk and dairy products Foods containing fat Foods/drinks containing sugar Meat, poultry, fish, dried beans, and eggs Fruit and vegetables	Yes	Participants had an adherence for most of the food groups below 45%, exception for cereal/cereal products that had an adherence of 71.8%. Sweets: 43.5% Cakes/Cookies: 44.2% Snacks: 33.0% Fast food/canned foods: 41.1% Lemonade/soft-drinks: 43.7% Fruits and vegetables: 33.4% Dairy products: 19.1% Meat/sausage products: 16.5% Fish/seafood: 32.1%

Table 2. *Cont.*

Reference	Dietary Guidelines	Pictorial Image	Food Groups	Include Physical Activity Messages	Summary Results
Louzada et al., 2018 [51]	Dietary Guidelines for the Brazilian population 2014	No	Unprocessed or minimally processed foods Processed culinary ingredients Processed foods Ultra-processed foods	No	Consumption of unprocessed/minimally processed foods was higher than the other groups: Prevalence of intake: Minimally or unprocessed foods: 58.1% Processed culinary ingredients: 10.9% Processed foods: 10.6% Ultra-processed foods: 20.4%
Tian et al., 2017 [55]	Chinese Food Pagoda	Pagoda	Water Cereals and tubers Vegetables and fruits Meat and Poultry; Aquatic products; Eggs Milk and dairy products; soybeans and nuts; Salt and Oils	Yes	Participants were consuming oils and fats above the recommendations, while fruits, eggs, aquatic products, and milk were below recommendations. Vegetables were the only group that meet the recommendations.
Batis et al., 2016 [41]	Mexican Dietary Guidelines	Plate	Fruit and vegetables Cereals Beans and animal protein sources	No	Low proportion adheres to the recommendations. Legumes: 1–4% Seafood: 4–8% Fruit and vegetables: 7–16% Dairy: 9–23% Sugar-sweetened beverages: 10–22% High saturated fat and added sugar products: 14–42% Processed meat: 7–23%

Table 2. *Cont.*

Reference	Dietary Guidelines	Pictorial Image	Food Groups	Include Physical Activity Messages	Summary Results
Chin Koo et al., 2016 [56]	Malaysian Dietary Guidelines	Pyramid	Rice, cereals, noodles, and tubers Vegetables and fruits Animal source of foods and legumes Fats, sugar and salt	No	Average consumption of the guidelines was below 40% for most of the food groups, with exception for "meat/poultry" with 84.8% Cereals/grains: 40.1% Fruits: 13.4% Vegetables: 9.5% Fish: 24.7% Legumes: 8.9% Milk/Dairy products: 5.5%
Verly Jr. et al., 2013 [42]	Dietary Guidelines for the Brazilian population 2006	Pyramid	Rice, bread, pasta, potato, cassava Fruits Vegetables Beans and nuts Milk, cheese, and yogurt Sugar and sweets Oils and fats	No	Participants were not meeting the recommendations for grains, fruits, vegetables, meat, oils, and sugars food groups. Participants were meeting the recommendations for milk and dairy, and beans/nuts groups.
Jayawardena et al., 2013 [57]	Food-Based Dietary Guidelines for Sri Lanka	Pyramid	Rice, bread, other cereals, and yams Fruits Vegetables Milk and/or Milk products Fish, pulses, meat, and eggs Nuts, oils, and seeds	No	Participants were exceeding the recommendations for grains, meats and pulses, and added sugars sources. Below recommendations for fruits, vegetables, and dairy.
Zang et al., 2012 [58]	Chinese Food Pagoda	Pagoda	Water Cereals and tubers Vegetables and fruits Meat and Poultry; Aquatic products; Eggs Milk and dairy products; soybeans and nuts; Salt and Oils	Yes	Majority of the participants were not meeting the recommendations for the following groups: Only 6.1%, 1.6% and 3.6% consumed the minimum recommendations for cereals, fruits, and vegetables. Participants consuming more than maximum recommendations for meats (65.4%). Dairy (67.4%), eggs (63.9%), and fish and shrimps (81.8%) were consumed less than the minimum recommendations.

4. Discussion

This review synthesized the evidence from observational and intervention studies reporting the adherence to national FBDGs in individuals from both HIC and LMIC. The 48 studies included in this review were conducted across 15 HIC and 4 LMIC, thus representing a broad perspective on this study objective. This review found that a large proportion of individuals in both HIC and LMIC are not meeting national dietary guidelines. Meat and alternatives, and discretionary foods were consumed above the recommended amounts, and vegetable intake was below the recommendations. A global review of 90 FBDGs found that most of the dietary guidelines demonstrated that the food groups that were most adhered to were the starchy staples (e.g., rice and potatoes) and the fruit and vegetables, while other groups were less adhered to across the countries [16].

Evidence from this review suggests that the global population may not be meeting the minimum dietary recommendations for FV and whole-grains, with more pronounced deficits in those from HIC. All national FBDGs have common themes that FV and whole grains should be incorporated in a healthy diet for the prevention of obesity, other chronic NCDs, and some nutrient deficiencies [11,12,76]. These food sources usually provide a low amount of fat, and are key sources of vitamins, minerals, and dietary fiber [77]. In some countries, particularly LMIC, where diets of nutritionally vulnerable groups (i.e., children, adolescent girls, women of child-bearing age, and older adults) continue to be inadequate, the co-occurrence of deficiencies from more than one micro-nutrient is common [76,78]. Thus, population-level interventions to improve dietary intake are urgently needed to reverse these global trends.

Findings from this review also demonstrated that discretionary foods and other high sugar and fat sources may exceed the recommendations in national FBDGs. However, it may be noted that most of the included studies assessing fat consumption only reported total fat intake or the combination of fats and oils, with the exception of one study that evaluated food groups and omega-3 fatty acid consumption after a nutrition education program [32]. Thus, most studies did not differentiate between the types of fat consumed in the diet, such as saturated fats, trans fats, and unsaturated fats (e.g., omega 3/omega 6 fatty acids). Given the importance of the associations between different types of fatty acid consumption in different age groups and prevention of several negative health outcomes, such as chronic NCD in adults and older adults [79] and cognitive development in children [80], this information might be valuable. For example, it would be beneficial to distinguish between the negative impacts of saturated/trans fats and positive effects of unsaturated fatty acids in the diet. Furthermore, the finding that the consumption of discretionary foods, such as SSB and sweet snacks, exceed recommendations (i.e., 1 serving = 600kj (143kcal)) [81,82] is crucial for researchers and practitioners given that consumption of these foods may contribute to unhealthy weight gain [83,84]. Unhealthy weight gain is associated with several risk factors for poor health outcomes, public health policies, behavioral-change strategies, and periodical updates on the national FBDGs are needed to tackle this problem.

The studies included in this review suggest that dietary intake patterns differ across age groups. For instance, children and adolescents usually consume fewer FV and other fiber sources [85,86] than adults. Notably, evidence from systematic reviews [87,88] showed that children and adolescents had lower adherence to national FBDGs, and that families play an important role in influencing their eating behaviors [89,90]. Thus, family aspects of eating behavior might be included as key messages on public health initiatives and other resources for the population.

The strengths of this systematic review include the examination of a topic that filled a gap in the existing literature. This systematic review aimed to identify adherence to national FBDGs and verify possible differences between HIC and LMIC. The studies included in this review were conducted in five different continents (North America, South America, Asia, Europe, and Oceania), providing a global perspective on the topic.

This study was not without limitations. Only studies including children older than 2 years, adolescents, and adults were included, as nutrition recommendations for younger children and older adults may differ. Only studies that directly compared intake to their national FBDGs were included; no other measurement tools that were based on the recommendations (e.g., Healthy Eating Indexes) or direct comparisons to international energy and nutrient recommendations (e.g., Institute of Medicine and World Health Organization) were included. This may have caused confirmation bias, when interpreting the studies [91]. Some studies were not performed in representative samples of the correspondent population, compromising their representativeness. Also, the methodology has its own limitations, as, some of the articles included evaluated the dietary intake with one 24hDR with limited items, which is not representative of the habitual diet. Nevertheless, this method is accepted for studying the intake in a large sample of population and estimating the mean nutrients intake [92]. Reported dietary intake may provide biased results (under or over-reporting by participants) due to social desirability. Furthermore, only English publications were included. Additionally, a greater proportion of the studies that evaluate adherence to the FBDGs were from HIC, especially from the USA, limiting the generalizability of the results to other countries. Finally, the selected studies included a variety of population sub-groups (e.g., sex, age, and weight status) that made it difficult to make conclusions across studies.

5. Conclusions

National dietary guidelines can be a useful tool to promote a healthy diet for different age groups. A diet based on these guidelines should provide adequate energy and nutrient intake and support a healthy weight status and positive health outcomes. The findings from this review demonstrate that individuals in both HIC and LMIC may be falling short in at least one recommendation from national guidelines. Overall, these results suggest that a substantial proportion of the population are not consuming enough FV and whole grains. Excess intake of discretionary foods was also observed, especially among younger populations from both HIC and LMIC, and the overall population in HIC. Thus, socio-demographic factors (e.g., age, sex, and income) may influence adherence to the guidelines. These findings can help inform the development of future health policies, behavioral-change strategies, and food-based dietary guidelines.

Author Contributions: The review protocol was developed by A.C.B.L. and J.H. Retrieval and screening of articles for inclusion criteria was undertaken by A.C.B.L. and S.H. The risk of bias assessment of undertaken by A.C.B.L. and S.H. Significant revisions were completed by J.H. Additional revisions were provided by R.M.F., and M.F. All authors have read and agreed to the published version of the manuscript.

Funding: This research was funded by São Paulo State Research Foundation (FAPESP), grant number 2015/20852-7. R.M.F. receives productivity funding from the National Council for Scientific and Technological Development (grant number 402674/2016-2; 301597/207-0). São Paulo State Research Foundation (grant number 2017/23115-9)

Institutional Review Board Statement: Not applicable.

Informed Consent Statement: Not applicable.

Conflicts of Interest: The authors declare no conflict of interest.

References

1. Lobstein, T.; Brinsden, H. *Obesity: Missing the 2025 Global Targets*; World of Obesity: London, UK, 2020.
2. Grech, A.; Sui, Z.; Siu, H.Y.; Zheng, M.; Allman-Farinelli, M.; Rangan, A. Socio-Demographic Determinants of Diet Quality in Australian Adults Using the Validated Healthy Eating Index for Australian Adults (HEIFA—2013). *Healthcare* **2017**, *5*, 7. [CrossRef] [PubMed]
3. Darmon, N.; Drewnowski, A. Does social class predict diet quality? *Am. J. Clin. Nutr.* **2008**, *87*, 1107–1117. [CrossRef] [PubMed]
4. Leme, A.C.; Muszynski, D.; Mirotta, J.A.; Jewell, K.; Caroll, N.; Hogan, J.; Yu, J.; Fisberg, R.M.; Ma, D.W.L.; Duncan, A.M.; et al. Diet quality of Canadian pre-school children at two to five years old from the Guelph Family Health Study: Family-based study. *Can. J. Diet. Pract. Res.* **2020**. [CrossRef]
5. Mello, A.V.; Pereira, J.L.; Leme, A.C.B.; Goldbaum, M.; Cesar, C.L.G.; Fisberg, R.M. Social determinants, lifestyle and diet quality: A population-based study from the 2015 Health Survey of Sao Paulo, Brazil. *Public Health Nutr.* **2019**, 1–12. [CrossRef] [PubMed]

6. Himmelgreen, D.A.; Cantor, A.; Arias, S.; Romero Daza, N. Using a biocultural approach to examine migration/globalization, diet quality, and energy balance. *Physiol. Behav.* **2014**, *134*, 76–85. [CrossRef]
7. Talukdar, D.; Seenivasan, S.; Cameron, A.J.; Sacks, G. The association between national income and adult obesity prevalence: Empirical insights into temporal patterns and moderators of the association using 40 years of data across 147 countries. *PLoS ONE* **2020**, *15*, e0232236. [CrossRef]
8. McKenzie, B.L.; Santos, J.A.; Geldsetzer, P.; Davies, J.; Manne-Goehler, J.; Gurung, M.S.; Sturua, L.; Gathecha, G.; Aryal, K.K.; Tsabedze, L.; et al. Evaluation of sex differences in dietary behaviours and their relationship with cardiovascular risk factors: A cross-sectional study of nationally representative surveys in seven low- and middle-income countries. *Nutr. J.* **2020**, *19*, 3. [CrossRef]
9. Gomez, G.; Fisberg, R.M.; Nogueira Previdelli, A.; Hermes Sales, C.; Kovalskys, I.; Fisberg, M.; Herrera-Cuenca, M.; Cortes Sanabria, L.Y.; Garcia, M.C.Y.; Pareja Torres, R.G.; et al. Diet Quality and Diet Diversity in Eight Latin American Countries: Results from the Latin American Study of Nutrition and Health (ELANS). *Nutrients* **2019**, *11*, 1605. [CrossRef]
10. Backholer, K.; Spencer, E.; Gearon, E.; Magliano, D.J.; McNaughton, S.A.; Shaw, J.E.; Peeters, A. The association between socio-economic position and diet quality in Australian adults. *Public Health Nutr.* **2016**, *19*, 477–485. [CrossRef]
11. World Health Organization. *Preparation and Use of Food-Based Dietary Guidelines*; Food and Agriculture Organization of the United Nations/World Health Organization: Geneva, Switzerland, 1996.
12. Tetens, I.; Birt, C.A.; Brink, E.; Bodenbach, S.; Bugel, S.; De Henauw, S.; Gronlund, T.; Julia, C.; Konde, A.B.; Kromhout, D.; et al. Food-Based Dietary Guidelines—Development of a conceptual framework for future Food-Based Dietary Guidelines in Europe: Report of a Federation of European Nutrition Societies Task-Force Workshop in Copenhagen, 12–13 March 2018. *Br. J. Nutr.* **2020**, *124*, 1338–1344. [CrossRef]
13. FAO; WHO. *Food-Based Dietary Guidelines*; Food Agriculture and Organization: Rome, Italy; World Health Organization: Geneva, Switzerland, 2020.
14. Mozaffarian, D.; Rosenberg, I.; Uauy, R. History of modern nutrition science-implications for current research, dietary guidelines, and food policy. *BMJ* **2018**, 361. [CrossRef] [PubMed]
15. FAO/UNU. *Influencing Food Environments for Healthy Diets*; Food Agriculture Organization of United Nations: Rome, Italy, 2006.
16. Herforth, A.; Arimond, M.; Alvarez-Sanchez, C.; Coates, J.; Christianson, K.; Muehlhoff, E. A Global Review of Food-Based Dietary Guidelines. *Adv. Nutr.* **2019**, *10*, 590–605. [CrossRef] [PubMed]
17. Micha, R.; Khatibzadeh, S.; Shi, P.; Fahimi, S.; Lim, S.; Andrews, K.; Engell, R.; Powles, J.; Ezzati, E.; Mozaffarian, D.; et al. Global, regional, and national consumption levels of dietary fats and oils in 1990 and 2010: A systematic analysis including 266 country-specific nutrition surveys. *BMJ* **2014**, *348*, g2272. [CrossRef] [PubMed]
18. Rippin, H.L.; Hutchinson, J.; Greenwood, D.C.; Jewell, J.; Breda, J.J.; Martin, A.; Rippin, D.M.; Schindler, K.; Rust, P.; Fagt, S.; et al. Inequalities in education and national income are associated with poorer diet: Pooled analysis of individual participant data across 12 European countries. *PLoS ONE* **2020**, *15*, e0232447. [CrossRef]
19. Booth, A.; Clarke, M.; Dooley, G.; Ghersi, D.; Moher, D.; Petticrew, M.; Stewart, L. The nuts and bolts of PROSPERO: An international prospective register of systematic reviews. *Syst. Rev.* **2012**, *1*, 2. [CrossRef]
20. Moher, D.; Liberati, A.; Tetzlaff, J.; Altman, D.G.; The, P.G. Preferred Reporting Items for Systematic Reviews and Meta-Analyses: The PRISMA Statement. *PLoS Med.* **2009**, *6*, e1000097. [CrossRef]
21. World Health Organization. *Nutrition for Older Persons: Ageing and Nutrition: A Growing Global Challenge*; World Health Organization: Geneva, Switzerland, 2020.
22. Ogata, B.N.; Hayes, D. Position of the Academy of Nutrition and Dietetics: Nutrition guidance for healthy children ages 2 to 11 years. *J. Acad. Nutr. Diet* **2014**, *114*, 1257–1276. [CrossRef]
23. Yang, L.; Bovet, P.; Ma, C.; Zhao, M.; Liang, Y.; Xi, B. Prevalence of underweight and overweight among young adolescents aged 12–15 years in 58 low-income and middle-income countries. *Pediatric Obes.* **2019**, *14*, e12468. [CrossRef]
24. Ford, N.D.; Patel, S.A.; Narayan, K.M. Obesity in Low- and Middle-Income Countries: Burden, Drivers, and Emerging Challenges. *Annu. Rev. Public Health* **2017**, *38*, 145–164. [CrossRef]
25. Armijo-Olivo, S.; Stiles, C.R.; Hagen, N.A.; Biondo, P.D.; Cummings, G.G. Assessment of study quality for systematic reviews: A comparison of the Cochrane Collaboration Risk of Bias Tool and the Effective Public Health Practice Project Quality Assessment Tool: Methodological research. *J. Eval. Clin. Pract.* **2012**, *18*, 12–18. [CrossRef]
26. Thomas, B.H.; Ciliska, D.; Dobbins, M.; Micucci, S. A process for systematically reviewing the literature: Providing the research evidence for public health nursing interventions. *Worldviews Evid. Based Nurs.* **2004**, *1*, 176–184. [CrossRef]
27. Schroeter, C.; Corder, T.; Brookes, B.; Reller, V. An incentive-based health program using MyPlate: A pilot study analyzing college students' dietary intake behavior. *J. Am. Coll. Health* **2019**. [CrossRef] [PubMed]
28. Ewers, B.; Marott, J.L.; Schnohr, P.; Nordestgaard, B.G.; Marckmann, P. Non-adherence to established dietary guidelines associated with increased mortality: The Copenhagen General Population Study. *Eur. J. Prev. Cardiol.* **2020**. [CrossRef] [PubMed]
29. Schuh, D.S.; Guessous, I.; Gaspoz, J.M.; Theler, J.M.; Marques-Vidal, P. Twenty-four-year trends and determinants of change in compliance with Swiss dietary guidelines. *Eur. J. Clin. Nutr.* **2019**, *73*, 859–868. [CrossRef] [PubMed]
30. Díaz-Méndez, C.; García-Espejo, I. Social Inequalities in Following Official Guidelines on Healthy Diet During the Period of Economic Crisis in Spain. *Int. J. Health Serv.* **2019**, *49*, 582–605. [CrossRef] [PubMed]

31. Rossiter, M.D.; Evers, S.E.; Pender, A.C. Adolescents' diets do not comply with 2007 Canada's food guide recommendations. *Appetite* **2012**, *59*, 668–672. [CrossRef] [PubMed]
32. Yen, W.-J.J.; Lewis, N.M. MyPyramid-omega-3 fatty acid nutrition education intervention may improve food groups and omega-3 fatty acid consumption in university middle-aged women. *Nutr. Res.* **2013**, *33*, 103–108. [CrossRef] [PubMed]
33. Kristjansdottir, A.G.; Johannsson, E.; Thorsdottir, I. Effects of a school-based intervention on adherence of 7–9-year-olds to food-based dietary guidelines and intake of nutrients. *Public Health Nutr.* **2010**, *13*, 1151–1161. [CrossRef]
34. Gambera, C.P.J.; Schneeman, B.O.; Davis, P.A. Use of the Food Guide Pyramid and US Dietary Guidelines to Improve Dietary Intake and Reduce Cardiovascular Risk in Active-Duty Air Force Members. *J. Am. Diet. Assoc.* **1995**, *95*, 1268–1273. [CrossRef]
35. Schwartz, J.L.; Vernarelli, J.A. Assessing the Public's Comprehension of Dietary Guidelines: Use of MyPyramid or MyPlate Is Associated with Healthier Diets among US Adults. *J. Acad. Nutr. Diet* **2019**, *119*, 482–489. [CrossRef]
36. Harrison, S.; Brassard, D.; Lemieux, S.; Lamarche, B. Consumption and Sources of Saturated Fatty Acids According to the 2019 Canada Food Guide: Data from the 2015 Canadian Community Health Survey. *Nutrients* **2019**, *11*, 1964. [CrossRef]
37. de Mestral, C.; Khalatbari-Soltani, S.; Stringhini, S.; Marques-Vidal, P. Perceived barriers to healthy eating and adherence to dietary guidelines: Nationwide study. *Clin. Nutr.* **2019**. [CrossRef] [PubMed]
38. Bel, S.; De Ridder, K.A.A.; Lebacq, T.; Ost, C.; Teppers, E.; Cuypers, K.; Tafforeau, J. Habitual food consumption of the Belgian population in 2014-2015 and adherence to food-based dietary guidelines. *Arch. Public Health* **2019**, *77*. [CrossRef] [PubMed]
39. Al Thani, M.; Al Thani, A.A.; Al-Chetachi, W.; Al Malki, B.; Khalifa, S.A.H.; Bakri, A.H.; Hwalla, N.; Naja, F.; Nasreddine, L. Adherence to the Qatar dietary guidelines: A cross-sectional study of the gaps, determinants and association with cardiometabolic risk amongst adults. *BMC Public Health* **2018**, 18. [CrossRef]
40. Chatelan, A.; Beer-Borst, S.; Randriamiharisoa, A.; Pasquier, J.; Blanco, J.M.; Siegenthaler, S.; Paccaud, F.; Slimani, N.; Nicolas, G.; Camenzind-Frey, E.; et al. Major Differences in Diet across Three Linguistic Regions of Switzerland: Results from the First National Nutrition Survey menuCH. *Nutrients* **2017**, *9*, 1163. [CrossRef] [PubMed]
41. Batis, C.; Aburto, T.C.; Sánchez-Pimienta, T.G.; Pedraza, L.S.; Rivera, J.A. Adherence to Dietary Recommendations for Food Group Intakes Is Low in the Mexican Population. *J. Nutr.* **2016**, *146*, 1897S–1906S. [CrossRef] [PubMed]
42. Verly Junior, E.; de Carvalho, A.M.; Fisberg, R.M.; Marchioni, D.M.L. Adherence to the food guide for the Brazilian population. *Revista Saude Publica* **2013**, *47*, 1021–1027. [CrossRef]
43. de Abreu, D.; Guessous, I.; Vaucher, J.; Preisig, M.; Waeber, G.; Vollenweider, P.; Marques-Vidal, P. Low compliance with dietary recommendations for food intake among adults. *Clin. Nutr.* **2013**, *32*, 783–788. [CrossRef]
44. Black, J.L.; Billette, J.M. Do Canadians meet Canada's food guide's recommendations for fruits and vegetables? *Appl. Physiol. Nutr. Metab.* **2013**, *38*, 234–242. [CrossRef]
45. Park, S.; Na, W.; Kim, M.; Kim, E.; Sohn, C. Correlation between Intake of Dietary Fiber and Adherence to the Korean National Dietary Guidelines in Adolescents from Jeonju. *Prev. Nutr. Food Sci.* **2012**, *17*, 254–260. [CrossRef]
46. Kirkpatrick, S.I.; Dodd, K.W.; Reedy, J.; Krebs-Smith, S.M. Income and race/ethnicity are associated with adherence to food-based dietary guidance among US adults and children. *J. Acad. Nutr. Diet* **2012**, *112*, 624–635.e626. [CrossRef]
47. Serra-Majem, L.; Ribas-Barba, L.; Salvador, G.; Serra, J.; Castell, C.; Cabezas, C.; Plasencia, A. Compliance with dietary guidelines in the Catalan population: Basis for a nutrition policy at the regional level (the PAAS strategy). *Public Health Nutr.* **2007**, *10*, 1406–1414. [CrossRef] [PubMed]
48. Tande, D.L.; Hotchkiss, L.; Cotugna, N. The associations between blood lipids and the Food Guide Pyramid: Findings from the Third National Health and Nutrition Examination Survey. *Prev. Med.* **2004**, *38*, 452–457. [CrossRef] [PubMed]
49. Munoz, K.A.; Krebs-Smith, S.M.; Ballard-Barbash, R.; Cleveland, L.E. Food intakes of US children and adolescents compared with recommendations. *Pediatrics* **1997**, *100*, 323–329. [CrossRef] [PubMed]
50. Cleveland, L.E.; Cook, D.A.; Krebs-Smith, S.M.; Friday, J. Method for assessing food intakes in terms of servings based on food guidance. *Am. J. Clin. Nutr.* **1997**, *65*, 1254S–1263S. [CrossRef] [PubMed]
51. Louzada, M.; Ricardo, C.Z.; Steele, E.M.; Levy, R.B.; Cannon, G.; Monteiro, C.A. The share of ultra-processed foods determines the overall nutritional quality of diets in Brazil. *Public Health Nutr.* **2018**, *21*, 94–102. [CrossRef]
52. El Ansari, W.; Samara, A. Adherence to recommended dietary guidelines and the relationships with the importance of eating healthy in Egyptian university students. *Int. J. Prev. Med.* **2018**, *9*, 73. [CrossRef]
53. Sousa, A.G.; da Costa, T.H.M. Assessment of Nutrient and Food Group Intakes across Sex, Physical Activity, and Body Mass Index in an Urban Brazilian Population. *Nutrients* **2018**, *10*, 1714. [CrossRef]
54. Steele, E.M.; Rauber, F.; Costa, C.D.S.; Leite, M.A.; Gabe, K.T.; Louzada, M.; Levy, R.B.; Monteiro, C.A. Dietary changes in the NutriNet Brasil cohort during the covid-19 pandemic. *Rev Saude Publica* **2020**, *54*, 91. [CrossRef]
55. Tian, X.; Huang, Y.; Wang, H. Deviation of Chinese Adults' Diet from the Chinese Food Pagoda 2016 and Its Association with Adiposity. *Nutrients* **2017**, *9*, 995. [CrossRef]
56. Koo, H.C.; Poh, B.K.; Lee, S.T.; Chong, K.H.; Bragt, M.C.; Abd Talib, R.; Group, S.M.S. Are Malaysian Children Achieving Dietary Guideline Recommendations? *Asia Pac. J. Public Health* **2016**, *28*, 8S–20S. [CrossRef]
57. Jayawardena, R.; Byrne, N.M.; Soares, M.J.; Katulanda, P.; Hills, A.P. Food consumption of Sri Lankan adults: An appraisal of serving characteristics. *Public Health Nutr.* **2013**, *16*, 653–658. [CrossRef] [PubMed]
58. Zhang, C.X.; Chen, Y.M.; Chen, W.Q.; Su, Y.X.; Wang, C.L.; Wu, J.N. Food group intake among adolescents in Guangzhou city compared with the Chinese dietary guidelines. *Asia Pac. J. Clin. Nutr.* **2012**, *21*, 450–456.

59. Jun, S.; Thuppal, S.V.; Maulding, M.K.; Eicher-Miller, H.A.; Savaiano, D.A.; Bailey, R.L. Poor Dietary Guidelines Compliance among Low-Income Women Eligible for Supplemental Nutrition Assistance Program-Education (SNAP-Ed). *Nutrients* **2018**, *10*, 327. [CrossRef] [PubMed]
60. McDaniel, J.C.; Belury, M.A. Are young adults following the dietary guidelines for Americans? *Nurse Pract.* **2012**, *37*, 1–9. [CrossRef]
61. Winham, D.M.; Florian, T.F. Hispanic women in EFNEP have low adherence with dietary guidelines regardless of acculturation level. *J. Hunger Environ. Nutr.* **2010**, *5*, 498–509. [CrossRef]
62. Krebs-Smith, S.M.; Guenther, P.M.; Subar, A.F.; Kirkpatrick, S.I.; Dodd, K.W. Americans do not meet federal dietary recommendations. *J. Nutr.* **2010**, *140*, 1832–1838. [CrossRef]
63. Kranz, S.; Mitchell, D.C.; Smiciklas-Wright, H.; Huang, S.H.; Kumanyika, S.K.; Stettler, N. Consumption of recommended food groups among children from medically underserved communities. *J. Am. Diet Assoc.* **2009**, *109*, 702–707. [CrossRef]
64. Pullen, C.; Noble Walker, S. Midlife and older rural women's adherence to U.S. Dietary Guidelines across stages of change in healthy eating. *Public Health Nurs.* **2002**, *19*, 170–178. [CrossRef]
65. Anding, J.D.; Suminski, R.R.; Boss, L. Dietary Intake, Body Mass Index, Exercise, and Alcohol: Are College Women Following the Dietary Guidelines for Americans. *J. Am. Coll. Health* **2001**, *49*, 167. [CrossRef] [PubMed]
66. Brady, L.M.; Lindquist, C.H.; Herd, S.L.; Goran, M.I. Comparison of children's dietary intake patterns with US dietary guidelines. *Br. J. Nutr.* **2000**, *84*, 361–367. [CrossRef] [PubMed]
67. Brassard, D.; Laramee, C.; Corneau, L.; Begin, C.; Belanger, M.; Bouchard, L.; Couillard, C.; Desroches, S.; Houle, J.; Langlois, M.F.; et al. Poor Adherence to Dietary Guidelines Among French-Speaking Adults in the Province of Quebec, Canada: The PREDISE Study. *Can. J. Cardiol.* **2018**, *34*, 1665–1673. [CrossRef]
68. Allen, J.P.; Taylor, J.G.; Rozwadowski, M.M.; Boyko, J.A.; Blackburn, D.F. Adherence to Canada's Food Guide among pharmacy students. *Can. Pharm. J.* **2011**, *144*, 79–84. [CrossRef]
69. St. John, M.; Durant, M.; Campagna, P.D.; Rehman, L.A.; Thompson, A.M.; Wadsworth, L.A.; Murphy, R.J.L. Overweight Nova Scotia children and youth: The roles of household income and adherence to Canada's food guide to health eating. *Can. J. Public Health* **2008**, *99*, 301–306. [CrossRef] [PubMed]
70. Irwin, C.; Desbrow, B.; Khalesi, S.; McCartney, D. Challenges following a personalised diet adhering to dietary guidelines in a sample of Australian university students. *Nutr. Health* **2019**, *25*, 185–194. [CrossRef]
71. Mishra, G.D.; Schoenaker, D.A.; Mihrshahi, S.; Dobson, A.J. How do women's diets compare with the new Australian dietary guidelines? *Public Health Nutr.* **2015**, *18*, 218–225. [CrossRef] [PubMed]
72. Schumacher, T.L.; Dewar, D.L.; Lubans, D.R.; Morgan, P.J.; Watson, J.; Guest, M.; Burrows, T.L.; Callister, R.; Collins, C.E. Dietary patterns of adolescent girls attending schools in low-income communities highlight low consumption of core foods. *Nutr. Diet.* **2014**, *71*, 127–134. [CrossRef]
73. Vandevijvere, S.; De Vriese, S.; Huybrechts, I.; Moreau, M.; Temme, E.; De Henauw, S.; De Backer, G.; Kornitzer, M.; Leveque, A.; Van Oyen, H. The gap between food-based dietary guidelines and usual food consumption in Belgium, 2004. *Public Health Nutr.* **2009**, *12*, 423–431. [CrossRef] [PubMed]
74. Stroebele-Benschop, N.; Dieze, A.; Hilzendegen, C. Students' adherence to dietary recommendations and their food consumption habits. *Nutr. Health* **2018**, *24*, 75–81. [CrossRef] [PubMed]
75. Niclasen, B.; Schnohr, C.W. Greenlandic schoolchildren's compliance with national dietary guidelines. *Public Health Nutr.* **2010**, *13*, 1162–1169. [CrossRef]
76. Molina, V. Guías Alimentarias en América Latina: Informe de la consulta técnica regional de las Guías Alimentarias. *Venez. Nutr.* **2008**, *21*, 31–41.
77. Chinese Nutrition Society. *Food-Based Dietary Guidelines—ChinaCh*; Ministry of Health: Beijing, China, 2016.
78. *Global Nutrition Policy Review 2016–2017: Country Progress in Creating Enabling Policy Environments for Promoting Healthy Diets and Nutrition*; World Health Organization: Geneva, Switzerland, 2018.
79. Ruel-Bergeron, J.C.; Stevens, G.A.; Sugimoto, J.D.; Roos, F.F.; Ezzati, M.; Black, R.E.; Kraemer, K. Global Update and Trends of Hidden Hunger, 1995-2011: The Hidden Hunger Index. *PLoS ONE* **2015**, *10*, e0143497. [CrossRef]
80. Amoroso, L. The Second International Conference on Nutrition: Implications for Hidden Hunger. *World Rev. Nutr. Diet* **2016**, *115*, 142–152. [CrossRef]
81. Ribeiro, P.V.M.; Andrade, P.A.; Hermsdorff, H.H.M.; Dos Santos, C.A.; Cotta, R.M.M.; Estanislau, J.; Campos, A.A.O.; Rosa, C.O.B. Dietary non-nutrients in the prevention of non-communicable diseases: Potentially related mechanisms. *Nutrition* **2019**, *66*, 22–28. [CrossRef]
82. Arnoldussen, I.A.; Zerbi, V.; Wiesmann, M.; Noordman, R.H.; Bolijn, S.; Mutsaers, M.P.; Dederen, P.J.; Kleemann, R.; Kooistra, T.; van Tol, E.A.; et al. Early intake of long-chain polyunsaturated fatty acids preserves brain structure and function in diet-induced obesity. *J. Nutr. Biochem.* **2016**, *30*, 177–188. [CrossRef] [PubMed]
83. Nicklas, T.A.; O'Neil, C.E. Development of the SoFAS (solid fats and added sugars) concept: The 2010 Dietary Guidelines for Americans. *Adv. Nutr.* **2015**, *6*, 368S–375S. [CrossRef] [PubMed]
84. Watson, W.L.; Kury, A.; Wellard, L.; Hughes, C.; Dunford, E.; Chapman, K. Variations in serving sizes of Australian snack foods and confectionery. *Appetite* **2016**, *96*, 32–37. [CrossRef] [PubMed]

85. Teo, P.S.; van Dam, R.M.; Whitton, C.; Tan, L.W.L.; Forde, C.G. Consumption of Foods With Higher Energy Intake Rates is Associated With Greater Energy Intake, Adiposity, and Cardiovascular Risk Factors in Adults. *J. Nutr.* **2020**. [CrossRef]
86. Mozaffarian, D.; Hao, T.; Rimm, E.B.; Willett, W.C.; Hu, F.B. Changes in diet and lifestyle and long-term weight gain in women and men. *N. Engl. J. Med.* **2011**, *364*, 2392–2404. [CrossRef]
87. Leme, A.C.; Baranowski, T.; Thompson, D.; Philippi, S.; O'Neil, C.E.; Fulgoni, V.L., 3rd; Nicklas, T.A. Food Sources of Shortfall Nutrients Among US Adolescents: National Health and Nutrition Examination Survey (NHANES) 2011–2014. *Fam. Community Health* **2020**, *43*, 59–73. [CrossRef]
88. Leme, A.C.; Baranowski, T.; Thompson, D.; Philippi, S.; O'Neil, C.; Fulgoni, V.; Nicklas, T. Top food sources of percentage of energy, nutrients to limit and total gram amount consumed among US adolescents: National Health and Nutrition Examination Survey 2011–2014. *Public Health Nutr.* **2019**, *22*, 661–671. [CrossRef] [PubMed]
89. Duncanson, K.; Shrewsbury, V.; Burrows, T.; Chai, L.K.; Ashton, L.; Taylor, R.; Gow, M.; Ho, M.; Ells, L.; Stewart, L.; et al. Impact of weight management nutrition interventions on dietary outcomes in children and adolescents with overweight or obesity: A systematic review with meta-analysis. *J. Hum. Nutr. Diet.* **2020**. [CrossRef]
90. Perez-Cueto, F.J.A. An Umbrella Review of Systematic Reviews on Food Choice and Nutrition Published between 2017 and-2019. *Nutrients* **2019**, *11*, 2398. [CrossRef] [PubMed]
91. Riebl, S.K.; Estabrooks, P.A.; Dunsmore, J.C.; Savla, J.; Frisard, M.I.; Dietrich, A.M.; Peng, Y.; Zhang, X.; Davy, B.M. A systematic literature review and meta-analysis: The Theory of Planned Behavior's application to understand and predict nutrition-related behaviors in youth. *Eat. Behav.* **2015**, *18*, 160–178. [CrossRef] [PubMed]
92. Srbely, V.; Janjua, I.; Buchholz, A.C.; Newton, G. Interventions Aimed at Increasing Dairy and/or Calcium Consumption of Preschool-Aged Children: A Systematic Literature Review. *Nutrients* **2019**, *11*, 714. [CrossRef]

10 people living outside major cities reported meeting recommendations for vegetable intake and fewer Australians living in rural areas meet fruit recommendations (47%) than their metropolitan counterparts (52%) [1]. However, the national health survey estimates food and nutrient information for the population based on a 24 h dietary recall, which may be less reflective of habitual dietary patterns than other dietary assessment techniques (such as a food frequency questionnaire (FFQ)). Additionally, the survey includes only limited sampling from rural populations and no sampling in very remote areas of Australia, identifying a clear opportunity to collect additional robust dietary data in these regions to strengthen our understanding of how dietary risk factors are driving rural health inequalities [7].

Growing evidence suggests that the gap in mortality from cardiovascular disease between rural and metropolitan Australians would be reduced if improvements in diet could be achieved in rural areas [4,8]. Alston et al. reported that the gap in ischemic heart disease mortality between rural and metropolitan Australia could be reduced by 38% if rural Australians were able to achieve the same risk factor levels for diet, alcohol, physical activity, and tobacco smoking as their metropolitan counterparts, with further gains if all public health recommendations were met [4,8]. This study identified the lack of dietary data collected from rural areas as a major barrier preventing further modelling in all rural and remote areas of Australia. Additionally, a recent review by Alston & Partridge identified a lack of evidence from intervention studies that aimed to improve dietary intake in rural Australia over the past 20 years and a major limiting factor was that dietitians and/or nutritionists were rarely involved in study design or delivery [9]. Given there is a lack of high level investment and progress made in addressing issues with healthcare access in rural and remote areas of Australia, interventions to reduce dietary risk factors are important to support the health of current and future generations. Clear identification of key priority areas for initiatives or policy change to reduce dietary risk factors in rural areas is required, in addition to an understanding of the current dietary intake patterns in these communities. With an absence of routine national-level monitoring of dietary intakes in rural and remote Australia, a synthesis of the evidence from published studies that characterize dietary intake patterns in rural communities is needed.

Therefore, this systematic literature review aimed to (i) synthesize the evidence characterizing dietary intake among adults residing in rural and remote areas of Australia, (ii) identify key priority areas for intervention and policy, and (iii) make recommendations for future research.

2. Materials and Methods

2.1. Protocol and Registration

This systematic review was conducted and reported following the Preferred Reporting Items for Systematic Reviews and Meta-Analysis (PRISMA) statement guidelines [10] (See Supplementary Information Table S1 for checklist and Figure 1 for flow diagram). A protocol for the review was submitted to the International Prospective Register of Systematic Reviews (PROSPERO) (Registration number CRD42020173340).

2.2. Eligibility Criteria

This review aimed to synthesize dietary intake data available from studies conducted in community settings outside of major cities of Australia (or MM2 and above, as classified by the Modified Monash Model (MMM)) [11], that included adults (defined as ≥18 years) defined by the Medical Subject Headings (MeSH) definitions. For ease, the term "rural" used throughout this paper refers to all areas classified as MM2 and above by the MMM [11].

Studies were included that met the following criteria:

- Study designs including
  - cross-sectional, longitudinal studies; and
  - randomised controlled trials, or before and after studies that included baseline dietary data;
- Dietary intake data including (but not limited to) serves of foods, food groups, and nutrient intake data collected using quantitative dietary assessment methods (e.g., FFQ, 24 h recall);
- All study settings were included (e.g., health care, community, home, or school-based settings) in areas classified as regional or remote based on the Australian Statistical Geographical Standard Remoteness Areas (ASGS-RA) [12] or categorized as MM2 or above [11]. If both rural and urban populations were included, dietary data must be stratified according to rurality;
- published in English due to a lack of translational resources;
- published on or after 1 January 2000 due to variation in the different remoteness classification systems being used over time [11,13].

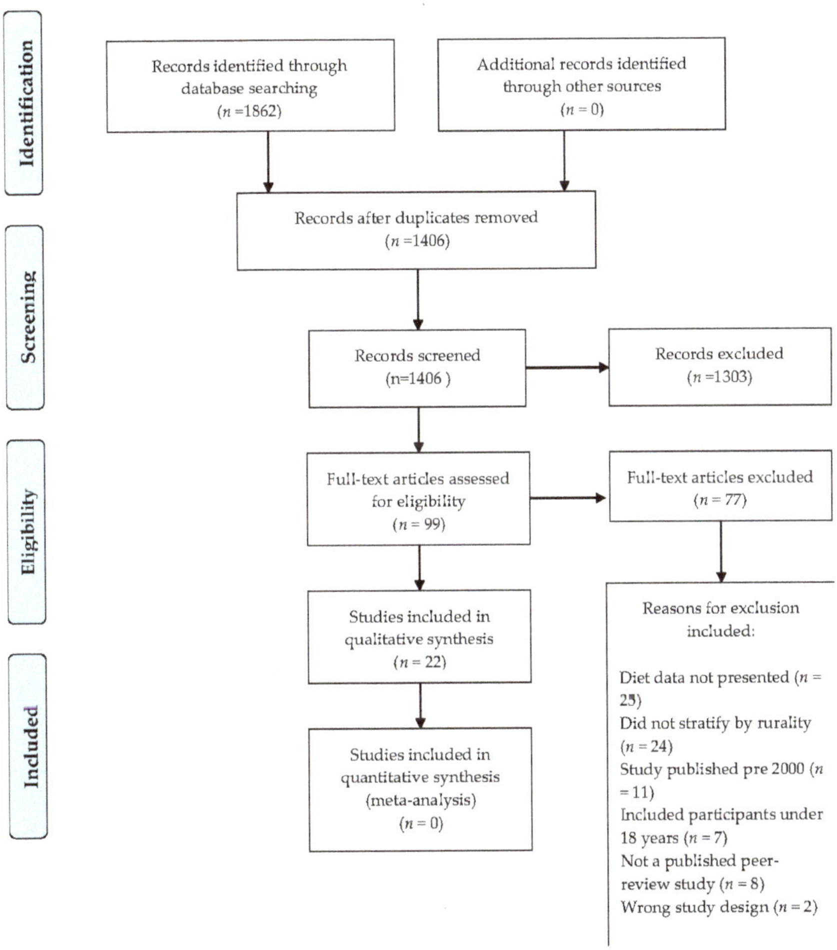

Figure 1. PRISMA flow diagram of included studies.

Studies were excluded if they met the following criteria:

- Study designs including case reports, reviews, editorials, letters to the editor, or qualitative research;
- Inclusion of people under 18 years, or if people under 18 years of age were included but the authors did not stratify outcomes according to age;
- Inclusion of populations living in metropolitan areas only (MM2 and above) or if metropolitan and urban populations were included and the authors did not stratify outcomes according to rurality;
- Dietary intake was measured using qualitative methods, apparent consumption data, food supply data, or similar; or
- Reported dietary intake following an intervention or changes only (i.e., no baseline data).

2.3. Literature Search and Study Selection

Five major electronic databases (CINAHL (EbscoHost), Medline (Ovid), EMBASE (Elsevier), Academic search premier (EbscoHost), and Rural and Remote Health database (INFORMIT), were systematically searched from 1 January 2000 until 30 April 2020 and online searching was conducted until 30 June 2020.

Search terms included combinations, truncations, and synonyms of the following:

- Diet*; Nutrition*; Nutrient*; Macronutrient*; Energy; Fib*; Micronutrient*; Vitamin*; trace element*; Mineral*; Intake*
- regional Australia; remote Australia; remote; regional; farming community; community; New South Wales; Northern Territory; South Australia; Tasmania; Western Australia; Queensland; Victoria; Australian Capital Territory.

Additional articles were obtained through a manual search of reference lists, conference proceedings, and abstracts and by contacting experts in the field.

An overview of the study selection is provided in Figure 1. One author (L.A.) carried out all electronic database searches, merged all search results into the reference management software (Covidence systematic review software; Veritas Health Innovation, Melbourne, Australia), and duplicate records were removed. Study selection followed the process described in the Cochrane Handbook of Systematic Reviews [14]. Two authors (L.A. and K.K.) independently screened all titles, abstracts, and full text articles to remove irrelevant studies according to the eligibility criteria. Any disagreements were discussed and resolved by consensus between two authors and there was no need for further consultation with a third author due to a high level of agreement between the two authors.

2.4. Data Extraction, Synthesis, and Quality Assessment

For studies meeting the inclusion criteria, information was extracted using a pre-designed electronic data extraction table that included details such as author, year of data collection, population and remoteness area (MMM) [11], number of participants, dietary data collection methods, dietary data characteristics, findings related to the dietary data, and strengths and limitations of the study. Additionally, it was determined whether the dietary outcomes were compared to or interpreted against recommendations made in the Australian Guide to Healthy Eating (AGHE) [15] and Australian Nutrient Reference Values (NRVs) [16]. Two authors extracted 50% of the data and conducted an independent cross-check of a random sample of 30% of the included studies for accuracy. When two or more articles reported results from the same study, all articles were considered together for complete data extraction. The researchers used the Australian Governments "Health Workforce Locator" (HWL) location classification database [17] to check the remoteness of each intervention based on information provided in the papers. If the location description was unclear, the lead author of the study was contacted to clarify the information in order to ensure correct remoteness classifications for both the ASGS and the MMM. If no response was received, an estimate of location remoteness was mapped using the HWL based on the information provided.

The Newcastle Ottawa tool for cross-sectional data was used to assess the quality of each study [18]. Using this tool, each study was evaluated based on the appropriateness of the study design and the quality of how the study was conducted. The checklist allows an objective rating (positive, neutral, or negative) to be given to each study. The CREATE tool was used to assess the quality of studies including Indigenous participants and was assessed by TW (who identifies as an Aboriginal Australian) [19]. The CREATE tool is designed to operate alongside other quality appraisal tools. It does not score numerically and defines studies based on 14 questions that consider the cultural context and safety of conducting Indigenous research based on Indigenous ways of knowing.

The key characteristics of the included studies were summarized in text form and tabulated using the information collected from the data extraction form.

3. Results

As summarized in the PRISMA diagram in Figure 1, the searches retrieved 1862 abstracts in total and after the removal of duplicates, a total of 1406 articles were screened for inclusion based on their title and abstract. Of these, the full texts of 99 articles were reviewed to find 22 articles that met the inclusion criteria. Reasons for exclusion (Figure 1) at the full-text stage included that the studies did not report on dietary intake data as part of the manuscript results, included participants under the age of 18 years, and did not stratify results by rurality (if metropolitan participants were included). Full details of the study designs, method of diet data collection, results, and conclusions of the studies are summarized in Table 1. Of the 22 studies, almost half included dietary data that were 10 or more years old (collected in 2010 or earlier) [20–28]. Three of the studies were intervention studies and baseline dietary data were extracted only [21,29,30]. An overview of the distribution of study characteristics is provided in Table 2, including dietary outcomes reported and dietary assessment instrument used and whether the authors compared dietary intakes with national public health recommendations.

Table 1. Summary of included studies.

Author and Year	Setting	Rurality (MM) *	Age Group	Diet Questionnaire Type	Form of Data Presented	Diet Data Benchmarked against Dietary Guidelines	Summary of Results and Authors Interpretation
Aoun, S. & Rosenberg, M., 2004	Rehabilitation/secondary prevention, intervention study	MM2	Adults over 18 years $n = 30$	Short fat dietary score questionnaire	Short fat dietary score as a mean and SD	✗	Dietary fat intake (as a score) was high in this rural sample. Authors commented that scores were high at baseline.
Brimblecombe et al., 2018	Indigenous remote communities cross-sectional design	MM7	Adults over 18 years ($n = 148$)	Culturally appropriate pictorial diet questionnaire	Fruit, vegetable, water, and soft drink intake	✓	Only a small number of participants met guidelines for fruit and vegetable consumption. Participants generally had low intake of fruit and vegetables at baseline.
Burgis-Kasthala et al., 2019	Community based cross-sectional design	MM3-MM5	Adults over 18 years ($n = 326$)	Standardised lifestyle questionnaire	Fruit and vegetable intake (cups)	✓	A relatively high proportion of participants reported meeting AGHE recommendations. The proportion of rural people meeting recommendations in this sample was high and sample size was small.
D'Onise et al., 2012	Indigenous remote communities cross-sectional design	MM7	Adults over 18 years ($n = 2583$)	Questioned intakes from the past 24 h	Mean fruit and vegetable serves	✗	A large majority did not meet the fruit and vegetable recommendations. Recommended improved nutrition should continue to be a focus to reduce the life expectancy gap between Aboriginal and Torres Strait Islander people.
Harrison et al., 2017	Cross-sectional study	MM3-MM6	Women 18–50 years ($n = 649$)	Cancer Council FFQ	Macronutrients stratified by BMI	✗	Detailed macronutrient data presented but not interpreted. Recommended future initiatives should aim to improve health-related behaviors, with focus on optimizing social support and community engagement for obesity prevention in rural women.

Table 1. *Cont.*

Author and Year	Setting	Rurality (MM) *	Age Group	Diet Questionnaire Type	Form of Data Presented	Diet Data Benchmarked against Dietary Guidelines	Summary of Results and Authors Interpretation
Lee et al., 2018	Cross-sectional study	MM3	Pregnant Indigenous women (n = 58)	Australian Eating Survey FFQ	Mean serves of each food group, whether or not meeting recommendations and overall dietary score	✓	None of the participants met all of the AGHE recommendations. Almost all (93%) exceeded recommendations for discretionary foods. Further, 29.3% met vegetable recommendations and 27.6% met fruit recommendations. A low proportion met the NRV for iron. Only a small proportion of the women met recommendations for the AGHE.
Lim et al., 2017	Cross-sectional study	MM5	Adults over 18 years (n = 1154)	Fruit and vegetable intake- "on a typical day how many serves of fruit and vegetables do you eat?"	Intake of fruit and vegetables serves/day	✗	11% had 0 serves of fruit; 34% reported 2 serves of fruit/day. Vegetable intake 21% report 2 serves/day, 55% reported 3 or more. Higher fruit and vegetable intake were associated with older age, being female, and having private health insurance.
Lombard et al., 2016	RCT	MM2-MM6	Females 18–50 years (n = 649)	Cancer Council Australia Food Frequency Questionnaire (FFQ)	Energy intake (kJ/day), Fruit g/day, Vegetables g/day, Snack food g/day, Takeaway food, g/day; Bread g/day, Breakfast cereal g/day, Alcohol g/day	✗	Study showed change as a result of the intervention and did not benchmark with NRVs/RDIs but showed grams of fruit and vegetables that were below AGHE guidelines. Women in this sample were not meeting AGHE guidelines for fruit and vegetables.
Martin, et al., 2018	RCT	MM3-MM6	Females 18–50 years (n = 230)	Cancer Council Australia Food Frequency Questionnaire (FFQ)	Total diet quality and variety score	✗	Diet quality was suboptimal at baseline. Diet quality was improved by the low intensity intervention in rural women.

Table 1. *Cont.*

Author and Year	Setting	Rurality (MM) *	Age Group	Diet Questionnaire Type	Form of Data Presented	Diet Data Benchmarked against Dietary Guidelines	Summary of Results and Authors Interpretation
Martin et al., 2017	Cross-sectional	MM3-MM6	Females 18–50 years (*n* = 394)	Cancer Council Australia Food Frequency Questionnaire (FFQ)	Macronutrient and micronutrient intake	✗	Higher macronutrient consumption pattern in this sample of rural women was potentially related to a higher lean meat intake.
McMahon et al., 2017	Cross-sectional	MM7	Indigenous adults (*n* = 1363)	24 h recall	Food groups (percentage energy from major and sub-major food groups), Cereals & cereal products, Sugar products & dishes, Meat/poultry/game products & dishes, Non-alcoholic beverages	✗	Vegetable and fruit intakes only made up a small % of energy.
Mishra et al., 2005	Cross-sectional study	Large rural sample-Rurality of residence was not further defined by modified Monash model.	women aged 50–55 years (*n* = 6020)	Cancer Council of Victoria food frequency questionnaires	Mean frequency of consumption per day of Bread, Breakfast cereals, Pasta/noodles, Sweets biscuits, Fast foods. Snack foods, Sugar products and dishes, Milk/flavored milk, Cheese, Ice cream, Yoghurt, Nuts/peanut butter of paste, Chocolate, Vegemite, Meat, Poultry, Fish (steamed, grilled, or baked)	✗	There were differences in the dietary intakes between rural and urban women. The most frequently consumed foods for rural women were processed foods.
Noble et al., 2015	Cross-sectional	Regional/rural NSW-Rurality of residence was not further defined by modified Monash model.	Adults ≥18 years (*n* = 377 attending Aboriginal Community Controlled Health Service (ACCHS))	Fruit and Vegetable Consumption Two items; "How many serves of fruit/vegetables do you usually eat each day?"	<two serves of fruit; and/or <five serves of vegetables daily	✓	The relatively small variation in fruit and vegetable intake and under-screening across the sample suggests that almost all people attending an ACCHS would benefit from improved diet and screening.

Table 1. *Cont.*

Author and Year	Setting	Rurality (MM) *	Age Group	Diet Questionnaire Type	Form of Data Presented	Diet Data Benchmarked against Dietary Guidelines	Summary of Results and Authors Interpretation
Nour et al., 2017	Cross-sectional	MM2-MM6	Adults 18–34 years inner regional (n = 408) and outer regional and remote (n = 335)	24 h recall data	Intakes and variety of fruit and vegetables	✓	Fruit and vegetable intake was suboptimal among Australian young adults. Young adults consumed a mean of 0·9 and 2·7 servings of fruits and vegetables daily. Less than a quarter of the population surveyed reported consuming 3–4 different vegetable categories on the day prior to the dietary recall.
O'Kane et al., 2008	Cross-sectional	MM3-MM5	Males 25–64 years, (n = 529)	Food Habit Score survey	Food Habit Score, serves of Fruit; Vegetables; Cereal or bread products; Milk; Visible fat on meat; Butter or margarine on bread; Bread; Cheese; Cooking oil; Milk	✗	Participants received a mean Food Habit Score of 12/20, close to that achieved by urban and rural men in the Western Australia (WA) study (Food Habit Score of 12.4/20). The men in higher skilled occupations had a better diet quality than those from lower skilled occupations.
Owen et al., 2020	Cross-sectional	MM3 & MM4	Adults aged 55–89 years (n = 458)	120 item semi-quantitative food frequency questionnaire	The Australian Recommended Food Score (ARFS), a diet quality index that captures the dietary quality of key food groups, was calculated from the AES FFQ	✓	50% of men and women did not meet recommended intakes of fiber, while 60% of men and 42% of women exceeded recommended dietary sodium intakes.
Peach et al., 2002	Cross-sectional	MM2	Adult ≥18 years (n = 131)	Self-administered, semi-quantitative food and beverage frequency questionnaire	Energy (kJ/day); Starch (g/day); Sugars(g/day); Fats (g/day); Cholesterol (mg/day); Alcohol (g/day); Dietary fiber (g/day); Vitamin C (mg/day); Iron (mg/day); Calcium (mg/day); Coffee (cups/month); Tea (cups/month)	✗	Authors did not make specific conclusions about diet. Descriptive data only.

Table 1. *Cont.*

Author and Year	Setting	Rurality (MM) *	Age Group	Diet Questionnaire Type	Form of Data Presented	Diet Data Benchmarked against Dietary Guidelines	Summary of Results and Authors Interpretation
Peach et al., 2000	Cross-sectional	MM2	Adults ≥18 years (n = 332)	Self-administered semi-quantitative food and beverage frequency questionnaire	Assessed calcium intake only	✓	Low dietary calcium intake was highly prevalent in both males and females in this regional setting.
Reinhardt et al., 2012	Intervention study	MM3-MM5	Pregnant women ≥18 years (n = 38)	The Cancer Council Victoria Food Frequency Questionnaire (FFQ) was utilized and has 74 items grouped into four food categories	Mean energy intake (mean of intervention and control group) Energy (kJ/day); fat (g/day); saturated fat (g/day); fiber (g/day); Carbohydrate (g/day)	✓	High % of saturated fat. Fiber intake below recommendations.
Simmons et al., 2005	Cross-sectional	MM2-MM5	Adults over 25 years (n = 1454)	Validated questions from the Victorian population health survey	Takeaways less than 1/month Use full-fat milk Use low-fat spread Cut fat off the meat Cut skin off chicken Dairy items 2+/day Fruit 2+/day Vegetables 4+/day	✗	This study found that the reported dietary intake was not related to obesity/BMI in this rural sample. There was a high % of rural people meeting vegetable intakes compared to more recent national health survey data.
Thorpe et al., 2016	Cross-sectional	MM2-MM6	Australian adults aged 55–65 years; (n = 1667)	111-item food frequency questionnaire and additional food-related behavior questions.	Score for compliance with the Australian Dietary Guidelines-DGI-2013	✓	Adults aged 55–65 years demonstrated poor diet quality according to the DGI-2013

Table 1. *Cont.*

Author and Year	Setting	Rurality (MM) *	Age Group	Diet Questionnaire Type	Form of Data Presented	Diet Data Benchmarked against Dietary Guidelines	Summary of Results and Authors Interpretation
Xu et al., 2019	Cross-sectional	MM6-MM7	Indigenous adults ≥18 years with Type 2 diabetes (n = 210)	FFQ with 10 response options	Vegetables; Fruit Fresh fish; Milk-based Drinks; Juice; Coffee or tea; Water; Homemade Meals; Takeaway; Snacks; Diet soft drinks/cordials; Regular soft drinks/cordials; Alcohol	✗	Self-reported vegetable and fruit intake was very low; no participant reported adequate daily vegetable intake and only 10% reported adequate fruit intake. If representative of diet quality in Indigenous Australians with diabetes, this is poorer than that of the Indigenous population nationally, in which a greater proportion reported adequate vegetable and fruit intake (5% and 43%, respectively) and poorer than that reported for remote communities in the 2015 Health and Welfare of Australia's Aboriginal and Torres Strait Islander peoples report. One in six reported consuming takeaways and 30% reported snacking at least twice weekly. This is slightly better than in the DRUID study of urban Indigenous Australians, 29% of whom reported consuming takeaway foods and 37% consumed snacks at least twice weekly. There was low fish intake, with only 4.3% meeting the CARPA guideline of two to three times per week.

AGHE = Australian Guide to Healthy Eating, MM = Modified Monash Model, NRV = nutrient reference values; * The Modified Monash Model measures remoteness and population size on a scale from MM 1 to MM 7, where MM 1 is a major city and MM 7 is very remote. A ✗ denotes 'not present', and a ✓ 'present'.

Table 2. Characteristics of included studies.

Characteristic	Number of Studies		References
	Visual representation	Number of studies (%)	
	Modified Monash Model classification		
MM2	••••••	6 (27)	[22,23,28,29,31,32]
MM3	•••••••••	9 (41)	[20,21,26,29,32–36]
MM4	•••••••••	9 (41)	[20,21,29,30,32–36]
MM5	••••	4 (18)	[20,21,29,30,32–35,37]
MM6	••••	4 (18)	[30,32,34,38]
MM7	•••••	5 (23)	[27,38–40]
Unclear but reported as rural and/or remote	•••••	5 (23)	[24,31,41–43]
	Sample size (rural/remote sample only)		
<100	•••	3 (14)	[21,26,28]
100–500	•••••••••••	11 (50)	[22,23,30,31,33,35,36,38, 39,42,43]
501–1000	••••	4 (18)	[24,29,32,34]
1001+	••••	4 (18)	[20,27,37,40]
	Dietary outcomes		
Food group serves/grams	•••••••••	9 (41)	[26,27,29,33,37,39,40,42, 43]
Macronutrient/s or energy	••••••••	8 (36)	[21,22,29,30,34–36,40]
Diet Quality Indices/Diet Score	•••••••	7 (32)	[24,26,28,30,32,35,36]
Non-quantifiable data (e.g., frequency of consumption)	•••••	5 (23)	[20,24,31,38,41]
Micronutrient/s	•••	3 (14)	[22,23,26]
	Dietary tool		
Non-validated questionnaire or short survey	•••••••••••	11 (50)	[20,22–24,27,28,31,33,37–39,42]
Validated Food Frequency Questionnaire	•••••••••	9 (41)	[21,26,29,30,32,34–36,41]
24 h recall	••	2 (9)	[40,43]
	Comparison to national public health recommendations		
None	••••••••••	10 (45)	[20,22,24,28,30,31,34,35, 37,40]
Australian Guide to Healthy Eating	•••••••••	9 (41)	[26,27,32,33,36,38,39,42, 43]
Nutrient Reference Values	••••	4 (18)	[21,23,26,36]

National Health and Medical Research Council (NHMRC) Australian Guide to Healthy Eating [15] and Nutrient Reference Values [16].

3.1. *Dietary Outcomes*

Dietary intake data were collected across all non-metropolitan classifications of the MMM, including areas classed as MM2-MM7, and most commonly in MM3 and MM4 (Table 2). Dietary data from a range of sample sizes were reported, ranging from 30–6020 people [28,41], most commonly with a sample size between 100–500 adults (Table 2). The studies presented the dietary data in a variety of ways. Most commonly, dietary data was reported as intake of food groups (e.g., grams or serves of fruit per day), followed by energy intake (total kJ/day) and information on macronutrient intake (in grams or kJ/day). Additionally, dietary data was presented using various diet quality scores, which compared dietary intake to adequacy of nutrient and/or food group recommendations. Non-quantifiable dietary data (i.e., without portion sizes) and micronutrient intake data were less commonly reported (Table 2).

3.1.1. Food Groups

Nine studies reported dietary intakes in consumption of foods and food groups [26,27,29,33,37,39,40, 42,43]. Fruit and vegetables were the most commonly reported food groups. However, a synthesis of the adequacy of dietary intakes of fruits and vegetables was not possible due to differences in the way studies reported dietary intake for these food groups (see Table 3 for differences in the reporting style for fruit and vegetables). Regardless, intakes of fruits and vegetables in rural populations were largely inadequate. For example, Nour et al. reported on the differences in intake between urban, regional, and remote young adults, showing that rural dwelling youth consumed less fruit and fruit juice and more starchy vegetables than their urban counterparts [43]. There was no significant difference in reported fruit and vegetable intake between people living in regional centers, large rural towns, and small rural towns in a cross sectional study of adults by Simmons et al. [20]. In this study, approximately half of respondents did not meet fruit intake recommendations and fewer (30%) respondents met vegetable recommendations. This study also reported that there was no relationship between eating takeaways monthly and risk of obesity [20]. Five studies presented non-quantifiable dietary intake data, most often reporting the frequency of consumption for particular foods (e.g., takeaway foods) (Table 2) [20,24,31,38,41].

Table 3. Comparison of outcomes for fruit and vegetable intake and the dietary assessment tool used among the included studies.

Reference	Fruit and Vegetable Consumption Reporting Style				Dietary Assessment Tool
	Mean or Median g/Day	Mean or Median Serves/Day	Mean or Median % Contribution to Energy/Day	% of Adequate or Inadequate Intake against Guidelines	
[39]	Fruit: 75 g/day Vegetables: 87 g/day				Non-validated questionnaire or short survey
[33]				Meeting fruit guidelines: 47% Meeting vegetable guidelines: 39%	Non-validated questionnaire or shor survey
[27]		Fruit 1.0 serves Vegetables 1.2 serves/day			Non-validated questionnaire or short survey
[26]	Fruit: 199.4 g/day Vegetables: 253.5 g/day	Fruit: 1.4 serves Vegetables: 3.4 serves/day		Meeting fruit guidelines: 16% Meeting vegetable guidelines: 17%	Validated Food Frequency Questionnaire
[37]				Fruit guidelines: 0 serves = 11%, 1 serve = 39%, 2 serves = 34%, 3 serves = 15%, Vegetable guidelines: 0 serves = 3%, 1 serve = 21%, 2 serves = 34%, 3 serves = 55%	Non-validated questionnaire or short survey
[29]	Fruit: 189 g/day Vegetables: 171 g/day				Validated Food Frequency Questionnaire
[40]			Fruit: 2.1% of energy Vegetables: 4.8% of energy		24 h recall
[42]				Inadequate fruit or vegetable intake: 84%	Non-validated questionnaire or short survey
[43]	Fruit: 128 g/day Vegetables: 205 g/day	Fruit: 0.9 serves/day Vegetables: 2.7 serves/day			24 h recall
Australian Public Health Recommendation [15]	Fruit: 300 g/day Vegetables: 375 g/day	Fruit: 2 serves Vegetables: 5 serves	-	-	

3.1.2. Nutrients

Eight studies reported on energy intakes and/or macronutrients intakes in their rural sample [21,22,29,30,34–36,40]. For example, Harrison et al. collected cross-sectional data in 2012–2013 from women (n = 649) residing in areas classed as MM3-MM6. The study described the mean nutrient intake of the sample, which was: mean energy intake of 7191 kJ/day, total fat intake of 74.3 g/day, saturated fat intake of 30.8 g/day, protein 88.0 g/day, carbohydrate 176.5 g/day, and 20.4 g of fiber per day [34]. Nutrient intakes in this sample were not compared with the AGHE or NRVs and instead, the associations between nutrient intakes and weight status were explored with the authors reporting that a higher BMI was associated with increased nutrient intakes [34]. Additionally, energy and macronutrient data was presented by Peach et al. for a sample of rural men (n = 131), showing that median energy intake was 11288 kJ/day, however dietary intakes were not compared with NRVs. Three studies reported micronutrient intake data (Table 2). Some studies were more targeted, reporting only micronutrient intakes in the absence of other dietary data. For example, Peach et al. 2000 used a self-administered quantitative food and beverage frequency questionnaire to determine calcium intake in 131 rural adults [23]. The authors presented dietary data as the proportion of respondents with low calcium intake against an identified cut off value, but did not report mean calcium intakes nor compare intake data clearly against the national NRVs [23].

3.1.3. Dietary Patterns

Seven studies reported diet quality scores or applied dietary patterns analysis on dietary data collected in their sample of rural adults [24,26,28,30,32,35,36]. Thorpe et al., used an 111-item version of the Cancer Council FFQ in a cross-sectional study of 1667 adults (men and women) and benchmarked dietary intake using a score of compliance (The Dietary Guideline Index) with the AGHE [32]. The study found that in this large rural sample, participants demonstrated poor diet quality when compared with the AGHE recommendations [32] and that rural men (but not women) had significantly poorer diet quality when compared with urban respondents. Mishra et al. undertook a cross-sectional study with 6020 females aged 50–55 years using a 100-item version of the Cancer Council FFQ, analyzed the dietary data using factor analysis, and presented the results as daily frequency of consumption of 15 food groups [41]. The study compared diets between urban and rural women and found that the most frequently consumed foods for rural women were processed foods [25]. O'Kane applied a non-validated Food Habit Score to 10 food consumption questions in their cross-sectional study of Australian rural men as an indicator of diet-quality. Respondents to their survey with lower Food Habit Scores were significantly more likely to report needing a health scare before changing their lifestyle [24].

3.1.4. Multiple Dietary Outcomes

Some studies collected high-quality dietary data and were able to report on multiple dietary factors. For example, Martin et al. (2018) presented baseline dietary data collected using the Cancer Council of Victoria FFQ from an RCT involving 230 females (aged 18–50 years) [30]. The study presented energy, macronutrient, and micronutrient intake and a score for diet quality using the "a priori" Dietary Guideline Index (DGI). Mean energy intake in the group was 8051.7 (SD 1827.6) kJ per day and diet quality scores were reported to be suboptimal at baseline [30]. Another study by Martin et al. (2017) presented cross-sectional data comparing the diets of rural women versus urban dwelling women [35]. Data presented showed that rural women consumed a mean of 7965.4 kJ of energy per day, 93.7 g of protein/day, 189.1 of carbohydrates per day, and 79.3 g of fat per day (41.1% being from saturated fat). The study did not benchmark the nutrient intakes against the NRVs, but hypothesized that women in rural areas had a higher meat intake than those in urban areas [35]. Lombard et al. collected dietary data as part of a randomised controlled trial at baseline, reporting energy intake (kJ/day) and daily intake (grams/day) of pre-defined food groups (fruit, vegetables, takeaway food, snack food, alcohol, and breakfast cereal). Although the study did not compare the reported dietary data with the AGHE, rural women in the sample were not consuming adequate fruit and vegetables according to AGHE recommendations [29].

3.2. *Comparison with Public Health Nutrition Guidelines*

Studies predominantly presented dietary data with no comparison against public health nutrition guidelines [20,22,24,28,30,31,34,35,37,40]. However, all of the studies that compared dietary intakes against public health nutrition guidelines showed that dietary intake was suboptimal in rural areas, except for one study, which found a high proportion of participants to be meeting the guidelines based on self-reported daily consumption of fruit and vegetables [33].

Nine studies compared food group intake to the Australian Guide to Healthy Eating (AGHE) [26,27,32,33,36,38,39,42,43] and only one study comprehensively interpreted dietary intakes against both the AGHE and NRVs [26]. For example, Brimblecombe et al. conducted a study with 148 Indigenous adults, using a culturally appropriate pictorial dietary questionnaire to understand patterns in fruit, vegetable, water, and soft drink intakes in a remote community [39]. Results were compared with recommendations in the AGHE and found that participants had low intakes of fruit and vegetables at baseline. Participants consumed an average of 75 g/day of fruit per day and 87 g/day of vegetables. Three other studies [26,29,43] also reported fruit and vegetable intakes in g/day, with each of these studies reporting that mean consumption fell below the recommendation of 300 g/day for fruits and 375 g/day for vegetables (Table 3).

Other studies did not explicitly report dietary intakes in g/day or serves/day but reported the percentage of the study sample who met public health guidelines (Table 3). For example, Noble et al. reported that 84% of their sample (n = 377 participants attending an Aboriginal Community Controlled Health Service) reported consuming inadequate fruit or vegetables compared with AGHE recommendations [42]. Similarly, Burgis-Kasthala et al. asked 326 adult participants how many cups of fruit and vegetables they consumed on a daily basis and found that a high proportion of participants were meeting fruit and vegetable recommendations [33]. Overall, 47.2% of participants met the recommended daily fruit guidelines (38.8% of males and 51.9% of females) and 39.5% met the daily vegetable guidelines (33.6% of males and 42.8% of females) [33]. Xu et al. undertook a cross-sectional survey using a non-validated FFQ with 10 response options for a sample of Indigenous adults with type 2 diabetes. The study found that when compared to national recommendations for diet, both vegetable and fruit intake was very low, with no participants reporting adequate daily vegetable intake and only 10% reported adequate fruit intake [38]. The authors noted that if the data was representative of diet quality in Indigenous Australians with diabetes, this is poorer than that of the Indigenous population nationally [38].

Four studies compared dietary intakes against NHMRC Nutrient Reference Values (NRVs) [21,23,26]. Lee et al. used the 120-item Australian Eating Survey FFQ (AES FFQ) to assess dietary intake in a small sample (n = 58) of Indigenous pregnant women and applied the Australian Recommended Food Score (ARFS) to compare dietary intakes against the AGHE. The study found that none of the women met all recommendations and only a small percentage of the women (a third of women or less) were meeting AGHE recommendations across each food group [26]. A study by Rheinhardt et al. also assessed the diets of a small sample (n = 38) of pregnant women participating in a pilot intervention using a 74-item Victorian Cancer Council FFQ. The study provided key macronutrient and micronutrient information for the sample and showed that the rural women had suboptimal fiber recommendations and a high intake of saturated fat [21]. The pregnant women were consuming a mean of 8910 kJ/day, 90 g/day of fat, 38 g/day of saturated fats, and 223 g/day of carbohydrates in the intervention group. Owen et al., 2020 conducted a cross-sectional survey of rural adults aged 55–89 years (n = 458) using the AES FFQ. The authors applied the ARFS to provide a diet quality score for the sample [36]. The study reported that 50% of men and women did not meet recommended intakes of fiber and 60% of men and 42% of women exceeded recommended dietary sodium intakes.

3.3. Dietary Tools

A variety of dietary assessment techniques and tools were used including non-validated questionnaires or short surveys [20,22–24,27,28,31,33,37–39,42], followed by validated food frequency questionnaires [21,26,29,30,32,34–36,41] and 24 h food recalls [40,43].

Most studies included in this review used non-validated dietary assessment tools or short surveys with limited generalizability. An example of this is an intervention study conducted by Aoun & Rosenberg who reported baseline dietary intake data for 30 participants, which were collected using a short fat dietary score questionnaire [28], however was unclear how this score represents actual fat intake. Additionally, Lim et al. conducted a cross-sectional survey of 1154 adults and asked participants "on a typical day, how many servings of fruit/vegetable do you eat?" [37]. This is not a validated technique and the study did not specifically benchmark the outcomes against fruit and vegetable recommendations in the AGHE.

Nine studies used validated food frequency questionnaires [21,26,29,30,32,34–36,41], with the number of food items ranging from 10 to 120 items (Table 1). The Cancer Council Australia Food Frequency Questionnaire was the most commonly reported tool, with each study reporting consumption of various food groups (both core and non-core foods), nutrient intake data, and diet quality scores. In other studies, the food frequency questionnaire tools were inadequately described [22,23].

Two studies utilized a 24 h diet recall method, which is a comprehensive and well-validated dietary assessment technique that can allow for high-quality food group and nutrient information to be reported. For example, a cohort study that included 2583 Indigenous adults used brief interviews to ask participants to recall their dietary intake from the past 24 h. On average, participants reported consuming 1.0 serve of fruit in the past 24 h and 1.2 serves of vegetables [27]. Conversely, McMahon undertook a cross sectional 24 h recall survey with 1363 Indigenous participants from very remote communities and reported the contributions of food groups to overall energy intake [40].

3.4. Quality Assessment

The methodological quality of the included studies varied (see Supplementary Tables S2–S4). Four studies received 5/10 stars [26,27,39,42], six studies [21,23,24,33,36,40] received 6/10 stars, and the remaining studies scored 7/10 stars or above (see Tables S2 and S3). The Aboriginal and Torres Strait Islander quality appraisal tool (CREATE) assessed six Indigenous-based studies [26,27,38–40,42] (Table S4). The majority of studies included either "unclear" or "no" answers to the CREATE 14 criteria, indicating room for culturally safe improvement in these papers, with a need to clearly report on study aspects such as "did the research demonstrate capacity strengthening for Aboriginal and Torres Strait Islander individuals", "did the research have Aboriginal and Torres Strait Islander research leadership", and "ensuring that the research is guided by an Indigenous research paradigm".

4. Discussion

This systematic literature review assessed the evidence characterizing dietary intakes in rural Australian adults. The review highlights a paucity of information, with only 22 studies that have collected relevant dietary intake data in non-metropolitan populations in Australia in the past two decades and almost half of the studies including data that are 10 or more years old. More than eight million people reside in rural Australia, with substantial evidence of diet-related rural health inequalities that affect these individuals [1,3,4,8], yet this review demonstrates that there is very little understanding of dietary intake patterns in these areas.

Dietary intake data collected from rural populations was captured and presented in multiple ways which limited the possibility of pooling and synthesizing the dietary data in a more comprehensive way. Most commonly, dietary data was presented as consumption of food groups, namely intake of fruits and vegetables. However, there were inconsistencies in the way in which dietary data were collected and presented (Table 3), meaning it is not currently possible to consolidate or make comparisons between the studies, along with heterogeneity issues of the sampled populations. Only one study [26] provided a comprehensive overview of dietary intakes in their study sample, including both food group and nutrient analysis in addition to interpreting the dietary outcomes clearly against public health recommendations. Therefore, this publication could be useful to inform ideal reporting practices for future research. Less than half of the studies [21,23,26,32,33,36,39,42,43] benchmarked the dietary data collected with existing public health nutrition guidelines, such as the AGHE, adding to the challenge of making assessments of dietary intake between studies and among rural areas. These issues mean that with the data available to date, clear priority areas for potential initiatives to improve dietary intakes in rural Australia are unable to be generated. Consistency in dietary data collection is needed to identify specific needs amongst different populations residing across all levels of remoteness according to the MMM, along with an understanding of the drivers of dietary intakes in these areas. Such data would be used by researchers, local health services, health promotion officers, dietitians, local governments, and policy makers to understand nutrition priorities for their individual communities in reducing the burden of diet-related diseases.

Overall, the studies showed that dietary intakes were suboptimal across all rural populations over the past 20 years, indicating that there is large potential for improvement in rural populations across Australia. While dietary data has been collected in relatively few rural Australian communities, it is likely that common challenges in rural food environments, such as poor food availability due to diminishing population sizes and lower food access as a result of needing to travel long distances to obtain food [44], mean that dietary intakes are likely to be suboptimal in most rural areas. Indeed, our investigation of fruit and vegetable intakes in the included studies (Table 3) highlights an average consumption between 87 and 199 g/day of fruit and 87 and 253 g/day of vegetables, which is substantially lower than public health recommendations (Fruit: 300 g/day and Vegetables: 375 g/day [15]). In line with previous research that shows that interventions targeting fruit and vegetable intakes should be the highest priority when seeking to reduce diet related chronic disease burden in rural Australian populations [4,8], only one study [33] showed a high proportion of participants were meeting fruit and vegetable guidelines. Almost half of the participants in this study met the recommended daily fruit guidelines and 39.5% met the daily vegetable guidelines. In contrast, data from the most recent National Nutrition Survey found that nationally, only 8% of adults reported meeting vegetable recommendations [45]. The authors explained that the discrepancy may be related to measurement error in the fruit and vegetable consumption data by using a non-validated, self-reported tool in addition to the fact that this study was conducted in a small sample in a single regional community that is not representative of the wider rural community. However, perhaps further research is warranted in this community to understand the drivers of higher fruit and vegetable intakes in a rural context.

Half of the studies included in this review (50%) used non-validated questionnaires or short survey tools when collecting dietary intake data [20,22–24,27,28,31,33,37–39,42], indicating a major issue when interpreting and comparing the results. It is plausible that the use of non-validated tools and short surveys used in these studies are a result of low resourcing, along with considerations around ease for participants. Additionally, it may reflect that the chosen method was developed to meet the need of the individual study and provided relevant outcome measures for that specific research. It is well recognized that selecting a dietary assessment method that is valid and acceptable to both respondents and researchers can be challenging, especially for non-specialists [46]. While it is strongly recommended that dietary data is collected in collaboration with nutrition experts, toolkits for different research contexts are available for non-nutrition experts [47] to ensure high-quality dietary data is collected and presented. When validated tools were applied, FFQs were the most common dietary assessment technique [21,26,29,30,32,34–36,41] and were generally comprehensive tools with over 100 items. This reflects the broader literature and the common use of FFQ in research seeking to measure dietary intakes [48], despite the known measurement errors, mainly under-reporting of dietary intakes. FFQ has been shown to have higher measurement bias than the more accurate 24 h recall method, which was used by only two studies in this review [40,43]. The 24 h recall method is frequently used in study sub-samples to calibrate findings from the easier to administer FFQs [49]. We did not identify any studies in rural populations that validated the FFQ results in the study, alongside collecting intake data. Future dietary intake research in rural Australian populations must consider the accuracy of different dietary intake measures in the design of studies, with the inclusion of some form of sub-population validation assessment, as the majority of data synthesized in this review may be subject to high levels of error and could be an overestimation of the quality of dietary intake in rural areas.

4.1. Recommendations for Future Research

In light of the findings of this review, it is important that researchers consider the implications around the scarcity of quality data collected on rural populations, the high levels of diet-related disease risks in these areas, and the potential future uses of dietary data that may lead to progress in addressing rural health disparities beyond the aims of individual studies. Where possible, collaborations should be established with nutrition professionals with expertise in dietary assessment methodologies to ensure valid, reliable tools are selected and that the outcome data is presented clearly, interpreted in the context of relevant research, and compared with national public health recommendations. A lack of high-quality dietary data collection and monitoring will contribute to inhibiting progress with the prevention of chronic disease in rural areas for future generations. Additionally, multidisciplinary rural health researchers should prioritize adding dietary outcomes to existing programs of health research, which could further our understanding of the environmental and/or health system factors relevant to diet-related disparities among rural populations. Future Australian research in rural communities should be conducted with representative populations; include standardized measures of rurality; use validated dietary assessment techniques; present comprehensive dietary outcome data; and clearly compare dietary intakes with relevant public health recommendations.

4.2. Strengths and Limitations

To our knowledge, this review is the first comprehensive synthesis of the literature using a systematic review methodology to synthesize the evidence on dietary intake data collected across rural Australia. A strength of this study is that we used broad search terms in multiple databases, across literature from the years 2000 to 2020. There are a number of limitations of this study, including that there was only a small number of highly heterogeneous studies that met the inclusion criteria, precluding a meta-analysis. As with all systematic reviews, the evidence synthesis here could be limited by publication bias, where studies with neutral or negative results may not be published, thus skewing results. Another limitation is that studies that included both rural and metropolitan populations but did not stratify results by remoteness were excluded, despite potentially showing efficacy and essential evidence for interventions in rural populations.

5. Conclusions

Despite the high level of preventable diet-related disease burden outside of major cities in Australia, there is a lack of high quality data available on the dietary intakes of rural dwelling adults to inform priorities for initiatives to improve dietary intake in these areas. Further and more frequent cross-sectional or longitudinal dietary data collection using robust dietary assessment tools is needed across all remoteness areas of Australia in order to adequately inform nutrition priorities and policy. Researchers need to consider the implications and potential future use of dietary data beyond individual studies to assist with progressing health and reducing diet-related chronic disease in rural areas.

Supplementary Materials: The following are available online at http://www.mdpi.com/2072-6643/12/11/3515/s1, Table S1. Preferred Reporting Items for Systematic Reviews and Meta-Analyses (PRISMA) Checklist; Table S2. Non-Indigenous studies quality assessment; Table S3. Indigenous based studies quality assessment; Table S4. CREATE quality assessment tool.

Author Contributions: Conceptualization, L.A. and K.K.; methodology, L.A. and K.K.; software, L.A.; trial registration: K.K.; database searching: L.A.; formal analysis, L.A. T.W., and K.K.; quality assessment T.W.; resources, L.A.; writing—original draft preparation, all authors; writing—review and editing, all authors; funding acquisition, L.A. All authors have read and agreed to the published version of the manuscript.

Funding: National Heart Foundation: 102530.

Conflicts of Interest: The authors declare no conflict of interest.

References

1. Australian Institute of Health and Welfare. Rural and Remote Health. Available online: https://www.aihw.gov.au/reports/rural-remote-australians/rural-remote-health/contents/health-status-and-outcomes (accessed on 30 October 2019).
2. Meier, T.; Grafe, K.; Senn, F.; Sur, P.; Stangl, G.I.; Dawczynski, C.; Marz, W.; Kleber, M.E.; Lorkowski, S. Cardiovascular mortality attributable to dietary risk factors in 51 countries in the WHO European Region from 1990 to 2016: A systematic analysis of the Global Burden of Disease Study. *Eur. J. Epidemiol.* **2019**, *34*, 37–55. [CrossRef] [PubMed]
3. Austalian Institute of Health and Welfare. Australian Burden of Disease Study: Impact and Causes of Illness and Death in Australia 2015. Available online: https://www.aihw.gov.au/reports/burden-of-disease/burden-disease-study-illness-death-2015-summary/contents/summary (accessed on 13 October 2019).
4. Alston, L.; Jacobs, J.; Allender, S.; Nichols, M. A comparison of the modelled impacts on CVD mortality if attainment of public health recommendations was achieved in metropolitan and rural Australia. *Public Health Nutr.* **2019**. [CrossRef] [PubMed]
5. Moayyed, H.; Kelly, B.; Feng, X.; Flood, V. Is Living near Healthier Food Stores Associated with Better Food Intake in Regional Australia? *Int. J. Environ. Res. Public Health* **2017**, *14*, 884. [CrossRef] [PubMed]
6. Whelan, J.; Millar, L.; Bell, C.; Russell, C.; Grainger, F.; Allender, S.; Love, P. You Can't Find Healthy Food in the Bush: Poor Accessibility, Availability and Adequacy of Food in Rural Australia. *Int. J. Environ. Res. Public Health* **2018**, *15*, 2316. [CrossRef] [PubMed]
7. Australian Bureau of Statistics. 4363.0.55.001—Australian Health Survey: Users' Guide, 2011–2013. Available online: https://www.abs.gov.au/ausstats/abs@.nsf/mf/4363.0.55.001 (accessed on 14 October 2020).
8. Alston, L.; Peterson, K.L.; Jacobs, J.P.; Allender, S.; Nichols, M. Quantifying the role of modifiable risk factors in the differences in cardiovascular disease mortality rates between metropolitan and rural populations in Australia: A macrosimulation modelling study. *BMJ. Open* **2017**, *7*, e018307. [CrossRef] [PubMed]
9. Alston, L.; Partridge, S.R. Limited dietary interventions in rural Australian communities: A systematic review. *Nutr. Diet.* **2020**. [CrossRef]
10. Moher, D.; Liberati, A.; Tetzlaff, J.; Altman, D.G. Preferred reporting items for systematic reviews and meta-analyses: The PRISMA statement. *Ann. Intern. Med.* **2009**, *151*, 264–269. [CrossRef]
11. The Australian Government Department of Health. Modified Monash Model. Available online: https://www.rdaa.com.au/documents/item/740 (accessed on 3 January 2020).
12. The Australian Bureau of Statistics. The Australian Statistical Geography Standard: Remoteness Structure. Available online: https://www.abs.gov.au/websitedbs/d3310114.nsf/home/remoteness+structure (accessed on 30 October 2019).
13. Australian Bureau of Statistics. Australian Standard Geographical Classification (ASGC). Available online: https://www.abs.gov.au/websitedbs/D3310114.nsf/home/Australian+Standard+Geographical+Classification+(ASGC) (accessed on 30 October 2019).
14. Cumpston, M.; Li, T.; Page, M.J.; Chandler, J.; Welch, V.A.; Higgins, J.P.; Thomas, J. Updated guidance for trusted systematic reviews: A new edition of the Cochrane Handbook for Systematic Reviews of Interventions. *Cochrane Database Syst. Rev.* **2019**, *10*, ED000142. [CrossRef]
15. National Health and Medical Research Council. *Australian Guide to Healthy Eating*; NHMRC: Canberra, Australia, 2013.
16. National Health and Medical Research Council. *Nutrient Reference Values for Australia and New Zealand Including Recommended Dietary Intakes*; Australia Government Publishing Service: Canberra, Australia, 2006.
17. The Australian Government Department of Health. Health Workforce Locator. Available online: https://www.health.gov.au/resources/apps-and-tools/health-workforce-locator/health-workforce-locator (accessed on 3 January 2020).
18. Modesti, P.A.; Reboldi, G.; Cappuccio, F.P.; Agyemang, C.; Remuzzi, G.; Rapi, S.; Perruolo, E.; Parati, G.; ESH Working Group on CV Risk in Low Resource Settings. Panethnic Differences in Blood Pressure in Europe: A Systematic Review and Meta-Analysis. *PLoS ONE* **2016**, *11*, e0147601. [CrossRef]
19. The Centre of Research Excellence in Aboriginal Chronic Disease Knowledge Translation and Exchange. CREATE Critical Appraisal Tool. Available online: https://create.sahmri.org/create-critical-appraisal-tool/ (accessed on 29 June 2020).

20. Simmons, D.; McKenzie, A.; Eaton, S.; Cox, N.; Khan, M.A.; Shaw, J.; Zimmet, P. Choice and availability of takeaway and restaurant food is not related to the prevalence of adult obesity in rural communities in Australia. *Int. J. Obes.* **2005**, *29*, 703–710. [CrossRef]
21. Reinhardt, J.A.; van der Ploeg, H.P.; Grzegrzulka, R.; Timperley, J.G. Implementing lifestyle change through phone-based motivational interviewing in rural-based women with previous gestational diabetes mellitus. *Health Promot. J. Aust. Off. J. Aust. Assoc. Health Promot. Prof.* **2012**, *23*, 5–9. [CrossRef] [PubMed]
22. Peach, H.G.; Barnett, N.E. Relationship between serum ferritin concentration and established risk factors among men in a population with a high mortality from cardiovascular disease. *Nutr. Diet.* **2002**, *59*, 97–102.
23. Peach, H.G.; Bath, N.E. Preventing fractures in large rural centres: Sociodemographic sub-groups at risk of osteoporosis from their lifestyle. *Aust. J. Rural Health* **2000**, *8*, 299–304. [CrossRef] [PubMed]
24. O'Kane, G.M.; Craig, P.; Black, D.; Sutherland, D. Riverina men's study: A preliminary exploration of the diet, alcohol use and physical activity behaviours and attitudes of rural men in two Australian New South Wales electorates. *Rural Remote Health* **2008**, *8*, 851. [PubMed]
25. Mishra, G.; Ball, K.; Patterson, A.; Brown, W.; Hodge, A.; Dobson, A. Socio-demographic inequalities in the diets of mid-aged Australian women. *Eur. J. Clin. Nutr.* **2005**, *59*, 185–195. [CrossRef]
26. Lee, Y.Q.; Collins, C.E.; Schumacher, T.L.; Weatherall, L.J.; Keogh, L.; Sutherland, K.; Gordon, A.; Rae, K.M.; Pringle, K.G. Disparities exist between the dietary intake of Indigenous Australian women during pregnancy and the Australian dietary guidelines: The Gomeroi gaaynggal study. *J. Hum. Nutr. Diet. Off. J. Br. Diet. Assoc.* **2018**, *31*, 473–485. [CrossRef]
27. D'Onise, K.; McDermott, R.A.; Leonard, D.; Campbell, S.K. Lack of folate improvement in high risk indigenous Australian adults over an average of 6.5 years: A cohort study. *Asia Pac. J. Clin. Nutr.* **2012**, *21*, 431–439.
28. Aoun, S.; Rosenberg, M. Are rural people getting HeartSmart? *Aust. J. Rural Health* **2004**, *12*, 81–88. [CrossRef]
29. Lombard, C.; Harrison, C.; Kozica, S.; Zoungas, S.; Ranasinha, S.; Teede, H. Preventing Weight Gain in Women in Rural Communities: A Cluster Randomised Controlled Trial. *PLoS Med.* **2016**, *13*, e1001941. [CrossRef]
30. Martin, J.C.; Moran, L.J.; Teede, H.J.; Ranasinha, S.; Lombard, C.B.; Harrison, C.L. Diet Quality in a Weight Gain Prevention Trial of Reproductive Aged Women: A Secondary Analysis of a Cluster Randomized Controlled Trial. *Nutrients* **2018**, *11*, 49. [CrossRef]
31. Brimblecombe, J.; Ferguson, M.; Barzi, F.; Brown, C.; Ball, K. Mediators and moderators of nutrition intervention effects in remote Indigenous Australia. *Br. J. Nutr.* **2018**, *119*, 1424–1433. [CrossRef] [PubMed]
32. Burgis-Kasthala, S.; Slimings, C.; Smith, M.; Elmitt, N.; Moore, M. Social and community networks influence dietary attitudes in regional New South Wales, Australia. *Rural Remote Health* **2019**, *19*, 5328. [CrossRef] [PubMed]
33. Lim, S.; Beauchamp, A.; Dodson, S.; O'Hara, J.; McPhee, C.; Fulton, A.; Wildey, C.; Osborne, R.H. Health literacy and fruit and vegetable intake in rural Australia. *Public Health Nutr.* **2017**, *20*, 2680–2684. [CrossRef] [PubMed]
34. Hossain, D.; Yuginovich, T.; Lambden, J.; Gibson, M.; Allen, R. Impact of Red Apple Healthy Lifestyles Programme on healthy eating behaviour of low socio-economic participants in rural and regional communities in Australia. *Int. J. Health Promot. Educ.* **2015**, *53*, 136–146. [CrossRef]
35. Noble, N.E.; Paul, C.L.; Turner, N.; Blunden, S.V.; Oldmeadow, C.; Turon, H.E. A cross-sectional survey and latent class analysis of the prevalence and clustering of health risk factors among people attending an Aboriginal Community Controlled Health Service. *BMC Public Health* **2015**, *15*, 666. [CrossRef] [PubMed]
36. Xu, D.; Jenkins, A.; Ryan, C.; Keech, A.; Brown, A.; Boffa, J.; O'Dea, K.; Bursell, S.E.; Brazionis, L. Health-related behaviours in a remote Indigenous population with Type 2 diabetes: A Central Australian primary care survey in the Telehealth Eye and Associated Medical Services Network [TEAMSnet] project. *Diabet. Med.* **2019**, *36*, 1659–1670. [CrossRef] [PubMed]
37. Harrison, C.L.; Teede, H.J.; Kozica, S.; Zoungas, S.; Lombard, C.B. Individual, social and environmental factors and their association with weight in rural-dwelling women. *Aust. N. Z. J. Public Health* **2017**, *41*, 158–164. [CrossRef]
38. Martin, J.C.; Moran, L.J.; Teede, H.J.; Ranasinha, S.; Lombard, C.B.; Harrison, C.L. Exploring Diet Quality between Urban and Rural Dwelling Women of Reproductive Age. *Nutrients* **2017**, *9*, 586. [CrossRef]

39. Mishra, G.; Ball, K.; Arbuckle, J.; Crawford, D. Dietary patterns of Australian adults and their association with socioeconomic status: Results from the 1995 National Nutrition Survey. *Eur. J. Clin. Nutr.* **2002**, *56*, 687–693. [CrossRef]
40. Owen, A.J.; Abramson, M.J.; Ikin, J.F.; McCaffrey, T.A.; Pomeroy, S.; Borg, B.M.; Gao, C.X.; Brown, D.; Liew, D. Recommended Intake of Key Food Groups and Cardiovascular Risk Factors in Australian Older, Rural-Dwelling Adults. *Nutrients* **2020**, *12*, 860. [CrossRef]
41. Thorpe, M.G.; Milte, C.M.; Crawford, D.; McNaughton, S.A. A Revised Australian Dietary Guideline Index and Its Association with Key Sociodemographic Factors, Health Behaviors and Body Mass Index in Peri-Retirement Aged Adults. *Nutrients* **2016**, *8*, 160. [CrossRef] [PubMed]
42. McMahon, E.; Wycherley, T.; O'Dea, K.; Brimblecombe, J. A comparison of dietary estimates from the National Aboriginal and Torres Strait Islander Health Survey to food and beverage purchase data. *Aust. N. Z. J. Public Health* **2017**, *41*, 598–603. [CrossRef] [PubMed]
43. Nour, M.; Sui, Z.; Grech, A.; Rangan, A.; McGeechan, K.; Allman-Farinelli, M. The fruit and vegetable intake of young Australian adults: A population perspective. *Public Health Nutr.* **2017**, *20*, 2499–2512. [CrossRef] [PubMed]
44. National Rural Health Alliance. *Food security and health in rural and remote Australia*; National Rural Health Alliance: Canberra, Australia, 2016; Available online: https://www.agrifutures.com.au/wp-content/uploads/publications/16-053.pdf (accessed on 14 November 2020).
45. Australian Institute of Health and Welfare. Poor Diet. Available online: https://www.aihw.gov.au/reports/food-nutrition/poor-diet/contents/poor-diet-in-adults (accessed on 13 October 2020).
46. Kirkpatrick, S.I.; Subar, A.F.; Krebs-Smith, S.M.; Thompson, F.E.; Reedy, J.; Schap, T.E.; Vanderlee, L.; Robson, P.; Csizmadi, I.; Boucher, B.A.; et al. Evaluation of Dietary Assessment Tools: Does 'Validated' Mean What We Think It Means? *FASEB J.* **2016**, *30*, 43–48. [CrossRef]
47. Dao, M.C.; Subar, A.F.; Warthon-Medina, M.; Cade, J.E.; Burrows, T.; Golley, R.K.; Forouhi, N.G.; Pearce, M.; Holmes, B.A. Dietary assessment toolkits: An overview. *Public Health Nutr.* **2019**, *22*, 404–418. [CrossRef]
48. Bassett, J.K.; English, D.R.; Fahey, M.T.; Forbes, A.B.; Gurrin, L.C.; Simpson, J.A.; Brinkman, M.T.; Giles, G.G.; Hodge, A.M. Validity and calibration of the FFQ used in the Melbourne Collaborative Cohort Study. *Public Health Nutr.* **2016**, *19*, 2357–2368. [CrossRef]
49. Kipnis, V.; Subar, A.F.; Midthune, D.; Freedman, L.S.; Ballard-Barbash, R.; Troiano, R.P.; Bingham, S.; Schoeller, D.A.; Schatzkin, A.; Carroll, R.J. Structure of dietary measurement error: Results of the OPEN biomarker study. *Am. J. Epidemiol.* **2003**, *158*, 14–21. [CrossRef]

MDPI
St. Alban-Anlage 66
4052 Basel
Switzerland
www.mdpi.com

Nutrients Editorial Office
E-mail: nutrients@mdpi.com
www.mdpi.com/journal/nutrients

www.ingramcontent.com/pod-product-compliance
Lightning Source LLC
Chambersburg PA
CBHW040757250926
51850CB00007BA/1022
9783036596921